The Greco-Persian Wars

THE
GRECO-PERSIAN
WARS

Peter Green

UNIVERSITY OF CALIFORNIA PRESS

Berkeley   Los Angeles   London

University of California Press
Berkeley and Los Angeles, California

University of California Press, Ltd.
London, England

© 1996 by
Peter Green

Library of Congress Cataloging-in-Publication Data

Green, Peter, 1924–
    The Greco-Persian wars / Peter Green.
        p.   cm.
    Rev. ed. of: Xerxes at Salamis. 1970.
    Includes bibliographical references and index.
    ISBN 0-520-20573-1 (alk. paper).—ISBN 0-520-20313-5 (pbk. : alk. paper)
        1. Salamis, Battle of, Greece, 480 B.C.   2. Xerxes I, King of Persia, 519–465 or
    4 B.C.   I. Green, Peter, 1934– Xerxes at Salamis.   II. Title.
    DF225.6.G7   1996
    938′.03–dc20

                                                                            95-46654
                                                                            CIP

Printed in the United States of America
9   8   7   6   5   4   3   2

The paper used in this publication meets the minimum requirements
of American National Standard for Information Sciences—Permanence
of Paper for Printed Library Materials, ANSI Z39.48-1984.

CONTENTS

ILLUSTRATIONS

(*Between pages 46 and 47*)

Themistocles portrait-herm discovered near the theatre of Ostia in 1939 (*Ostia Museum: photo James Austin*)

The 'Troezen Decree' (*American School in Athens: photo Alison Frantz*)

Kallidromos, the pass over the mountains behind Thermopylae (*photo R. Schoder, SJ*)

(*Between pages 78 and 79*)

The 'Aristion stele', an Attic burial marker (*National Museum Athens: photo Hirmer*)

Late-archaic torso of Greek hoplite (*Sparta Museum: photo Mansell Collection*)

The Marathon plain, from the summit of the Burial Mound (*photo David Beal*)

Salamis: the Megara Channel looking eastward (*Archeological Institute of America*)

(*Between pages 174 and 175*)

Xerxes as Crown Prince: detail from the Treasury Frieze at Persepolis (*Museum Teheran: photo Rene Percheron*)

Persepolis: the east stairway of the Apadana (*Museum Teheran: photo Rene Percheron*)

The 'Serpent Column', a memorial dedicated at Delphi (*photo R. Schoder, SJ*)

The city-walls of ancient Plataea (*photo R. Schoder, SJ*)

MAPS

Maps drawn by Design Practitioners

ABBREVIATIONS

AASH	*Acta Antiqua Academiae Scientiarum Hungaricae*, Budapest [Akadémiai Kiadó]
Aesch.	Aeschylus
	Pers. = *The Persians*
AHR	American Historical Review
AJA	American Journal of Archaeology
AJPh	American Journal of Philology
ALUB	*Annales littéraires de l'Université de Besançon* [section classique]
Anc. World	*The Ancient World*
ANSP	*Annali della Scuola Normale Superiore di Pisa. Classe di Lettere e Filosofia*
Ath. Pol.	Aristotle's *Athenaion Politeia*, or *Constitution of Athens*
AUB	*Annales Universitatis Budapestinensis de Rolando Eötvös nominatae.* Sectio Classica
BICS	Bulletin of the Institute of Classical Studies, London
Bull. Corr. Hell.	*Bulletin de correspondance hellénique*
Burn, PG	A. R. Burn, *Persia and the Greeks*
CAH	*Cambridge Ancient History*
Chron. d'Ég.	*Chronique d'Égypte*
CJ	Classical Journal
Class. Ant.	*Classical Antiquity* [formerly *CSCA*, q.v.]
CPh	Classical Philology
CQ	Classical Quarterly
CR	Classical Review
CRHA	*Centre de recherches d'histoire ancienne*
CSCA	*California Studies in Classical Antiquity*
CW	Classical Weekly
DHA	*Dialogues d'Histoire Ancienne*
Diod.	Diodorus Siculus, *The Universal History*
Diss. Abs.	Dissertation Abstracts
GRByS	Greek, Roman and Byzantine Studies
Grundy, GPW	G. B. Grundy, *The Great Persian War and its Preliminaries*
Hdt.	Herodotus
Hignett, XIG	C. Hignett, *Xerxes' Invasion of Greece*

ABBREVIATIONS

HWComm	W. W. How and J. Wells, *A Commentary on Herodotus*
IJNA	*International Journal of Nautical Archaeology and Underwater Exploration*
Iran. Ant.	*Iranica Antiqua*
JCS	*Journal of Classical Studies* [Kyoto University, Japan]
JHS	Journal of Hellenic Studies
Macan	R. W. Macan, *Herodotus, the Seventh, Eighth and Ninth Books*
Mus. Helv.	*Museum Helveticum*
Nepos	Cornelius Nepos
	Arist. = *Life* of Aristeides
	Them. = *Life* of Themistocles
Paus.	Pausanias, *Description of Greece*
PCPhS	*Proceedings of the Cambridge Philological Society*
Pind.	Pindar
	Pyth. = *Pythian Odes*
Plut.	Plutarch of Chaeronea
	Arist. = *Life* of Aristeides
	Camill. = *Life* of Camillus
	MH = *De Herodoti Malignitate*
	Moral. = *Moralia*
	Pelop. = *Life* of Pelopidas
	Them. = *Life* of Themistocles
PP	*Parola del Passato*
RBPh	*Revue Belge de Philologie et al Histoire*
REA	Revue des Etudes Anciennes
REG	*Revue des Études grecques*
Rev. Hist.	*Revue Historique*
RFIC	Rivista di filologia e di Istruzione Classica
RIL	*Rendiconti dell' Istituto Lombardo*. Classe di Lettere, Scienzi morali e storiche
Riv. Stud. Class.	*Rivista di Studi Classici*
TAPhA	Transactions and Proceedings of the American Philological Association
Thuc.	Thucydides
Xen.	Xenophon
	Anab. = *Anabasis*
	Hell. = *Hellenica*
ZPE	*Zeitschrift für Papyrologie und Epigraphik*

INTRODUCTION TO
THE 1996 REPRINT

OF all the books I have written, this one is most closely and pleasurably linked in my mind with the physical and emotional experience of long-term residence in Greece. My biography of Alexander began in Macedonia but then took off for the East; my Sappho novel *The Laughter of Aphrodite* never really moved beyond the magical ambience of Lesbos. But the history of the Persian Wars will for ever be associated in my mind with exploration, mostly on foot, of Athens, Phaleron, Piraeus, Aigina, Salamis, Marathon, Thermopylae, Plataea, Delphi, Cithaeron, Corinth, the Tempe gorge, the hill-track over Kallidrómos, the Isthmus and the Peloponnese. I used to lecture on both Marathon and Salamis *in situ*, which was fun for me and (I hope) for my students; they certainly enjoyed the Marathon outing, on which the late (and by me sorely missed) Robin Burn and I (who had very different ideas about how the battle was fought) conducted – hopefully for the students' benefit – a running debate of our own, arguing all the way from Schoinià beach to the Soros. Topographical expeditions into Attica, amid early spring flowers or in the golden ember days of late September – what Greeks call 'the little summer of St Demetrios' – were enhanced by the company of such knowledgable friends as Alan Boegehold, C. W. J. Eliot, and Gene Vanderpool. Kevin Andrews was always there in his big, shabby old house near the top of Loukianoù Street (long since demolished to make way for the inevitable high-rise) to talk Greek politics, ancient or modern (these being mostly indistinguishable). My reading of Aeschylus and Pindar, Homer and Herodotus, was interlaced with forays into modern Greek writers such as Cavafy, Seferis, Elytis, Sikelianòs. Past and present coalesced in a way that Ritsos (a poet I hadn't then discovered) has so uniquely and potently evoked.

It was inevitable that, when I embarked on a study of the confrontation between a handful of Greek states and the Achaemenid empire of Persia, these influences would make themselves felt. Looking back over the quarter-century between now and then, I find *The Year of Salamis* (the title of the first edition) very much a hands-on book, full of sun and sea, limestone landscapes, sweat and physical exhaustion, with an intense consciousness throughout of Greece's ever-present and all-important physical context. But there were other factors involved too. While I was doing my research and writing it up, we moved from the third to the fourth year of the Colonels' dictatorship: the symbol of the risen phoenix was everywhere and most people found it hard to see any end in sight. I used to argue – presciently, as things turned out – that what we should pray for was an economic recession: nothing would cut the ground from under the feet of a *tyrannos* (who, after all, succeeded by delivering the goods) more rapidly or effectively. This argument was pooh-poohed by those classicists, still numerous, who found economic arguments either suspect (evidence of Marxism?) or irremediably vulgar; but of course it found its way into my treatment of the Peisistratids.

I think many of us, too, were – for obvious reasons – more receptive then than we might otherwise have been to the fundamental Herodotean concept of freedom-under-the-law (*eleutheria, isonomia*) making its great and impassioned stand against Oriental despotism. Indeed, the one major change in attitude to the subject since 1970 has been the emerging view of the Greek notion of 'the Barbarian Other' as a rhetorical and propagandistic device, the prime object of which was the achievement of self-definition.[1] We know now substantially more about the Achaemenid world than we did then (even if little of that knowledge has a direct bearing on the Persian Wars), and the insistent lessons of multiculturalism have forced us to take a long hard look at Greek 'anti-barbarian' propaganda, beginning with Aeschylus's *Persians* and the whole thrust of Herodotus' *Histories*. Yet even so Herodotus is as likely to praise Persian or Egyptian as Greek (a habit for which he was taken severely to task by Plutarch in a famously splenetic essay: see Bowen), and for much of Persia's dealings with the West he remains almost our sole witness. What is more, on those comparatively few occasions when we can cross-check him against Achaemenid evidence (mostly epigraphical) he shows reassuring accuracy, sometimes indeed echoing the official record (Martorelli; Lewis *ap.* Burn 1984, 599; Dandamaev 1985).

It remains true that probably the most useful work done in the past twenty-five years for any would-be historian of the Persian Wars (or for anyone planning, as I am, to revise an earlier narrative) lies in two main areas: Achaemenid studies generally and Herodotean exegesis. Even if one's narrative of *events* is largely unaffected by the vast outpouring of recent Iranian scholarship (e.g. the publications of the successive *Achaemenid History* workshops organised by Heleena Sancisi-Weerdenburg or of the Briant-Herrenschmidt conference on *Le tribut dans l'empire perse*)[2] the fresh light shed by that scholarship on Achaemenid society, religion,

imperial administration, fiscal policies, and economics in general cannot but illuminate the underlying *motives* of much that before was uncertain or obscure. The Ionian Revolt provides an excellent example. The
economic pressures exerted upon the Ionian Greeks by Darius' fiscal
policies and expansion into Europe, which as a result deprived them of
profitable markets, are now much clearer (Murray, 477–80). So, even
more intriguingly, are the complex links and sympathies between the
Ionian and Persian aristocracies (Austin, 289–306; Murray, ibid.) that
played so crucial, yet unstated, a role in Aegean history. The phenomenon of 'medism' (pro-Persian treachery) turns out to be as ambiguous
and nuanced as any Cold War spy-catcher could predict (Arnush; Gillis;
Graf 1979 and 1984; Holladay; Jouanna; Wolski 1971 and 1973).

The prime achievement in Herodotean scholarship has been the
splendid Italian edition – revised text, parallel translation, full documentation and commentary, ample bibliography, one large volume
to each Herodotean book – commissioned by Mondadori of Milan.[3]
Books VIII and IX, both by Agostino Masaracchia, came out first, in
1977 and 1978 respectively (VIII reached a second edition in 1990).
After that David Asheri brought out Book I in 1988, and Books II–V
have followed at irregular intervals (1989–94). (A handy modern Greek
edition of Book V, by Christos Xydas, appeared in 1991.) Unfortunately
for the historian of the Persian Wars, Book VI (Nenci) and Book VII
(Lombardo), the two most important books, are still awaited. Nothing
comparable exists in English, where the most recent complete commentary is still that of How and Wells (1912). It is also true, as A.W. Gomme
pointed out long ago (Boedeker 1987, 5), that Herodotus 'more than
most writers is one to read, not to talk about'.[4] Could this be why, as
Waters complained a decade ago at the beginning of a not entirely successful attempt to remedy the situation (Waters 1985, Foreword), 'no
satisfactory book on Herodotos has been published in the last two generations' (for a good deal longer than that, I would argue), in the sense
of 'one which the general reader can understand, which will aid com-
prehension and appreciation of the vast achievement represented by the
History'?

It is certainly true that though the academic industry on Herodotus
has never flagged, the results have been for the most part particularist.
Details, details: though overviews are lacking, I have learned a great
deal since I wrote this book, in mosaic fashion, not only about Herodotus but also about almost every aspect of the Persian Wars. I now (Boedeker, 185 ff.) keep a wary eye out for subtexts, not least when studying
renegade Spartan kings. I have always suspected that much of the *History* had at least the secondary function of offering Athens an uncom-

fortable object-lesson in the perils of imperial expansionism: that belief has been reinforced (Raaflaub, 221 ff.). Yet when I finally produce a second edition I cannot see my basic conclusions changing all that much. More time to think, yes. Scope for more documentation, certainly. But on the big issues I haven't come up against any new evidence or thesis that has induced a radical change of mind.

To take an obvious and large example: in 1970 it was clear to me, from many of the arguments advanced (Lewis 1961 was particularly cogent, not least on telltale archaisms) that the so-called Themistocles Decree, though a third-century text that had edited, omitted, revised and up-dated many incidentals, still presented the essential core of the Decree (or possibly extracts from more than one) promulgated in June of 480.[5] Yet many scholars were prepared to argue that the Decree was an elaborate forgery devised to whip up patriotic fervor in the Social War of 357 – 355, or against Philip of Macedon or during the Lamian War of 323/2 against Antipater. The plain improbability of producing so oddly detailed an antiquarian document for propaganda purposes (not to mention making a naval appeal where the crying need was for a land-based defence) was compounded by general ignorance of how and why forgers go about their business. This ignorance was thrown into glaring prominence by those who triumphantly pointed to supposed *discrepancies* between Herodotus and the Decree as proof of inauthenticity. In fact, these were among the surest guarantees of precisely the opposite: the last thing forgers ever dream of doing (being *inter alia* unimaginative people – one reason for becoming addicted to forgery in the first place) is to arouse suspicion by going against their main source of information.[6]

The protracted early debate on authenticity made it clear that a point had very soon been reached where logic had been replaced by committed faith (a situation that occurs in scholarship rather more often than one likes to think). Perhaps this is the reason why so few articles have been devoted to the problem in recent years. After 1971 (which saw yet another argument in favor of fourth-century anti-Macedonian propaganda, this time by Prestianni) there was virtual silence for over a decade, except for a broadside by Robertson (1976), consigning to the alleged busy forgers of Athens' Second Naval Confederacy, between 375 and 368, not only the Themistocles Decree, but also, for good measure, the Oath and Covenant of Plataea, the Festival Decree, the Peace of Callias, the Ephebic Oath, and Pericles' Congress Decree. Just what effect this odd collection was supposed to have, and why the perpetrators would prefer to invent nonsense rather than evoke the actual past, were problems never squarely faced. By 1982 Robertson had at least

xvi

(and at last) acknowledged the obvious fact (1982, 30) that 'in c. 380 as at any other time in the fourth century it is impossible to conceive of a patient audience for all the antiquarian details with which the compendious decree embellishes the theme of Athenian sea-power'. But instead of abandoning his theory, he simply moved on to another century in search of an audience that *would* be patient of antiquarianism, and came up with Ptolemy Philadelphos, who, despite his own naval power, was unlikely, to say the least, as the son of one of Alexander's veteran marshals, to be stirred to high emulation by wartime arrangements made in Athens over two hundred years earlier. J. F. Lazenby (of whom more in a moment), though conceding that the problem was unlikely ever to be settled, in 1993 wrote (102 n. 4) that 'to my mind, this virtually proves that the decree is not authentic'. It does? Here (though we differ as to basic chronology) I find Hammond's arguments for authenticity far more compelling and made with a genuine understanding of forgers' psychology.[7]

I also figured it might be a useful and badly needed lesson in humility to search out the academic reviews of *The Year of Salamis* and see how they disposed of my younger, brasher, less professional self. It was an interesting experience, not always quite in the way I had expected.[8] Edouard Will (a historian for whose work I have the utmost respect) advised the reader that, though he might find me an enjoyable read, he would be well advised 'to abandon at the outset any sort of *cuistrerie*', an admonition I had cause to remember since of course *cuistrerie* means not only 'pedantry' (which I am sure was what Will had in mind) but also 'ungentlemanly behavior', 'caddishness'. Will, having disarmingly admitted to being bored stiff by strategy or tactics, went on – he was not alone in this – to invoke my fiction-writing *alter ego* as having improperly meddled in professional historiography, first, by romanticizing my characters (i.e., making them too real), and second, more importantly, by revealing a historical novelist's distaste for lacunas. His main complaint, however, was that I had 'over-isolated the episode of the Persian Wars from its deeper background: the great *Why* of the whole matter is not explored in depth'.

Since *le grand pourquoi* (the 'great *Why?*') was for me, as for Herodotus,[9] one of the main reasons for writing my book, this hit hard. I thought I had brought out the dangers of an Achaemenid policy of westward expansionism into Europe (especially when linked to oppressive taxation); the levelling wind of democratic change blowing from mainland Greece to topple *tyrannoi*; the crippling of Anatolian Greek trade; the consequent disenchantment of many Ionian leaders (who had previously colluded very comfortably for thirty years and more with their Persian overlords) to the point of launching a concerted revolt; the escalation of hostilities after the burning of Sardis (face-saving and the territorial imperative were now involved); the impact of Marathon, bringing a sense of pride and stubbornness to Athens; Xerxes' weak vulnerability to the ambitious plans of relatives and courtiers;[10] and finally, the ability of just enough of the factious and quarrelsome Greek states to rise above medism, self-interest, social in-fighting, and the eternal round of beggar-my-neighbor for just long enough to stand off the assault of a juggernaut whose sheer size not only terrified but also produced acute logistical and command-structure problems. I can only promise to stress these and other factors even more emphatically next time.

Some critics, of course, will do anything for a good punch-line (in Frank Frost's case, several of them). On page 26 I quote Plutarch's graphic anecdote of Themistocles' father Neocles on the beach of Phaleron with his young son, pointing to the rotting hull of an old trireme and saying: 'That, my boy, is just how the Athenian people treat their leaders when they have no further use for them.' *Ben trovato* if not necessarily true. Frank's comment (we have since become good friends) was: 'When the reader realizes that the democracy had only been in existence for ten years or so, he must surely credit Neocles with awesome foresight.' But when was democracy ever an indispensable ingredient of perennially vicious Greek politics? This is on a par with the assumption that my take on these politics is based on 'a conflation of Plutarch, Marx [!], and Toynbee [!!]'. The inclusion of Marx I suspect to have been occasioned by my analysis of the bitter conflict in Athens between the landed aristocracy (plus those more affluent farmers who served as *hippeis*) and the lower orders who rowed the triremes and formed the backbone of Athens' emergent thalassocracy. Frank argued that this conflict did not exist. It is hard to read the passage in Plato's *Laws* that I quote from briefly (p. 39) and still think so.[11]

There are, inevitably, a number of slips and errors that I need to put right. Even though I knew very well that, before the development of Piraeus, Phaleron beach served as the Athenian naval base, I still absentmindedly made Themistocles frequent the waterfront taverns of the former at least a year (494) before he began building the port. Thessaly in 510 was not allied to Sparta (p. 16). It is misleading (p. 17) to talk of Hippias' 'government-in-exile' (even though Persia regarded Hippias as the legitimate ruler of Athens). Xanthippus (p. 45) was *strategos* in 480/79; there is no solid evidence for his having served in this capacity in 489/8. Callixeinos, one of the mysterious characters known only from pottery shards, or *ostraka* (*ostraka* found on the Acropolis describe him as 'traitor', show him to have been an Alcmaeonid, and in quantity are second only to those attacking Themistocles),[12] cannot be shown to have been exiled in 483/2, or at any other point in the 480s, though the likelihood remains considerable. The Greek hoplite's leather jerkin was probably *not* bronze-stripped. My scepticism about Themistocles' tutor Mnesiphilus (p. 293 n. 4) has been overcome by new *ostraka*, which confirm his existence and residence in Themistocles' deme (Lazenby, 157 with n. 12). I am less confident than I was about the ability of a trireme to shear off the oars of a ship as it passed it. Twenty-four, rather than twenty, states were brigaded together at Plataea (p. 262), and an unfortunate phrase on the following page led one scholar (and, thus, possibly other readers) to assume, wrongly, that I think Pausanias, Captain-General of the Hellenes, was a Spartan king rather than regent for his uncle Leonidas' son Pleistarchus.

In general, I would agree with Frost and Briscoe that my treatment of the complex political scene in Athens, particularly between Marathon and Xerxes' invasion, is oversimplified and too schematic, especially with regard to the ostracism victims during that decade. Though an interesting number of them were indeed Alcmaeonids, they were not *necessarily* all opponents of Themistocles (though I still think this highly probable).[13] Like Lewis (*ap.* Burn 1984, 603–5; cf. Lewis 1974), I have to concede, regretfully, that 'a historical reconstruction is not yet possible' – or at least not secure – for the 9000-odd *ostraka* found (1965–68) in the Kerameikos. Of these about half (4647) were cast for Megacles son of Hippocrates, 1696 for Themistocles, and 490 for Cimon (only a boy in 489 B.C. when he paid his father Miltiades' fine). These three are linked by joinable *ostraka*, and Lewis leaned towards dating them in the 470s (though he backed off his earlier belief that they formed a unified cache). It still seems very likely to me that the Megacles-Themistocles confrontation *is* that of 486, as was originally supposed (Cimon's presence does not rule out this possibility). As Lewis says, this earlier dating, if true, would destroy Badian's thesis that Themistocles was of little importance before 482; but I have never believed this anyway. Xanthippus' ostracism in particular remains puzzling: Aristotle (*AP* 22.6) claims that he was the first victim to be exiled in those years, not as a 'friend of the tyrants', but simply as one who 'seemed to be too great': but surely his marriage into the Alcmaeonid clan had to have been a factor (Ostwald, 342)? The ambiguities here cannot but put one in mind of Vichy France and (as I suggested earlier) the looking-glass world of Cold War espionage.

This brings me to one of the more important general points raised by the reviewers not only of this book (Weiler, Will, Frost, and Meyer) but also of a more recent work such as *Alexander to Actium*, regarding my record of drawing parallels between the ancient and modern worlds: a practice condemned as historiographically unsound and in every sense misleading to the reader. Some (perfectly logical) reasons for so doing will not recommend themselves to academics, in particular, the fact that if one is writing for an audience that includes non-specialist readers, it becomes tedious (for author as well as audience) to have no recognizable points of reference. Thus known modern parallels, even if not precise, enable the uninformed reader to get an approximate picture of what is going on. No reasonable person would suppose for one moment that such parallels were advanced as exact (e.g. to anticipate a point discussed below, that the use of modern military nomenclature might somehow give the impression that hoplites at Plataea functioned like a WWII army brigade). On the other hand human nature – as historians from Herodotus on were all too well aware – has an uncomfortable habit of repeating itself (whether as tragedy or farce), and I no more regard it as historiographically unsound to search out such recurrences than did Thucydides when he wrote of 'clearly examining [τὸ σαφὲς σκοπεῖν] both past events and those that will, in all human likelihood, happen in much the same or similar manner'.[14] As I learned from my Hellenistic researches, such parallels have a great deal to teach us.[15]

Of equal importance is the matter of source-criticism. As we saw, Will attributed to me (correctly, and I think the same is true of most historians, as of papyrologists) a distaste for lacunas – which is not to say that I always believe they can be filled. Frank Frost made the principles behind this kind of complaint very clear:

> One of the details that we expect of the historian of the Persian Wars is an explanation of how he intends to treat the evidence. We may not agree with an Obst, or a Pritchett, or a Hignett, but at least we know what they are going to do with Herodotus, and with the testimony that supplements or contradicts Herodotus. Here there is not a word about sources. . . . At times, for instance, G. will tell an anecdote as though it were well-established fact [Plutarch's anecdote of Themistocles, Neocles and the rotting triremes is cited]. . . . When faced with a number of conflicting sources, G. will find a way to reconcile them and use them all, once again without annotation or explanation. (Frost, 264)

To take the simplest point first: the absence of detailed annotation was not a matter of choice, but an economy wished on me to avoid unnerving the hypothetical 'common reader'. Had I insisted, as I did later for my revised biography of Alexander, I might well (I suspect now, looking back) have gotten my way. Here is one good reason for an eventual second edition, in which, I am confident, my documentation will, given the controversy surrounding the topic, be at least as massive as that for *Alexander to Actium*.

Basic to Frost's case is the demand for a prior statement of principles governing the evaluation of sources. This, again, I omitted largely because I was supposed not to be writing an academic text, but also because my ideas about source-criticism were and still are, given current fashion, heterodox, and in 1970 I did not see this book as the proper forum for academic debate. Today, however, I am more than happy to make my position clear. It is not, I think, irrelevant that I was originally trained as a textual critic, and that when I turned to history I found what I had learned no less apposite for the evaluation of historical sources. The kernel of my thinking lies in a famous passage by A. E. Housman:

Open a modern recension of a classic, turn to the preface, and there you may almost count on finding, in Latin or German or English, some words like these: 'I have made it my rule to follow *a* wherever possible, and only where its readings are patently erroneous have I had recourse to *b* or *c* or *d*.' . . . Either *a* is the source of *b* and *c* and *d* or it is not. If it is, then never in any case should recourse be had to *b* or *c* or *d*. If it is not, then the rule is irrational; for it involves the assumption that wherever *a*'s scribes made a mistake they produced an impossible reading.[16]

As Housman went on to make clear, the only occasion on which ('in the same spirit of gloomy resignation with which a man lies down on a stretcher when he has broken both his legs') we invoke the 'better' manuscript is to decide between a pair of equally possible readings: 'We cherish no hope that it will always lead us right: we know that it will often lead us wrong; but we know that any other MS would lead us wrong still oftener' (xv).

Applying these lessons to historiography can be most interesting, not least in the present case. Substitute 'author' for 'manuscript' and you do not have to look far to find Housman's prime fallacy flourishing unchecked. In his opening chapter on the evidence, Lazenby writes: 'It seems almost always legitimate to reject the secondary sources when they conflict with Herodotus' (pp. 15 – 16). But the fact that Herodotus is *the* prime early source by no means sanctions this kind of rule-of-thumb treatment. Worse still, Lazenby argues that since the late testimonia often tell tall stories (quite true; but then so does Herodotus), we should *therefore also discredit them when their testimony is plausible*: 'If Plutarch believes fifth-century Athenians capable of human sacrifice, why should we believe his story of the dawn wind at Salamis?' He claims to be working according to 'rational principles', but this is to stand reason on its head. We know that other early material on the Persian Wars existed; we have virtually no notion of how the tradition was handed down or which authentic details managed to survive along with the imaginative dross. In other words, these much-despised 'late sources', like the Alexander-Romance, while they quite obviously are stuffed with every sort of rhetorical garbage, may also contain valuable material along with the rubbish, and we should not fall into the obvious fallacy (Housman again) of assuming that everything they recorded *must inevitably* be false. In every case we have to use our reason and historical judgment to sort the true from the false (or, more often, the plausible from the fatuous): there are no generic short cuts.

The problem is complicated by a familiar scholarly phenomenon: the common need to prove one's critical ability through scepticism, which in some cases seems to exploit a deep and passionate affinity, well beyond reason, with the demolition of 'myth' *per se*. The Themistocles Decree has suffered several such assaults: so, by a nice paradox, has that 'prime source' Herodotus himself. Armayor [17] has devoted a great deal of time and trouble in attempting to prove (for the most part through discrepancies with reality [18]) that this supposed great traveller never in fact went to Egypt or the Black Sea, but simply patched together his evidence from suspect literary sources; while Fehling goes even further, accusing Herodotus of systematic lying, of inventing his alleged 'sources' wholesale, and dismissing the matter they present as worthless fabrications. [19] No one would argue that Herodotus did *not* contain errors and inconsistencies; but, as Murray remarked, in criticism of Fehling, 'to postulate deliberate and wholesale deception . . . rather than faulty execution, requires an answer to the question, who invented the model which Herodotus is thought to have abused? It implies a proto-Herodotus before Herodotus'. [20]

These are extreme, and in the case of Fehling almost pathological, examples. But the attitude they imply, even if only moderately expressed, is in part at least responsible for the doubts aroused by my suspect ability to reconcile apparently conflicting sources (the Themistocles Decree offers a fair instance of this). What critics want me to do is reject testimony, especially late testimony, on principle. But the evaluation of evidence strictly in the light of inherent probability (what Greek rhetoricians and courtroom lawyers described as ἀπὸ τοῦ εἰκότος), together with the abandoning of rule-of-thumb dismissal, will indeed tend to admit more material, and if witnesses at first sight discrepant can, on examination, be reconciled, so much the better for the difficult business of historical retrieval.

The objection to modern army terms mentioned earlier was made –

and directed primarily, though not exclusively, at *The Year of Salamis* – by J. F. Lazenby, in what I have found, to my astonishment, to be the only book-length treatment of the Persian Wars (as far as I know) published since my own.[21] Bearing in mind the fact that the Greek victory in the Persian Wars is routinely described as a fundamental turning point in European history (advocates of this view don't quite argue that today, had things gone the other way, mosques and minarets would dominate Europe, but you can sense the unspoken thought in the air), this omission seems all the more inexplicable. Alexander's conquests mark the other great Hellenic milestone, and think of the endless books devoted to *him*. What is more, *The Defence of Greece 490 – 479 B.C.* (1993), as its title makes clear, and its author's other publications confirm,[22] is very much a *military* history, with all the limitations that this implies. There is no serious attempt to deal with what Will called 'the great *Why?*'. Economics seldom enter into Professor Lazenby's scheme of things.[23] Instead, we get the highly debatable thesis, advanced in the first two chapters and exploited throughout, that both on land and at sea Greeks were tactical and strategic innocents with no military or naval sense beyond the very simplest manoeuvres or 'square-bashing', and that commanders were appointed on the basis of social prestige rather than military experience.[24] There is a nice pay-off here: the supposed naïveté of Herodotus is excused and explained by the argument that he simply reports what he heard and saw, that the naïveté is not his, but that of his characters (Lazenby, 14). To render this verdict even more incongruous, the Persians collect high praise (Lazenby, 29 – 32) for all those sophisticated functions the poor Greeks are regarded as too naive or inexperienced to master: intelligence-gathering, diplomatic warfare, meticulous planning, engineering expertise, siege-works, and land operations.

Thus it comes as an unexpected surprise when we read how successful the Persians had been – '*until they came up against the mainland Greeks*' (Lazenby, 32: my emphasis). Lazenby's lead-up emphasizes the paradox (for him, one feels, an intellectually annoying one[25]) that these untrained ignoramuses somehow contrived to upset so well-organised a military machine, not to mention the safe predictions of Delphi. But Lazenby's argument is simply not true: however rudimentary their preparation, the Greeks, for whom fighting one another was the prime occupation of life, were far more sophisticated and flexible in military as in naval affairs than Lazenby wants to believe. The victory at Marathon is one outstanding example; the Corinthian decoy movement at Salamis is another; and in both cases Lazenby either fudges the Greek or willfully ignores modern scholarship in an effort to avoid any admission of sophisticated strategical planning.[26] After all, the hoplite phalanx, which required very careful coordination, had been in existence at least since 700, while naval manoeuvres such as the *diekplous* (Hdt. 8.9) were already in use during the Persian Wars.[27]

Thus on several counts I am very glad to see a reissue of *The Year of Salamis*, not least since nothing comparable, apart from Lazenby's strictly military survey, has been published in the interim. This is not to say that *The Defence of Greece 490–479 B.C.* is not in many ways a useful and stimulating book, primarily in its generally meticulous treatment of detail. On points of chronology, as on troop and fleet numbers, Lazenby has much to offer, which future writers (myself included) will ignore at their peril; and his flirtation (p. 169) with the idea that Themistocles may have been ready to medize in earnest I find both intriguing and seductive.[28] But there will also be innumerable points to argue: some simple (e.g. the timing of Xerxes' mole: before or after the battle? surely both – begun in advance and reutilized later),[29] some decidedly complex (e.g. Lazenby's assertion, which I would dispute, that the Persians could have afforded to bypass Salamis altogether).[30] I look forward to such discussions.[31] Certainly this book has sharpened my resolve to produce a second edition of my own. But I suspect that the changes, apart from at last supplying my narrative with a full support-structure of documentation, will be almost entirely particularist on points of detail or newly discovered evidence.[32]

There is, however, one omission which I must put right now. In an otherwise kindly review Willie Eliot pointed out (p. 87) that though I had acknowledged earlier scholars in the field, I had not paid proper tribute to my greatest benefactor: Herodotus himself. Such was certainly not my intention. For me Herodotus is one of the best-loved texts, most often read, most greatly admired, in the whole classical canon: a lifelong companion, a more congenial – and, I believe, a better – historian than Thucydides, like him a 'possession for ever', but not ashamed of giving pleasure too. Perhaps the best proof of my attitude is that a very large part of my retirement will be spent translating, editing, and writing a new commentary on this wise, shrewd, tolerant, cosmopolitan, and in many ways most modern of ancient writers, a task to which I look forward with zestful anticipation.

Austin, Texas   PETER GREEN
1 September 1995

PREFACE AND
ACKNOWLEDGMENTS

WHEN my publishers asked me to write a book on *The Year of Salamis*, perhaps neither they nor I quite realised that what would emerge was a full-scale history of the Persian Wars. Yet in a sense this was inevitable. It is impossible to understand Salamis or Plataea without having first studied Marathon, and impossible to understand Marathon except against a general background of sixth-century Greek and Persian history. The actual Athenian archon-year 480–79, during which the battles of Thermopylae, Artemisium and Salamis were fought, does, nevertheless, occupy the greater part of my narrative – though Xerxes' invasion, we should remember, was well under way before it opened, while Plataea and Mycale both took place after it closed. If ever there was a true turning-point in European history (as I hope to have made clear) it was during those crowded and tumultuous months when all Greece, to borrow a memorable phrase publicised at the time, stood on the razor's edge. No excuse is needed for yet another study of the Great King's expedition, particularly since it continues to arouse a quite remarkable degree of controversy and disagreement among modern historians.

The list of great scholars who have worked in this field is an imposing one, and I am more than usually conscious of the debt I owe to them. The books and articles of such specialists as Goodwin, Grundy, Hauvette, How, Kromayer, Labarbe, Macan, Munro, Pritchett and Wells (to name but a few) have all, in their various ways, made the task of anyone who follows in their footsteps a great deal easier. Two recent full-scale accounts of the Persian Wars, A. R. Burn's *Persia and the Greeks* and C. Hignett's *Xerxes' Invasion of Greece*, have travelled with me throughout my own investigations; without either of them this book would have been immeasurably the poorer, and far harder to write. Mr Burn's lucid common sense and masterly grasp of strategy and topographical detail make a neat complementary balance to Mr Hignett's acute (and often refreshingly contemptuous) critical insights – not to mention his enviable familiarity with all scholarly literature on the subject published during the last half-century. My debt to these two continually illuminating and provocative books is perhaps best measured by the number of occasions on which I disagree with their findings (almost as often, indeed, as they disagree with each other). A particularly important case in point concerns the authenticity of the Troezen Decree. When Burn and Hignett published their books (in 1962 and 1963 respectively), the controversy over this newly discovered inscription [see below, p. 98 ff.] was still at its height. By now, I hope, the dust has settled far enough to allow a reasonably balanced appraisal. My original intention was to write a special appendix on the historical problems arising from discrepancies between the Decree and Herodotus. However, the monstrously large literature which this inscription has already called forth demands a stringent application of Ockham's Razor – *essentia non sunt multiplicanda praeter necessitatem* – and it now seems to me that anything useful I have to say on this vexed topic is best discussed in my main narrative. Otherwise I have little to add to the admirable articles (with which I am in substantial agreement) of Jameson, Berve, Meritt, Lewis, Schachermeyr, Treu, Cataudella, and Fornara.

Living permanently in Greece gives one very special advantages and insights for writing a book of this kind. It would be a bold man, today, who claimed that a knowledge of modern Greek politics did not help us to understand ancient Greek history. Above all, there is the ubiquitous feeling of physical immediacy, of the past obtruding into the present like those great rocky outcrops which here and there rise from the Athens asphalt, bleakly austere, to humble our human pretensions. Most of the places mentioned in this book, and all the major battlesites, I know well from frequent personal exploration at every season of the year. I have sailed round the bays and inlets of Salamis, and walked over lonely mountain goat-tracks above Thermopylae and Plataea. Marathon, for me, is not merely an abstract historical label or atlas diagram, but a favourite weekend retreat for swimming and picnics. When I write about such places, I can *see* them in my mind's eye; familiarity may not breed contempt, but it does put a curb on the romantic (or scholarly) imagination. One still remembers, as a kind of awful warning, the cheerful way in which Munro and Bury, from their studies, beached the Greek fleet at Salamis on some highly uncomfortable rocks.[1]

I would like to express my gratitude to Professor Eugene Vanderpool for much help and advice, not least during several long topographical expeditions, on foot, through the hills of Attica. To the Directors of the American School of Classical Studies and the British School of Archaeology in Athens I must once again express my warmest thanks for making me free of their excellent libraries, which provide the most congenial conditions imaginable for research work. The Librarians of both Schools, Mrs Philippides and Mrs Rabnett, have, as always, given me

advice and assistance far beyond the call of duty. Mr Joseph Shaw, of
the American School of Classical Studies, most generously made available to me unpublished surveys of Plataea and Thermopylae, without
which it would have been a much harder task to construct remotely
adequate maps of either area, and in the case of Plataea virtually impossible (for Thermopylae I have also drawn freely on Pierre MacKay's
excellent survey, published in the *American Journal of Archaeology*). I owe a
great deal to stimulating discussions, on Marathon and Salamis especially, with my pupils of College Year in Athens, and in particular to
Miss Elizabeth Knebli, who went to much trouble to obtain photostats
of rare articles on my behalf. My affectionate and grateful thanks go to
George and Ismene Phylactopoulos for many things, not least for helping so signally to solve my transport problem. Professor C. W. J. Eliot
read an earlier and very different draft of parts of this book; he is in no
way responsible for the views expressed in the final version. Nor is
Mr A. R. Burn, who read my entire typescript and saved me from many
errors, thus placing me doubly in his debt. My greatest debt of gratitude,
however, is to my publishers, whose farsighted generosity has made it
possible for me to devote my full energies to this and several other long-
cherished projects which, without their support, might never have seen
the light of day.

Methymna, August 1969   PETER GREEN

Copyright Acknowledgments

All translations of Herodotus, unless otherwise stated, are from the Penguin Classics version by the late Aubrey de Selincourt; those of Plutarch
are from Ian Scott-Kilvert's *Plutarch: The Rise and Fall of Athens*, in the
same series; and those of Diodorus Siculus from the Loeb Classical
Library edition by C. H. Oldfather. The translations of Aeschylus are
my own.

The translation of the Troezen Decree on p. 98 ff. is that first published by Prof. M. H. Jameson, *Historia* 12 (1963), 386.

The translation of the Oath of Plataea on p. 240 is that by A. R. Burn,
first published in *Persia and the Greeks* (1962), 513.

In memory of all those
who have given their lives for Greece

PART ONE

DARIUS
AND THE WEST

THE great conflict between Greece and Persia – or, to be more accurate, between a handful of states in mainland Greece and the whole might of the Persian empire at its zenith – must always remain one of the most inspiring episodes in European history. As Aeschylus and Herodotus clearly saw (despite the obfuscations of national pride and propaganda) this had been an ideological struggle, the first of its kind known to us. On one side, the towering, autocratic figure of the Great King; on the other, the voluntary and imperfect discipline of proudly independent citizens. In Herodotus's account, Xerxes' soldiers are driven forward to fight under the lash; the recurrent Persian motif of flogging, mutilation and torture throughout his narrative repays study. The Greeks, on the other hand, fought because they had a personal stake in victory: their struggle was to preserve a hard-won and still precarious heritage of freedom.

In Aeschylus's play *The Persians*, produced only eight years after the crowning mercy of Salamis, and written by a man who had fought in the battle himself, what matters is not so much the picture of the Persians – an inevitable caricature: no Greek ever really understood Achaemenid ethics – so much as the spirit, the ideal, which Aeschylus shows us animating the Greeks. The Queen Mother Atossa, Darius's widow, asks a Royal Councillor various questions concerning Athens, and finally (as one might expect from a dowager in her position) quizzes him on the Athenian power-structure, which she assumes to be a replica, *mutatis mutandis*, of that at Susa.

'What man rules them?' she asks. 'Who is in command of their armies?' The answer surely drew a round of applause from that all-too-partisan Athenian audience: 'They say they are no man's slaves or dependents.' This to Atossa suggests incompetent anarchy, a view which the Athenian *demos*, in its more perverse moments, might seem to confirm. 'Then how,' she enquires, 'could they stand against a foreign invasion?' – a feed-line if ever there was one. 'So well,' the Councillor tells her, 'that they destroyed the great and magnificent army of Darius'.

Aeschylus, like most Athenian patriots, may have exaggerated the

3

military significance of Marathon, but hardly its psychological impact. David had taken on Goliath, against all reasonable odds, and won. That Juggernaut, the Persian war-machine – nothing so formidable had appeared since the collapse of the Assyrian empire – was not, after all, invincible: the lesson went home. Ten years after Marathon, when Greece faced invasion on a scale that made this previous landing look like a mere border raid, the memory of victory still kept Athens, Sparta and her allies fighting. It was, by any rational calculation, an insane piece of intransigence. Those who thought of themselves as long-term realists – including the priests of the Delphic Oracle, and the leaders of nearly every Northern Greek state and Aegean island – argued, like French Vichy politicians in 1940, that resistance was hopeless, and collaboration the only logical answer to Persia's threat. Logically, they were quite right. But great victories of the human spirit against fearful odds – as both Themistocles and Churchill so clearly saw – are not won, in the last resort, by logic. Reason alone is not enough.

About the middle of the sixth century BC, just before the Persian conqueror Cyrus overran Ionia, Phocylides of Miletus wrote: 'A little *polis* living orderly in a high place is stronger than a blockheaded Nineveh.' Though Ionia fell, and Miletus – alone of Ionian cities – made a treaty with the invader, Phocylides, in the long view, was absolutely right. This is a shining central truth which we should never forget when studying the Graeco-Persian wars. In recent years, thanks to spectacular work by Oriental scholars and archaeologists, our knowledge of Achaemenid Persia has increased out of all recognition. Today we are in a position to assess Darius, Xerxes, and their civilisation with greater insight and less *a priori* bias than was possible for even so open-minded an enquirer as Herodotus. Our picture is no longer the xenophobic libel produced by Greek witnesses: what we now have to watch out against is a mood of indiscriminate over-enthusiasm.

Those with a naturally authoritarian cast of mind tend to be fascinated by the Achaemenid empire for just the reasons which induced the Greeks to hold out against it: monolithic (if not always efficient) administration, theocratic absolutism, lack of political opposition (except for the occasional bloody-minded palace intrigue), and easygoing provincial administration by the satraps (provided their subjects made no trouble and paid their taxes regularly). Arnold Toynbee has even suggested that it would have fared better with the Greeks had they lost the Persian Wars: enforced unity and peace might have stopped them dissipating their energies on absurd internecine feuding (and parochial lost causes) until they were absorbed by the benevolent *pax Romana* of Augustus.

4

What such arguments fail to appreciate is that the whole concept of political and intellectual liberty, of the constitutional state – however individually inefficient or corrupt – depended on one thing: that the Greeks, for whatever motive, decided to stand out against the Oriental system of palace absolutism, and did so with remarkable success. Modern Europe owes nothing to the Achaemenids. We may admire their imposing if oppressive architecture, and gaze in something like awe – from prostration-level, as it were – at the great *apadana* of Persepolis, with its marvellous bas-reliefs. Yet the civilisation which could produce such things is almost as alien to us as that of the Aztecs, and for not dissimilar reasons. Achaemenid Persia produced no great literature or philosophy: her one lasting contribution to mankind was, characteristically enough, Zoroastrianism. Like Carthage, she perpetuated a fundamentally static culture, geared to the maintenance of a theocratic *status quo*, and hostile (where not blindly indifferent) to original creativity in any form.*

Against this monolithic opposition the Greek achievement stands out all the more clearly, an inexplicable miracle. We sometimes take it for granted that democratic institutions should have evolved in the city-states from Solon's day onwards, reaching their apogee in the Persian Wars and the fifty years which followed. Nothing could be further from the predictable course of events. Free scientific enquiry, free political debate, annually appointed magistrates, decision by majority vote – all these things ran flat counter to the whole pattern of thought in any major civilisation with which the Greeks had to deal. Their achievement, however brought about, and for whatever self-seeking or otherwise disreputable motives, becomes all the more extraordinary when viewed against such a background.

It would be hard to labour this crucial point too much, especially since the story which follows is, in detail, often far from inspiring. For one Greek Churchill there are a dozen Greek Lavals. Cowardice, self-interest, treacherous double-dealing and political in-fighting, between cities and factions within those cities, meet us at every turn. Hostile propaganda and the calculated smear-technique are commonplaces: not even Herodotus wholly avoids suspicion here. Even the most glorious and best-known of actions often turn out, on close inspection, to have singularly mixed motives behind them. Yet nothing, in the last resort, can tarnish the splendour of that marvellous achievement, when,

* This attitude is characteristic of all the Near East civilisations, even (despite a more striking artistic achievement) of Egypt. Theocratic absolutism applied here with equal rigour; and the one Pharaoh – Akhnaton – who attempted to buck the system had no more long-term success in his crusade than Julian the Apostate.

as Pindar (a Theban, not an Athenian) wrote, 'the sons of Athens laid a bright foundation-stone of freedom'.

'The Persian empire', it has been well said, 'was created within the space of a single generation by a series of conquests that followed one another with a rapidity scarcely equalled except by Alexander, and by the Arabs in the first generation after the death of Mohammed'. It also survived, with its boundaries intact, and under the same ruling house, for over two hundred years, which is more than can be said for Alexander's *oikoumené* – or, strictly speaking, for Islam. In the mid-sixth century the Near East was parcelled out into several small empires: those of Media, ruled over from Ecbatana by Astyages; Babylonia, and Lydia, where Croesus held sway. At this time the inhabitants of Parsa were mere upland tribesmen, hardy fighters but little known – and probably without power – beyond their own domains.* Yet a bare twenty-five years later this limited region (now Fars, centred on modern Shiraz) controlled a greater empire than that of Assyria at her apogee: the largest single administrative complex that had ever existed in the ancient world hitherto. For this achievement one man, ultimately, was responsible.

In 559 Cyrus son of Cambyses (more correctly Kurash son of Kambujiwa, but Herodotus's Greek transliterations have become too familiar to abandon) ascended the throne of Anshan, a Median vassal kingdom lying north and east of Susa. Cyrus's house, founded by Achaemenes [Hakamanish] had for some time held sway in Parsa and its environs; but Cyrus himself was a man of more far-reaching ambitions, and fully endowed with the military and political genius necessary to achieve them. He united the various Parsa tribes under his leadership; he built a new Achaemenid capital, Pasargadae; and he made a profitable alliance with Nabonidus, who had usurped Nebuchadnezzar's throne in Babylon. After thus preparing the ground, he launched a full-scale rebellion against Astyages – who, like so many weak rulers, was both cruel and unpopular.

The first army Astyages sent against Cyrus deserted *en masse* to the Persians – largely at the instigation of their commander, Harpagus, whose son Astyages had previously executed in a most unpleasant fashion. The Median King then took the field himself. Outside Pasargadae his troops mutinied, and turned him over to Cyrus. This was in 550. Cyrus proceeded to capture the Median capital, Ecbatana, which

* Herzfeld (see Bibliography) has recently argued that Parsa's large eastern expansion was already an accomplished fact. His speculations are intriguing (Kambujiwa indeed sounds like an Indian name) but not conclusive.

yielded him a fabulous amount of booty. From now on Media lost its independence, and in fact became the first satrapy of the new Persian empire. In order to have a secure base for further expansion, Cyrus took no punitive measures against Media, and for all intents and purposes placed the Medes on an equal footing with his own people. Harpagus was only the first of many Median nobles to hold high civil or military office under Cyrus and his successors: ironically, where we would speak, generically, of 'the Persians', Herodotus and other Greek writers always refer to 'the Medes'.

By conquering Astyages Cyrus also laid claim – *ex officio*, as it were – to all Media's satellite dependencies: Mesopotamia, Syria, Armenia, Cappadocia, the *disiecta membra* of the old Assyrian empire. Here, of course, he came into direct conflict with Nabonidus, who had ambitions to recover some at least of the lost glories of the old Babylonian empire. But Cyrus, far from giving away Mesopotamia or Syria to a potential rival, meant, ultimately, to absorb Babylon itself. There were too may vultures circling the carcase already – including Croesus of Lydia, who in 547 marched east across the Halys River in the hope of picking up a few more outlying provinces. He had been encouraged in this action by the Delphic Oracle, which informed him, with classic ambiguity, that if he crossed the Halys he would destroy a great empire. So he did; but it happened to be his own. His cavalry horses fled in terror from the rank and unfamiliar smell of Cyrus's camels. In 546, after a fortnight's siege, the Lydian capital Sardis fell, and Croesus probably committed suicide by self-immolation to save himself worse indignities. Various popular legends about his end – such as Apollo's miraculous intervention to save him from the flames – look like self-exculpatory propaganda put out by Delphi after the event.

Cyrus himself merely recorded, with sinister brevity, that 'he marched to the land of Lydia. He killed its king [?]. He took its booty. He placed in it his own garrison.' This process, with variations, was to be repeated in a good many places. Between 546 and 539 Cyrus systematically mopped up the coastal cities of Greek Ionia and the Dardanelles: only the half-savage Lukku (Lycians) offered more than a token resistance to his seemingly invincible armies. During the same period he subjugated the whole of the great Iranian plateau, penetrating far beyond the Caspian, to Samarkand and the Jaxartes River (now the Syr-Darya, flowing from the mountains of Tien-Shan to the Aral Sea). Finally came the absorption of Babylonia. Nabonidus had been unwise enough to form a private alliance with Croesus: whether this made any difference to his ultimate fate is debatable. While he held court in Arabia, his son Belshazzar was left to govern Babylon. Nabonidus, an archaising religious dilettante, had contrived to offend the powerful priesthood of Bel-Marduk: his capital seethed with discontent and treachery. It hardly needed a Jewish prophet to spell out the meaning of the writing on the wall for Belshazzar's benefit. On 29 October 539 Cyrus made a ceremonial state entry into Babylon without a blow being struck against him, and the following year his son Cambyses was installed as Viceroy.

Cyrus now found himself undisputed master of the greatest empire the Near East had ever seen. What was more, he showed himself a most subtle and sophisticated conqueror. He was the first Oriental autocrat to realise that toleration and benevolence, far from being signs of weakness, could be made to pay handsome dividends: that more could be done by clever conciliatory propaganda than through any amount of iron-fisted terrorisation. In Babylon there were no pogroms or deportations, while local deities were treated with scrupulous respect – in return for which, naturally enough, Cyrus claimed to have their divine backing. 'When I made my gracious entry into Babylon,' he announced, 'Marduk, the great lord, turned the noble race of the Babylonians towards me, and I gave daily care to his worship. My numerous troops marched peacefully into Babylon. In all Sumer and Akkad I permitted no unfriendly treatment.' For modern readers, however, Cyrus's most famous example of religious toleration is probably his edict for the rebuilding of the Temple in Jerusalem (537). Whenever possible, he believed in placating minorities. It cost little, and it paid handsome dividends.

The remaining eight years of his life Cyrus devoted, for the most part, to organising this great and heterogeneous empire he had acquired. He divided it into about twenty provinces, each under a viceroy whose Persian title – *khshathrapavan*, 'Protector of the Kingdom' – was transliterated by the Greeks as *satrapes*, and has given us the generic term 'satrap'. Two of these satrapies contained Greek subjects: Lydia, with its governmental seat at Sardis, included the Ionian seaboard, while Phrygia covered the Dardanelles, the Sea of Marmara [Propontis], and the southern shore of the Black Sea. These satraps, especially in the vast eastern provinces, wielded enormous power. They not only concentrated all civil administration in their own hands, but acted as military commander-in-chief as well. Such centralisation of authority was convenient, but had obvious dangers – not least that some ambitious governor might become too big for his satrapal boots, and attempt to usurp the throne. To avoid such a contingency, the Chief Secretary, senior Treasury official, and garrison commanders of each province were appointed by the Great King, and directly responsible to him. More sinister was the travelling inspector, or commissar, known as 'the

Great King's Eye', who made a confidential yearly report on the state of every imperial province.

Cyrus spent much time at Pasargadae, his new capital, where he built himself a great palace – its audience-hall alone was 187 feet long – and a walled park, the lodge-gates of which were guarded by Assyrian-style winged bulls. Above, he had cut the proud trilingual inscription: 'I am Cyrus, the King, the Achaemenid.' Pasargadae stands some 6,000 feet above sea-level, a chill upland plateau: the coda to Herodotus's *Histories* describes a move on the part of the Persian aristocracy to relocate their capital in a milder region. This proposal, however, was flatly vetoed by Cyrus, and his nobles agreed, choosing rather 'to live in a rugged land and rule than to cultivate rich plains and be slaves'. Here, too, Cyrus built his tomb, perhaps in premonition of what was to come: work on the palace was still unfinished when, in 530, he marched east to fight the wild tribesmen beyond the Syr-Darya, and was killed in battle. His career – astonishing enough in sober truth – soon acquired an overlay of heroic myth, to which admiring Greek writers contributed more than their share. Xenophon's *Cyropaedia*, that remarkable essay in historical fiction, shows how far the process had gone by the fourth century BC.

Cyrus's son Cambyses ascended the throne without incident in September 530, after some years' training as Viceroy of Babylon. The hostile picture of him drawn by our sources aroused some suspicion in Herodotus, and is almost certainly much exaggerated. Neither the Egyptians whom he conquered, nor his ultimate successor Darius, as we shall see, had much good reason to praise him in retrospect. Modern research suggests that the atrocities he was said to have committed – in a fit of insanity – after his invasion of Egypt were, for the most part, invented by Egyptian priests summarily deprived of their rich temple perquisites. In fact Cambyses seems to have gone out of his way, as Culican says, to 'adopt the titles of Egyptian royal protocol and to put himself in proper relationship to the Egyptian gods'. Here he was clearly carrying on Cyrus's successful policy elsewhere. But even if not the sadistic, heavy-drinking paranoiac of tradition, Cambyses proved a tougher, less paternalistic despot than his father, and made numerous enemies in consequence. Apart from Egypt (where he spent most of his short reign) he obtained the submission of Cyrene and Cyprus and, most important, of the Phoenician states. Persia thus acquired at one stroke what hitherto she had notably lacked: a strong fighting navy.

About March 522, while Cambyses was still abroad, rebellion broke out in Media, led by a man who claimed to be the King's younger brother. Cambyses hurriedly left Egypt, but died, in somewhat suspicious circumstances, when he had got no further than Syria. The rebellion was put down by a junta under Darius [Darayavaush] son of Hystaspes, who belonged to a collateral branch of the Achaemenid family, and had actually been serving as a staff-officer with Cambyses in Egypt. Darius afterwards claimed, in his self-laudatory Behistun inscription, that the would-be pretender was no Achaemenid, but a Magian priest named Gaumata. Modern scholars believe that he may well have been Cambyses' brother after all, and that the true struggle lay between rival Median and Persian claimants for the throne. Darius's *ex post facto* account is highly suspicious in places. How did an impostor come to rally all the central provinces behind him – let alone contrive to deceive his own putative mother? And if Darius's achievement was to rid Persia of a hated usurper, it is remarkable how hard the job proved. A pogrom against the Magi merely triggered off further revolts: in a single year Darius fought, and won, nineteen major battles. But in July 521 the main fighting was over, and before 520 Darius had established control, however precariously, over almost all of Cyrus's former domains.

These events, which completely transformed the balance of power in the Near East for centuries to come, at first made singularly little impression on the city-states of mainland Greece. One of the oddest, and surely the most significant, facts about Graeco-Persian relations is the abysmal ignorance, tinged with contempt, which each civilisation maintained concerning the other. Even so sympathetic a student as Herodotus knew virtually nothing of the Persian aristocratic ideal, though in many ways it much resembled that upheld by Homer's heroes. Burn's description is admirable:

> The Persian gentleman of the great days was ... encouraged by his religion to be manly, honourable, athletic and courageous; devoted to hunting and the promotion and protection of agriculture; contemptuous of trade, and shunning debt, which 'led to lying'; dignified in his manners, even a little prudish.

There is little here that would be recognised by a reader of Aeschylus. Zoroaster [Zarathustra] had promulgated the doctrine that all men must work for the establishment of God's Righteous Order on earth, a clarion-call for would-be imperialists in any age, and especially attractive to Darius. To begin with he underestimated the Greeks no less ludicrously than they did him; but not for long. What should, by any normal calculation, have been a minor frontier campaign was blown up, ultimately, into war on the grand scale, East against West in a conflict that rocked the empire of Darius and Xerxes to its very foundations.

The degree of mutual ignorance may be gauged from a delightful anecdote told by Herodotus. When Cyrus, operating on the divide-and-rule principle, confirmed Croesus's previous treaty with Miletus, the other Ionian cities, fearing the worst, appealed for aid to Sparta. The Spartans had recently emerged as the most powerful military state in the Peloponnese, perhaps in all Greece. Two long and grinding wars had – for the time being, at any rate – broken the spirit of their rebellious Messenian serfs. A league of Peloponnesian states had been established under Spartan leadership. If any power in Greece could save Ionia, it was surely this iron-hard militaristic régime. But whether the Spartans would commit themselves was quite another matter. Constant fear of revolt at home made them singularly reluctant to send Spartan troops over the frontier: the present crisis proved no exception. The Ionian spokesman dressed himself in purple (a psychological error, one feels) and made a long speech, which fell very flat indeed. The Spartans refused to give Ionia any military aid.

Nevertheless, a single fifty-oared galley was dispatched across the Aegean: best to see just what was going on. Furthermore, 'the most distinguished of the men on board . . . was sent to Sardis to forbid Cyrus, on behalf of the Lacedaemonians, to harm any Greek city upon pain of their displeasure'. (Isolationism, then as now, formed an excellent breeding-ground for megalomania.) Cyrus, perhaps a little disconcerted despite himself by such sublime effrontery, asked who on earth the Spartans might be, that they dared address him thus. On being told, he made a reply to their herald which, whether authentic or not, pin-points the radical split in temperament between Greek and Persian. 'I have never yet,' he said, 'been afraid of men who have a special meeting-place in the centre of their city, where they swear this and that and cheat each other'. Herodotus goes on to explain that this was because the Greeks had market-places, whereas the Persians did not: a revealing admission. Persia, in fact, was still a basically feudal society, which most of Greece had not been for a century or so: this constituted the deepest socio-economic cleavage (religion apart) between the two cultures.

What Cyrus, as a feudal aristocrat, despised most about the Greeks, over and above their banausic addiction to trade, was the free exchange of opinions that went with it. To a Persian, the Great King *was* the State, in a sense which no Bourbon monarch could have apprehended, and which is demonstrated by the pattern of all Achaemenid inscriptions. The solar radiance of the King's presence also illuminated – in his penumbra, as it were – a few high kinsmen and Court officials; beyond lay outer darkness, a wilderness of faceless, prostrate peasants. This attitude, on both political and religious grounds, was anathema to the Greeks. The Greek word *agora*, 'market', meant originally 'place of assembly'; there was no clear differentiation between the two. The more advanced Greek city-states had long since got rid of their hereditary noble rulers, together with the *tyrannoi* who succeeded them, and were feeling their way towards some sort of democratic government. (One unexpected exception was Athens, where Solon's cautiously conservative reforms had been followed by an aristocratic dictatorship under Peisistratus.) Ironically, Cyrus delivered his snub to men whose régime had a good deal in common with Persian feudalism: many diehard Dorian nobles would have applauded his sentiments.

The conquest of Ionia taught Persian officialdom some useful lessons about the Greeks – while at the same time minimising the very real danger they constituted. It did not take long for Cyrus and his commanders to realise that, man for man, the Greek hoplite or marine was a formidable fighter: from now on Greeks commanded a high price as Persian mercenaries. But it was equally obvious (to judge by the sorry defence the Ionians put up) that Greek *polis* government formed the worst possible basis for any kind of concerted action, whether civil or military: here the monolithic Achaemenid command-structure came into its own. There were always rival factions in every Greek city-state, to be bribed, exploited, and played off against each other. Greek oracles, like Greek politicians, turned out to be far from incorruptible. *Docet experientia*: with cynical aplomb Cyrus swallowed up the Ionian cities piecemeal, and installed in each a cooperative Greek *tyrannos* – perhaps 'quisling' would be too strong an equivalent – to run it on behalf of the local satrap. Free trade was encouraged, and most commercial concessions granted by the Lydians left intact. A minority (composed for the most part of free-thinking intellectuals, such as Pythagoras or Xenophanes) emigrated rather than compromise with Persian overlordship; the rest stayed put, sized up their situation realistically, and set themselves – with some success – to make it show a handsome profit.

This honeymoon between Ionia's merchants and the Great King began to come under increasing strain from the moment of Darius's accession in 522. That same year Polycrates, the powerful tyrant of Samos, was lured to the mainland and executed by Oroetes, the satrap of Lydia. Though Oroetes himself was afterwards put to death by Darius, the Persians took care to install a puppet-ruler on Samos. The first stepping-stone across the Aegean had been captured: others were soon to follow. After a preliminary reconnaissance expedition, Darius took a large army over the Bosporus on a bridge of boats, marched north to the Danube, crossed it, and invaded the wild northern steppes of Scythia. Though this expedition was by no means a complete success, from now on (513) it became increasingly clear that Persia meant business in Europe. Darius's general Megabazus captured town after town in Thrace. Amyntas, King of Macedon, gave earth and water in token of vassalage. Otanes, who succeeded Megabazus as 'Captain-General of the men along the sea', subdued the rebellious key ports of Byzantium and Chalcedon, at the Black Sea entrance to the Propontis.

Persia now controlled all sea-traffic through the Straits. For the first time, there was a real threat to the food-supply of mainland Greece. Darius had lost no time in recapturing Egypt, with its vast wheatfields. If he closed the Dardanelles, traffic to the Black Sea and South Russia would be cut off as well. Now for fifty years at least Athens, in particular, had been faced with a problem of rising population. Perhaps as early as 594 it had been made illegal to export grain from Attica – which was, in any case, a bad area for growing wheat. Home consumption soon began to soar above the amount produced. By the end of the sixth century BC something like two-thirds of Athens' wheat had to be imported from abroad, and the proportion rose steadily as time went on. The two best grain-markets in the Near East were, precisely, Egypt and South Russia; Darius now controlled access to both of them. In addition, he possessed unlimited supplies of gold, which the Crimean corn-barons often insisted on by way of payment. Thus Darius was also in a position to outbid other competitors in the open market, and force prices up to a level the Greeks could not afford. From now on the threat of the Barbarian, a vast horrific shadow, loomed constantly over the Greek world.

The degree of actual danger would clearly depend very much on the personal character and policies of the Great King. In this respect Darius gave small cause for optimism. All the signs were that he meant to extend Persia's sphere of control into Europe: just how far, no one could tell. Herodotus describes a Persian naval intelligence mission sent out to survey the coasts and harbours, not only of mainland Greece, but also of southern Italy. From the very beginning Darius showed himself a formidable administrator, with strong commercial interests: not for nothing did Iranian noblemen refer to him, half admiringly, half in well-bred scorn, as 'the huckster'. He dug a forerunner of the modern Suez Canal, 150 feet wide, and deep enough to carry large merchantmen. At the same time he sent a Greek captain, Scylax of Caryanda, to explore the sea-route to India by way of the Persian Gulf. These two moves, taken together, reveal a shrewd eye for profitable areas of trade. He reorganised the satrapies, improved provincial communications, set up an efficient civil service, and adapted the Babylonian legal code for Persian use. Nor was he modestly reticent about his achievements. 'What is right I love,' he proclaimed, 'and what is not right I hate'. No one was likely to contradict him.

13

Above all, Darius initiated extensive financial and fiscal reforms: the benefit of these has been overrated. To standardise weights and measures was sensible enough; so was the introduction of an official gold and silver coinage. But the Great King's economic reputation is hardly

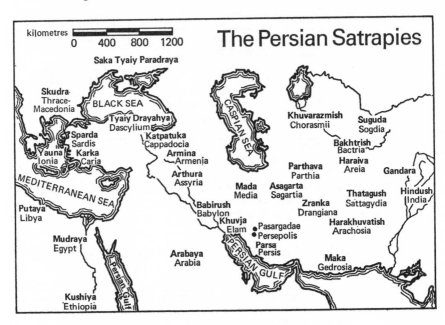

The Persian Satrapies

enhanced by his attitude to credit, tribute, and the flow of capital within the empire. The total revenue from imperial taxes payable in precious metal has been calculated at 14,560 Euboic talents, which – taking the talent at $57\frac{1}{2}$ lb weight – represents an enormous sum: 'something like twenty millions of dollars with purchasing power several times greater,' says Olmstead. Yet very little of this bullion was even coined, let alone fed back into circulation. For the most part it was melted down into ingots, and stored in the vaults at Susa, which thus became something like the Fort Knox of antiquity. Darius seems neither to have known nor cared that this policy was progressively draining the Empire of gold and silver, with obvious, inevitable results: chronic inflation, spiralling prices, and, after a time, the near-collapse of Persian agriculture in a welter of unpaid debts and unredeemed mortgages. His idea of credit was restricted to specie, and he saw no reason why the safeguard which it represented as reserve capital should not remain a royal monopoly.

In modern terms, any such programme would be regarded, rightly, as pure economic lunacy; yet Darius and his successors clung to it with unswerving faith. Long-term financial planning was something unknown in the ancient world. What the Great King saw was that he could outbid all competition for the purchase of desirable commodities (such as mercenaries or wheat), finance the construction of new palaces, and in general retain a comforting margin of solvency, large enough to deal with any foreseeable crisis. His near-monopoly of gold and silver also offered ample scope for economic blackmail, as the Greeks soon learnt to their cost. It never seems to have struck him that he might eventually exhaust the Mediterranean's resources of precious metal altogether; if one goose stopped laying golden eggs (so the argument ran) another could always be found. This was merely one more reason, as Darius saw it, for extending Persian rule westward across the Aegean.

The Great King's short-sighted avarice had peculiarly disastrous consequences in Ionia. If Darius had not been so hedged about with theocratic delusions of grandeur, he would surely have realised that these rich commercial cities would only collaborate so long as he made it worth their while to do so. Instead, he slapped heavy taxes on them, severely curtailed their free trade with the Black Sea, and refused to change their system of government – though the whole concept of rule by tyrants, let alone puppet tyrants, had been abandoned by the free Greek world. Since about 535, moreover, Carthage and Etruria between them had closed the Western Mediterranean to Greek shipping. Ionia, in fact, was beginning to feel the pinch. The tribute exacted from 'the Greeks of Asia', together with Caria, Lycia and Pamphylia, was 400 talents, or 2,400,000 drachmas – as much as fifth-century Athens made out of her whole sea-empire. When Sybaris, that proverbially rich Greek city of southern Italy, was destroyed by her neighbour and rival, Croton (511–10), the Milesians shaved their heads and wept: they were mourning not only lost friends, but fat lost profits. Sooner rather than later, Ionian resentment at Darius's new-broom policies was liable to boil over in active rebellion. In 513 Histiaeus of Miletus and other Greek leaders had held the Danube bridge for Darius during his Scythian expedition. By 499 it was quite another story.

This ominous march of events made singularly little impression on the Greek mainland states, which, as usual, were preoccupied with their own parochial affairs to the virtual exclusion of all else. The fate of Polycrates, the fact that Persia now controlled a large Phoenician fleet, the softening-up by Darius's generals of Thrace and the Dardanelles – here was the writing on the wall with a vengeance, yet few, until much later, were willing to recognise it as such. At best, the Persian

B

situation (it was thought) added a new dimension to the domestic power-game.

In Sparta, King Cleomenes kept a watchful eye on Sparta's old rival Argos, and gave cautious encouragement to a group of Athenian exiles who were planning the overthrow of the Peisistratid government. Peisistratus himself had died in 528–7; one of the two sons who succeeded him was assassinated in 514, while the survivor, Hippias, was thus turned into a frightened, cruel despot. Amongst those banished by him, and lucky to escape a worse fate, was a remarkable family of aristocratic opportunists, the Alcmaeonidae, who remained at the centre of Athenian political life for the next century (both Pericles and Alcibiades were related to them). Like the Cecils under Elizabeth I, the Alcmaeonidae were interested in two things only, wealth and political power, but these they pursued relentlessly. If, while taking over the Athenian government, they could also win renown for having rid Athens of an obnoxious tyranny, so much the better. Exile was nothing new to them, and they made the most of it, winning the support of Delphi, whose priests now prefaced every Spartan oracle with the injunction to 'free Athens'.

Cleomenes can have had few illusions about the Alcmaeonidae and their leader, Cleisthenes; but at least they both wanted the same thing, even if for very different reasons. Cleomenes was not, as is sometimes suggested, Hellas's champion against the threat of Persian aggression. This would imply a considerable degree of both altruism and foresight, two characteristics in which Spartan foreign policy was singularly deficient. In fact, some of Sparta's closest allies at the time – Thessaly, Aegina, Delphi, Boeotia – had Persian sympathies *ab initio*, and later emerged as wholehearted *collabos*. What is more, when Ionia finally revolted, and appealed for aid to the homeland, Sparta, as so often, stayed neutral, preferring to keep her forces for an all-out attack on Argos. Nothing could have been more selfish or short-sighted; pan-Hellenic patriotism was nowhere in sight here. Cleomenes wanted the Peisistratids out, not because of their known tie-up with Persia – much less through any ideological opposition to tyranny as such – but because a strong Athens might well become a commercial and military threat to the Peloponnese.

The Alcmaeonids' first attempt at a take-over flopped embarrassingly. They occupied a stronghold on Mt Parnes, in northern Attica, where some of their friends from Athens joined them. But if they expected their countrymen at large to welcome them as deliverers, they were in for a disappointment. Most people must have reasoned (and who could blame them?) that there was little to be gained by changing one noble junta for another. The invasion fizzled out. A year later (511)

Cleomenes was persuaded to send a somewhat inadequate naval task-force to Phaleron. Hippias got wind of its approach well in advance, hired a force of Thessalian cavalry, and drove the Spartans off, with heavy losses, almost as soon as they had disembarked.

This spectacle of rival Athenian factions slugging it out with the aid of foreign troops must have produced a certain weary cynicism among the local peasantry. King Cleomenes, on the other hand, took Sparta's humiliation very hard indeed, and in 510 launched a full-scale invasion by way of the Isthmus. Hippias shut himself up on the Acropolis, with good defences and plentiful supplies; but by a stroke of bad luck his family was captured at the frontier, and he had to surrender. Granted a safe-conduct, he left Athens for his estates at Sigeum, on the Dardanelles, where he soon set up a government-in-exile. Since the Spartans were supposed to be 'liberating' Athens, they could neither choose their own junta nor keep an occupation force on the spot indefinitely – a very modern dilemma. The moment they pulled out, a savage struggle for power began.

Cleisthenes had returned from exile under the Spartan military umbrella: to get back into power by constitutional means, once that umbrella had been removed, was a far trickier business. The conservative group, led by Isagoras, son of Teisander, fought hard – and with considerable initial success – to prevent an Alcmaeonid take-over. They began their campaign by scrutinising the electoral roll, and getting a good many of Cleisthenes' 'new immigrant' supporters disenfranchised on technical quibbles. But they soon saw that it would pay off better, in the long run, to capture the popular vote rather than antagonise it. A law was passed abolishing the judicial use of torture against Athenian citizens; other similar measures followed; for two years Isagoras had things very much his own way. The electorate showed no sign whatsoever, at this stage, of welcoming Cleisthenes as a great democratic reformer, for the very good reason that no such idea had yet entered his head.

In 508, however, Isagoras (a good friend, incidentally, of Cleomenes) was elected Chief Archon. Cleisthenes had already held this office, and was thereby debarred from standing again. Something had to be done: as a desperate measure Cleisthenes, to borrow Herodotus's ambiguous phrase, 'took the people into partnership'. This probably meant a radical extension of the franchise: to put it bluntly, Cleisthenes bribed the citizen-body to support him by offering them their first real stake in the government, a government that he intended to lead by means of their block vote. The proposal was rushed through the Assembly; and so, by a somewhat singular *accouchement*, Athenian democracy finally struggled to birth. The child proved noisy, healthy and troublesome almost before it could walk; which was lucky, since otherwise its chances of survival would have been slim.

Isagoras, no longer in control of the very people who had elected him Archon, and seeing his power at an end, appealed once more to Sparta. A Spartan regiment marched into Athens; Cleisthenes and the Alcmaeonidae were expelled. They went quietly; they could afford to wait. The Spartans then blacklisted some 700 Athenian families (of known or suspected radical tendencies), and attempted to set up a puppet ruling council composed of conservative yes-men. At this point the newly democratised Athenians decided they had had enough. There was a sudden, violent, and surprisingly successful riot. Isagoras, the Spartans, and their supporters found themselves besieged on the Acropolis. The Spartans were eventually allowed to leave Attica, and smuggled Isagoras out with them; the rest surrendered, and stood trial before a people's court, which demonstrated its democratic solidarity by condemning them to death. Cleisthenes returned home in triumph, to the cheers of his supporters. This time there was no opposition. On the other hand, some large political promises had to be fulfilled, or there would be a swift reversion to factional anarchy.

Cleisthenes did more than fulfil them; once in power he proved himself a far-sighted administrator, whose various reforms (including a complete overhaul of Attica's tribal system) were to reshape the pattern of Athenian political life for centuries to come. How far he was a genuine idealist, let alone planned the long-term consequences of his legislation, is highly debatable. He certainly aimed to break the power of Athens' leading aristocratic families; at the same time, he had every intention of keeping his own in power. His attitude to the *demos* was simple and traditional: he had rewarded them for their support, and now, like any noble patron, expected their gratitude. That within a few decades this same *demos* would be in a position to sway Athens' destiny Cleisthenes, I am convinced, neither foresaw nor intended. Yet in the context of Near East political life, the fact that he carried such reforms through at all is extraordinary enough; and the consequences of the Athenian people thus discovering their collective identity and power were momentous. Herodotus saw this very clearly:

Thus Athens went from strength to strength, and proved, if proof were needed, how noble a thing freedom is, not in one respect only, but in all; for while they were oppressed under a despotic government, they had no better success in war than any of their neighbours, yet, once the yoke was flung off, they proved the finest fighters of them all. [5.78: the Penguin version has 'in the world' for the last three words, which is incorrect.]

It is interesting, by way of contrast, to study the apologia which Herodotus puts in the mouth of Sparta's exiled king Demaratus, now adviser to Xerxes:

When the Spartans fight singly they are as brave as any man, but when they fight together they are supreme among all. For though they are free men, they are not free in all respects; law is the master whom they fear, far more than your subjects fear you. They do what the law commands and its command is always the same, not to flee in battle whatever the number of the enemy, but to stand and win, or die. [7.104.5]

These subtly contrasting ideologies (or ethnic myths) give one much food for thought. How far can freedom go before it degenerates into anarchy, or authority before it becomes mere authoritarianism? Anyone who cares to pursue fifth-century Greek history for another fifty years or so will find somewhat dusty answers to both these questions: Herodotus was wise to end his *Histories* at the point he did. Athens may have gone on to more dazzling achievements, but she never quite recaptured that early mood of buoyancy and dedication. In the immediate surge of self-confidence generated by Cleisthenes' programme, a Spartan king who rode roughshod over free Athenians had been thrown out for his pains. Within a very few years that new spirit would enable Athens to face, and conquer, an invading host far greater – in numbers at least – than any force she could muster against it. Athenian parish-pump politics did, after all, play a crucial part (if only psychologically) in winning the Persian Wars.

Fifth-century propaganda tried to portray this new democratic Athens as staunchly anti-Persian from the very beginning. In point of fact the Cleisthenic régime lost no time in sending an embassy to Darius's brother Artaphernes, satrap at Sardis, with the object of securing the Great King's recognition and alliance. They had very little choice in the matter; Hippias was busy pressing his own claim from Sigeum. Artaphernes was co-operative enough when Cleisthenes' envoys approached him, but made short work of their pretensions. First he enquired who the Athenians were, and where they dwelt; then he forced the ambassadors to offer earth and water in token of submission. This earned them a severe reprimand when they got back home – though no one can have expected Darius to grant Athens his support on more favourable terms, and the whole episode strongly suggests public face-saving by the government.

On the other hand, the merest suspicion of an Athenian *démarche* with Darius was enough to cause considerable alarm at Sparta. Cleomenes and Demaratus, the two Spartan kings, raised a Peloponnesian army and marched from the Isthmus: their declared objective was to restore a safe conservative régime at Athens, under Isagoras. (Cleomenes was said to be involved with Isagoras's wife, but this sounds like a typical Alcmaeonid slander.) Athens prepared to face yet another crisis, which, oddly, did not materialise. Near Eleusis the Corinthian allies had a change of heart and went home, Cleomenes quarrelled with Demaratus, and the whole expedition collapsed: it looks uncommonly as though someone in Athens had laid out a massive bribe at the eleventh hour. Three or four years later (504) the Spartans were in so nervous a state about this all-too-independent Athenian government that they actually suggested restoring Hippias, the exiled Peisistratid. Their cynical *volte-face* was too much for Sparta's Peloponnesian allies, who vetoed the proposal out of hand. The Spartans had been neatly hoist with their own anti-tyranny propaganda, and were now expected to stick by the principles they preached. All Cleomenes wanted at Athens was a reasonably subservient government, of any sort so long as it was manageable; what he got was a blast of moral obloquy, which forced him to back down in public.

Sparta's dilemma was partially solved in about 500, when Darius, after a decade of enjoyable fence-sitting, decided to recognise Hippias's government-in-exile. *My enemy's enemy is my friend*: for the time being, at least, Sparta and Athens stood, if not in the same camp, at any rate on the same side of the fence. Then, a year later, Ionia's long-smouldering discontent burst, at last, into fiery rebellion. Some of Darius's Greek 'tyrants' were lynched, while others, with remarkable aplomb, transformed themselves overnight into revolutionary generals. During the winter of 499–8 their leader, Aristagoras of Miletus, visited both Sparta and Athens trying to drum up support for his cause. The response was something less than enthusiastic. Cleomenes refused to commit Sparta: his isolationism saw no further than Argos. Non-intervention at this juncture was not only pure selfishness, but may well have ensured the failure of the revolt. With a few more squadrons from mainland Greece, Ionia could at least have held her three great naval bases – Lesbos, Chios and Samos. The resultant combined fleet would have been strong enough to deter Darius from invading Europe at all.

In Athens Aristagoras did somewhat better. The Athenians, after escaping a Spartan invasion, had proved equally firm with Artaphernes. Not at any price, they said, would they have Hippias back. In thus defying the Great King they were taking a big risk, and knew it. The revolt in Ionia must, to begin with, have looked like a godsend: as well be hanged for a sheep as a lamb. Aristagoras's speech before the

Assembly was typical anti-Persian propaganda, still going strong nearly two centuries later, in Alexander's day. The Persians were hopeless soldiers, he said. The country was loaded with loot. The whole campaign would be a walk-over. His audience gave him a mixed reception. Some wanted the whole fleet sent out: total commitment. Others were for following Sparta's example and staying neutral. In the end a squadron *was* dispatched to Ionia – but one of twenty ships only: perhaps all they could muster, more likely that most lethal of phenomena, a democratic compromise. 'The sailing of this fleet,' says Herodotus, 'was the beginning of trouble not only for Greece, but for the rest of the world as well'.

The trouble, as should by now be clear, had begun long before; but Athens' role in that initial expedition certainly precipitated it. The combined Greek fleet sailed to Ephesus, and from here the rebels' land forces marched to Sardis. They quickly captured the city, though the Acropolis held out. Their hopes of sacking it, however, were disappointed. Most of the houses were reed-built, and even those of brick had reed roofs. A soldier set one house on fire, and the whole city went up like tinder. Persian forces were approaching in strength, and the Ionians hastily pulled out. The Persians overtook them on the coast, at Ephesus, and defeated them with severe losses. At this point the Athenians, seeing which way things were going, hastily withdrew their squadron, sailed back home, and refused to take any further part in the revolt. But it was already too late. The burning of Sardis came as an affront which the Great King could neither forget nor forgive.

The story goes [says Herodotus] that when Darius learnt of the disaster, he did not give a thought to the Ionians, knowing perfectly well that the punishment for their revolt would come; instead, the first thing he did was to ask who the Athenians were, and then, on being told, gave orders that his bow should be handed to him. He took the bow, set an arrow on the string, shot it up into the air and cried: 'Grant, O God, that I may punish the Athenians.' Then he commanded one of his servants to repeat to him the words, 'Master, remember the Athenians,' three times, whenever he sat down to dinner [5.105].

Darius's confident optimism about the outcome of the rebellion was not misplaced. After some initial Ionian successes, the ponderous Persian war-machine lumbered into action. By 495 most resistance had been crushed. In 494 the Ionian fleet, 353 strong, was utterly defeated in a sea-battle off the island of Lade, in the gulf opposite Miletus. Miletus itself was captured and sacked. The men were mostly killed, the women and children enslaved. The whole southern quarter of the city was wiped out. Now Darius could say that the burning of Sardis had been avenged; yet this was no more than the prelude to his reprisals. The following spring the Persian fleet concluded its mopping-up operations. Chios, Lesbos, Tenedos and the Thracian Chersonese fell in turn. The cities on the eastern shore of the Dardanelles had already been recaptured, together with Byzantium and Chalcedon, which the Ionians had briefly held. All through the straits smoke curled blackly up from burning townships. Refugees fled everywhere – many of them to Sicily and Italy. Young boys and girls were sent off to servitude as palace eunuchs and members of the Royal Harem. The Ionian Revolt was over, and the invasion of mainland Greece had, by that fact alone, become inevitable.

The most interesting casualty of this *débâcle* was an enigmatic Athenian aristocrat named Miltiades. In about 555 his uncle had been sent out by Peisistratus – the Athenian tyrant, Hippias's father – to rule the Thracian Chersonese, the long peninsula which forms the European side of the Dardanelles. Here he established a species of family dynasty, whose benevolent but autocratic rule much resembled that of the 'White Rajahs' in Sarawak, and whose function, clearly, was to safeguard Athenian interests in the Dardanelles area. Miltiades himself became head of the family about 514. His position was ambiguous, to say the least of it: just where he stood, at any given point, with Persia, or Hippias, or the Ionians, or the government in Athens, is almost impossible to determine. In 514–3, he claimed, he had urged the destruction of the Danube bridge while Darius and his Persian army were cut off in Scythia. But the bridge survived; and so, significantly, did Miltiades. Thrown out of the Chersonese by the Scythians in 511, he managed to reinstate himself at the time of the Ionian Revolt – only to become a refugee when resistance collapsed. The Great King put a price on his head, and he only just escaped capture by the victorious Persian fleet. His son, in a following vessel, was not so lucky – at least, from the Greek viewpoint, since he was treated humanely by his captors, and finally 'went Persian'.

Naturally enough, Miltiades made for Athens, but his arrival there (summer 493) must have caused some embarrassment in official circles. He belonged to one of the most distinguished families in Athens, the Philaids, and therefore must be handled carefully. On the other hand, he was that most obnoxious of creatures in the eyes of Athens' new-style democrats – a tyrant. Worse still, he owed his appointment in the Chersonese to Peisistratus and Hippias. But, it could be argued by his supporters, his vast knowledge of Persia would be invaluable for Athens at this critical time. A thoroughly shady record, said some: prosecute him. Exactly the commander we need, said others: appoint him to the Board of Generals. There was no one who watched this debate more closely, or weighed up the odds with greater care, than the newly appointed Chief Archon. At the age of thirty-one – just above the minimum for eligibility – Themistocles, son of Neocles, from the Phrearri deme, had been elected to the highest civil office in Athens.

Oddly, we know almost nothing about Themistocles' early life. Herodotus first mentions him just before Salamis, in 480, when he is introduced as 'a man in Athens who had recently made a name for himself – Themistocles, more generally known as Neocles' son'. It is Dionysius of Halicarnassus [6.34] who reveals that he held the archonship,* and Plutarch [*Arist.* 5.3] from whom we learn that he fought, with distinction, though probably in the ranks, at Marathon. We may well have to blame Herodotus's aristocratic informants – not least the Alcmaeonidae – for the deliberate suppression of Themistocles' early career, and his systematic denigration throughout the *Histories*. His record during the Persian invasions was too brilliant and famous for anyone to forget; but at least it could be slanted in as unfavourable a light as possible. Herodotus never misses a chance of emphasising how selfish, greedy, and unprincipled a man Themistocles was. Like all the best propaganda, this picture contains more than a grain of truth; for a more generous, and more reliable, estimate we are lucky to have the magisterial summing-up by Thucydides.

Themistocles was born in 525 or 524 BC. His mother was a foreigner (Thracian, Carian or Acarnanian: accounts differ) but his father, Neocles, belonged to a distinguished aristocratic family, the Lycomidae. The hostile tradition that Neocles was a *novus homo*, without family or background, may depend on nothing more solid than casual etymologising – his name means 'newly famous' – or it may be true that he came from some wealthy *parvenu* family that had married into the Lycomidae. There must have been *something* in the rumour, because Themistocles – to judge from his portrait – did not look at all like a

---

* A few modern scholars, in fact, hold that Themistocles was Chief Archon in 483, and died in 449. As it happens, not only the two big Persian invasions of Greece (490 and 480) but also two major Athenian expeditions to Cyprus and Egypt (459, 449) were exactly ten years apart. Themistocles was traditionally supposed to have died at the age of sixty-five, and his death is associated with an Athenian expedition to Cyprus and Egypt. His age as Archon is given as thirty or thirty-one. An ancient writer trying to square these facts *might* have misdated all the events of his life by ten years. But this means assuming either that Dionysius made a glaring mistake (which considering the evidence he worked from is unlikely) or else that *another* Themistocles was Archon in 493 – surely too much of a coincidence? And it still leaves his early life a blank.

B*

horsebreeding Athenian gentleman; and as this story will show, he seldom behaved like one. All the anecdotes we have about him point in the same direction. They show us a plain, blunt, practical man, with a marvellous flair for strategy and political in-fighting, indifferent to art or culture, immensely ambitious, and far better acquainted with the hard facts of trade and commerce than most of his aristocratic opponents, who thought such things beneath them.

The Ostia herm[1] [see plate opp. p. 46] portrays a most striking personality, and one which exactly matches the impression conveyed by our other sources. An influential group of scholars and art-historians now maintains, rightly as I would hold, that this bust derives from an original portrait made towards the end of Themistocles' life, about 460 BC. Till recently it was taken as axiomatic that no true 'likenesses', in the modern sense, existed for almost another century. This view is now undergoing considerable revision and modification, for which the Themistocles bust itself is in no small part responsible. That big round head, simple planes recalling the early cubic conception, poised squarely above a thick, muscular, boxer's neck; the firm yet sensuous mouth, showing a faint ironic smile beneath those drooping moustaches; wiry crisp hair lying close against the skull – all tell an identical story. What we have here is the portrait of a born leader: as Gisela Richter wrote, 'a farseeing, fearless, but headstrong man, a saviour in time of stress, but perhaps difficult in time of peace'. There is, surely, nothing conventional or stylised about that broad forehead and bulldog jaw; they have an ineluctably Churchillian quality. Indeed, of all modern statesmen, Churchill is the one whose career parallels that of Themistocles in so many ways that coincidence will hardly suffice as an explanation. Both possessed the unpopular gift of being right when their more intellectual contemporaries were wrong. Both had a streak of that dazzling yet suspect histrionic genius which can transcend and transform a national emergency. Both were voted out of office with uncommon speed when the crisis they surmounted was over. Under Themistocles' leadership the Athenians, too, lived through their finest hour.

Like everyone else, Themistocles must have watched the Great King's increasing interest in Europe with some alarm. But unlike most of the aristocratic in-group whose members – even under a democracy – were regularly elected to high office,* he had a very shrewd idea what it implied. Darius not only intended, eventually, to conquer European Greece, but to soften up the city-states beforehand by fifth-column

* Whatever their political views, the men who actually wielded power in Athens – at least until 425 BC – more often than not came from about half a dozen intermarrying families. In this sense Themistocles *was* an outsider.

infiltration and, worse, by applying simple economic pressure where it would hurt most. After the collapse of the Ionian Revolt in 494–3, it looks very much as though the Great King debarred Athenian and Ionian shipping from the Black Sea grain-route. Ever since the Scythian expedition in 514/3, this must have been a fear that hit the Athenian man-in-the-street with increasing urgency. After 493 it became stark fact. An invasion one could march out and meet with sword and spear. Famine was quite another matter. Obviously, the up-and-coming politician who would be sure of popular support was the man who somehow guaranteed Athenians their daily bread.

But where was the bread to be found? Here our archaeological evidence helps us. We know that Athens' largest single import was wheat. We also know that her main export was fine pottery. In a known wheat-growing region, then, it is a fair assumption that Athenian pottery-sherds will represent payment for grain-imports. The heavier the sherding at any particular stratigraphical level, the more grain Athens will have imported during that period. Now the deposits of sherds in Egypt, Thrace, South Russia, Cyprus and the Eastern Mediterranean – all Persian-controlled areas – fall off to a mere trickle shortly before the Persian Wars. This is just what we might expect, and the natural consequence of Darius's restrictive policies. But when we look to the West it is another matter. In Sicily, South Italy, and the Northern Adriatic (Po Valley) there is an enormous increase of Athenian pottery-deposits, which reaches its peak between 450 and 430. All these were famous wheat-growing areas in antiquity: it was here, beyond a doubt, that Athens found her alternative market. Indeed, by 490 Athenian merchants had already built up bigger trade-links with the West than any they had previously achieved nearer home.

After the Ionian Revolt this supply-line was no longer a matter of *laissez-faire* economics; it rapidly acquired political importance as well. Athens' life-blood now depended on it, and its fluctuations could not be left exclusively in the hands of merchants. Some far-sighted statesman undoubtedly saw that from now on, at least until the Persian threat was removed, trade with the West must be treated as a public issue of government, and not abandoned to private enterprise. Even if we did not possess evidence confirming his strong interest in Sicily and Magna Graecia,* it would be almost inevitable to identify that statesman as

---

* Hdt 8.62.2 shows Themistocles threatening to lead a mass Athenian migration to Siris in the Bay of Taranto ('it has long been ours, and the oracles say we must found a colony there'); cf. p. 171 and note *ad loc.* He named two of his daughters Sybaris and Italia (Plut. *Them.* 32.2). When he was an exile on the run, his first thought on reaching Corcyra was to make for the court of Hiero in Sicily (*ibid.* 24.4,

Themistocles. We can imagine him talking to his friends down in the Piraeus taverns – where no self-respecting aristocrat would deign to go. There would be long, careful interrogation of merchant skippers and Sicilian brokers, discreetly placed bribes, deals arranged over a bottle of wine. During this period he must have seemed not so much a politician as a hustling import-export agent. But the work he did saved Athens during the Persian Wars, no less surely than his more famous achievement at Salamis.

So gradually this ambitious young merchant-politician got himself established as a public figure. He knew every citizen by name – a characteristic trick of the professional ward-heeler. He always had a smile and a handshake for those he met on the street; he never missed an opportunity of making useful contacts or of getting himself talked about. To borrow an expressive modern phrase, he knew how to project his own image. He persuaded one famous musician to practise at his house, chiefly as a bait for visitors. On top of his other activities, he set up as a private lawyer: in so litigious a society any good courtroom attorney could do very well for himself. This profession was also a popular way (then as now) into politics. Themistocles not only learnt to speak persuasively, which stood him in good stead later; he also made some very useful friends among the influential clients he got acquitted.

Neocles knew the dangers of a life in politics, and tried to warn his son off this dangerous ambition. Surely, he said, it was safer to be a merchant, or to work your estate? One day he and Themistocles were strolling together along the beach at Phaleron, where Athenian ships used to be slip-hauled before Piraeus harbour was built. Neocles pointed to the rotting hulls of some old triremes, lying there abandoned on the shore. 'That, my boy,' he said, 'is just how the Athenian people treat their leaders when they have no further use for them'. In later life Themistocles had good cause to remember those words; but now he was young, and too ambitious to heed the voice of experience. What young man in a hurry ever did? Besides, his ambitions were on the point of

citing Stesimbrotus). His connection with Corcyra itself is suggestive. He gave judgement in favour of the island when called to arbitrate between Corcyra and Corinth (*ibid.* 24.1), and was recognised as a public benefactor there in consequence. His concern with Corcyraean affairs seems to have been of long standing. According to Cornelius Nepos (*Them.* 2.1–3), a late and inferior but on the whole pro-Themistoclean source, the 'first step in his public career' had to do with putting down trouble on Corcyra and ridding the Straits of Otranto of pirates – both of which activities suggest strong Athenian interest in maintaining safe communications with the West. Modern scholars tend to assume that Nepos here wrote 'Corcyra' when he really meant 'Aegina'; on the practice of solving awkward historical problems by arbitrary textual emendation see below, p. 297, n. 13.

fulfilment. He may have been poison to aristocratic diehards, but the average man found something solid, earthy and reassuring about him. With Ionia lost, and the Great King's vengeful wrath-to-come hanging over Attica, a strong leader was needed. Perhaps – so the word must have run in Athenian political circles – perhaps the thrusting young man from Phrearri would fill the bill? So, in the spring of 493, Themistocles found himself elected Chief Archon of Athens; and for a while, as the Persian crisis steadily mounted, he had more urgent things on his mind than trade with the West.

Facing up to the Great King would have been a tough enough assignment in itself, even if Athens had been united; but united was precisely what Athens was not. A powerful pressure-group – including those versatile band-waggon jumpers the Alcmaeonidae – wanted nothing better than to do a deal with Persia. Like most shabby collaborators in any age (French Vichy politicians offer a good modern parallel) the Alcmaeonidae regarded themselves as long-term realists. Perhaps, if they agreed to take back Hippias, they might avoid the indignity of a Persian occupation force, but that was the best they could hope for. Darius's overlordship in Greece, they argued, was inevitable. To fight the Persian war-machine struck them as pure suicidal lunacy. Against them, unswayed by rational considerations, stood the plain, decent, stupid men: farmers and craftsmen and sailors who were not clever enough to know in advance when they were beaten, men who still placed honour above calculation. These took a very different line; they also (no doubt at Themistocles' instigation) gave it some forceful publicity.

In the early spring of 493 the dramatist Phrynichus put on a play called *The Capture of Miletus*, vividly depicting the collapse of the Ionian Revolt. (It may have been the first time that recent historical events, as opposed to myths, were represented in the Athenian theatre.) The effect was remarkable: Phrynichus saw his audience weep tears of grief and patriotic shame. Stung into swift action, the pro-Persian lobby got the play banned: when in doubt, fall back on censorship. Phrynichus himself was fined 1,000 drachmas, almost three years' pay for the average working-man. But the idea of subservience to Darius, however reasonable it might be, now rapidly lost ground. The proof of this is Themistocles' own election in the spring – on a tough-line-with-Persia ticket. About midsummer, with an all but theatrical sense of timing, Miltiades arrived in Athens. Themistocles and he had almost nothing in common except a determination to fight; but that, for the moment, was enough. Miltiades knew both Darius and Hippias personally. For

27

twenty years he had lived in or near the Chersonese, and during that time he had become a seasoned field-commander – something Athens conspicuously lacked in 493. If there was going to be real trouble with Persia, who better to handle it? Charges brought against him were summarily dismissed (perhaps by Themistocles in person) and soon afterwards – 'by popular vote', Herodotus says – he was elected general of his tribal division. Sometimes the *demos* chose better than it knew.

Meanwhile alarming reports were coming in of the Great King's projected invasion plans. It was clear that the defence of Athens had to be organised without delay. Themistocles argued – and time, as we shall see, did nothing to change his view – that the best course was to fortify Piraeus, abandon Athens, and stake everything on a strong navy. This policy ran into violent and predictable opposition from the whole aristocratic-conservative group. To abandon Athens and Attica, for however strategically impeccable a motive, was bound to offend not only the great landowners, but all those with an old-fashioned sense of honour about defending hearth, home, and the shrines of their ancestors. Themistocles had the whole weight of prejudice and tradition against him. No one, except in the direst emergency, would support such a motion, especially when the direct result was bound to be the destruction of all farms and estates in Attica. Moreover, Themistocles' main support came from the much-despised 'sailor rabble'; when his naval plans eventually went through – in the greatest crisis of Athens' history – people said that 'he had deprived the Athenians of the spear and shield and degraded them to the rowing bench and the oar'. In 493–2 his naval development programme was defeated; but the Assembly nevertheless voted for the fortification of Piraeus, and its development as the port of Athens. Work on the great triple harbour began at once, and was not completed for another sixteen years. The fortifications alone were a gigantic undertaking: solid ashlar walls on which two waggons could pass abreast. Themistocles aimed to make Piraeus so strong that a small reserve garrison could easily hold it – thus releasing more able-bodied men for the fleet. By Pericles' day Piraeus was not only Athens' main arsenal, but also the greatest commercial port in the Aegean.

It soon became clear that Athens was going to need all the defences she could muster. In the spring of 492 Darius sent out his son-in-law Mardonius with a large fleet and army: the burning of Sardis was to be avenged. Mardonius was young, shrewd, and ambitious. He also knew very well that one of the main reasons for the Ionian Revolt had been Persia's practice of ruling through Greek tyrants. Before he ferried his forces across the Dardanelles, he threw out the puppet dictators who had been restored in Ionia, and, with exquisite cynicism, set up a series of puppet democracies instead. This soothed Greek opinion, and cost him nothing. His autocratic temper made little distinction between putative forms of government; as far as he was concerned, it all came to the same thing in the end. On the other hand, he had no intention of letting another revolt break out behind him while he was in Greece. Fate smiled sardonically, and dealt him a smart back-hander to lower his self-assertiveness. On the borders of Macedonia his camp was beaten up by a hairy and hitherto unheard-of Thracian tribe, and he himself wounded. About the same time the Persian fleet ran into a severe storm while rounding Mt Athos: many of the ships were driven ashore and wrecked. Mardonius wisely pulled out the remainder of his force and returned to Persia, where he was temporarily relieved of his command.

The following spring (491) Darius decided to test the morale of the various Greek states. While his shipyards were busy turning out fresh warships and horse-transports, he sent envoys round the Aegean and mainland Greece, demanding earth and water in token of vassalage. Athens and Sparta refused. In Herodotus's words, 'at Athens they [the messengers] were thrown into the pit like common criminals, at Sparta they were pushed into a well – and told that if they wanted earth and water for the king, those were the places to get them from'. But all the islands, Aegina included, and a number of mainland cities, especially in the north, submitted without protest. The Thasians were told to dismantle their walls. They did so. With most of the North Aegean from Thessaly to the Dardanelles in his power, Darius felt ready to strike. Early in 490 a new fleet and army assembled near Tarsus, on the Cilician coast opposite Cyprus, and sailed westward for Ionia. Darius had replaced Mardonius with his own nephew, Artaphernes, and a Median noble called Datis. 'Their orders,' says Herodotus, 'were to reduce Athens and Eretria [a city of Euboea which had also taken part in the Ionian Revolt] to slavery, and to bring the slaves before the king'. The exiled Hippias also sailed with them, in high hopes – though now nearly eighty – of returning to Athens as dictator once more.

From Ionia the fleet moved westward through the Cyclades. There was to be no risk of another shipwreck off Mt Athos. Naxos, which had survived an attack ten years before, was now captured and sacked. The inhabitants of Delos heard the news and fled. Datis, who knew the value of propaganda, sent them reassuring messages: he would never, he said, harm the island in which Apollo and Artemis were born. He also burnt ostentatiously large quantities of incense on Apollo's altar as an offering. (This policy of religious toleration paid off well – so well, indeed, that the Delphic Oracle subsequently became little more than a mouthpiece for Persian propaganda.) Soon after he left the island it experienced a major earthquake, which perhaps rather spoilt the effect he had intended – a warning of trouble on the way, men said – but his gesture undoubtedly got widespread publicity. The Persian fleet advanced from island to island, commandeering troops and picking up children as hostages. At Carystus, the southernmost town of Euboea, they met with a flat refusal, upon which they laid siege to the town and began burning the crops in the surrounding countryside. Datis and Artaphernes had a fighting force of at least 25,000 men; by now their total numbers, rowers and conscripts included, were over 80,000. To transport them they had some 400 merchantmen, with a minimum escort of 200 triremes.[2] The Carystians, understandably, gave in.

At Eretria doubt and confusion reigned. Some were for fighting it out. Others wanted to abandon their city to the Persians, take to the hills, and (like their modern descendants) harry the enemy with guerilla operations. Others again, the inevitable quislings, were secretly preparing to sell out to Datis for Persian gold. Four thousand Athenian colonists had come from neighbouring Chalcis to help defend the threatened city. One of the Eretrian leaders warned them what was afoot, and advised them to get out while the going was good. They withdrew to Athens, where their services as hoplites soon proved more than welcome. Eretria held out for a week, then was betrayed from inside the walls. In accordance with Darius's orders, all the city's temples were burnt as a reprisal for the burning of Sardis. A few days later, says Herodotus, 'the Persian fleet sailed for Attica, everyone aboard in high spirits and confident that Athens would soon be given the same sort of medicine'. There is an understandably ironic relish about the way he puts this. The Persians' immediate destination was the Marathon plain, some twenty-four miles north-east of Athens itself, on the coast opposite Eretria.

It was old Hippias who had suggested Marathon as the Persian beachhead. Datis wanted room to use his cavalry, and Marathon offered just the right conditions – a long flat strip between the mountains and the sea, with easy through access to Athens by way of the Hymettus-Pentele gap. There were marshes at the north-east end, and clumps of trees and scrub dotted the plain. Better still, there was a fine shelving sandy beach (lined today with dunes and umbrella pines) on which to haul up the Persian warships and disembark horses. The invasion fleet beached at the north-east end of the bay, between the marshes and the long promontory known as Cynosura, or the Dog's Tail. Here Datis had natural protection on his landward side, an easy line of retreat by sea, and good grazing for his horses. The main Persian camp was probably established near Trikorinthos [modern Káto-Soúli], where, then as now, a good spring provided plentiful water. There were only two narrow approaches to this position from the west, along the shore-line and under the lee of Mt Stavrokoraki [see map, p. 33]. Datis and Artaphernes, having landed at dawn, lost no time in securing the road leading north to Rhamnous. Cavalry patrols explored the plain. The Persians were in an extremely strong position.

From the heights of Mt Pentele the beacon flared, telling Athens that enemy forces had landed. A fast runner was sent off to Sparta with the news. Athens was threatened; reinforcements were urgently needed. The runner, Pheidippides, left Athens while it was still dark, and reached Sparta by the following evening, having covered something like 140 miles over bad roads. (On the way, he afterwards swore, he had a vision of Pan. We can, if we like, explain this as a hallucination induced by exhaustion and lack of sleep.) The Spartans were full of sympathy, but regretted that they could not put troops into the field until after the full moon – that is, on 11–12 August. To do so would have meant breaking a religious taboo, probably in connection with the Carneian Festival, sacred to Apollo. It was now 5 August.[3] Reinforcements could not be expected for another ten days. The Spartans were, beyond any doubt, sincerely pious and old-fashioned traditionalists: we have no right, without strong supporting evidence, to accuse them of practising religious hypocrisy for political ends. Yet it is undeniably curious how often such taboos happened to fit in with their practical plans. An expeditionary force was in readiness at the frontier, prepared to move as the moon, or the luck of battle, dictated. Meanwhile the Spartan government avoided committing itself.

From the moment the fall of Eretria became known, a succession of fierce debates had taken place in the Athenian Assembly. Some were for sitting tight and holding the city against siege. Others, Miltiades in particular, insisted that the citizen-army should go out and fight. A siege would cut them off from Spartan reinforcements (the famous Long Walls were not yet built), and increase the risk of treachery within the walls. Just who might be in touch with Hippias and the Persians at this juncture no one, except the conspirators themselves, could tell; but the existence in Athens of a large pro-Persian pressure-group was an accepted fact, and those who meant to fight ignored it at their peril. When the news of the Marathon landing reached Athens, it was Miltiades' policy which won the day. Clearly he argued that their only hope – especially against cavalry squadrons – was, in modern terms, to 'contain the beach-head': that is, to prevent enemy forces from fanning out and advancing inland. A famous resolution, to 'take provisions and march', was approved by the Assembly: tradition makes Miltiades the proposer, and tradition may well be right.

So the heavy-armed infantrymen of Attica, some 10,000 strong, set off along the quickest route to Marathon, through the Hymettus-Pentele gap and along the coast,* their ration-bags loaded on mules or donkeys, slaves carrying their body-armour. The commander-in-chief, or War Archon [*polemarchos*] was Callimachus of Aphidna. Miltiades, though almost certainly responsible for the strategic and tactical plan which won the battle, and earned him well-merited fame, served as one of the ten divisional commanders; among his colleagues was Aristeides, Themistocles' great rival, known as 'the Just'. When the Athenians reached the southern entrance to the Marathon plain, between Mt Agrieliki and the sea, they took up their position by a precinct, or grove, sacred to Heracles, a little beyond the Brexisa marsh [see map opposite].[4] By so doing they effectively blocked any Persian advance on Athens. As a defence against Datis's cavalry they felled a number of trees and set them in position across the plain, with their branches facing the enemy. At this point they were joined, unexpectedly, by a volunteer force of between six hundred and a thousand Plataeans. Plataea was a small town in Boeotia, to the north of Attica, and an old ally of Athens. Every available man there had turned out to help repel 'the Barbarian'.

For several days (7–11 August) nothing happened: the two armies sat facing one another, two or three miles apart, and made no move. Both sides, in fact, had excellent reasons for playing a waiting game. The Athenians, who possessed neither archers nor cavalry, were unwilling to operate in the open plain, where Datis's squadrons would have them at a severe disadvantage. They still hoped, too, that Spartan

---

* There are many reasons for not accepting Hammond's alternative route, by the hill-track from Kephissià to Vraná (*Hist. Greece* p. 216 with n. 2; repeated in JHS 88 (1968) 36–7, with n. 107). The most obvious, surely, is that such a move would leave the coast-road – the only approach to Athens easily negotiable by cavalry – wide open, a bonanza Datis and Artaphernes could not possibly have missed. Miltiades' dash to Marathon was designed to forestall, or block, just such an attack. This end would hardly be achieved by straggling over the hills (where cavalry could not operate) and totally ignoring the coastal gap. Nor would any commander in his right mind have first stripped Athens of defenders, and then obligingly left the front door open, as it were, while he led his troops up the back lane. One alert Persian scout on the hills, and Datis's squadrons could have ridden into Athens while Miltiades' hoplites were still stumbling down the track above Vraná. For other critical objections see Burn, PG pp. 242–3, with n. 14.

reinforcements might reach them in time. After four days the moon would be full, and a Spartan army – with any luck – on its way to join them. The longer the Athenians sat tight, the better their chances.

The Persians, too, had their own motives for not wishing to force an immediate engagement. If the Athenians were shy of encountering Persian cavalry, Datis and Artaphernes, conversely, had no wish to

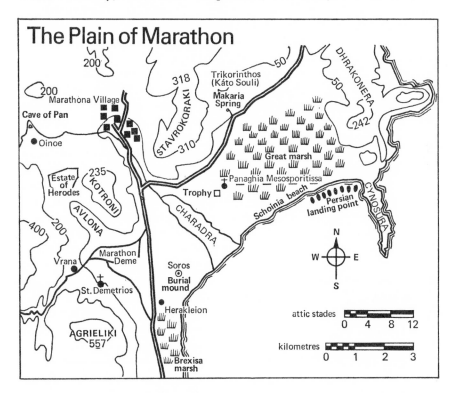

The Plain of Marathon

launch their own weaker infantry against Greek hoplites holding a prepared position. More important, they were in touch, through Hippias, with a group at Athens who had promised to betray the city to the Persian invader. Those slippery opportunists the Alcmaeonidae were, almost certainly, among the ringleaders. When everything was ready, the conspirators would flash a shield on Mt Pentele. Just what did this signal imply? There is very little hard evidence: what follows is a reconstruction, based for the most part on late and often dubious sources.

If the flashing shield meant that the traitors were ready to open the gates of Athens, then the response to it must have been an advance on the city itself. The Persians, we may assume, would send the bulk of their fleet off round Cape Sunium, and make a landing in Phaleron Bay. The cavalry, or a large part of it, would accompany this assault group, and act as a spearhead for the advance on Athens. The gates would be opened from the inside. Meanwhile, of course, Attica's entire citizen army would still be immobilised at Marathon by Artaphernes' holding force. (If they tried to withdraw, in the confusion they would at once be attacked in the rear by the Persians and forced to fight at a severe disadvantage.) As soon as Athens fell, Datis's troops would march out along the same coast road as the Athenians had taken, and cut off their line of retreat. Callimachus would thus be compelled to fight a simultaneous frontal and rearguard action, between the mountains and the sea, against vastly superior numbers. Until this trap was sprung, the Persian force at Marathon need do nothing – unless the Athenians either attacked or attempted to withdraw.

Day followed day, and still there were was no sign of a Spartan army, no shield-signal from the mountain-top. Herodotus reports that the Greek divisional commanders reached a five-a-side deadlock over their immediate course of action. One group argued that the Athenian army could not possibly win a pitched battle against such odds. They were heavily outnumbered; they had no cavalry or archers, whereas the Persians were well-supplied with both; the only logical course was to fall back on Athens. Miltiades and his friends had already countered such arguments in the debate which ended with the decision to go to Marathon. If the generals did in fact fight this debate all over again, then Miltiades, it is clear, proved equally firm. Withdrawal, moreover, would be suicidal in the circumstances. Callimachus needed little or no persuasion to stay where he was. Perhaps he acted on a hunch; perhaps he had learnt something of Datis's plans from spies or deserters.*

Datis and Artaphernes must have known all about those Spartan reinforcements, and the alleged reason for their delay. Once the moon was full, further waiting might prove highly dangerous. Yet there was still no signal from the pro-Persian party in Athens by 11 August. A crucial decision now faced the Persian commanders; and it looks very much as though they made up their minds to take a chance, and go ahead with their planned operation regardless. In that case, Datis will have sailed for Phaleron Bay on the night of 11–12 August, under cover of darkness, taking the bulk of the cavalry with him: not all, since at

---

* Athens' ten divisional commanders each took a turn, in rotation, as 'General Officer of the Day', or operational second-in-command to the War Archon. The four commanders who had backed Miltiades all, as a gesture, surrendered their stint to him – a nice instance of democratic institutions yielding before superior know-how.

least some token cover would be needed for Artaphernes' holding force. This body, to be on the safe side, must have substantially outnumbered the Athenians, though not so far as to weaken the assault group: 15,000 seems a likely figure. Even so, it is clear that neither Datis nor Artaphernes expected their opponents to risk an attack without archers or cavalry: when they in fact did so, the Persians' first reaction was that the poor fellows must have taken leave of their senses.

The Persians may have hoped to benefit by treachery, but it was the Athenians who actually did so. Some Ionian scouts serving with Artaphernes noticed the absence of Datis's task force, and slipped across to the Athenian lines before dawn, bearing a message which afterwards became proverbially famous – 'the cavalry are away'. (Treachery or Panhellenic patriotism? As so often in Greek history, it is hard to know where the dividing-line should be drawn.) Miltiades realised, as soon as he heard the news, that here was the one possible chance for Athens to snatch a victory. Even with a strong following wind, Datis could not reach Phaleron by sea in less than nine or ten hours: twelve would be a more likely estimate. He was unlikely even to begin disembarking his troops and horses till late afternoon. Artaphernes was now very short on cavalry, though he still had his corps of archers. He had also, for safety's sake, redeployed his forces no more than a mile from the Athenian lines. If the Athenians could bring him to battle and beat him, they might just get back to Athens in time to deal with Datis. Even so, it would be – as the Duke of Wellington said on another occasion – a damned close-run thing. Battle-weary troops could hardly hope to march those twenty-four* miles in much less than seven or eight hours. By nine o'clock at the latest they would have to be on the road. Callimachus agreed with Miltiades and, as Commander-in-Chief, decided to risk an engagement. It was about five-thirty a.m.

The troops were now drawn up in battle order. Callimachus himself commanded the right wing, where he had placed his own tribal division. The left wing was held by the Plataeans. The Leontid and Antiochid tribes were placed in the centre, with the remaining Athenian divisions spread out on either side of them. It was in the centre that the toughest fighting took place. (Themistocles was a Leontid, and Aristeides an Antiochid, so they were both in the thick of it.) Now if Callimachus had massed his troops eight deep, in the normal way, the Persians would easily have outflanked him. A front of 1,250 infantrymen, allowing a yard per man, is not all that wide, and once the Athenians

* Not twenty-six, as is generally supposed. This error has been caused by measuring the distance to the modern village of Marathóna rather than to the actual site of the battle.

left their entrenched position for the open plain they would become doubly vulnerable. (The sea has retreated since 490 BC, but even then the plain was wide enough to constitute a formidable hazard.) Callimachus and Miltiades therefore made a virtue of necessity. They deliberately thinned out their centre, widening the space between each man, and reducing the number of ranks to three or four at most. Their most powerful striking force they massed on the wings. Here Miltiades' intimate and detailed knowledge of Persian military customs proved invaluable. He must have guessed that Artaphernes, like all Persian commanders, was liable to place his crack troops in the centre, and his conscript levies on the wings. To risk – indeed, to invite – a Persian breakthrough in the centre was taking a calculated risk indeed. But if Callimachus and the Plataeans could knock out Artaphernes' wings quickly, and then wheel about to reinforce their own weakened centre, the battle was as good as won.

So they faced each other on that August morning – the 12th, in all likelihood – between the mountains and the sea. It was about six o' clock, and the sun had just risen across the water, above the Euboean hills. Bronze armour glinted; feet shuffled and stamped. Then came the shrill note of a trumpet, and the Athenian ranks moved forward, marching briskly, spears advanced: men with a job of work to do. There was no shouting, no battle-song: they needed all the breath they had. Artaphernes' troops were drawn up in line, waiting for them, a stationary barrier reaching from Mt Kotroni to the shore, archers deployed in front, cavalry – what there was of it – on the wings. As the Greeks came within range of the Persian archers (at about 150 yards distance) they broke into a double, to get through that murderous hail of arrows as fast as possible, and engage.

The Persian order of battle was just as Miltiades had anticipated. Artaphernes' best troops – Iranian guardsmen reinforced by picked tribal warriors from the eastern frontier – were placed in the centre. His less reliable units, the satellite battalions of the empire, had been relegated to the wings. Amongst these were Ionian levies: Greek arrayed against Greek, and (as the events of the previous night suggest) probably not too happy about it. The Athenians had several other advantages to compensate for their lack of numbers. Greek discipline, Greek tactics, Greek weapons and body-armour were all very much superior to those of the Persians. It was long spear against javelin, short sword against dagger or scimitar, bronze-lapped cuirasses against quilted jerkins, bronze-faced shields against wicker targets. The Athenians had a first-rate battle-plan; best of all, they were not imperial conscripts, but free men fighting to preserve their freedom.

In the centre, predictably, the Persians had the best of it. Step by hard-fought step, sweating and gasping, the Athenian hoplites were forced back – 'towards the Mesogeia', as one of the survivors told Herodotus: by which he meant, not 'inland', as is generally supposed, but more or less along the line of their previous advance through the coastal gap, in the direction of southern Attica. (Local inhabitants still call this region 'the Mesogeia'.) Here was where the brunt of the Persian attack fell; and it was here, in the front ranks of their respective divisions, that Themistocles and Aristeides fought. Meanwhile on the wings the Greeks had carried all before them. Many of the fleeing Persians stumbled into the Great Marsh and were drowned: their total death-roll reached the staggering figure of 6,400, and it was here that they incurred their heaviest casualties. (Afterwards the Athenians erected a white marble column by the edge of the marsh to commemorate this wholesale slaughter: fragments of it still survive *in situ*.) Other fugitives retreated along the narrow gap between the marsh and the shore, making for the ships hauled up in the lee of the Dog's Tail.

At this critical point Greek discipline once more proved its worth. There are few things harder to control than a military rout and pursuit. Yet both Athenians and Plataeans, once victory was secure, disengaged according to plan. 'Having got the upper hand,' says Herodotus, 'they left the defeated Persians to make their escape, and then, drawing the two wings together into a single unit, they turned their attention to the Persians who had broken through in the centre'. The tactical skill which this complex movement implies is quite extraordinary. The Persian advance was contained and halted somewhere near the great mound which marks the burial-place of 'the men of Marathon'. The Athenian and Plataean wings about-faced, and hastened back the way they had come. They did not take the Persians in the rear (tempting though this must have been) because to do so might well have meant sacrificing their own hard-pressed centre altogether in the process. Instead, they outflanked the battle in a double-pincer movement, which strengthened the Athenian line with massive reinforcements, and, eventually, brought Artaphernes' advance to a standstill. Then the tide of battle turned, and the Persian line broke. Those who could forced their way through to the sea, and retreated along the foreshore, where their ships were launched and ready for departure.

The Athenians pursued them closely, cutting down stragglers in the shallows till the water ran red with blood, calling back to their camp-followers for torches to set the Persian vessels on fire. It was during this stage of the battle the Athenians suffered most of their astonishingly few casualties: only 192 all told. Callimachus the War Archon was killed, together with one of his divisional commanders; and as they reached the Dog's Tail, Cynegirus, the brother of Aeschylus the playwright, 'had his hand cut off as he was getting hold of a ship's stern, and so lost his life'. During the last stand by the Persian centre Artaphernes had had time to get most of his other surviving troops aboard, and to save a large part of his naval squadron. He lost only seven ships to the Athenians: with the rest he stood out to sea. It was at this point – better late than never – that the long-awaited signal was flashed from the mountains above Marathon. The Persians set course for Sunium and Phaleron, no doubt hoping to find Athens already occupied by Datis – or at least to arrive before the Athenian army. It was about nine in the morning, perhaps even earlier: the battle and pursuit had taken something under three hours.

As if they had not done enough already, the Athenians once again achieved a near-miracle. Aristeides and the Antiochid division were left behind to guard the prisoners and booty. The rest at once set off back to Athens, each man for himself: 'as fast as their feet could carry them', Herodotus says, and one can well believe it. When they reached Athens, they took up a defensive position at Cynosarges, to the south of the city, facing Phaleron and the sea. They can scarcely have got there before four in the afternoon, and Datis's squadron may well have sailed into Phaleron roads an hour or less later. Yet that hour made all the difference, in more ways than one. The reappearance of the Marathon warriors – grim, indomitable, caked with dust and sweat and dried blood – not only gave Datis pause for thought; it also, obviously, came as an unexpected shock to the Alcmaeonidae and the pro-Persian party. A lot of people in Athens must have silently switched sides in a hurry: Datis would get no help from within the walls now.

His fleet rode at anchor for a while, presumably long enough to let Artaphernes and his battered survivors rejoin the main body. Then the entire Persian expeditionary force set sail, and retreated, somewhat ignominiously, to Asia, leaving 6,400 dead and an unrecorded number of prisoners behind them. Callimachus, on behalf of the State, had vowed a kid to Artemis for every enemy soldier killed. The Athenians were forced to pay the debt by instalments, at the rate of five hundred a year. For the time being at least, Greece was rid of the Barbarian.

After the battle came the feasting, the epigrams, the propaganda, the tall stories: almost before the dead were buried, Marathon had become a legend. Giant warriors and ancestral heroes had, men said, fought in the Athenian ranks. Offerings of Persian spoils and armour flowed in to the temples of Olympia and Delphi. Statues were set up, hymns of thanksgiving composed. Those who died in the battle were sumptuously commemorated by the mound – originally over fifty feet high – which still marks their last resting-place. The Persian dead got less ceremonious treatment. Their bodies were shovelled pell-mell into a great trench, and Pausanias, the Greek travel-writer, could find no grave-stone marking where they lay. It was left for a nineteenth-century German military surveyor to turn up 'huge masses of bones lying in disorder in the area of the Mesosporitissa Chapel and over as far as the marsh': grim witness to that last dreadful mud-slimed holocaust.

Practically speaking, Marathon was no kind of final solution: it merely postponed the day of reckoning. On the other hand, this un-precedented victory gave an enormous boost to Athenian morale. It showed that a well-trained Greek army could beat the Persians *on land* – something the Ionians had never contrived to do. Psychologically speaking, the legend became almost more important than the actual battle. It also very soon turned into a rallying-cry for conservatives and traditionalists of every sort. The 'men of Marathon', the heavy-armed soldiers who had saved Athens, alone and unaided except for one Plataean contingent, were all property-owning landowners or farmers. They came in after years to embody every known or remembered conservative virtue: selfless public service, old-fashioned morality, hard work, thrift, respect for one's parents and the gods. They seemed to demonstrate – against increasing opposition – the natural superiority of the upper classes. Small wonder that, in the years which followed, reactionaries clung so fiercely to their memory.

This mixture of aristocratic snobbery and anti-naval military roman-ticism proved surprisingly powerful and long-enduring. We shall meet it at every turn during the latter stages of the Persian Wars. Nor did it end with Xerxes' final defeat. A survey of literary evidence from Aeschylus's day to Plato's (Aristophanes is a crucial witness here) amply confirms Macan's verdict that 'Marathon was all along for all Athenians the prime victory'. As another modern scholar points out, landowners and agrarians 'resented historical conceptions which attributed, in their opinion, too much of the liberation of Hellas to the common people'. In Plato's *Laws* it is, significantly, the Athenian who asks: 'How can a political constitution be a good one which is based on the sea-folk?... We assert that the battle of Marathon began and the battle of Plataea completed the salvation of the Hellenes, and, moreover, that the land-battles made the Hellenes better men, and the sea-battles the reverse.' This stubbornly chauvinistic *cri de coeur* testifies eloquently to the persistence of the 'Marathon myth' – long after it had ceased to bear any relation to reality.

Indeed, Marathon was the swan-song of the old régime. From now on the real power came to lie, not with yeoman-hoplites or aristocratic cavalrymen, but with the 'sailor rabble' who manned Athens' fleet and merchant marine. It was a new world, both socially and politically, a revolution that transformed far more than modes of warfare. Class-conscious landowners hated it, and did all they could to smear the man who brought it about.* Yet through Themistocles, and the powerful navy he built, Athens not only faced the ultimate challenge from Persia, but went on to reach the very summit of her power and achievement. If we still talk, today, about the glories of Periclean Athens, it is Themistocles rather than the Marathon warriors whom we have to thank for it.

A Spartan army, two thousand strong, was sent off as promised the moment the moon was full, on 12 August – which happened to be the day on which Marathon was fought. Herodotus says that they 'were so anxious not to be late that they were in Attica on the third day after leaving Sparta [14 August]. They had, of course, missed the battle; but such was their passion to see the Persians, that they went to Marathon to have a look at the bodies. After that they complimented the Athenians on their good work, and returned home.' Curiously, whether the Spartans acted in good faith, or missed the battle on purpose, they still played a vital part in ensuring a Greek victory. The mere fact that they were, or might be, on the move forced both Datis and the pro-Persian group in Athens to act before they were ready. From this all else followed. The gates of Athens remained closed to the invader. There was no treacherous *coup* inside the city, by the Alcmaeonidae or anyone else. Datis did not even land his cavalry, let alone take Miltiades in the rear; and old Hippias had lost his last chance of re-establishing the Peisistratid dynasty in Athens. He sailed away with the Persian fleet, and died on the voyage back to Sigeum. Age and disappointment between them had finished him off: he had nothing left to live for.

* On the probability of Alcmaeonid treason at Marathon, and the blatantly biassed account of the mistocles given by Herodotus, see now the brilliant article by Daniel Gillis, 'Marathon and the Alcmaeonids', GRByS 10 (1969) 133–45, which only reached me after this book had gone to press.

PART TWO

THE LEGACY
OF MARATHON

MILTIADES was the popular hero of the hour. All Athens rang with praise for his courage, foresight and generalship. On the other hand, Marathon seemed to affect Themistocles in the most peculiar way. He began to avoid company. He was no longer seen at nightly drinking-parties. He suffered from insomnia, 'kept to himself and seemed completely wrapped up in his own thoughts'. When friends asked him what was the matter, he said 'he could not sleep for thinking of Miltiades' triumph'. Now Themistocles had as much driving ambition as the next man; but his remark hints at something more than mere jealous envy. In his view Miltiades was wrong, and dangerously wrong, all along the line. He – and the whole aristocratic-conservative group which he represented – exaggerated the long-term effects of Marathon, thus lulling Athens into a false sense of security. They refused to back the naval development programme. They still clung obstinately to the outdated notion that a patriotic citizen-army could solve all Athens' defence problems. Worst of all, the public showed signs of believing them.

'Now the rest of the Athenians,' Plutarch reports, 'supposed that the Persian defeat at Marathon meant the end of the war. Themistocles, however, believed that it was only the prelude to a far greater struggle . . . sensed the danger while it was still far away, and put his city into training to meet it.' The wisdom of hindsight enables us to assert, confidently, that Themistocles was right, and everyone else wrong. This is one of the highest tributes we can pay him: at the time few could have predicted future events with such confidence and clarity. Like Churchill between the two World Wars, he was a voice crying in the political wilderness, an odd man out preaching what no one wanted to hear. Yet the signs were there for all who cared to read them. After Marathon Darius's son Xerxes – who for eight years had been an active and efficient Viceroy of Babylon – was chosen over the head of his elder brother as Crown Prince. The Great King may have begun by regarding the Greeks as a mere peripheral nuisance (his new satrapy-list made no special mention of them) but the defeat of Datis and Artaphernes was a humiliation not to be taken lightly.

Preparations for a new and far more elaborate expedition now got under way. Darius's messengers sped out along the Royal Roads to every province, with requisition orders for men, ships, transports, horses, grain and other commissariat supplies. 'For the space of three years,' says Herodotus, 'the whole continent was in an uproar'. It would be strange indeed if echoes of this empire-wide commotion had not reached Athens. As early as the winter of 490–89 it was clear – at least to Themistocles and his supporters – that the Persian menace, far from vanishing, now loomed larger than ever. To meet this threat, Themistocles was convinced, meant building up a first-class fighting navy, larger than any fleet Athens had previously possessed. Fifty triremes was still about the maximum the city had in commission at any one time. If Themistocles had his way, this figure would be quadrupled. Yet such a project could not possibly win endorsement from the Assembly so long as the conservatives, and above all Miltiades, remained a dominant majority. Miltiades himself had to be somehow eliminated. He was too popular to attack directly: best to let him go off on some risky campaign, where with any luck he would either get himself killed, or else do so badly that he could be prosecuted on his return. He was, of course, still a general: his year in office would not be over until June 489. In the event the Assembly voted him a fleet of seventy ships (twenty bought for a nominal price from Corinth) to carry out reprisals against 'the islands that had given help to the barbarians'.

His main target was Paros, a Cycladic island which possessed rich marble quarries, and lay on one of the busiest Aegean sea-routes. The Parians had sent one trireme to help the Persian war-effort at Marathon: it was a good enough excuse. Unfortunately for himself, Miltiades seems to have spent some time bullying various lesser islands back into the Greek fold first. This was excellent strategy,* but destroyed the element of surprise. The Parians can hardly have doubted that they were on the list too: apart from anything else, Miltiades had a personal score to settle with one of their leaders. While the Greek fleet busied itself elsewhere, they had ample time to prepare their defences. In due course Miltiades arrived, blockaded the port, cut off its supplies, and pitched

---

* Burn [PG p. 258] makes a most percipient comment on such operations: 'Owing to the short range of ancient warships, which, like the fighter aircraft of 1940, were built for speed and not for long endurance without "refuelling" (filling up, especially with drinking water for a large crew of thirsty rowers), the possession of islands had some of the same significance for galleys in the Aegean as for the forces of World War II in the vast Pacific.'

the price of withdrawal at a hundred talents – enough to pay all his crews through a short spring campaign. (This suggests that one motive for the expedition was, quite simply, plunder in the form of protection-money: we find Themistocles conducting an identical type of operation after Salamis.) The islanders refused, and the siege was on.

For nearly a month Miltiades did everything he could to crack Paros's defences, but without success. He tried siege-engines; the defenders doubled the height of their outer wall at its weakest point. Finally he fell back on secret negotiations, through the agency of a captured priestess. Here he seems to have had better luck: it was, after all, the kind of game at which he had proved himself an expert in the Chersonese. Yet once more luck was against him. At the very last moment, when surrender had actually been agreed on, a forest fire broke out on nearby Myconos. The Parians at once assumed that this was a beacon-signal from some Persian admiral, telling them relief was at hand. They thereupon broke off discussions, and decided to stick out the blockade a little longer. On top of all his other setbacks, Miltiades had received a wound in the leg, and this wound now turned gangrenous. Finally he gave up, burnt his siege-engines, and sailed back home. 'All he had achieved,' says Herodotus, 'was to destroy the crops in the countryside; he had failed to annex the island, and he did not bring home a single penny'. It was just the kind of disaster for which his enemies had been praying.

In the annual elections for 489 Aristeides had been elected Chief Archon, while Pericles' father Xanthippus joined the Board of Generals. If Aristeides was a moderate conservative, Xanthippus, as subsequent events showed, wholeheartedly supported the naval programme, and thus stood in opposition to the aristocratic group backing Miltiades. Nor was it difficult to spread the rumour that this too-successful, too-popular nobleman nursed dictatorial ambitions: aimed, in fact, to make himself a second Peisistratus. Public opinion – always jumpy on this explosive topic – had swung round somewhat since Marathon. At all events, Miltiades ran into serious trouble when he got back home, and his associates, significantly, were powerless to save him. Xanthippus prosecuted the great general on a charge of 'defrauding the people'. It was even suggested that the Great King had bribed him to abandon the siege of Paros; no doubt the old charges of 'tyrannical behaviour' in the Chersonese were taken out and given a fresh airing, too.

By now Miltiades was so ill that he had to be carried before the jury on a stretcher, and could not even conduct his own defence. The prosecution demanded the death-sentence, and this, incredibly, was avoided by no more than two or three votes. Miltiades' brother and friends spoke up on his behalf, asking the jury to remember his distinguished war-record. In the end he was condemned to pay a fine of fifty talents – per-haps as recompense for the Treasury's losses over Paros. It was, of course, far more than he could raise, and he was thrown into prison, where, shortly afterwards, the spreading gangrene in his leg killed him.

So died the victor of Marathon, scarcely a year after his immortal triumph: in Athenian politics yesterday's hero was all too likely to become tomorrow's scapegoat. His downfall, however providential for the opposition, must surely have caused his enemies some misgivings. The will of the people was, to say the least, unpredictable: there, but for the grace of God, went any statesman in Athens. Themistocles, now thirty-five, must surely have remembered what his father had said to him, long ago, as they walked together along the beach at Phaleron, and looked at the old, rotting, abandoned triremes: *That, my boy, is just how the Athenian people treat their leaders when they have no further use for them.*

In 489 Athens was still almost wholly unprepared for total war, and had little enough time in which to build and train an adequate defence force. Two or three years was the most her leaders could count on: after that the Great King would surely return to Greece, and this time with the whole vast resources of the empire at his command. Themistocles had his own plans for confronting this emergency; but before he could imple-ment them, there were several crucial preliminary problems to be resolved. The first, and perhaps the most urgent, concerned the method of choosing high public officials. Whereas a modern English government may exercise power up to a maximum of five years before seeking re-election, no fifth-century Athenian statesman could hold unbroken office for more than one year at a time. In the case of the Archons, an even more crippling qualification applied: election was by vote – *but limited to one term only*. As a result, many first-class leaders were inevitably wasted, since they had twelve months, and no more, in which to exercise effective control over the city's public affairs. It is true that after serving his term, an Archon was admitted, *ex officio*, to life-membership of the Areopagus. This venerable council, originally the King's advisory committee, should, on the face of it, have exercised considerable authority. Until Solon's day it was (according to Aristotle) largely res-ponsible for day-to-day administration. It scrutinised the conduct of magistrates, and sat in judgement on cases of homicide. Solon himself made it the 'guardian' of his new constitution. Yet its actual influence on public affairs (at least from the sixth century onwards) seems to have been minimal. The real centre of power lay, inevitably, with the executive – which, hitherto, had meant the Archonship.

Themistocles: portrait-herm discovered near the theatre of Ostia in 1939. Roman copy of a Greek original which may have been executed during Themistocles' lifetime (see p. 289).

The 'Troezen Decree': inscribed stele of the third century BC, containing an edited recension of Themistocles' emergency mobilisation orders, ratified in June 480 (see p. 98).

Kallidromos: the hidden upper pass over the mountains behind Thermopylae, revealed to Xerxes by the traitor Ephialtes, and the eventual instrument of Leonidas's destruction.

Now to defeat Persia called for long-term planning of the first order; and long-term planning was impossible without continuity of office. This was something which Themistocles, Xanthippus, and everyone else in the anti-Persia, naval development group saw very clearly. Some constitutional device must be found which would allow important posts to be held by the same men, or group of men, year after year. The answer lay in the Board of Generals. These divisional commanders (one for each of the ten Cleisthenic tribes) could be re-elected indefinitely. They formed a conveniently sized group, representing every section of the community. Themistocles and his friends now set about transforming the Board into a formidable instrument of government, with the combined powers of the Cabinet and the General Staff.

The quickest (indeed the only) way of increasing the Board's authority by legitimate means was to reduce that of the Archons. So in 487/6 a measure was carried in the Assembly, laying down that henceforth the Archons were to be chosen *by lot*, from a preliminary list submitted by the demes, or local electoral divisions. A high property qualification was still insisted upon; but when any dunderheaded citizen of means might, with luck and a little influence, find himself Archon, clever and ambitious men would soon seek office elsewhere. Previously, both the Chief Archon and the War Archon had been chosen from the city's ablest generals or politicians; now, inevitably, both posts soon dwindled into insignificance. The real power, as Themistocles had anticipated, was transferred to the Board of Generals; and the reform of the Archonship had other long-term consequences, not so immediately apparent, but surely foreseen by those who planned it. At present the ex-Archons who composed the Areopagus may have been a group of crusty, ageing traditionalists; but they were also men of vast experience, intelligence, and prestige. Their brand of entrenched aristocratic conservatism was still, however indirectly, a force to be reckoned with. In a few years, however, all this would be changed. By then the Areopagus would be packed full of nonentities, and its prestige correspondingly reduced.

So the Board of Generals was moulded into a flexible executive group, handling administration, finance, foreign affairs, and the armed forces. Either now or a little later its members were relieved of their original military commands: these were henceforward held by ten deputy *taxiarchoi*, or brigadiers. The change both centralised Athenian government and increased its efficiency; the right of annual re-election, properly handled at voting time, made some degree of continuity at least possible. On the other hand, this was not an adequate weapon in itself with which to combat potential traitors. Nothing could be left to chance: those leading conservatives who, for whatever motive, were

c

prepared to collaborate with Persia must, somehow, be eliminated while there was still time. Here is where the curious institution of ostracism came in: the right, on a 'potsherd vote' of six thousand citizens or more, to banish anyone, without loss of civil rights, for a statutory ten-year period.

Most of our ancient sources claim that ostracism had been first placed on the statute-book by Cleisthenes in 508, but remained a dead letter until 487; which strongly suggests that Themistocles – that sharp professional lawyer – rediscovered it during his constitutional researches, and saw just how formidable a political weapon it could become in the hands of any ruthless pressure-group. For the next sixty years and more it was employed regularly and effectively – by no means always for personal or party ends. On many occasions (we shall observe one instance shortly) it gave Athenians the chance to break a dangerous political deadlock, even perhaps to avoid the ever-lurking danger of civil war. Despite its too-easy abuse, this odd device did function, in a very real sense, as the escape-valve of democracy, which at Athens more than in most places tended to operate with too high a pressure of factional steam.

In 488–7, it is clear, the most influential opponents of Themistocles' policy, Miltiades being dead, were the wealthy, well-connected Alcmaeonidae, who, among other things, enjoyed considerable influence at Delphi. Their treachery during the Marathon invasion may not have been proved, but most Athenians assumed it. Any friend or relative of the Peisistratid dynasty was also naturally suspect, since it was from their ranks that the Persians were most likely to form a quisling government. Themistocles and his political group now went to work on public opinion, with remarkable results. The first ostracism took place in 487: its victim was Hippias's brother-in-law Hipparchus, a former Chief Archon. In spring 486 Megacles – Cleisthenes' nephew and a leading Alcmaeonid – suffered the same fate. Another Alcmaeonid, Callixenus, appears to have been banished in 483–2. All this time, as one might expect, the aristocrats and conservatives were making equally strenuous efforts to ostracise Themistocles himself.* But all their efforts, at this period, proved in vain: the burly, arrogant radical from Phrearri had the *demos* behind him, and went on from strength to strength.

---

* There even existed 'party headquarters' which issued prepared *ostraka* with the names ready inscribed, for the benefit of illiterate or wavering voters. A dump of 191 sherds, all bearing Themistocles' name, has been found in a disused well on the Acropolis. Recently two *ostraka* turned up, one bearing the name of Themistocles, the other that of Megacles, which make a perfect join with each other – thus proving that Themistocles and Megacles were candidates for exile at the same ostracism.

So gradually, during the crucial decade between the first and second Persian invasions, the administration was overhauled, and political opposition disarmed. This still left the most important problem of all: finance. Athens badly needed to boost her revenues and put them on a firmer long-term basis. There was nothing, as yet, remotely resembling a modern national budget: the city lived, almost literally, from hand to mouth. It was true that for some years now there had been a steady increase in overseas markets for Athens' exports: wine, oil, marble, high-class ceramic ware. There was also Themistocles' Piraeus project – the vast new harbour complex now under construction, naval arsenal and commercial port combined. Piraeus would, in course of time, become the largest, most flourishing centre of maritime trade in the whole Aegean; but the work was still only half-finished, and meanwhile much of the trade which might otherwise have come to Athens was being handled by her neighbour and long-standing rival, the island of Aegina. Some other secure source of income was needed, and needed fast: in 486 the problem must have seemed well-nigh insoluble.

The news from abroad continued ominous. That summer Darius increased taxation throughout the Persian empire, and no one doubted that his main motive in so doing was to finance his projected large-scale invasion of Europe. To make matters worse, the loyalty of many Greek states was highly suspect. The Aleuadae, Thessaly's current ruling dynasty, would welcome a Persian invasion, if only to prop up their own tottering régime. From that rich northern plain, through which any invading army would have to pass, more than one ambassador made his way to the Great King's court at Susa. Darius found himself extending hospitality to every kind of Greek exile, from the Spartan ex-king Demaratus to the Peisistratids and their hangers-on – all dreaming of the day when a successful invasion would float them back into power at home.

However, the winter of 486–5 brought Greece an unexpected and highly welcome respite. Darius's new taxes triggered off a major rebellion in Egypt. Grain deliveries were totally disrupted, and the reconquest of this vital province at once took top priority. The insurrection was not brought completely under control for another year; and meanwhile in November 486, after a month's illness, Darius died, at the age of sixty-four, having ruled as Great King for thirty-six years. He had already designed his own last resting-place at Naqsh-i-Rustam, a vast tomb hollowed out horizontally from the living rock, its ornately decorated front cut in the shape of a Greek cross, some sixty feet wide by seventy high. Here he was buried, with all traditional ceremony, to be succeeded on the throne by his chosen heir Xerxes, on his mother's side Cyrus's true-born grandson, now thirty-two years old. For a time, inevitably, the Greek invasion hung fire.

Xerxes' first concern after his accession was to bring Egypt under firm control once more. By January 484 his armies had crushed the rebellion. He then, deliberately and systematically, 'reduced the country to a condition of worse servitude than it had ever been in the previous reign', scorning even to take the native title of Pharaoh – a significant break with Achaemenid tradition. This act was all too characteristic of his general policy towards the subject nations: he showed himself equally high-handed in dealing with Babylon, a country which, like Egypt, had hitherto enjoyed specially privileged status. Arrogant and autocratic in a way that Darius had never been (or needed to be), Xerxes treated these once-proud kingdoms as though they stood on a par with his barbarous Asiatic satrapies. Many Greeks must have asked themselves – and with good reason – whether such a monarch would deign to change his ways when he crossed over into Europe.

Our traditional picture of Xerxes is a caricature, put together from hostile, and faintly contemptuous, Greek propaganda. We see him as a small, blubbering, effeminate Oriental, a cowardly despot ruled by his women and his eunuchs (did he not turn Darius's treasury at Persepolis into a harem? and what about his treatment of Masistes' wife?), cruel in victory, spineless in defeat. Persian sources (no doubt equally prejudiced in the opposite direction) reveal a very different man. Tall, regal and handsome he stands in the Persepolis reliefs, and his proclamations have a ringing dignity which echoes down the ages:

A great god is Ahura-Mazda, who created this earth, who created man, who created peace for man; who made Xerxes king, one king of many, one lord of many ... I am Xerxes the great king, king of kings, king of lands containing many men, king in this great earth far and wide, son of Darius the king, an Achaemenid, a Persian, son of a Persian, an Aryan, of Aryan seed ... When Darius my father passed away, by the will of Ahura-Mazda I became king.'

Modern scholars, whether classical historians or Orientalists, disagree sharply over Xerxes' character and achievements. Some deny him the military ability, let alone the statecraft, of his predecessors; others praise him as a remarkable soldier, administrator, and reformer. This depends, by and large, on their relative assessment of Greek and Persian propaganda. Somewhere between these two extremes – between *The Persians* and Persepolis – the truth must lie: Herodotus, as so often, presents a more balanced picture than most. His Xerxes is a munificent and compassionate monarch, with the true Persian appreciation of natural beauty – our word 'Paradise' was, originally, the Iranian term for a park – but also uncontrolled in his passions and appetites, emotionally unpredictable, intolerant of criticism, and fundamentally weak-willed. As a character-sketch this sounds convincing. The defeat in Greece testifies, in detail, to the less attractive side of his personality; but there is much solid and indisputable evidence which balances the portrait. Contrary to general belief, his record contains a long list of striking military successes. He himself emphasises that he was *chosen* as Darius's successor. Harsh yet efficient, he could claim with justice of his many provinces that 'I governed them, they brought tribute to me, they did that which was commanded them by me; the law which was mine, that held them firm'. When they revolted, retribution was swift and terrible. On top of all this Xerxes was a remarkable religious reformer, and a scarcely less remarkable patron of the arts. The chief glories of Persepolis – the spacious architecture, the proud and virile reliefs – we owe to Xerxes rather than Darius. Our Greek sources, Aeschylus in particular, hardly enhance their national triumph by presenting this man as a contemptible weakling. The true measure of Themistocles' achievement only becomes apparent when we realise what a formidable monarch he contrived to defeat.*

Xerxes himself seems to have been in two minds about going on with Darius's plan for the invasion of European Greece; but there were many individuals and groups with powerful motives for encouraging such a venture, and these put constant heavy pressure on him to undertake it. His cousin Mardonius – the son of Gobryas and Darius's sister, the commander whose fleet had been wrecked while rounding Mt Athos [see above, p. 29] – had ambitions to become Governor-General of Greece, and exercised great influence over Xerxes. As might be expected, he thought up endless arguments in favour of the expedition. By all means, he agreed, settle the Egyptian rising first. 'But when you have tamed the arrogance of Egypt,' Herodotus reports him as saying, 'then lead an army against Athens. Do that, and your name will be held in honour all over the world, and people will think twice in future before they invade your country.' Besides, he went on, Europe was a beautiful land which produced 'every kind of garden tree' – an argument calculated to excite that strong horticultural instinct which seems to have been endemic among the Iranian nobility.

* This point is made with some force, in a different context, by Lucian (*How to Write History* 14.2, cf. 20.3). Describing some sedulous scribbler's account of Lucius Verus's campaign against the Parthians, in AD 165, he writes: 'A little further on he compared our general to Achilles, and the Persian King to Thersites, not understanding that Achilles would have been a better name for him if he was killing a Hector rather than a Thersites.'

Others were equally plausible and persuasive. There were the aristocratic rulers of Thessaly, promising full collaboration with an invading
army. There were the exiled Peisistratids, still dreaming of their
triumphal restoration to power in Athens, who hung around the court
at Susa working on Xerxes through a bogus oracle-monger. 'Any
prophecy which implied a setback to the Persian cause he would carefully omit, choosing for quotation only those which promised the
brightest triumphs, describing to Xerxes how it was foreordained that
the Hellespont should be bridged by a Persian, and how the army
would march from Asia into Greece.' Invidious comparisons with the
achievements of Darius formed an obvious element in this psychological
pressurising. In *The Persians* [vv. 753–8] Aeschylus makes Atossa blame
her son's folly on

> . . . the false friends that he mixed with. 'Impetuous Xerxes!'
> They used to say that *you* [Darius] won great wealth for your sons
> At the spear's point, but he from cowardice
> Did his fighting at home, and added nothing
> To his father's treasures. Hearing such bitter taunts
> Time and again from these villains, he was stung into action:
> This it was led him and his army on the road to Greece.

This passage rings uncommonly true, and suggests inside information –
perhaps obtained from captured high-ranking Persian officers. Europe
(we can hear all these ambitious sycophants urging) would be a most
profitable addition to the empire, a fresh glory for its conqueror.
Caught between duty and vanity, Xerxes gave in.

Once the Great King had made his momentous decision, preparations
went ahead on a vast scale, and with a degree of organised, rational
planning far beyond anything which the Greek city-states had ever
envisaged, let alone put into practice. Xerxes' top generals and adminis-
trators were well acquainted with the supposedly modern science of
logistics: they brought meticulous staff-planning to every aspect of this
gigantic operation. Here, of course, the monolithic, centralised structure
of the empire proved invaluable. No measures had to run the gauntlet
of a critical assembly; orders were unquestioningly obeyed; the Great
King's word was law. Persia's imperial resources, whether in cash,
matériel, or manpower, were virtually unlimited, a pool on which Xerxes
could, and did, draw *ad infinitum* for the most grandiose schemes, labours
of Hercules which his innumerable toiling subjects soon turned into
sober fact.

By 484–3 the most alarming reports began to reach Athens. Xerxes
had not only confirmed, but intensified, all his father's plans for

launching a major expeditionary force. In all the shipyards of the empire, in Egypt, Phoenicia and Cyprus, along the coastline of Southern Anatolia, from Lycia to the Troad and the southern shore of the Black Sea, galleys and transports were being built by the hundred for the Great King's armada. Nor could there be any doubt as to their destination. An advance fleet, carrying thousands of labourers, was established at a base in the Dardanelles; from here shifts were ferried over in rotation to Athos, and set to work cutting a canal through the peninsula, wide enough for two triremes rowed abreast. The workmen were divided into teams according to their nationality, and each team made responsible for a marked section of ground. As the cut got deeper, the soil was passed up in buckets, from one ladder to another. Though work was pushed ahead under the lash, there seems to have been little overall planning. Only the Phoenicians had sense enough to begin their trench at double the prescribed width, and slope it down to the bottom; everyone else cut sheer, so that constant landslides doubled their labour.

This project, though inefficiently carried out, was of great practical value. It both saved time – Herodotus is ludicrously wrong in saying ships could just as easily be hauled across the isthmus – and obviated the risk of damage from sudden storms. Xerxes did not intend to court another disaster like the wrecking of Mardonius's fleet in 492, while sailing round the Athos peninsula; nor, one imagines, did Mardonius. At the same time, Ephorus may well be right when he asserts that Xerxes was also 'hoping by the magnitude of his exploits to strike the Greeks with terror before his arrival'. Psychological warfare – primitive, but nonetheless effective – was a Persian speciality. Transport and commissariat, however (those twin bugbears of any commander-in-chief, in any age or country), were patently the Great King's prime concern. Apart from digging the Athos canal, his engineers had orders to bridge the Strymon [Struma]; while experts from Egypt and Phoenicia were assembling special material – including massive papyrus and esparto-grass[1] cables over a mile long – for two giant pontoon-bridges across the Dardanelles. Finally, food-dumps of grain and salted meat were set up at various strategic points – White Cape and Tyrodiza on the west shore of the Propontis [Sea of Marmara], Thracian Doriscus, Eion at the mouth of the Strymon, Therma and other places in Macedonia – which virtually flagged out the proposed line of the Persian army's advance. Throughout the empire troops were on the move. It would take a miracle to save Athens now.

And then, in the winter of 484–3, the miracle happened.

In the Maroneia district of Laurium, near Cape Sunium, was a group of silver-mines, which the Athenians, says Xenophon, had worked 'since time immemorial'. These mines appear to have been state-owned, and leased out in concessions to speculators, who shared the resultant profits. Intensive development had only begun half a century or so before, during the economic boom ushered in by Peisistratus. Even then the yield was very small in return for the outlay involved:

> The extraction and refining of the ore was an expensive business in terms of manpower, for even after the initial costs of driving the shafts and galleries, the ore had still to be extracted by primitive means (by child labour according to the size of the galleries uncovered), then crushed by hand, milled, washed, and smelted, before finally separating the silver from the lead in the remaining amalgam. [French p. 78]

The shafts were between two and three feet in diameter, with minuscule winding galleries (to crawl through them is an eerily claustrophobic experience) where slave-miners, branded, naked, and in chains, worked ten-hour shifts, day and night, by the light of guttering oil-lamps.

Modern research has revealed three strata of ore, each covered by a layer of limestone. The top deposit was probably revealed as a result of surface erosion, and worked by open-cast methods. Since Peisistratus's day, however, deep-level workings had become necessary. How far such explorations were backed, much less initiated, by the government is hard to decide. We may, however, note that the Laurium mines offered about the only potential economic bonanza which Athens could hope to acquire without territorial expansion. The city's basic exports (as every reformer since Solon had realised) were fundamentally inadequate. Wine and oil were easily come by throughout the Mediterranean, and Attica had no monopoly of good marble. With a rising population Athens could not go far on pottery alone. It is hard to believe that Peisistratus (who had studied mining techniques in Thrace) did not bequeath Athens a tradition of state-capitalised research at Laurium; and shrewd operators like Themistocles, all too well aware of the financial crisis which a Persian invasion would precipitate, must surely have maintained very close liaison with the mining community. At all events, in 484–3 the second limestone crust was pierced (presumably by a trial shaft) and a deep, rich, seemingly inexhaustible lode of silver brought to light. This most providential discovery was not (one strongly suspects) due to nothing but coincidence. Behind the bare facts of the case human skill, foresight and perseverance can be detected. It is tempting to guess – though a guess it must remain – that here, as so often during the dark days which followed, Themistocles contrived to give Fate a nudge in the right direction.

The strike, in fact, was so rich that after a year's exploitation – one can picture a minor version of the Klondike gold rush taking place – the profits were 100 talents, or some two and a half tons, of pure silver, with perhaps an equal amount going to those who had leased concessions. How was the public half of this windfall to be applied? It soon became clear that there was a radical division of opinion on the subject. One large and influential group, including the conservative farmers and landed gentry, the 'men of Marathon', wanted these mining royalties distributed among the whole adult citizen body, at the rate of ten drachmas a head. In other words, Laurium was to be regarded as a kind of public utility, from which every Athenian, by virtue of his civic status, was entitled to draw dividends as a shareholder. The chief spokesman for this group was Aristeides, and it may well be that such a scheme (which was by no means so intrinsically ridiculous as is often assumed) had some kind of traditional precedent behind it. It could certainly be given a fine democratic flavour, and was bound to appeal to the lower-income groups.

An equally influential and determined group, headed (as we might expect) by Themistocles, bitterly opposed this squandering of public funds. Themistocles wanted ships, not a civic dole: a fleet with which to beat the Aeginetans, and after them the Persians. However, he was sensible enough not to scare his fellow-citizens with the immediate prospect of a trial of strength against the Great King. (Besides, those who stood to benefit most from a hand-out – that is, the 'sailor rabble' – were also precisely the group on whose vote Themistocles normally relied: a decidedly awkward dilemma.) In his speech before the Assembly, therefore, he played safe, proposing simply that the surplus income from the mines 'should be set aside and the money used to build triremes for the war against Aegina'. This carried an immediate appeal. The conflict with Aegina was primarily economic in origin: not for nothing did Pericles afterwards label that all-too-visible island 'the eyesore of Piraeus'. What was more, the Aeginetans had just defeated Athens crushingly at sea, and their superior navy meant that trade which might otherwise have gone to Piraeus was being handled by Aegina instead. Themistocles, in fact, was overbidding his conservative opponents' appeal to public cupidity.

Plutarch understands very well what was in his mind. 'There was no need', he explains, 'to terrify the Athenians with the threat of . . . the Persians, who were far away and whom few people seriously imagined would come and attack them. He had only to play upon the enmity and the jealousy the people felt towards the Aeginetans to make them agree to the outlay.' Yet even to take such a stand called for courage as well as diplomacy. No one who asks people to give up a free bonus is ever

C*

exactly popular: his counter-arguments need to be very persuasive indeed. The Athenian man-in-the-street still much preferred not to think about invasion at all, on the well-tried principle that if you turn a blind eye to something unpleasant for long enough, it may conceivably go away. After a sharp and hard-fought debate Themistocles got his allocation – but for one year only. The accumulated profits from Laurium were earmarked to build a hundred new triremes – ostensibly as a counter-measure against Aeginetan naval superiority, for which purpose they would be quite adequate. But to face Xerxes' armada was quite another matter. Themistocles' secret estimates called for a fleet at least double the size, and free access to Laurium's income for the duration of the emergency. Instead, he found himself blocked at every turn by his political opponents. During the latter months of 483 continual arguments raged to and fro in the Assembly, with neither side yielding an inch. It soon became clear that the only way to resolve this deadlock was by holding yet another ostracism. Either Themistocles or Aristeides had to go.

This was no time for squeamishness: Themistocles was fighting not only for his career, but for the freedom of Athens as well. His position was still by no means secure: under a democratic régime it never could be. In 484 he was driven to get rid of his own associate Xanthippus, who was Megacles' brother-in-law, and thus in the last resort liable to side with his Alcmaeonid relations-by-marriage. To manipulate the 'potsherd vote' called for political in-fighting of a specially ruthless kind. Themistocles ran a clever smear-campaign against Aristeides, suggesting that his supposedly incorruptible opponent was aiming at a dictatorship. After Hippias, Athenians had become understandably jumpy on the subject of tyranny: some of the mud was bound to stick.

So, on a spring morning in 482, Athens' citizens assembled to decide what may well have been the most crucial issue in their history. The Agora was fenced in for the occasion, except for ten gates – one allotted to each tribe – through which the voters passed. There was a holiday mood in the air, yet a tense atmosphere underlying it. No one went home after casting his vote, even though the result was not to be announced until late in the afternoon. One illiterate peasant, from some outlying corner of Attica, presented Aristeides with a blank sherd, and asked him (not knowing who he was) to write his own name on it. Aristeides, curious, asked why. 'Because,' said the peasant, with understandable irritation, 'I'm so sick and tired of hearing everybody call him "the Just" '. Aristeides duly obliged, without comment. Perhaps there were many ordinary people who felt as that peasant did; on such minor illogicalities, all too often, hang the fates of men and nations. At all events, when the trumpet finally rang out, and the herald called for silence, it was Aristeides' name that the listening citizens heard, Aristeides who was condemned to leave Athens for ten years.

Themistocles had his ships.

It has been calculated that the shipwrights of Phaleron and of Piraeus could, working at top pressure, launch between six and eight triremes a month. This would produce up to two hundred in the period July 483 – May 480; between then and July 480 perhaps another dozen were laid down. The total number available at the outset of the campaign was over 250 [see below, p. 109]; the balance must have been made up with the best of the fleet already in existence. That so much was achieved in so short a space of time – a crash building programme if ever there was one – is a remarkable tribute to Athenian resourcefulness and perseverance. Crews were mustered and trained. Skilled craftsmen poured into the Piraeus dockyards. Contracts were placed abroad for ropes and sails and – above all – first-class timber. Two hundred triremes, for instance, would require no less than 20,000 oars, cut from best pine or fir. (It was no accident that throughout the fifth century BC the King of Macedon figured so prominently on the Athenian VIP list.) Attica's trees were being used up faster (what with goats and charcoal-burners) than the forests could re-grow themselves, so that almost all lumber had to be imported. The Athenian government found itself more and more deeply involved in foreign trade diplomacy – but now, for the first time, Athens could be sure of paying her way in the open market.

At one point in *The Persians* Atossa, Xerxes' mother, asks her counsellors what resources the Athenians possess apart from brave fighting men. 'Have they sufficient wealth in their homes?' she enquires, and the answer comes: 'They possess a treasure underground, a fountain of silver.' This goes straight to the heart of the matter. It was the Laurium strike which, quite literally, made the defence of Athens against Xerxes possible: not all Themistocles' skill and strategy would have been worth anything without it. But the 'fountain of silver' had other, more far-reaching results. It flooded the market with first-class Athenian currency – four-drachma silver pieces so good that they soon became standard exchange throughout the Aegean. (The mild resultant inflation at Athens was an added attraction to foreign traders, since the purchasing value of silver remained higher abroad.) It paid for military and other governmental expenses. Most important, it closed Athens' export gap; sometimes, indeed, it was exported itself. The Egyptians, who had no silver of their own, were willing to supply wheat and flax in exchange for it.

The Laurium bonanza had one very welcome and perhaps unlooked-for result: the breaking of Aegina's trade-monopoly. The Aeginetans, unlike the Athenians, possessed no silver of their own for coining, but purchased it, at a highly competitive price, from Siphnos. The rates they paid very soon debarred them from competing with a city that dug the stuff up, as it were, in its own backyard. Athens, however, was not the only state to acquire an unexpected windfall about this time. In August 482 a native pretender, Belshimanni, killed Xerxes' satrap in Babylon, and 'took the hands of Bel-Marduk' as King, according to ancient custom. Xerxes dispatched his brother-in-law Megabyxus, one of Persia's toughest generals, to smash the rebellion and make what profit he could out of it. Megabyxus, true to his reputation, did an appallingly thorough job. Nebuchadnezzar's towering fortifications and ziggurat were demolished. Babylon's great estates were turned over piecemeal to Persian landowners. The whole country was looted and ravaged. Supreme insult, the eighteen-foot statue of Bel-Marduk, almost eight hundred pounds of solid gold, was carried off and melted down into bullion. Xerxes had scorned to 'take the hands' of Bel-Marduk; nothing less than total possession and overlordship would satisfy him. Babylon's theocratic monarchy was destroyed, and the city lost its last vestige of political independence. At a more mundane level, Megabyxus's *Blitzkrieg* showed a handsome profit. If Laurium had enabled Themistocles to lay down a new fleet, Xerxes could now partially finance his projected frontier expedition on the proceeds of the Babylon campaign.

What was the actual size and composition of the force with which Xerxes invaded Greece? Even though Herodotus had access to the official Persian army roster, his overall figures (for the land forces at any rate) are flatly incredible: 1,700,000 infantry, 80,000 cavalry, 20,000 chariots and camels, and 300,000 Thracians and Greeks picked up *en route* – which latter figure, as Burn says, 'might be tolerable as a guess at the whole manpower of the Balkan peninsula'. Reducing these astronomical totals to reasonable proportions has kept scholars and military historians busy for many years, without any final consensus of opinion being reached.[2] However, it may be possible to arrive at a rough estimate. The Persian command structure operated – at least, up to corps level – on the decimal system, with officers commanding units of 10, 100, 1,000, and 10,000 men. One attractive theory suggests that Herodotus may have confused the Persian terms for chiliarch and myriarch (the two highest ranks in this list), thus automatically multiplying all his figures by ten. Strike a nought from every total given above, and the picture at once becomes far more plausible:

170,000 infantry
  8,000 cavalry
  2,000 chariots and camels
 30,000 Thracians and Greeks

––––––––

210,000 total

––––––––

It remains to check this figure against estimates reached by different methods, and to integrate it, if possible, with Herodotus's allotment of the various army corps to thirty divisional generals under six field-marshals.

According to Munro and others, the thirty generals were in fact myriarchs, commanding a total of 300,000 men: this figure was then increased to 360,000 on the assumption that each general also had 2,000 cavalry at his disposal. Taking the Herodotean figure of 60,000 [8.126; 9.96] as the paper strength of a Persian army corps, Munro divided his total of 360,000 between the six field-marshals. From various slight indications (e.g. the division of the expeditionary force into three operational columns) he assumed that Xerxes took no more than half his available military reserves – i.e. three full army corps – into Greece, thus reaching a provisional invasion total of 180,000 men. This theory has been criticised in detail – most telling is Burn's comment that, if we accept Herodotus's list of regional contingents, the thirty divisions cannot possibly have been uniform in size – but it does agree substantially with the figures produced by decimating the Herodotean total. General Sir Frederick Maurice tackled the problem in a quite different manner, by travelling over the Gallipoli Peninsula, observing local conditions (the availability of water in particular), and applying his knowledge of military logistics to work out how large a task force Xerxes' known route could possibly have supported. He concluded that the Persian army, at most, numbered 210,000 (of which perhaps 150,000 would be fighting men), together with perhaps 75,000 cavalry horses and pack animals.

Thus, by several independent methods, we reach a very fair modicum of agreement over absolute totals. As regards general troop-availability, we know that several army corps stayed behind on garrison duty throughout the empire: Greeks were too prone to credit the Persians with their own practice of total emergency conscription. Xerxes' six marshals each probably commanded a corps of about 30,000 men, with two corps forming an operational field army. Herodotus's thirty generals (*archontes*, a significantly vague term), command forty-six regional contingents between them. Fourteen of these are large enough to rate a commander of their own, while the remaining thirty-two are brigaded into fifteen operational units. Bearing Burn's criticisms in mind, it seems better to posit a varying strength for each command – as we would expect considering their nature – rather than to start from the assumption that these generals were myriarchs in any but a titular sense. We know that Hydarnes, the commander of the Immortals – Xerxes' crack Guards Division – did, in fact, have 10,000 men under him; but this was a special case, and Herodotus goes out of his way to emphasise, as a fact worthy of note, that the Immortals were always kept up to strength, with reserves ready to replace battle-casualties or those who died of disease. Other units, it is clear, did not enjoy such favoured treatment. Any of Hydarnes' twenty-nine colleagues who had six thousand men on his muster-roll probably considered himself lucky.

When we turn to the question of Xerxes' fleet, we find a far less intractable problem confronting us: there are difficulties, true, but none that cannot be resolved by the application of logical (or logistical) arguments. Aeschylus, our earliest source, places the total number of warships at 1,207; this figure agrees with Herodotus's estimate for the period *before* any Persian naval losses had been sustained, whether by storms or enemy action. (Aeschylus himself retains it – a pardonable piece of propaganda – for the fleet which the Greeks defeated at Salamis.) It is clearly distinguished from any estimate of transport-vessels, which Herodotus reckons at a round three thousand, and we are given a detailed break-down, by squadrons, which bears every mark of authenticity:

Phoenicia	300
Egypt	200
Cyprus	150
Cilicia	100
Pamphylia	30
Lycia	50
Caria	70
Asiatic Greeks:	
Ionia	100
Dorians	30
Aeolians	60
Hellespontines	100
Cycladic islands	17
Total	1,207
Thrace and the islands [Hdt. 7.185]	
also provide an estimated	120
Overall total	1,327

This total is by no means impossible as a general estimate of total available resources; but all our evidence suggests that it is far too large for the actual fleets which fought at Artemisium and Salamis. The Persian admiral Achaemenes, speaking after Artemisium, makes it clear that the detachment of three hundred (?) vessels for an attack on the Peloponnese *would lose Xerxes numerical superiority over the Greeks;* and this superiority, as Herodotus admits in a unguarded moment, was no more than barely maintained at Salamis [Hdt. 7.236; 8.13]. Now the highest serious estimate for the Greek fleet, that of Thucydides [1.73–4] is four hundred triremes; the figure given by Aeschylus, who fought in the battle himself, is 310 [*Persians* 341–3]. Herodotus seems unhappily aware of this discrepancy; by assuming storm-losses of six hundred [!] he brings the operational total down to 720, and we can further reduce this by postulating 100+ casualties at Artemisium. Most modern scholars agree that Xerxes' fleet numbered somewhere between eight hundred (Munro) and six hundred (Tarn, Hignett and others) at the time of Artemisium, and perhaps 450+ when Salamis was fought. Once we have whittled the overall total down to Munro's estimate, all further losses can be attributed, as our sources indicate, to a combination of bad storms and enemy action. Yet this still leaves over six hundred vessels which unaccountably vanish from the record. How are we to explain such a discrepancy?

It may be helpful, at this point, to ask ourselves just how the Greeks (and, in due course, Herodotus) obtained all their highly detailed and circumstantial intelligence concerning the strength and composition of Xerxes' forces. The simple answer is that they got it from Xerxes himself, who was very much alive to the psychological impact of sheer strength and numbers as propaganda. During the winter of 481–80, when he and his host were wintering at Sardis, three Greek spies were caught prowling round the camp. Far from executing his prisoners, the Great King had them taken on a conducted tour of every unit under his command. They were then released, and sent home to report what they had seen – furnished, no doubt, with muster-rolls, naval lists, and other hand-outs from the Quartermaster General's staff. At this time many Greek city-states were still dithering between resistance and collaboration: Xerxes doubtless hoped to influence their decision by some well-timed publicity. He felt confident, says Herodotus, that the spies' report on 'the magnitude of the Persian power would induce the Greeks to surrender their liberty before the actual invasion took place, so that there would be no need to go to the trouble of fighting a war at all'.

Here, surely, we have the original source from which Herodotus drew his comprehensive survey of Xerxes' invasion force. (Significantly, the naval armada is described with far less vividness of detail than are the land-based contingents – just as we might expect, seeing that the former had assembled at Cyme and Phocaea on the Ionian coast, whereas the spies were arrested in Sardis.) If this is true, two important conclusions follow. Firstly, the likelihood of all figures being exaggerated is very great: Xerxes would inflate his strength in the interests of psychological warfare, while the Greeks would compound any such error (rather than correct it) to magnify their own achievement in retrospect. Secondly, even where these figures are genuine estimates or returns, they will refer to the period *before Xerxes crossed over into Europe*. No Greek intelligence officer – much less Herodotus – was likely to reduce them in the light of subsequent events, and thus minimise the glory of Greece's heroic triumph against barbarism.

Such a line of argument at once suggests where we should look for over six hundred missing ships. Like G. K. Chesterton's postman, they have remained invisible through being taken for granted. Xerxes' plans called for the construction of two pontoon bridges across the Dardanelles – the one fact, it is safe to say, which almost everybody remembers about his invasion. To float them required no less than 674 galleys and triremes [see below, p. 75] – indeed, the overall figure may have been much higher, since a storm smashed up both original bridges 'and carried everything away'. The ships which went into this remarkable project were doubtless provided by the Ionians, Hellespontine Greeks, Phoenicians, and other maritime provinces of the empire. They will also, one may surmise, have figured on the putative 'naval strength' of each area before the actual crossing was accomplished. What the Greek spies brought back – to be preserved for Herodotus and posterity – was this cumulative but seriously misleading total. No one, however, would want to spoil so dramatic a contrast by pointing out the non-combatant, not to say static, role which almost half of Xerxes' vast flotilla had played in the drama of the Persian Wars. If we subtract 674 from 1,327 we obtain a net figure of 653: this agrees admirably with most scholarly estimates of the Persian fleet's actual size before Artemisium.

It was indeed a vast, colourful, and motley host through which the three Greeks spies – dazed with astonishment to find themselves still alive – were led on their tour of inspection. Pride of place went to Xerxes' 10,000 Immortals, all Persians, Medes or Elamites, splendid in gold-woven raiment. These élite troops were accompanied on the march (a unique privilege) by covered waggons containing their servants and concubines; they also received special rations, which were carried on a train of camels and mules specially earmarked for this purpose. Encaustic tile friezes from Susa, now in the Louvre, show us these proud and barbaric guardsmen on parade, just as the Greeks must have seen them. They stand in something very like the 'present arms' position, one foot advanced, the ceremonial spear, with its silver blade and silver pomegranate-butt, held stiffly upright in both hands, quiver and bow slung over the left shoulder, hair bound with a regulation rope fillet, beard trimmed short and square. The close-fitting military tunic falls neatly from neck to ankles, gathered up in a shallow inverted V between the legs, with wide hanging sleeves and a vertical stripe running down the centre of the body. Surprisingly, this uniform comes in every sort of colour, from old gold to pale purple, and with endless variety of decoration – barred brown squares, blue-and-white rosettes, yellow stars, white circles. Viewed *en masse*, the Immortals must have presented a unique and awe-inspiring spectacle.

Yet they formed no more than a fraction of the levies who had mustered at Xerxes' command, from every satrapy in the empire. There were trousered Persian and Median infantrymen, with embroidered tunics and fish-scale armour, regulation dirks slapping their right thigh as they walked. There were turbaned Elamites, and bearded Assyrians who wore bronze helmets and carried wicked iron-studded cudgels, and Scythians with their murderous battle-axes, and Indians in cotton dhotis, who used cane bows and cane arrows tipped with iron. There were Caspian tribesmen with leather jackets and curved scimitars, and thighbooted Sarangians, and fierce Arabs, already wearing the long flowing burnous, then known as the *zeira*. There were black Ethiopians, who smeared themselves with white and vermilion war-paint before going into battle, and wore horses' scalps with the ears and manes still attached. There were Thracians in fox-skin caps, and crimson-putteed Pisidians, and Moschians, who wore cumbersome wooden helmets. The whole camp was a Babel of outlandish tongues; everywhere one had to raise one's voice against endless shouted orders, the tramp of marching feet, hee-hawing mules and donkeys. The smell of camels and heavily spiced exotic food hung in the air.

All this the Greek spies took in, and subsequently reported. Whether their tale made quite the impression Xerxes hoped it would is another matter. The Great King had undoubtedly amassed a very large expeditionary force; but its quality and striking power were, to say the least, variable. Units like the Immortals had to be taken seriously, but the general lack of battle-training and cohesive military discipline must have been as obvious to a trained Greek observer as the rudimentary nature of even the Iranian contingents' defensive armour. Conscript levies, many of them mere Stone Age savages, who had to be driven into battle under the lash, would' present no great problem to a veteran hoplite phalanx of Spartans or Athenians. Nor were democratic Greeks likely to be over-impressed by a command-structure in which almost every key post was held by one of Xerxes' numerous Achaemenid relatives, including no less than ten other sons of Darius: nepotism carried to this extent became merely risible.[3] The real danger lay in the Imperial Fleet, of which the bulk was supplied by traditionally maritime nations from the Eastern Mediterranean. There were no better sailors than the Phoenicians and Egyptians; the latter also filled their warships with boarding-parties of marines, who 'wore reticulated helmets and were armed with concave, broad-rimmed shields, boarding-spears, and heavy axes'. The Cypriots (apart from the fact that their princes affected turbans and their matelots peaked caps) were as Greek in temperament and naval skill as the Ionian or Hellespontine contingents. If Xerxes was planning an amphibious operation, it was the naval side of it which would, almost certainly, give his opponents most trouble.

Yet here, too, there was something to be said on the other side. Whatever this fleet may have been, it was certainly not Persian. The Persians themselves, bred on an inland plateau, had no navy and no tradition of maritime skill: indeed, crossing salt water was against their religious faith, a taboo which still survives among certain Hindu sects. For Xerxes' invasion of Europe, however, the fleet would be of paramount importance; and how far its loyalty could be relied upon in a crisis must have caused some heart-searching at Susa. The Phoenicians could almost certainly be trusted; but which other major contingent had an unblemished record of allegiance to Achaemenid rule? The major rebellions of Egypt, Cyprus and Ionia were still fresh in living memory; who could guarantee that, given favourable conditions, they would not be repeated? No one had forgotten that during the Ionian Revolt, in 497, the Persian fleet (if such we may call it) had been soundly trounced by Greeks and Cypriots. It had, to be sure, redressed the balance at Lade in 494; but even here treachery had done as much to ensure its success as any display of naval expertise. The Greek spies' report, then, was by no means entirely discouraging. Xerxes might have many subjects; but his harsh taxes and generally despotic attitude were not calculated to transform them into the best of invasion troops, whether by land or sea.

In the spring of 481, his vast and complex preparations at last complete, Xerxes set out from Susa, and the invasion of Europe was under way. On 10 April, just before his departure, there had been an eclipse of the sun. The Persian soothsayers hurriedly explained away this bad-luck omen by asserting that the sun represented the Greeks, while the eclipsing moon stood for the Persians. While the naval contingents were assembling at Cyme and Phocaea, on the Ionian coast, the land forces gathered – from the furthest corners of Xerxes' vast empire – at Critalla, somewhere in southern Cappadocia. (The exact site of this town is unknown. It must have been at the junction of several main trunk roads: Tyana seems the likeliest choice.) Here Xerxes himself joined them. When mobilisation was complete, the whole vast host set out westward. As Herodotus says, 'there was not a nation in all Asia that he did not take with him against Greece; save for the great rivers there was not a stream his army drank from that was not drunk dry'.

Whatever this army's military capacities, it must have presented a splendid spectacle on the march. When it was moving in column through non-hostile territory, the order of march was as follows. First went the baggage-train, with half the infantry divisions as escort. Then a gap was left, to keep this common riff-raff from any contact, even symbolic, with the person of the Great King. Next there came two crack brigades, of cavalry and infantry, each a thousand strong, the infantry marching with spears reversed, a golden pomegranate agleam on the butt-end of each spear. These were followed by ten thoroughbred stallions, magnificently caparisoned, and the sacred chariot of the god, Ahura-Mazda, with eight white horses to draw it. The charioteer went behind on foot, holding the reins – 'for no mortal man,' says Herodotus, 'may mount into that chariot's seat'. Behind the god rode Xerxes himself, in his royal war-chariot, standing beside the charioteer – though from time to time, when weary, he would travel for a while in a covered waggon. There followed him, as escort, two more brigades of the finest cavalry and infantry (the latter, again, with either golden pomegranates or golden apples on their spear-butts). After them came the rest of the Immortals, and the column ended with another body of 10,000 horsemen (this figure may well be exaggerated) plus the remaining infantry divisions.

Their route lay through Phrygia, by way of Celaenae: a town of springs and caves and ravines, at the junction of the Marsyas and Maeander rivers.* Here Xerxes was entertained by Pythius, the wealthiest man in Lydia, who had previously given Darius two legendary presents, a golden plane-tree and a golden vine. He now declared his intention of turning over his entire fortune, two thousand silver

---

* Xenophon [*Anab.* 1.2.9] reports that as late as his day – c. 400 BC – the skin of Marsyas, flayed after his flute-contest with Apollo, still hung in the grotto where the river named after him had its source.

talents and no less than 3,993,000 gold darics, to the expedition's war-chest. 'I myself,' he hastened to explain, 'can live quite comfortably on my slaves and the produce of my estates'. Xerxes, in an expansive mood, refused Pythius's proffered gift; instead (true to his character as the Munificent Prince) he presented his would-be benefactor with the 7,000 darics needed to bring his resources up to a round four million. From Celaenae he moved on through the Lycus gorge, by tamarisk-haunted Callatebus [Ine Göl] and the Tmolus mountains, reaching Sardis about September. Somewhere *en route* he 'came across a plane-tree of such beauty that he was moved to decorate it with golden ornaments and to leave behind one of his Immortals to guard it' – a nice blend of Achaemenid ostentatiousness and the instinctive Persian feeling for natural beauty.

By now there could be no possible doubt about Xerxes' intentions. His declared object was to punish Athens for the part she had played in the Ionian Revolt; but his real ambition, as Herodotus saw, 'was in fact the conquest of all Greece', and its absorption as yet another satrapy in the empire. This became all too clear when his heralds crossed over to the mainland from Sardis that autumn (481), with the usual request for earth and water, 'and a further order to prepare entertainment for him against his coming'. Only two city-states, ominously, were excepted from the Great King's ultimatum: Athens and Sparta, both of which had broken the law of nations in 491 by executing Darius's emissaries like common criminals [see above, p. 29]. As usual, this move was primarily a *ballon d'essai*, designed to find out whether those who had previously held out against Darius would now be scared into submission. For Athens and Sparta, however, no such loophole existed: their prospects were thus considerably more bleak. Having been made the immediate target for Persian reprisals, they could hardly hope to avoid the Great King's wrath by timely collaboration, even if they were willing to countenance such a step. This fact is crucial, and should be borne in mind throughout the events which follow. Cities which have nothing to gain by surrender are *ipso facto* more likely to put up a heroic last-ditch defence. This does not detract in any way from their courage and resolution; but it goes a very long way towards explaining them.

What the Delphic Oracle thought of Greece's chances at this juncture can be deduced, all too clearly, from various responses that were given to Athens, Crete, Argos, and perhaps also to Sparta, in the summer or autumn of 481. It has often been alleged that Delphi 'medised' before and during the Persian Wars: most of the northern states connected with the shrine supported Xerxes, the temple and its treasures remained mysteriously immune to enemy action, the oracles issued were master-pieces of pessimism. On the other hand it can be argued, with equal plausibility, that it was the priests' business to prophesy as truly as they knew, without regard for the consequences: and who, at this point, could have predicted anything except a Persian walk-over? In that case, to preach non-resistance and neutrality was the merest common sense. Why encourage the senseless waste of lives to no good purpose? (Jeremiah took a very similar line with the Jewish nationalists in Jerusalem; but he had no Themistocles to upset his calculations, and thus suffered no loss of prestige after the event.) Moreover, Delphi's survival through a year and more of Persian domination in northern Greece need not imply active medism as a *quid pro quo* for immunity. It was Achaemenid policy to respect alien shrines, as Datis had long ago made clear at Delos [see above, pp. 29–30], and Xerxes would hardly take tough measures against so useful – and encouraging – a centre of free propaganda. Like most rich and established corporations, Delphi was instinctively conservative (though not averse to playing the field over home politics) and in an emergency preferred realism to heroics. But the way in which the Oracle's reputation survived after a Greek victory precludes any likelihood of public collaboration with the invader.

Argos, Sparta's traditional enemy and rival, had already been privately approached by an emissary from Xerxes, offering her special favours and privileges in return for neutrality. The Argive government, well aware that they would soon be asked to join in the defence of Greece, and anxious to avoid doing so without loss of face – they were far more interested, as Xerxes knew, in ousting Sparta from leadership of the Peloponnese – consulted Delphi as to their best course of action. The priestess, very obligingly, gave them this advice:

> Loathed by your neighbours, dear to the immortal gods,
> Hold your javelin within and sit upon your guard.
> Guard the head well, and the head will save the body.

The Cretans were similarly counselled to preserve strict neutrality. Sparta, as one might expect, received a less encouraging prognostication:

> Hear your fate, O dwellers in Sparta of the wide spaces;
> Either your famed, great town must be sacked by Perseus' sons,
> Or, if that be not, the whole land of Lacedaemon
> Shall mourn the death of a king of the house of Heracles,
> For not the strength of lions or of bulls shall hold him,
> Strength against strength; for he has the power of Zeus,
> And will not be checked till one of these two he has consumed.

It is interesting that the response describes Xerxes' countrymen as descended from Perseus – precisely the same claim as was put forward by the Great King himself when approaching the Argives. This piece of fictitious genealogising formed, it is clear, a key element in Xerxes' invasion propaganda, and its admission by Delphi is significant. It also militates against the popular modern belief that this oracle was an *ex post facto* invention, forged by the Ephors at Sparta to explain away the death of King Leonidas [see below, p. 139 ff.], and condoned by Delphi as a convenient face-saver. In any case, whatever the Spartan envoys heard is unlikely to have given them grounds for optimism.

The grimmest warning of all, however, without a scintilla of hope to relieve it, was that received by the Athenians: Delphi 'had never given such a crushing pronouncement of disaster.'[4] Herodotus's version runs as follows:

> Why sit you, doomed ones? Fly to the world's end, leaving
> Home and the heights your city circles like a wheel.
> The head shall not remain in its place, nor the body,
> Nor the feet beneath, nor the hands, nor the parts between;
> But all is ruined, for fire and the headlong God of War
> Speeding in a Syrian chariot shall bring you low.
> Many a tower shall he destroy, not yours alone,
> And give to pitiless fire many shrines of gods,
> Which even now stand sweating, with fear quivering,
> While over the roof-tops black blood runs streaming
> In prophecy of woe that needs must come. But rise,
> Haste from the sanctuary and bow your hearts to grief.

All this suggests that the priests were politically well-informed, and watching events with a cautious eye. The varying tone of the responses marks a calculated – and appropriate – attitude to each individual applicant. For Crete and Argos, tactful neutrality would suffice. Sparta's outlook was by no means bright, but she might, with luck, escape total annihilation. Athens' one chance for survival lay in a mass exodus of her citizens – perhaps to southern Italy. One ingenious scholar [Labarbe, *Loi navale* p. 118 ff.] has suggested that this horrific warning was deliberately engineered by Themistocles. It would, he hoped – so the argument runs – unite his own naval party and those who genuinely favoured evacuation (ships, after all, could be used to run as well as fight), thus creating a *bloc* large enough to defeat the landed conservatives who still hoped for a repetition of Marathon. But this is to be over-wise after the event. We have no real reason to doubt that the oracles given when Xerxes was on the march represent Delphi's honest estimate of the situation. If they offered small grounds for hope, that was, quite simply, because to do otherwise would have been whistling in the dark.

Nevertheless, a determined nucleus of resistance did exist, centred – as we might expect – on Athens and Sparta, and drawing the bulk of its support from Sparta's Peloponnesian allies. During the autumn of 481, soon after Xerxes had taken up winter quarters at Sardis, an emergency meeting of this self-styled Hellenic League was held at Corinth, on the Isthmus, to discuss the formation of a common front against Persia's impending attack. A good many of the delegates came from cities which subsequently medised, and the general atmosphere seems to have been one of panic and pessimism. (Only the quislings, who expected to do well out of a Persian occupation, remained cheerful at this point.) There were far too few ships in Greece, it was argued, to stop Xerxes' advance – this sounds like a counter-argument against Themistoclean policy – and most Greek states, even if not actively collaborating with the enemy, were 'unwilling to fight and all too ready to accept Persian domination'. Most people regarded the prospect of invasion, not as a common threat to be faced by a united Hellas, but rather as an inevitable if unpleasant disruption of their own personal existence. Such quietism is typified by the anonymous Megarian poet of the *Theognidea*, who wrote, with disarming candour: 'We want to make music, to drink and chat and not fear the War of the Medes.' This is an understandable human sentiment – as those who cheered Neville Chamberlain at the time of the Munich Agreement should be the first to admit. Every city's first concern was for its own security: Panhellenism came a very poor second to *sauve qui peut*. What united the Isthmus delegates was the same feeling that inspired Benjamin Franklin to remark, at the signing of the Declaration of Independence: 'We must indeed all hang together, or most assuredly we shall all hang separately.'

It must have been clear, from the time of the League's very first meeting, that any defence force raised against Xerxes would depend, substantially, on Peloponnesian land-forces – the Spartans and their allies – reinforced by Athens' new fleet. No other alignment made political or strategical sense. Ideally, as Themistocles emphasised, the Barbarian should be met and held as far north as possible; but such a strategy, to be effective, called for a strong united front, the absence of which cost the Greek allies dear during the early stages of their campaign. How far any northern state could be trusted, when it came to the crunch, was highly uncertain. Whatever Thessalians *en masse* might think about the invasion, their present rulers, the Aleuadae of Larissa, were openly pro-Persian. Macedonia had long ago given earth and water to Darius. Whether or not Thebes and the other cities of Central

Greece sent delegates to Corinth at this stage is still under dispute;[5] but even if they did, no strategy which stood or fell by their loyalty had much chance of success. This made it all the more important to win over neutral Argos, the one uncertain state south of the Isthmus.

It also helps to explain the general atmosphere of the conference – not to mention certain items on the agenda. All the emphasis at this point was, inevitably, on Sparta and her allies, if only because they controlled a majority of the votes. (There is even a tradition according to which the delegates [*probouloi*] first met, not at Corinth but at Sparta, in a special building known as the Hellenion.) An eminently reasonable proposal that Athens should command the joint allied fleet – put up, presumably, by the Athenian *proboulos* – ran into violent opposition. All other delegates (which meant, in effect, the Peloponnesian *bloc*) declared that rather than serve under an Athenian, they would abandon the defence of Greece altogether. The Athenians thereupon 'waived their claim in the interest of national survival' – a notable sacrifice, since their High Admiral was Themistocles himself. The 'sailor rabble' of Piraeus put up with this affront for the time being; but when faced with the prospect of action, they nearly mutinied at the idea of being commanded by some Spartan landlubber [see below, pp. 110–11], and only Themistocles' diplomacy saved the day.

Plutarch, indeed, claims for this extraordinary man that 'the greatest of all his achievements was to put an end to the fighting within Greece, to reconcile the various cities with one another and persuade them to lay aside their differences because of the war with Persia'. This task was of obvious and paramount importance, and recognised as such by the delegates, whose first unanimous motion called for the suspension, *sine die*, of all quarrels between member-states. (The most serious was that involving Athens and Aegina.) Such a decision, however, was more easily taken than implemented. If Themistocles really succeeded in smoothing over the endemic feuds and creeping parochial jealousies which kept every Greek state at loggerheads with its neighbour, he achieved something unique in fifth-century history. Superficially at least, this seems to have been the case. The delegates exchanged oaths and mutual assurances, guaranteeing each other alliance and support. They were, however, realistic enough to see that their main problem lay with the uncommitted states, whose neutrality might at any moment lapse into defection. Embassies were therefore sent to the most important (including Argos, Crete, and Corcyra) urging them to join the common struggle for freedom. At the same time a motion was proposed, and carried, that after the war was won (no one would admit the possibility of defeat) any state which had voluntarily taken the Persian side should be 'tithed' by the victors, and this tribute offered to Apollo at Delphi. Such a threat was, on the face of it, quite practicable; how effective it proved as a deterrent is another matter.

What the League Congress achieved, during this initial session, was the establishment of a somewhat primitive and ill-disciplined (but nonetheless effective) military command-structure.[6] One ancient source claims that members paid contributions into a common war-chest, but this sounds like an anachronism. The normal practice was for each city to support its own forces: only much later did the idea of a joint treasury emerge. Member-states do not appear to have enjoyed the right of secession – though it is hard to see how such a provision could be enforced. Nothing, in fact, was possible except on the basis of voluntary cooperation. The position of the allied commander-in-chief was particularly difficult, and therefore, perhaps, not too closely defined. During a campaign almost all decisions of high policy, let alone strategy, would have to be taken on the spot. When councils of war virtually replaced the League Congress, member-states such as Athens, whose military strength far exceeded their voting-power, could, and did, cause the High Command considerable embarrassment. Senior Spartan officers, accustomed all their lives to barking orders which were at once obeyed, now found themselves struggling with the unfamiliar skills of round-table diplomacy. Still, it was about the best system that could be thought up at short notice, bearing in mind the intractable (not to say anarchic) nature of the Greek psyche; and on its main purpose, at least, all were agreed. The Persian invasion must be met and halted. How, where, and when – those explosive imponderables – could be decided in due course.

It was, in point of fact, impossible to settle on a firm plan of campaign until the overall strategic picture became much clearer. When the League Congress met that autumn, no one, it is safe to say, had any real idea of the allies' total resources, let alone of the actual size or composition of Xerxes' expeditionary force. To compile accurate intelligence reports on both was clearly a matter of some urgency. Spies were therefore chosen and dispatched to the Persian camp at Sardis, with what results we know [see above, p. 61], and envoys went round soliciting support, not only from the neutralist states of Greece, but also – a most interesting development – from that remarkable, rich, and enlightened despot, Gelon of Syracuse, in Sicily. To carry out these various missions, it was calculated, would take up most of the winter – a close season for warfare in antiquity, and thus largely devoted to the joys of diplomatic intrigue. The Congress now broke up, its task for the moment done. The delegates agreed to reassemble at the Isthmus in the early spring of 480, when they would consider reports from their agents, and decide all major issues of policy for the coming campaign. 'For the first and last time in Greek history,' writes Brunt, 'consciousness of community in race, language, religion and customs formed the basis for common political action, prompted by a common danger'. Disgruntled, mutually suspicious, propaganda-ridden and out for the main chance, the states of the League now lurched – with more unanimity than competence, with more courage than unanimity – into the first great ideological conflict of European history.

PART THREE

WAITING
FOR THE
BARBARIAN

By March 480 both the ship-canal through the Athos peninsula and the double bridge of boats across the Dardanelles were complete. Both were pilloried, with derision, by ancient writers as prime examples of Xerxes' megalomania; both have been enthusiastically defended by modern military historians, who know very well what the Persian High Command was about. (Ask any transport officer, faced with a wide river, whether he would prefer one bridge, however primitive, or a fleet of boats, however numerous, when it comes to shifting troops – let alone camels, mules and artillery – up to the front in a hurry.) It is true that the Great King was not a patient man. When the original bridges were destroyed by a storm, Xerxes not only executed the engineers responsible, but vented his spleen on the Hellespont itself. He had a pair of fetters thrown into the water, which was then given three hundred lashes and branded with red-hot irons.

Whether this act should be regarded as a piece of symbolic magic, or mere childish *folie de grandeur*, or a mixture of the two, is very hard to determine. The insults which Xerxes' minions were commanded to shout at the water while executing sentence can be construed in either sense;* so can his reputed letter to Mt Athos, threatening to topple it into the sea if it caused any trouble. Harpalus, a Macedonian contractor, who took on the bridging project after his predecessor's decapitation, clearly had every intention of keeping his own head firmly on his shoulders. He lashed vast numbers of triremes and fifty-oared galleys together, bows-on to the current: 360 for the bridge nearest the Black Sea, laid north-east from Nagara Point, and some 4,220 yards in length; 314 for that towards Maidos, across the narrows, which measured a

---

* Hdt [7.35] quotes them verbatim, on what authority is not clear: 'You salt and bitter stream, your master lays this punishment upon you for injuring him, who never injured you. But Xerxes the King will cross you, with or without your permission. No man sacrifices to you, and you deserve the neglect by your acrid and muddy waters.' On this Herodotus comments: 'A highly presumptuous way of addressing the Hellespont, and typical of a barbarous nation.'

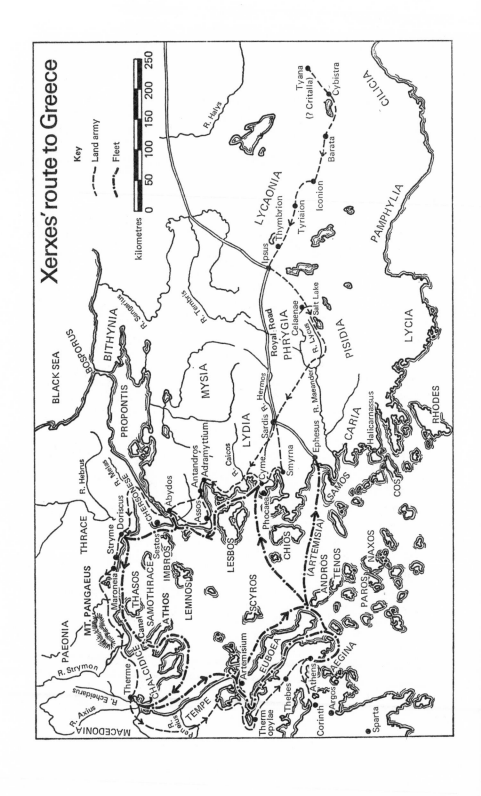

Xerxes' route to Greece

Key

- – · – Land army
- – · · – Fleet

kilometres

0 50 100 150 200 250

little over two miles. Both positions had excellent landing-points. Each boat was held in place by two specially-designed anchors, strong enough to withstand gales from either the Black Sea or the Aegean. Across these boats, from shore to shore, were laid huge cables, two of flax and four of papyrus to each bridge, the former weighing about two hundredweight a fathom. When they were secured at all points, Harpalus had them winched taut with huge wooden windlasses. The structure at this point somewhat resembled a railway line laid on its sleepers. Planks were then cut to match the floats, and cross-tied, close-lapping, over the cables. This surface was first covered with a layer of brushwood, and finally hard-packed with earth. Last of all, a parapet was built along either side, to prevent animals falling off, or panicking at the sight of the water below them. At three points on each bridge the pontoons could be floated out to allow merchantmen passage under the cables: presumably this involved unstepping their masts.

As soon as news came that both canal and bridges were ready, Xerxes marched from Sardis, probably towards the end of March, a little after the spring equinox. The local dry season was already beginning: he could not afford to delay much longer. The army's departure was marked by a peculiarly macabre incident. Pythius the Lydian, Xerxes' would-be benefactor, feeling himself securely in favour at court, begged for at least one of his five sons to be released from service with the expedition. He clearly had no idea just how Orientally capricious a monarch Xerxes could be when crossed. The Great King flew into a furious temper at this presumptuous request. Far from granting it, he 'gave orders that the men to whom such duties fell' – an ominous phrase – 'should find Pythius's eldest son and cut him in half and put the two halves one on each side of the road for the army to march out between them'. The Great King's wrath, like his gratitude, tended to be both arbitrary and overwhelming.

The bridges had been constructed between Abydos and Sestos. From Sardis, then, the Persians marched north, past Atarneus and the Gulf of Adramyttium, round the eastern foothills of Mt Ida towards the Troad. The most serious mishap that befell them during this march was a violent electric storm, during which a number of men were struck by lightning. Homer's Scamander was the first stream which failed to supply them with sufficient drinking-water.* While this advance was proceeding – that is, during the first fortnight in May – Xerxes himself

---

* At least a week's marching time separated the front units from the rear. Maurice [p. 215] suggests that 'each division of the army on arriving at the Scamander halted at the river for two nights and the intervening day to fill up with water and then advanced to the bridges'. Even so the Scamander 'ran dry' [sic].

made a detour to Troy. After ascending the citadel and being shown its antiquities, he 'sacrificed a thousand oxen to the Trojan Athene, and the Magi made libations of wine to the spirits of the great men of old'. Which great men? Not, one imagines, the Greeks. Herodotus emphasises, at the very beginning of his *Histories*, that Persia regarded the Trojan War as a standing *casus belli* – a tradition which is unlikely to predate Darius's invasion in 490, and may very well have originated as diplomatic propaganda. In this case Xerxes' actions at Troy will have been designed to publicise the invasion as a legitimate war of revenge. Mythological excuses for aggression always went down surprisingly well in Greece, and Xerxes still hoped – not without justification – to reap a bumper crop of collaborators.

Legend soon got busy with the Great King's stay at Abydos, on the Asiatic shore of the Dardanelles. He was said to have reviewed his entire expeditionary force there, rather than at Doriscus – though the region could not supply such a host with water for one day, let alone a week. Nor is it remotely probable that his whole armada was there to cover the crossing; if he ordered a rowing-match or regatta, as Herodotus claims, it will have involved only a few picked squadrons. We hear of him moralising to old Artabanus over the brevity of human life (it suddenly struck him that not one member of his expedition would be alive in a hundred years' time), refusing to eat Attic figs until he reached Attica, and taking no steps to prevent grain-ships sailing through to Aegina and the Peloponnese, on the grounds that they were saving him trouble. 'Are we not bound ourselves for the same destination?' he exclaimed. 'I do not see that the men in those ships are doing us any harm in carrying our grain for us.' This last anecdote, apocryphal or not, is very much to the point. So is the (unheeded) warning of Artabanus, that Xerxes' greatest enemies would be the land and the sea: absence of good harbours, shortage of supplies, unpredictable storms, ever-lengthening lines of communication.

Artabanus's reward for his sage counsel was to be sent back to Susa as Viceroy during Xerxes' absence. The actual crossing began about 10 May. On the previous day the Great King addressed his senior commanders, employing such well-worn platitudes as – then or now – are *de rigueur* on these occasions ('Let each and all of us exert ourselves to the utmost; for the noble aim we are striving to achieve concerns every one of us alike', etc.). The next morning, before dawn, incense was burnt on the bridges, and the road-surface strewn with myrtle-boughs. When the sun rose, Xerxes poured a libation into the Hellespont from a golden chalice, praying at the same time 'that no chance might prevent him from conquering Europe or turn him back before he

Late-archaic torso of Greek hoplite in Corinthian-type helmet with ram's-head cheekpieces. Found at Sparta, and plausibly identified as the memorial statue of Leonidas.

left The 'Aristion stele', an Attic burial marker: Greek hoplite, armed for battle. Equipment such as this – helmet, cuirass, greaves – was worn by the 'men of Marathon'.

top The Marathon plain, from the summit of the Burial Mound (Soros). In the background (from left to right): Mt Agrieliki, Vrana, Avlona, and Mt Kotroni.

bottom Salamis: the Megara Channel, looking eastward. It was this channel that the Egyptian squadron blocked before the battle (see pp. 181–2).

reached its utmost limits'. After this the chalice, together with a golden bowl and a Persian *acinaces*, or scimitar, was cast into the water: perhaps as a hopeful apology for those 300 strokes of the lash. The crossing then began, led by Xerxes' 10,000 Immortals, all wearing wreaths. Combatant troops passed over the upper bridge, nearer the Black Sea, while the other was kept for 'pack-animals and underlings' – perhaps the first recorded instance of what we may term the Tradesmen's Entrance principle.

By 12 May the crack units of the Royal Household were all safely across, and *en route* for their first major assembly-point, Doriscus, on the River Hebrus in Thrace. Here they had limitless water, abundant grazing, and the first of Xerxes' previously prepared food-dumps awaiting them. For at least four more days the crossing continued, as unit after unit tramped into Abydos [Chanak] – ill-disciplined tribal levies, slow-moving camel-trains and baggage-waggons, foul-mouthed drunken muleteers – to be hurried over the Dardanelles by the Great King's military police. Tradition claims that they crossed under the lash. If they did – and if the congestion bore any resemblance to that produced by a column of modern troops on the march – the whips will have been wielded most freely at the two Abydos bridgeheads, and even then, for the most part, on recalcitrant pack-animals. At about the same time as the last of the army and commissariat train set foot on European soil (*c.* 16 May), Xerxes' advance guard was already approaching Doriscus, having marched 134 gruelling miles from the Scamander. During their advance through Thrace, the Persians' ranks were swelled by numerous local volunteers, both Thracian and Greek – an ominous warning of things to come.

By 22 May the entire invasion force, fleet included, had reached Doriscus. With commissariat requirements in mind, a rough check on overall numbers was now made. Over and above this, some kind of unitary reorganisation seems to have been carried out before advancing into hostile territory. Maurice [*op. cit.* p. 226 f.] assumes the formation at Doriscus of twenty-nine active-service brigades (the Immortals making up the thirtieth), each with a muster-strength of between 3,000 and 5,000 men. Burn [PG p. 329] further suggests that these brigades may now have had 'smaller forces of "expendable" barbarians attached to them, like *auxilia* to Roman legions'. Both suggestions seem highly plausible. The most interesting move, however, and one which reveals considerable foresight, concerns the fleet. All squadrons, on arrival, were beached near Cape Serreum [Makri] and given a thorough drying-out, which doubtless included recaulking. Here Xerxes took full advantage of the initiative which his role as aggressor gave him. The Greeks, never certain when an attack might materialise, and outnumbered even at full strength, dared not take any of their squadrons out of commission for careening. As a result they found themselves heavier and slower in the water than their opponents – though both sides were equipped with very similar triremes. This loss of speed was a major factor in determining naval strategy and tactics throughout the subsequent campaign.[1]

By the end of the second week in June all preparations were complete, and Xerxes held a general review of his sea and land forces. The latter he inspected from a chariot, contingent by contingent, chatting with various officers and asking them questions, 'the answers to which were taken down by his secretaries'. The fleet was drawn up in battle-line, some little way out to sea, bows facing the shore, sailors and marines paraded on deck in full armour. Xerxes cruised slowly past aboard a Sidonian vessel, enthroned under a cloth-of-gold canopy. His inspection complete, he turned to the exiled Spartan king Demaratus (who was accompanying him as Greek military adviser) and asked, with evident self-satisfaction, whether he thought the Greeks would dare to put up any kind of fight against such overwhelming superiority of numbers.

Such a question obviously expected an awed and flattering negative by way of response; but Demaratus – renegade or not – was still very much a Spartan at heart, and did not take kindly to the role of court spaniel. The whole exchange is often dismissed as apocryphal, and so it may be; but it is still worth quoting for the light it sheds on the Greek 'psychology of resistance'. Demaratus's proud and dramatic claim that Spartans would always die rather than surrender is not borne out by the facts of history; but some of his other remarks (even if only what Herodotus thought he might have said) deserve our consideration: 'Poverty is my country's inheritance from of old, but valour she won for herself by wisdom and the strength of law. By her valour Greece now keeps both poverty and bondage at bay.' The Spartans, he insists – but the claim surely has wider application – 'will not under any circumstances accept terms from you which would mean slavery for Greece . . . They are free – yes – but not entirely free: for they have a master, and that master is Law, which they fear much more than your subjects fear you.' Xerxes, we are told, turned the whole incident off with a laugh – another example, presumably, of his imperceptive *hubris*. Then, leaving the faithful Mascames behind as Governor of Doriscus, he set out on his long march through Thrace and Macedonia. The date of his departure was about 16 June.

Meanwhile, probably in April, the Congress of the Hellenic League reassembled at Corinth. During the winter Themistocles had kept the

Piraeus shipwrights working to schedule: by now the bulk of Athens' new fleet was built, while many old triremes had been overhauled and refitted. On the other hand, Themistocles' own official position, as always, continued highly precarious. Even at this late stage his policies still aroused violent opposition – so much so that it was by no means certain whether or not he would secure election to the Board of Generals for the year 480–79. (The actual elections took place about February, but *strategoi* did not assume office until the end of June.) A rival candidate, Epicydes the son of Euphemides, actually looked like winning the place for the Leontid tribe: Themistocles – with that odd blend of ambition and public-spiritedness which marks so many of his actions – bribed this unwelcome candidate to stand down, and duly won a seat on the Board. Immediately after election he began canvassing hard for his long-prepared defence plan: man the triremes, evacuate Attica, and 'meet the barbarians at sea as far forward in* Greece as possible'.

Such a policy was by no means entirely new. Herodotus's historical predecessor Hecataeus had similarly – though without success – advocated it for Miletus, at the outbreak of the Ionian Revolt. The islanders of Thasos had been using the profits from their gold-mines to build up a strong fleet (and impregnable fortifications) ever since 494–3. If Themistocles hoped to convince his fellow-delegates at the Isthmus, however, he had first to obtain a clear mandate from his own Assembly in Athens. This, for the time being at least, he failed to do. The landowners and conservatives closed ranks against him: they could, and doubtless did, argue that with those superb soldiers the Spartans for allies, such a fearful sacrifice as Themistocles proposed was not only repugnant but strategically unnecessary. If they meant to destroy Xerxes, let them do it by land, as the Marathon warriors had so gloriously done before them. The fact that Xerxes himself was planning an amphibious assault, with the closest liaison between fleet and army, seems not to have discouraged such military diehards in the very least.

This was the situation – and the prevalent mood in Greece – when the League's delegates gathered to hear reports from their ambassadors, and, on that basis, to implement an immediate joint defence policy. A long winter had been spent in hard diplomatic bargaining, but with few concrete results. Corcyra had indeed promised sixty ships, a notable contribution; but (for whatever reason) this squadron never in fact materialised. The Cretans flatly refused to become involved at all, and could produce a Delphic oracle endorsing their decision [see above, p. 67]. The Argives, perhaps because they had decided to wait on

* Not 'away from', as the Penguin and other translations have it: see Burn PG p. 341, n. 13.

events (which meant, in effect, staying neutral unless, or until, a Persian victory made open collaboration respectable) did not take quite so uncompromising a stand. They declared themselves willing to fight – provided that they shared the direction of the war on equal terms with Sparta. Their condition, as they must have foreseen, was rejected out of hand. This, however, was not necessarily its intention. No one could expect an Argive force to put itself unreservedly at the disposal of such bitter and long-standing enemies, however urgent the crisis.

Gelon of Syracuse, likewise, had good reasons for holding aloof from the mainland's struggle against Xerxes: not out of weakness – during the past decade he had made himself perhaps the most formidable ruler in the whole Greek-speaking world – but because there were equally dangerous enemies to be dealt with nearer home. Gelon's steady climb to wealth and power in Sicily revealed a despot whose brilliance was only matched by his ruthless ambition. He left a litter of broken promises and democracies behind him: at his word cities were abandoned and whole populations transferred. He had taken over Syracuse in 485, and was allied by marriage to another powerful tyrant, Theron of Acragas [Agrigento]. Both of them won impressive victories at Olympia, while playing less reputable political games at home. By 483, when Theron wrested northern Himera from its own petty dynast, Terillus, these two between them controlled almost the whole of Greek Sicily except for Selinus [Selinunte] and Messina. Even here the prospects for continued independence looked far from healthy. However, Anaxilas of Rhegium [Reggio] happened to be Terillus's son-in-law (tyrants intermarried as much for safety's sake as anything else), while Terillus himself was a guest-friend of the Carthaginian *suffete*, or chief magistrate, Hamilcar. Both Anaxilas and Terillus now appealed to Carthage for military intervention.

This at once introduced a new, and highly inflammable, element into Sicilian power-politics. Hitherto the main contact between Greeks and Phoenicians in the West had been one of trade rivalry. Sixth-century Greek expansion to Marseilles and Spain was cut short about 540, when a combined Etruscan and Carthaginian fleet drove out the intruders from Corsica, and established a virtual monopoly over all Western Mediterranean commerce. But by 483 Carthage's ties with Etruria were weakening. Rome had emerged, in 509–8, as an independent power; Greek-inspired piracy around the Straits – directed exclusively against Etruscan and Carthaginian shipping – had become a serious threat; and the ambitions of despots such as Gelon, not content with absorbing their own Greek neighbours, now looked towards the Phoenician outposts established in Western Sicily. It follows that any appeal from a Sicilian power for Carthaginian support was most unlikely to be ignored. Nothing, at this stage, could have suited the Carthaginian government better than a watertight excuse to destroy Gelon's empire before it got completely out of hand. Gelon had always been the aggressor; if left to expand unchecked, there was no telling what he might not achieve.

His military resources were formidable. If he was not boasting to the Hellenic League's envoys when they sought aid from him in the winter of 481–80 – his reported estimates certainly sound on the steep side – he could, at need, contribute 200 triremes, 20,000 hoplites, and of archers, cavalry, slingers and light horse, a round 2,000 in each category. Figures on this scale, if true, hint at a vast population – which Syracuse's natural wealth and freedom from external pressure could well have brought about. Gelon, in fact, would make a dangerous enemy, and an equally desirable ally; he also happened to be a Greek. If the fleet and army of Syracuse were thrown into mainland Greece's struggle against Persia, they might well prove the decisive factor. No one knew this better than Xerxes. As a matter of course he maintained close diplomatic relations with Carthage (Phoenicians, after all, supplied the bulk of his navy); and when he finally decided to invade Europe, he at once sent an embassy to Carthage, with plans for concerted and simultaneous action. While Persia dealt with the mainland, he proposed, 'the Carthaginians should at the same time gather great armaments and subdue those Greeks who lived in Sicily and Italy'. In this way it would be made impossible for either East or West Greeks to send each other reinforcements.[2]

Self-interest alone was enough to make Carthage fall in with such a plan. During the years which followed (483–80) her leaders set about preparing almost as formidable an expeditionary force as that of Xerxes: it looks very much as though the ultimate goal envisaged was a Perso-Phoenician empire of the seas throughout the entire Mediterranean. Vast sums were earmarked for the invasion of Eastern Sicily: mercenaries flocked in from as far afield as Gaul and Spain and Liguria. In addition, thousands of free citizens were recruited (Libya too sent her contingent) and perhaps two hundred warships laid down. These preparations will hardly have escaped Gelon's vigilant eye. They seem to have had precisely the effect, in the first instance, which Xerxes hoped they would – that is, to make the tyrant of Syracuse think twice about committing his forces in mainland Greece.

Gelon's dealings with the League ambassadors, as Herodotus reports them, have been largely overlaid with romantic fiction; but one or two fundamental facts do emerge from his account. Gelon, like the Argives, laid down patently unacceptable conditions for helping Athens and Sparta – indeed, his terms were more or less identical with those proposed by Argos, which makes one wonder whether the two states had not come to some private agreement beforehand. He, Gelon, must be given the command of either fleet or army, if not of both. The ambassadors at once vetoed his stipulation, without even referring it back to the League Congress. In point of fact, he would have been highly embarrassed had they done anything else. Gelon's problem was very simple: he wanted to save face. He was well aware that he would need every man and ship he could raise to meet the threat from Carthage; yet his self-projected image as the Magnificent Nabob required his resources to appear infinite, and his generosity unbounded. To admit that he could not (rather than would not) help his countrymen was unthinkable. He therefore, with genial aplomb, both exaggerated the help he was in a position to give, and made quite sure that his generous offer was turned down. The ambassadors, seemingly unaware of the realities behind this smooth performance, came back to Corinth fuming and empty-handed.

The general failure of these diplomatic missions must have produced a despondent atmosphere in the newly reassembled League Congress. The most unwelcome consequence, however, for Themistocles and all who shared his views, was that such failure greatly strengthened the position of the anti-naval militarists. They could now argue – and with some show of reason – that while a Greek army might yet fight Xerxes to a standstill in the passes, the Greek allied fleet was (on present intelligence) too heavily outnumbered to avoid eventual defeat. Those powerful naval reinforcements on which such hope had been placed were, clearly, not going to materialise. Neither Crete nor Syracuse had furnished a single trireme; and how far Corcyra's promised squadron could be relied on only time would tell. Better, surely, to concentrate the League's resources on building up a land-based defence line? Since Themistocles, at this stage, did not even have home backing for his naval strategy he was in no position to out-argue the militarists; the most he could do was emphasise that such a line must be far up in Northern Greece, and not (as many Spartans surely hoped) on the Isthmus itself. The question of naval support could be thrashed out later.

With most of the central and northern states either committed to Persia or, at best, uneasily neutral, the dangers of holding a forward position were obvious. Above all, the local inhabitants could never be trusted in an emergency. Auxiliary troops were liable to fade away at short notice, or not to appear at all. Any Greek commander holding a mountain pass might wake up one morning to find himself outflanked, the enemy having meanwhile procured some more knowledgeable and cooperative native guide than he had. However, unexpected support for this risky strategy now appeared, in the form of a delegation from Thessaly. Its envoys did not represent the Aleuadae of Larissa (who had, as we know, long since sold out to the Persians); they spoke for a 'resistance group' of various rival dynasts, centred on other cities in the Thessalian plain, prominent among them being the Echecratids of Pharsalus. Disinterested patriotism is unlikely to have been their foremost motive: clearly they had ambitions to replace the Aleuadae as dynasts-in-chief.

This meant getting strong Greek support, which they were unlikely to do by telling unpalatable home-truths about the situation up north. As a result, in their address to the Congress they exaggerated both the extent and the intensity of Thessalian enthusiasm for resistance, while remaining tactfully vague about geographical hazards such as alternative passes into central Greece.* Their proposal, then, was that a strong allied task-force should be dispatched to hold the Tempe gorge, between Ossa and Olympus, a few miles north of the ill-defined Macedonian frontier. If this was done, the Greeks could count on solid Thessalian support. Otherwise, the speaker concluded, with disarming candour, 'we give you fair warning that we shall come to terms with Persia. We are in an exposed position, and cannot be expected, alone and unassisted, to give our lives merely to save the rest of you.' This sounded reasonable enough; the League's serious mistake was to assume that the delegation spoke, if not for Thessaly as a whole, at any rate for a strong and united war-group. On-the-spot investigation soon made it clear how alarmingly wide of the truth such an assumption was.

A force of 10,000 allied hoplites (was it coincidence that the same number had trounced the Barbarians at Marathon?) marched north, as requested, to hold the Tempe gorge. Its commanders were a Spartan nonentity named Euaenetus, and Themistocles, who probably went along with this ill-conceived plan, however reluctantly, on the grounds that any forward defence was better than none. Plutarch – himself a Boeotian and all too conscious of his country's medising record – claims that Thebes sent a contingent of five hundred men on this expedition. If she did, they were almost certainly picked – as subsequent events made clear – from the right-wing government's political opponents.

---

* Westlake, JHS 56 (1936) 12–24, esp. 16–21, believes the Congress knew about the other passes (e.g. those of Petra and Volustana) but was led into believing that they would be held by Thessalian levies. This not only ignores the testimony of Herodotus (7.173) but considerably underestimates Greek parochialism. How many Peloponnesians had ever travelled as far north as Tempe in their lives? How many have done so today?

Conscription for front-line service was a simple, well-tried method of removing trouble-makers: Uriah the Hittite was neither the first nor the last man to die in battle because some official fancied his wife or disfancied his politics. What the Congress thought of Boeotia's reliability at this point can be deduced from the fact that their army, instead of marching through central Greece in the normal way, was routed by sea as far as Halus, on the Gulf of Pagasae. The choice of port is equally suggestive. Pagasae itself, close to modern Volos at the head of the Gulf, would have been far more convenient: one can only surmise that the local dynast of Pherae had proved no more cooperative than the Aleuadae up in Larissa. Halus, on the other hand, belonged to the barony of Pharsalus: it was here, if anywhere, that a genuine resistance movement existed. But the very idea of holding Tempe – what we may call the 'Olympus line' – presupposed a strongly united front. It must have been all too obvious, from the moment of disembarkation, that Thessaly was teeming with *collabos*, while the great barons were more concerned to outsmart each other than outfight a Persian army.

Fearing the worst, but unwilling to give up so early – an immediate withdrawal would be hard to explain convincingly at the Isthmus – the Greeks marched north to Tempe, and set about digging themselves in. (It would be interesting to know what sort of reception they got *en route* at Larissa. The Aleuadae were in no position to tell them to go back home, so presumably turned a blind eye until they were safely through town.) At least this expedition had time on its side. The force reached Tempe in early May, before Xerxes had even begun his crossing of the Dardanelles. Themistocles and Euaenetus now did some intensive reconnoitring and intelligence work, to assess their chances of holding the position. What they learnt was by no means encouraging. There were at least two negotiable passes west of the Olympus massif, those of Petra and Volustana, besides the nearer hill-track to Gonnus. Blocking these effectively would call for guerilla tactics on a large scale. Apart from the fact that Greeks in 480 knew little about this specialised type of warfare, to employ it effectively depended on obtaining a high degree of loyalty and cooperation from the local inhabitants. But the hill-tribes of Perrhaebia and Northern Achaea and the Magnesian coastal strip – even those as far south as the Malian Gulf – could no more be relied upon than could the cattle-barons down in the plain. One source, indeed, claims that they medised *en masse* while the Greeks were still holding Tempe – about as cogent a reason for withdrawal as could well be imagined. Apart from this, Persian spies and fifth-column agents had been infiltrating Northern Greece for months; the only volunteers who joined the Greeks were some cavalry detachments, probably from

Pharsalus. Not even the most optimistic commander could envisage them holding the central passes on their own.

It was that charming but shifty rogue King Alexander I of Macedon (known, with ironic ambiguity, as 'the Philhellene') who finally made up the Greeks' minds for them. The message he sent them was brief and to the point. Their present position was untenable. They would be cut off and massacred by Xerxes' vastly superior forces. The only sensible course was for them to pull out while they still had the chance. Alexander's motives in giving them such advice were far from disinterested. His philhellenism was given a somewhat dubious flavour by the fact that his brother-in-law happened to be a Persian general, a connection he was at some pains to explain away; but his main concern had little to do with nationalism or ideologies. What really bothered Alexander was the prospect of Xerxes' army being held up indefinitely in Macedonia, a plague of human locusts stripping the granaries bare, decimating herds and flocks. The sooner they were on their way the better; and that meant ensuring that they found no entrenched opposition awaiting them at Tempe. The Greeks, however, needed very little pressurising. No one in Thessaly could be trusted, the whole country was rotten with medism, and their chances of holding the central passes were virtually nil. The longer they sat still in this atmosphere and did nothing, the worse their morale would become. Successive reports of Xerxes' triumphal advance, which lost nothing in the telling, hardly improved matters. Themistocles had never liked the Tempe project anyway, and was anxious to put his own plan into operation while there was still time. So at some point before the end of May, this imposing force abandoned Tempe and marched back south, while the enemy they were supposed to be keeping out of Greece was still several hundred miles distant.*

Xerxes' fleet and army set out from Doriscus about mid-June. Their immediate destination was the Athos ship-canal, which lay just south of Acanthus, on the easternmost prong of the Chalcidic peninsula. For the first stage of this journey, as far as the River Nestus [Mesta], just beyond Abdera, they were following a broad coastal plain. This meant that Xerxes could greatly reduce the length of his unwieldy column by dividing it into three separate corps, each under two marshals. These corps marched parallel to one another, between the sea and the foothills: the exact route which the up-country division took is uncertain. Meanwhile the fleet cruised westward with them, just offshore. Local tribesmen were conscripted for service – and, no doubt, as hostages – at

* Damastes fr. 4 (Jacoby) states that 'Alexander informed the Greeks of the treachery of Aleuas [sic] and of the Thessalians', a detail which sounds convincing. Cf. Westlake op. cit., p. 19.

each settlement they passed. Several rivers were drunk dry. Soon after crossing the Nestus, the pack-animals (less choosy, it would seem, than their masters) contrived to drain a *salt-water* lake four miles in diameter. Skirting Mt Pangaeus, with its gold and silver mines, Xerxes' host reached the Strymon [Struma] about the beginning of July. Here pontoon-bridges had been made ready, at a point some three miles inland. (It was known, then, as Nine Ways, but later [437] became famous when Athens colonised it under the name of Amphipolis.) The Magian priests accompanying Xerxes propitiated this great river by the sacrifice of a white horse, cutting its throat into a pit so that there should be no pollution of running water.* Then the army began its crossing. By the time the last contingents were over the Strymon, the advance guard was far down the coast towards Argilus.

Recruits were not the only benefit Xerxes obtained during this march through Thrace. Since the cities all owed him allegiance, each in turn 'had to entertain the Persian army and provide a dinner for the king'. One disgruntled citizen of Abdera remarked that it was lucky Xerxes did not make a habit of eating two dinners a day: otherwise they would all be ruined. Even so, this system of purveyance (equally prevalent, and equally unpopular, in mediaeval England) caused immense hardship. When Xerxes sat down to a meal, he had no less than 15,000 regular guests at table with him – his entire officer corps, by the sound of it. Such a banquet is said to have cost 400 silver talents, or about £100,000 – perhaps inclusive of rations for other ranks as well. Nor were the wretched local officials left to tackle this gargantuan catering problem in their own way. Long before Xerxes' actual arrival, a spate of precise and fussy instructions would descend on them from the royal stewards – so much grain to be requisitioned, so much flour to be ground, so many geese and poultry, so many head of fat livestock. The bowls and drinking-cups for the King's table had to be specially made of gold and silver. A suitable pavilion must be set up, ready for the Great King's repose.

But further exactions were in store. When the army moved on next day – or at least, that section of it containing the royal entourage – astonished burghers found that their self-imposed guests took all this paraphernalia with them: pavilion, gold tableware, everything. Alexander of Macedon, who no doubt heard about Xerxes' travelling habits from his friends in the Thraceward regions, had good reason for wanting

---

* Herodotus (7.114.2) adds that when they learnt the name of the place, the priests also buried alive nine local boys and girls. This sounds like atrocity propaganda. Human sacrifice was no part of Zoroastrianism (though some Thracian tribes practised it) and Xerxes would hardly provoke trouble in so good a recruiting area. See HW Comm., vol. 2, p. 169.

to speed the Persian army on its way as fast as possible. Herodotus reports, *en passant*, that the fine road which Xerxes' engineers drove through the forests and rocky outcrops of northern Greece still survived in his own day: the Thracians, he says, 'hold it in profound reverence and never plough it up or sow crops on it'. Small wonder: it was the one tangible benefit they got from Xerxes in return for their quite monstrous outlay on his commissariat, and they had every intention of keeping it. Indeed, Xerxes' famed munificence would seem, at this critical stage of his campaign, to have been cut very much on the cheap. His behaviour on arrival in Acanthus, at the eastern end of the newly completed ship-canal, provides a good example. No Greek city had been more sedulous in support of the invasion, or worked harder to ensure that the canal was ready on time. Loyal collaboration now reaped its due reward. Xerxes 'issued a proclamation of friendship to the people and made them a present of a suit of Median clothes'. Who, one wonders, was entitled to wear it?

Xerxes' pleasure in these harmless junketings was only marred by the sudden death, after a short illness, of his relative Artachaeës, a shambling giant (reputedly eight feet tall) with the loudest voice in Persia. This Stentorian monster, appropriately enough, had been general overseer of the canal workmen. He received a magnificent funeral, and the whole army helped to raise a great mound over his grave. By Herodotus's day the local inhabitants were already sacrificing to Artachaeës 'as to a demi-god', and invoking his name during their prayers. Why not? He had been larger, and louder, than any of them. One commentator remarks that 'respect for mere size is an Oriental characteristic', citing the Mamelukes' surprise at Napoleon's shortness; but there is something very Greek about this metamorphosis too. In the increasingly anthropocentric world of the fifth century BC – 'Man is the measure of all things', said Protagoras – nothing could have been more logical, when one comes to think of it, than to worship an outsize human being.

At Acanthus, army and fleet parted company for a while: a coastal rendezvous was fixed at Therma, on the eastern edge of the great Vardar plain, near the site of modern Thessalonika. While Xerxes' warships sailed two by two through the Athos canal, and then cruised round the other 'prongs' of the Chalcidic peninsula, picking up fresh reinforcements as they went, the land forces followed a more direct route, through the wild hill country of the interior [see map, p. 90]. Just how tough going they found it can be deduced from the fact that the fleet reached Therma well before them. Among other annoyances

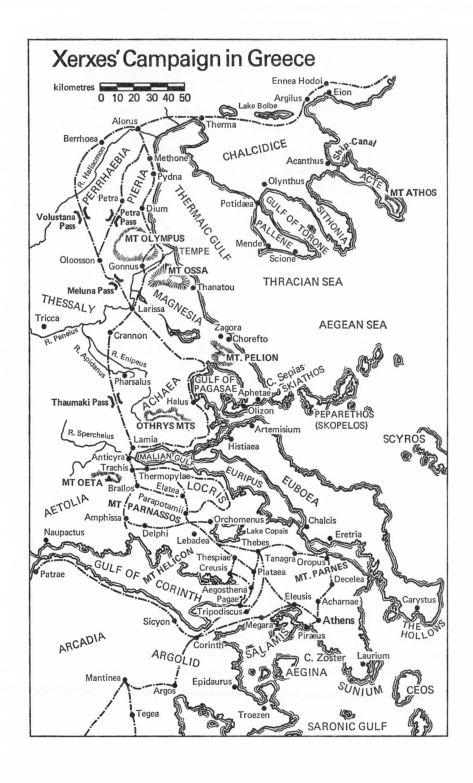

Xerxes' Campaign in Greece

kilometres
0 10 20 30 40 50

Ennea Hodoi
Argilus
Lake Bolbe
Eion
Alorus
Therma
Berrhoea
CHALCIDICE
Ship-Canal
Methone
ACTE
Acanthus
MT ATHOS
PERRHAEBIA
PIERIA
Pydna
Olynthus
R. Haliacmon
Petra
Potidaea
GULF OF TORONE
Volustana Pass
Petra Pass
Dium
THERMAIC GULF
SITHONIA
PALLENE
MT OLYMPUS
Mende
Oloosson
Gonnus
TEMPE
Scione
MT OSSA
THRACIAN SEA
Meluna Pass
Thanatou
MAGNESIA
THESSALY
Larissa
AEGEAN SEA
Tricca
Zagora
Crannon
Chorefto
R. Peneius
R. Enipeus
MT. PELION
R. Apidanus
C. Sepias
SKIATHOS
Pharsalus
GULF OF PAGASAE
Aphetae
Thaumaki Pass
ACHAEA
Halus
Olizon
PEPARETHOS (SKOPELOS)
OTHRYS MTS
Artemisium
SCYROS
R. Spercheius
Lamia
Histiaea
Anticyra
MALIAN GULF
Trachis
EURIPUS
MT OETA
Thermopylae
EUBOEA
Brallos
Elatea
LOCRIS
Parapotamii
MT PARNASSOS
Amphissa
Orchomenus
Chalcis
Naupactus
Delphi
Lake Copais
Eretria
Lebadea
Thebes
Patrae
Thespiae
Tanagra
Oropus
GULF OF MT HELICON
Creusis
Plataea
MT. PARNES
Aegosthena
Decelea
CORINTH
Pagae
Eleusis
Carystus
Tripodiscus
Acharnae
THE HOLLOWS
Sicyon
Megara
Athens
Piraeus
ARCADIA
Corinth
SALAMIS
C. Zoster
Laurium
ARGOLID
AEGINA
Mantinea
SUNIUM
CEOS
Argos
Epidaurus
Tegea
Troezen
SARONIC GULF

encountered *en route* were mountain lions, which preyed on the baggage-train and became especially partial to lagging camels. The head of the column reached Therma about 24 July, and a halt of some days was made there. Xerxes' bivouacs – the Persian army, apart from the Great King himself, seems to have had no tents – spread out for some twenty miles along that lush coastal plain. With two great rivers, the Axius [Vardar] and Haliacmon [Vistritsa] available, a water-shortage was unlikely; yet the tail of the column, away to the east on a smaller stream, the Echeidorus, once more drank its source dry.

Xerxes had several good reasons for making a fairly lengthy halt at this point. First and foremost, he was awaiting the return of his various agents from Greece, with detailed information as to which city-states were, or were not, ready to collaborate. Secondly – and conditional, in part at least, on the results of this investigation – he had to plan his advance into what might well prove actively hostile territory. He now began to appreciate the force of Artabanus's statement [see above, p. 78] that his two greatest enemies would be the land and the sea. Eastward from the Pindus, a great rampart of mountains protected Greece's northern frontier: the points at which an army might penetrate or circumvent this natural barrier could be counted, literally, on the fingers of one hand. The most attractive, in theory, was the Tempe gorge, through which the coast road threaded its way, to debouch straight on to the Thessalian plain, north-north-east of Larissa. This route offered three distinct advantages. It followed the line of a major river, the Peneus; it avoided a difficult trek over the mountains; and it hugged the coast until the last possible moment – a vital factor, this, since close liaison between fleet and army was essential to Xerxes' strategy. Last but not least, thanks to Alexander of Macedon's machinations, the Tempe gorge was now undefended. Xerxes' military advisers, however, had serious objections to this route: Xerxes therefore decided to go and inspect it himself. On a clear summer day, at dawn, Olympus and Ossa were visible from the head of the Thermaic Gulf; and Tempe had the reputation of being a famous beauty-spot. It would make a pleasant diversion to spend a few days studying the landscape: aesthetic and strategic considerations seldom coincided so happily. The royal Sidonian galley was made ready, and Xerxes set off.

Herodotus remarks, drily, that 'the appearance of the river mouth, on his arrival there, was a great surprise to him'. We may well believe it. On one side towered snow-capped Olympus, almost 10,000 feet high; on the other the lower, but scarcely less formidable peaks of Ossa and Pelion. Between them ran the pass through which he hoped to lead his army: some four and a half miles long, and at many points no more than a hundred yards wide – effectively even less, in fact, since most of this space was taken up by the river-gorge, leaving the road a perilous passage between rock-face and chasm. The eyewitness account by Polybius, in Livy's paraphrase [44.6] is both accurate and impressive: 'Tempe is a defile, difficult of access, even though not guarded by an enemy; for besides the narrowness of the pass for five miles, where there is scarcely room for a beast of burden, the rocks on both sides are so perpendicular as to cause giddiness both in the mind and eyes of those who look down from the precipice.' Xerxes, with commendable restraint, merely observed that damming this cleft would turn Thessaly into a lake; but he must also have seen the dangers of trying to funnel his large army, or even part of it, through the gorge. It would be a horribly slow process, in extended file (of all dispositions the most vulnerable for marching troops), and from start to finish wide open to ambushes, road-blocks, rock-rolling, or any other form of guerilla action. The pass might at present, thanks to Alexander's machinations, be clear of Greek troops; that was no guarantee against their sudden reappearance. The risks attendant upon using this route so far outweighed the advantages that Xerxes abandoned the whole idea on the spot.

Nevertheless, his decision meant striking inland much further north – either along the line of the Haliacmon River, and then south-east over the Volustana Pass, or else from Dium by way of Petra [see map, p. 90]. These two routes met at Oloösson [Elassona], in the Perrhaebian mountains; from there the road wound down through the Meluna Pass to the plain, approaching Larissa from the north-west. The only other alternative was a steep and rugged hill-track, which branched inland shortly before Tempe, to emerge at Gonnus – thus by-passing the Peneus gorge. Herodotus seems to assume that this was the route Xerxes actually took (and indeed he may have sent a few light mountain troops that way to protect his flank); but it was far too rough for any large-scale expeditionary force, especially with numerous cavalry units and a cumbersome baggage-train to be considered. Once Tempe had been ruled out, Xerxes had little choice but to settle for the two central passes, which in turn meant a prolonged separation from the fleet.

He could, however, console himself with the reflection that this was a hazard which he would have to face whatever his route. While the fleet sailed sixty long miles down the mountainous and inhospitable coastline of Magnesia, the army would be marching well inland, by one of the two main roads to Lamia, at the head of the Malian Gulf. It was physically impossible [see map, p. 90] for sea and land forces to be reunited before Pagasae. This, however, after his visit to Tempe, must have struck Xerxes as very much the lesser of two evils, especially since his agents from central Greece now came in with excellent news. Nearly all cities and tribes in the area were ready to collaborate, including Thessaly, and the whole of Boeotia except for Thespiae and Plataea. Xerxes' course was now clear; his mind once made up, he took prompt and effective action. One-third of all his land forces, perhaps 60,000 in number, were ordered into the mountains of Macedonia, where they set about clearing and widening the old forest trail to the Volustana Pass. Xerxes himself sailed back to base headquarters at Therma in a mood of buoyant and justifiable confidence. Northern Greece had caved in without a blow being struck. Athens' position was untenable, and public opinion there seriously divided. The odds against the Peloponnesians attempting to defend anything except their own frontiers had lengthened immeasurably. Once Xerxes' fleet had turned the Isthmus land-defences, Argos could declare openly for Persia, thus cutting Sparta's communications with Corinth. After that, each state could be dealt with separately and at leisure. It was an alluring dream, which, had it not been for one man's genius and determination, would almost certainly have come true.

The Hellenic League's army had evacuated Tempe a few weeks earlier, in late June. It was shortly after their withdrawal – as we might expect – that the bulk of the central Greek states, including Boeotia and Thessaly, defected to Xerxes. Euaenetus and Themistocles marched their grumbling troops back south to the Gulf of Pagasae, where they were re-embarked for Corinth. It is tempting to hazard a guess that Themistocles himself went back home by the overland route, and paid a discreet visit to Delphi on the way. He was now more than ever determined to get his naval defence scheme accepted by the League, before it was too late. First, however, it was essential that he win a mandate from his own countrymen – something which so far, except for the creation of the fleet (over which the Assembly was deliberately misled) he had failed to do. Athens, after all, would supply by far the largest contingent of ships, and it was on those ships that his entire strategy depended. Time enough to worry about the Congress vote when he had dealt with the powerful and articulate opposition at home. Ingrained prejudice against evacuation, on both patriotic and religious grounds; the class-hatred which most landowners and aristocrats felt for the 'sailor rabble' who manned the fleet; a stubborn belief in the possibility of defeating Xerxes by land alone, the 'Marathon solution' that was equally popular at Sparta, and had been directly responsible for the Tempe fiasco – all these considerations made it highly unlikely that

Themistocles, even now, would carry a vote in the Assembly except by the very narrowest of margins. Any special pressure which he could bring to bear on the electorate was worthy trying. A *bona fide* oracle from Delphi had more chance than most things of working effective propaganda on his behalf.

Another persuasive line of attack was to scare the Assembly with the prospect of betrayal by Sparta and the Peloponnesian League, which would leave Athens exposed, in isolation, to the full advancing might of the Persian war-machine. That Themistocles believed this to be a real possibility we need not doubt for one moment; subsequent events made it all too clear how strong the grounds for suspicion were. Our greatest handicap in appreciating the events of 480 is, quite simply, the fact that *we know how it all turned out*. We are lulled by too-perfect hindsight, wise – and over-confident – after the event. No one, not even Themistocles, could be sure, that June, which way things would go, who would medise, who stand firm. Delphi's pronouncements in the late summer of 481 had been both realistic and plausible.* Few Peloponnesian states, least of all Sparta, had any overriding reason to love Athens; only those who shared Themistocles' views *ab initio* would understand that the Athenian fleet was indispensable for any plan to defend the Isthmus. Cynics at Sparta, it could be argued, might well sacrifice Athens to Xerxes (a rival well out of the way) and let Persia annex northern Greece by agreement. We know, now, that the Peloponnesian *bloc* (though with many misgivings) did in fact hold firm: this was by no means self-evident before the event. No one could guess, with any certainty, how the League Congress would vote in a few days' time on the burning question of defence – or even whether the resultant decision would be honoured by all member-states.

Sparta's long-cherished isolationism, her trick, even when she *did* send support, of sending it too late (no one in Athens was likely to have forgotten Marathon), her growing suspicion of Athenian maritime ambitions – none of these things can have given Themistocles much grounds for confidence; nor can the oracle-mongers, urging neither land-defence nor naval strategy, but incontinent emigration. The latter, it was true, might be turned to some advantage, since ships were essential for evacuation, whether to Salamis or south Italy; but Themistocles could not afford to argue his case at the Isthmus without having first, before he left Athens, taken out an insurance policy against possible

---

* A close modern parallel may be found in the predictions of England's imminent defeat put out (1940–1) by Radio Vichy – an organ which, in its blend of reasoned intellectual pessimism, time-serving self-interest, and cash-conscious religiosity, much resembled Delphi during the latter's pro-Persian phase.

defeat or betrayal. In other words, he had to plan comprehensive emergency defence measures for Athens and Attica *independently of the League*: measures which could, at a pinch, be implemented either with or without allied backing. The Athenians, to borrow an expressive phrase from 1940, must be prepared, if necessary, to go it alone. If the new Delphic oracle which was now[3] brought back to Athens did, in fact, depend on material supplied by Themistocles, such considerations surely lay behind it. Since it played so crucial a part in the debate which followed, it is worth quoting in full:

> Not wholly can Pallas win the heart of Olympian Zeus,
> Though she prays him with many prayers and all her subtlety;
> Yet will I speak to you this other word, as firm as adamant:
> Though all else shall be taken within the bound of Cecrops
> And the fold of the holy mountain of Cithaeron,
> Yet Zeus the all-seeing grants to Athene's prayer
> That the wooden wall only shall not fall, but help you and your children.
> But await not the host of horse and foot coming from Asia,
> Nor be still, but turn your back and withdraw from the foe.
> Truly a day will come when you will meet him face to face.
> Divine Salamis, you will bring death to women's sons
> When the corn is scattered, or the harvest gathered in.

That this was a genuine oracle, not one fraudulently concocted after the event, there seems little room for doubt.[4] The forger of *ex post facto* pronouncements can afford to be confidently explicit: he is dealing with the past, not the future. But the response which Athens' anxious envoys received was packed with all the old familiar caveats and ambiguities. Delphi carefully refrained from saying *which* women's sons would suffer death at Salamis – most Athenians, in fact, took this to indicate a Greek defeat – and was not even prepared to specify the date of the coming encounter, let alone its upshot. 'When the corn is scattered, or the harvest gathered in' could refer to virtually any point in a normal campaigning season: no Greek in his right mind would fight a battle at midwinter. Even the crucial presumed allusion to fighting at sea ('the wooden wall') could be, and was, taken in a quite different sense by Themistocles' opponents. All this suggests a genuine, typically hedging pronouncement. Perhaps someone at Delphi had seen that Themistocles' naval strategy did stand just a chance of coming off; but the resultant oracle could hardly be said to predict a Greek victory. This adequately disposes of the view that Themistocles somehow *dictated* Delphi's response. Had he been in the position to do so, he would undoubtedly have made a more straightforward and efficient job of it. At this stage, far from calling the shots, he had to take what he could get out of Delphi, and be grateful. The oracle, in fact, was just what might have been expected in the circumstances. It offered Athens a scintilla of hope, but took great care, at the same time, not to give open offence to the Persians.

What has aroused most discussion is the explicit allusion to Salamis. Some regard this as a proof of forgery; others argue that Themistocles' plan, from the very first, was to fight the decisive engagement in Salamis straits, that Thermopylae and Artemisium were never intended as more than holding actions. Both these extreme views seem to me mistaken. What Themistocles wanted divine endorsement for, above all, was the evacuation of Attica, a proposal which aroused more bitter opposition than any other point in his programme. There was no secret, either, about his plan to use Salamis as an emergency naval base, administrative centre, and overspill area. He was always urging his views before the Assembly, and Delphi must have been well acquainted with them. To advise withdrawal, and predict some kind of engagement at Salamis (without being specific about either its nature or its outcome) was as far as the Oracle would go, whether in response to private solicitations or not. From this lukewarm and ambivalent utterance Themistocles – faced with the most critical debate of his entire career – had to squeeze what poor shreds of support he could. He was already doing his best with signs and portents – 'just as a poet introduces a *deus ex machina* into his tragedy', Plutarch remarks. There was, for instance, the business of Athena's sacred snake on the Acropolis. First it mysteriously went off its food. Next – even more mysteriously – it vanished from the enclosure where it was kept. The priests then announced, on Themistocles' instructions, that 'the goddess Athena had abandoned her city and was showing them their way to the sea'.

The formal debate on this oracle – which was, in effect, a debate on Athens' entire future war-policy – took place towards the end of June. It is safe to say that a more crucial issue never came before the Athenian Assembly: all was at stake indeed, not for Greece alone, but – though no one there could have foreseen this – for the whole future of European civilisation as we know it. No one who has ever stood on the Pnyx, Athens' open-air Parliament Hill, could fail to revisualise the tense excitement and stress of that momentous occasion: packed ranks of citizens craning towards the speakers' platform below them, anxious not to miss a word, while beyond – a sublime background for any human drama – stood the Acropolis, that natural citadel, framed against the diamond-bright, heat-hazed landscape of Attica. To the Athenian voter it was all so familiar that he scarcely noticed it: a huddle of houses and temples, the encircling smoke-blue mountains – Parnes, Hymettus, the hazy outline of Pentele, its slopes freshly gashed by marble-quarriers, and, invisible beyond the horizon, the Marathon plain, where once before Athens had met, and defeated, a Persian invader. But on that day, in June 480, it was the big, thickset, burly figure of Themistocles which dominated the scene: arguing, pleading, cajoling, rhetorical and, finally, triumphant.

He still had conservative opinion – the priests and soothsayers, the crustier aristocrats, elderly diehards of every kind – solidly against him. These now produced their own interpretation of the oracle. For them the 'wooden wall' was the wattle palisade which, in bygone times, had fenced in the summit of the Acropolis, and they argued that it was the Acropolis which would escape destruction. This implies a last-ditch defence of the traditional sort. Themistocles' alternative – evacuation and defence by the fleet – came under heavy fire from the professional seers. These gentlemen took a gloomy view of the oracle's two closing lines: 'Divine Salamis, you will bring death to women's sons/ When the corn is scattered, or the harvest gathered in.' The meaning of this, they alleged, was that if the Athenians fought at sea, they would suffer defeat off Salamis. Like their colleagues at Delphi, they were against offering resistance at all, either by land or sea, and urged that the only feasible course, now, was to 'abandon Attica altogether and seek a home elsewhere'. This *fainéant* attitude probably did a good deal, unintentionally, to help Themistocles' cause: neither the Marathon warriors nor the sailors of the fleet could stomach mere tame capitulation.

Themistocles did what he could, which was not much, with the oracle. If Apollo was hinting at an *Athenian* defeat, surely he would not have applied the epithet 'divine' to Salamis? Would not something like 'hateful' have been more likely? Thin stuff indeed – but there were many anxious to believe it: the common men, the unthinking patriots, above all the young, untrammelled by reactionary tradition or dogmatic platitudes, glimpsing, better than their elders, where Athens' true future greatness lay. We can imagine the mood of the Assembly changing as Themistocles gathered himself for his final peroration. The State, he cried, was not mere walls and buildings – these had little significance in themselves – but the sum of its citizens. What matter if Athens was destroyed? A city could be rebuilt. To make good the loss of human freedom and integrity was a harder matter. So, years before, that intransigent poet Alcaeus: 'It is not fine houses or stout walls or canals or dockyards which make a *polis*, but men able to use their opportunities.' Finally, as the climax of his speech, Themistocles put before the Assembly a formal motion, embodying the essence of his war-strategy. When he stopped speaking, Athens' citizens rose and cheered him. The show of hands was overwhelmingly in his favour. He stood there, a heavy, dogged, indomitable figure: one man with the fate of Greece on his broad shoulders. Common sense had triumphed over upper-class traditionalism. He had appealed to the people, and he had won. It was, indeed, his finest hour.

We know, today, the gist – if not the *ipsissima verba* – of that famous motion which Themistocles put forward, and the Assembly, to its eternal credit, ratified. In 1959 Professor Michael Jameson of Pennsylvania found a third-century BC copy of the draft decree at Troezen in the Argolid – a town which, as we shall see, befriended many Athenian evacuees during the Persian Wars. Over two centuries and more, intervening generations had edited and modernised the original text, much as we nowadays will modernise the spelling or diction of an early writer such as Chaucer or Piers Plowman. The decree also diverges somewhat in substance – though far less than is commonly supposed – from our soundest historical account of these events, that by Herodotus. Fierce scholarly debate still continues over the inscription's authenticity: many scholars regard it as a late forgery, perhaps intended to whip up patriotic feeling against Macedonia. Many others, however – including the present writer – believe that the fragmentary inscription does, in fact, give us something very close to Themistocles' actual proposals, though it may possibly run together several motions passed on different days. I quote it here (with one small textual change) in the revised version published by Professor Jameson:[5]

The Gods
Resolved by the Council and People
Themistocles, son of Neocles, of Phrearri, made the motion
To entrust the city to Athena the Mistress of Athens and to all the other Gods to guard and defend from the Barbarian for the sake of the land. The Athenians themselves and the foreigners who live in Athens are to send their children and women to safety in Troizen, their protector being Pittheus, the founding hero of the land. They are to send the old men and their movable possessions to safety on Salamis. The treasurers and priestesses are to remain on the acropolis guarding the property of the gods.

All the other Athenians and foreigners of military age are to embark on the 200 ships that are ready and defend against the Barbarian for the sake of their own freedom and that of the rest of the Greeks along with the Lacedaemonians, the Corinthians, the Aeginetans, and all others who wish to share the danger.

The generals are to appoint, starting tomorrow, 200 trierarchs [captains of triremes], from among those who have land and house in Athens and legitimate children and who are not older than fifty; to these men the ships are to be assigned by lot. They are to enlist marines, 10 to each ship, from men between the ages of twenty and thirty, and four archers. They are to distribute the servicemen [perhaps 'petty officers' would be more accurate: see Morrison and Williams, *Greek Oared Ships*, p. 253 ff.] by lot at the same time as they assign the trierarchs to the ships by lot. The generals are to write up the sailors[6] ship by ship on white boards, (taking) the Athenians from the lexiarchic registers [citizen-rolls], the foreigners from those registered with the Polemarch [formerly C.-in-C. of the armed forces (see above, p. 32), now a senior magistrate]. They are to write them up assigning them by divisions, two hundred of about one hundred (men) each, and to write above each division the name of the trireme and the trierarch and the serviceman [petty officer], so that they may know on which trireme each division is to embark. When all the divisions have been composed and allotted to the triremes, the Council and the generals are to man all the two hundred ships, after sacrificing a placatory offering to Zeus the Almighty and Athena and Nike [Victory: perhaps we should read 'Athena Nike' here] and Poseidon the Securer.

When the ships have been manned, with a hundred of them they are to meet the enemy at Artemisium in Euboea, and with the other hundred they are to lie off Salamis and the coast of Attica and keep guard over the land. In order that all Athenians may be united in their defence against the Barbarian those who have been sent into exile for ten years are to go to Salamis and stay there until the People come to some decision about them, while [? those who have been deprived of citizen rights are to have their rights restored . . .]

The stone breaks off at this point, but it is probable that we have the larger part of it. We are left with a brief, vivid glimpse of Athens preparing to meet her crisis – and of the practical, far-sighted statesman who brought her safely through the storm.

One cardinal fact should never be forgotten. This decree was a strictly *internal* measure, passed by and for Athenians alone. It had no direct connection with the League Congress, a fact which makes its dating of some importance. Herodotus [7.174] suggests that the Greek force under Themistocles and Euaenetus went straight from Tempe to the Isthmus, where it was voted, in full session, to defend the Thermopylae-Artemisium line. The natural deduction from this evidence – and so taken, to the best of my knowledge, by all scholars – is that the 'Troezen Decree' was passed *after Themistocles returned from the Isthmus*. Jameson's version of events is typical: 'The decision must have been reported by Themistocles and his colleagues to the Athenians, and put into effect by them in this decree.'[7] In that case what, one wonders, would have happened if the Athenian Assembly, in one of its more perversely whimsical moods, had thrown the motion out? Never in its chequered history – and now least of all – do we find that unpredictable body acting as a mere rubber stamp. Quite apart from this, Themistocles' previous experience could scarcely have led him to believe that so controversial a measure would win automatic approval, crisis or no crisis. He had failed before; he might well fail again.

One interesting point about the 'Troezen Decree' is that it mentions Artemisium, but not Thermopylae. Themistocles, of course, knew very well from the beginning that only an amphibious defence-line, with close liaison between fleet and army, stood any real chance of success. Whether he could sell this basic strategy at the Isthmus, however, was by no means certain. He clearly intended that the fleet (to which Athens contributed by far the largest individual contingent) should play the dominant role in these combined operations, while the army merely acted as a subservient holding force. Such a concept of their respective functions was unlikely to prove popular with Spartan militarists. Indeed, when it came to the point, Nepos tells us, 'many of the states did not approve of Themistocles' plan, but preferred to fight on land' – the old, stubborn chimaera created by Marathon. The obvious inference from this is that when the 'Troezen Decree' was voted, no one actually knew whether Athens' unpredictable Peloponnesian allies would endorse it or not. In other words, it must be dated to a time *before* the League Congress met for its final decision on the defence of Greece.

One last but important point. Whatever policy Themistocles advanced at the Isthmus, he was, clearly, acting in his capacity as Athenian *proboulos*. Our evidence for the nature and functioning of the League is sadly sketchy; but I have always thought it odd that no modern study, not even the most exhaustive,[8] has fully considered the matter of the League's executive authority. Could its decisions be carried out at once, without subsequent ratification by the governments of member-states? In other words, did the *probouloi* have plenipotentiary powers? The answer must, surely, be in the affirmative. The object of the League was to take fast collective action against Persia. Such action would be impossible – especially in Greece – if every vote was referred back to member-states for debate, with the chance of veto rather than ratification. The *probouloi* must have had full powers to act on behalf of the states they represented, and the League's majority decisions will have been binding on all members. Now if Themistocles, as *proboulos*, spoke for Athens, at least one point covered by the 'Troezen Decree', mobilisation of the fleet, would not have required ratification at all; and the other two main clauses – the evacuation of Attica, the recall of political exiles – though domestic in application, stand or fall by this first one.

If, then, we date the decree *after* that final meeting at the Isthmus, its logical *raison d'être* is severely reduced – to the point, indeed, where it becomes virtually nonsensical. But if we place it *before* the League Congress, immediately after Themistocles' return from Tempe, it takes on a very different complexion. It is not only Themistocles' original mandate as Athenian *proboulos*, the policy for which he was obliged to win Assembly approval (and without which approval, no doubt, Athens would have had a different representative at the Isthmus). It is also an emergency measure designed to cover Athens' betrayal or abandonment by the Peloponnesian League. The decision to fight for freedom 'along with the Lacedaemonians, the Corinthians, the Aeginetans, and all others who wish to share the danger' is no more than a hopeful acknowledgement of the League's existence: it does not imply any preconcerted policy. No one could guess how the voting at the Isthmus would go. Sparta's isolationists might well carry the day; in which case Themistocles, and Athens, would find themselves out on a north Greek limb, while their allies busied themselves with the defence of the Peloponnese. That this was no idle fear became all too obvious after the defeat at Thermopylae, when the Peloponnesians, predictably, were found to be 'fortifying the Isthmus, and letting all else go'; it took tough Athenian pressurising to bring them back north in time for Plataea [see below, p. 229 ff.].

The 'Troezen Decree', then, was passed by the Athenian Assembly after the retreat from Tempe, but prior to the final meeting of League delegates at the Isthmus: in the archonship of Hypsichides, which means before the end of June. Xerxes was still little farther than Doriscus, and Athens had ample time to take full defensive measures against his coming. The League army's calamitous experience up north had demonstrated, beyond any shadow of doubt, that if Xerxes was to be stopped in central Greece, it would not be by land alone. Themistocles, we need not doubt, made the most of this point. The return of Athens' contingent meant that just about enough men were now available to man the fleet. Two hundred triremes (and these were only the front-line vessels) called for an ideal complement of 40,000 men. The decree – if Jameson's restoration here is correct – allots no more than a hundred citizens and resident aliens to each vessel: half the normal crew, in fact. The likeliest explanation is that this deficiency was made good by conscripting slaves, as Athens did at every crisis in her history from Marathon to Arginusae. The important point, however, is that there *was* a manpower shortage. The crews which fought at Artemisium were reinforced by Plataeans, while no less than twenty Athenian triremes had volunteer crews from Chalcis: at full strength this represented an addition of four thousand men. In other words, every Athenian, bond or free, who could bend an oar was now pressed into service with the fleet. From this two inevitable consequences followed. First, Athens could contribute no land-forces to the defence of the north, and in any case (as we have seen) was probably relying on naval strategy alone. All military action, then, would be Sparta's responsibility. Secondly, the evacuation of Attica now became inevitable, since mobilisation of Themistocles' new fleet would leave the frontiers totally undefended, except by boys and old men.

Here, of course, is where the 'Troezen Decree' would seem to diverge most radically from Herodotus's version of events. In the latter, the abandonment of Athens is a last-minute, scrambling, *sauve qui peut* affair, carried out only after the collapse of the Thermopylae-Artemisium line, with a Persian breakthrough imminent. This is almost certainly untrue. To evacuate the whole of Attica in perhaps no more than forty-eight hours[9] would be neither provident nor, indeed, physically possible. If we then ask how Herodotus came to believe the story as he tells it, the answer is, almost certainly, that his aristocratic informants were to blame. It was they who prejudiced him in so astonishing a fashion against Themistocles: it is not hard to see why. The great statesman had been largely responsible for ruining the careers of many highly distinguished noblemen [see above, p. 47–8], and their descendants were not liable to give any enquirer an unbiassed picture of him. Themistocles' principal victims, moreover, had all been Alcmaeonidae; and to judge by the way Herodotus goes out of his way to give any Alcmaeonid the benefit of the doubt, this family had proved most cooperative when he sought their help in collecting material for the *Histories*. The inference is obvious. But that is not, I suspect, the whole story. Herodotus's friends in Athens were all old-fashioned conservatives, well-bred gentlemen who could not bear the shame of Athenians having actually *voted* to abandon hearths, temples and ancestral shrines without a fight – and in favour, what was worse, of that ultra-plebeian institution the fleet. An emergency evacuation was somewhat less of a blot, as they saw it, on the civic scutcheon. What made these diehards so angry in retrospect, however, was the underlying belief that this appalling sacrifice had been quite unnecessary. If heavy-armed Spartan and Athenian infantrymen could break a Persian army at Plataea, surely they could equally well have done so before Salamis? The mild juggling of historical fact which the decree reveals in Herodotus's narrative does not affect any vital issue, and is all too understandable in terms of upper-class Athenian prejudice.

It is clear that this complex operation consisted, in fact, of two quite separate stages. First came the general transfer of civilians and movable property: a precautionary measure, carried out (in theory at least) immediately Themistocles' measures became law. At the same time the fleet was mobilised to defend Euboea, the coastline of Attica, and Salamis. This evacuation, however, was by no means total. A skeleton administrative staff had to remain in Athens. Shops, farms, and public services must have carried on. As usual on such occasions, many people simply ignored the decree, preferring to wait on events: quite enough to account for the chaotic last-minute flight so dramatically chronicled by Herodotus and Plutarch. Even then, so strong was the force of inertia or stubborn indifference, no less than five hundred prisoners were taken by the Persians during their advance through Attica. However, a very large proportion of the noncombatant population did remove to Troezen or Salamis during that July, taking their goods and chattels with them.

One can sympathise with their predicament. Even if the Peloponnesian states stood firm, any defence which rested on the fleet still left Attica itself fatally vulnerable. The decision to hold Thermopylae may have reassured some; but others, while welcoming it, doubtless saw the danger of this new defence line being turned, sooner or later, through central Greece. It has, indeed, been argued that Thermopylae-Artemisium was never planned as more than a long-term holding action – as Jameson says, 'to give time for the building of the Isthmus wall and the rallying of naval units'. Most Athenians, on this showing, must have believed that the final choice lay between a last-ditch campaign off Salamis, and mass emigration to Southern Italy. There may be something in this, but it ignores the possibility (which Themistocles surely at least considered) of snatching a quick naval victory at Artemisium while Xerxes was held up before the Hot Gates. Such an outside chance, however, could not be relied on, much less made the guarantee for innumerable Athenian lives. So the refugees sailed from Piraeus, like all Greek travellers, then or now, amid a great clutter of baskets, baggage, goats, hen-coops and babies, to receive a most hospitable welcome across the water. The citizens of Troezen even 'voted to maintain the refugees at the public expense; they gave each family two obols a day, allowed the children to pick the fruit wherever they pleased as soon as it was ripe, and went so far as to pay schoolmasters to teach them' – an odd anticipation of Welfare State procedure.

Themistocles might not have won over Athens' elderly tories – one can imagine the outcry with which they greeted the passing of his controversial decree – but at least he seems to have made some impression on their sons. While many Athenians were still wavering, Miltiades' handsome young son Cimon organised a public demonstration, of a somewhat unusual kind. He led a procession of his friends, all young noblemen serving with Athens' *élite* cavalry corps, from the Cerameicus up to the Acropolis. Each of them carried a horse's bridle. When they reached Athena's temple they dedicated these offerings to the goddess, 'in token of the fact that what the city needed at the moment was not knightly valour but men to fight at sea'. After Cimon himself had dedicated his bridle, and made a prayer to the goddess, he took one of the shields hanging on the temple wall; then he and his friends trooped down to Piraeus and the ships – probably to serve as marines. Whether this incident was organised propaganda or not, it had the desired effect. Just as rival city-states had sunk their differences in the face of a common danger, so Athens now abandoned – at least for the duration of hostilities – that social factionalism which the development of the fleet merely served to exacerbate, until it became ugly and irremediable class-hatred. Cimon, as his subsequent career proved, was a true reactionary at heart, and politically naïve into the bargain; but this patriotic gesture of his youth, made long before he had become the white hope of Athens' *ultras*, should never be forgotten when judging him.

Another emergency measure outlined in the 'Troezen Decree', and known to us from several literary sources,[10] is that providing for the recall of political exiles, 'in order that all Athenians may be united in their defence against the Barbarian'. This phrase is something of a euphemism: what everyone feared was that the exiles – all brilliant men of great talent and experience – might offer their services to Xerxes instead. Most of them had little reason to love Themistocles, the chief if not the only begetter of their ostracism: one could only hope that patriotism would prove stronger, at such a moment of crisis, than mere personal resentment. The odd (yet somehow characteristic) thing about this clause in the decree is that it demands, unconditionally, what could not in fact be enforced. As Burn says, 'Athens asserted her rights over her citizens temporarily exiled, as she did over those at home and liable for service'. It is all rather like the famous exchange between Glendower and Hotspur: 'I can call spirits from the vasty deep.' 'Why, so can I, or so can any man; but will they come when you do call for them?' Xanthippus and Aristeides did: as a reward for civic devotion, and in recognition of their proven abilities, they were not only exonerated but made generals for the forthcoming campaign. Hipparchus, on the other hand, did not. By now he was a known quisling with the Peisistratids at Xerxes' court; the Assembly arraigned him for treason, and he was condemned to death *in absentia*. His bronze statue on the Acropolis (probably an *ex-voto* commemorating his archonship) was melted down and made into a pillar, on which, afterwards, the names of all traitors were engraved. To guard against any similar defection, a decree was passed prescribing (under penalty of absolute loss of citizenship) the area within which an exiled person might live. It did not include Persian territory.

While the front-line triremes, together with any others in good enough condition for active service, were being fitted out and allotted their permanent crews, Themistocles left Athens for Corinth, where the League was once more in session. Most of July was wasted in futile bickering and interminable debate. Disagreement over strategy – where should the joint defence-line be drawn? how should it be held? – was only one among many bones of contention. The Spartans, in particular, had their usual religious objections to campaigning at such a season. Their chief festival, the Carneia, fell on or about 20 August, at the time of the full moon; so, that year, did the quadriennial Olympic Games, during which all warring Greek states sunk their differences and competed together in relative amity. To us such scruples, in such an hour of crisis, may appear flatly incredible: Xerxes would hardly carry respect for local customs to the point of honouring the Olympic truce. Yet, half a century later, an educated *Athenian* general lost his entire army through refusing to march after an eclipse of the moon. Could anyone expect Spartans, of an older generation, and unenlightened by Periclean rationalism, to show themselves more progressive?

Oddly enough, when it came to the point, they did. Themistocles was a highly persuasive man; but it was the news that Xerxes' pioneers had actually begun road-clearing operations in Pieria which at last shocked the League into unanimous and decisive action. Themistocles' long-advocated plan for holding the Thermopylae-Artemisium line was now formally ratified. Allied naval contingents made ready to sail north, while the Spartans mobilised a small advance force under King Leonidas – including three hundred picked Spartiate warriors – for the immediate defence of the Hot Gates. These arrangements concluded, the delegates at once 'broke up from the Isthmus and proceeded to their new positions'. The chips were down at last.

PART FOUR

THE
CORNER-STONE
OF FREEDOM

THE allied Greek fleet, with a total strength of 271 front-line vessels (as against the Persians' 650+), sailed for Artemisium late in July. By far the largest single contingent was that provided by Athens. In addition to a round hundred of Themistocles' new triremes, the Athenians had equipped some forty-seven 'graveyard refits' as emergency support. Twenty of the latter were crewed by volunteers from Chalcis, and most of the rest by Plataeans: at a full complement of 200 men to a trireme [see above, p. 101], Athens was literally scraping the bottom of the barrel. (It is no coincidence that those states which contributed ships, sailors and marines did not, on the whole, send hoplite contingents to Thermopylae: the reverse is also true. The allied war-fleet absorbed up to 65,000 men all told, of whom not more than five per cent were marines.) Of the Plataeans Herodotus observes, drily, that their courage and patriotism 'led them to undertake this service in spite of their ignorance of everything to do with the sea'. Nobody in his right mind – let alone Themistocles – would entrust such tyros with any but strictly expendable vessels. Athens apart, the Peloponnesian states contributed a hundred triremes, the cities of the Argolid thirteen, and the islands eleven. There were also a few fifty-oared galleys. A reserve fleet was left behind to guard Salamis, Attica, Aegina and the Argolid. Its exact strength is unknown, but was probably two hundred at the outside. Here, again, Athens' contribution was by far the largest: two full squadrons, one of fifty-three vessels to patrol the Attica coastline, and another, perhaps fifty-seven strong,* to guard the sea-lanes round Salamis. A large proportion of the rest were probably supplied by Aegina, whose fleet – one of the most powerful in the Aegean – contributed no more than eighteen triremes to the defence of Artemisium.

Taking only iron rations with them – 'barley meal and a relish of

* Taking Ctesias's statement [§26, Henry p. 31] that the Athenians took 110 triremes to Salamis in conjunction with the prescription of the Troezen Decree (lines 41–4) that 100 front-line vessels were to be reserved for home defence: the extra ten triremes will then have been refits.

onions and cheese': there was little storage space in a trireme, even for drinking-water – the main allied fleet rowed from the Saronic Gulf past Cape Sunium, and then northwards, under a blazing sun, through the narrow straits between Euboea and the mainland. A day or two later, about the beginning of August, they established their base camp at Artemisium. The position they chose was a flat, sandy plain, about ten miles long, backed by shallow folded hills. Here and there small streams drained seaward through clumps of reeds, and the gritty, shelving beach was littered with drifts of salt-white stones – mute witness to those raging on-shore gales which still blow up-channel from Skiathos with the *meltemi*. In bad weather Artemisium could be an uncomfortable station. Strategically, however, it gave the Greeks just what they needed: a long strand, on which hundreds of triremes could be drawn up without difficulty, a position from which patrols could keep watch, simultaneously, on the sea-lanes by Skiathos and Skopelos, and the entrance to the Malian Gulf. Xerxes' Phoenician squadrons would not advance into the channel without first eliminating this threat to their flank (similar considerations dictated their strategy at Salamis); nor, since the Persian army was largely dependent on them for supplies, would they sail *en masse* down the east coast of Euboea, by-passing the Greek position altogether. But there was another point which Themistocles had foreseen when choosing this position: the need, at all costs, to prevent a Persian landing on the island. If Xerxes achieved this, he could march south as far as Chalcis, where the channel between island and mainland narrows to about forty yards, and block the Greek line of retreat both by land and sea. While his engineers dammed the channel, his advance guard would hurry back by the coast road through Phocis, and take Leonidas in the rear.

No sooner had the Greek fleet reached Artemisium, however, than fresh trouble [see above, p. 70] blew up over the vexed question of the High Command. The Athenians, since they contributed more triremes than any other member-state, had felt all along that Themistocles should be allied commander-in-chief; civic pride apart, they were liable to see action any day now, and no man there had a better right, or was better qualified, to lead them in battle. The idea of fighting under a Spartan admiral struck them as something worse than a bad joke. They would not, they now declared, accept Eurybiades' leadership. Themistocles, with unwonted tact, affirmed his own readiness to do so, 'and soothed the Athenians' pride by promising them that if they proved their valour in the fighting, he would guarantee that the rest of the Greeks would accept their leadership later on.' He also, it would seem, gave them a pretty broad hint that Eurybiades' office was decorative rather than functional, being mainly designed to satisfy the touchy pride of their Peloponnesian allies. Diodorus sums up the arrangement to perfection: Eurybiades was admiral, but Themistocles gave the orders. Once again a breakdown of the allies' always precariously united front had been averted in the nick of time. Placated and mollified, they were now at leisure to consider the question of their defences. Skiathos was made the base for an advanced naval reconnaissance unit, while look-outs with fire-beacons were posted on the mountain-tops both there and in Northern Euboea. A thirty-oared galley, under Habronichus son of Lysicles – Themistocles' trusted lieutenant, and later his fellow-ambassador to Sparta – was specially detailed for liaison duties with Leonidas at Thermopylae: an essential precaution, since the two bases were about forty sea-miles apart. Though their normal method of communication was by beacons or smoke-signals, these would be something less than adequate in a crisis.

Leonidas got his advance force into position later – though not much later – than the fleet: soon enough to repair an ancient Phocian defence wall [see plan, p. 113], and for news of his arrival to reach Xerxes while that dilatory monarch was still in Thessaly. If the intelligence report was accurate in its assessment of numbers, no Persian staff officer is likely to have lost much sleep over it. When Leonidas marched north for the Isthmus, he had no more than 4,000 men with him, over half of whom were Arcadian peasants. Sparta herself contributed a bare 300 warriors (though these were drawn from her *corps d'élite*), and perhaps three times that number of Helots to serve as batmen and to die at their masters' side if the need arose. Why, we may well ask, were the Peloponnesian states so niggardly at this critical point? It is clear that they had no intention, now or ever, of committing *all* their available troops in the north: a reserve must be held back to defend the Peloponnese itself. If Themistocles' ambitious and daring strategy went awry – as many conservatives feared – there could still be a last-ditch stand at the Isthmus. On the other hand no one – least of all a Spartan military expert – could have regarded Leonidas's little army as capable of putting up more than a temporary stop-gap defence unaided. It was *an advance guard only*: so it is treated by Herodotus, so Leonidas himself described it. Its main purpose, in cooperation with the fleet, was to encourage the wavering states of central Greece to stand firm rather than medise, and, at most, to fight a holding action at Thermopylae until the main Peloponnesian army came up with reinforcements.

We have no good reason, in fact, to accuse either the Spartans or their allies of treachery and bad faith, as modern scholars have all too often done.[1] Herodotus, on this vital point, is clear and unambiguous:

... The intention was, when the Carneia was over (for it was that festival which prevented the Spartans from taking the field in the ordinary way) to leave a garrison in the city and join the confederate army with all the troops at their disposal. The other allied states proposed to act similarly; for the Olympic festival happened to fall just at this same period. None of them ever expected the battle at Thermopylae to be decided so soon – which was the reason why they sent only advance parties there. [7.206]

This is surely no more than the plain truth. The Spartans always intended to send reinforcements, and when Leonidas assured various prospective allies that help was on the way he meant what he said. The Peloponnesians were probably glad enough to use the Carneia and the Olympic festival as an excuse for some days' delay, if only to see which cities in central Greece – Boeotia above all – could be relied on, and which could not. Such an attitude does not discredit their serious determination to hold the Thermopylae-Artemisium line. They clearly regarded this strategy with some apprehension; there would always be a minority whose first instinct in a crisis was to barricade themselves behind the Isthmus. But that they acted in bad faith is a wholly unwarrantable assumption. They were well aware that Leonidas could not hold out indefinitely, but this does not mean that they callously left him to his fate. Their faults were those characteristic of Spartans throughout Spartan history: over-cautious conservatism, slowness to move in a crisis. Because of unforeseen factors, Thermopylae fell much sooner than had been anticipated: the staff commanders of the League, far from being guilty of Machiavellian self-interest, were, quite simply, caught on the wrong foot. But once the line had collapsed, no good purpose would be served by sending a valuable field army north to try and shore it up. From there, unfortunately, it is an easy step to the assumption that no one ever intended to send an army at all. When Leonidas marched, he did so in the confident – and justified – belief that the whole mobilised strength of the Peloponnese was behind him.

From the Isthmus he made for Boeotia, where he got a polite but lukewarm reception – except from Thespiae, a little town which, like Plataea, was stubbornly determined to resist absorption by the Thebans or anyone else, and therefore mustered 700 hoplites, probably her entire fighting force. Thebes proved rather less generous. Leonidas, it was clear, wanted to make the Thebans show their hand: the Thebans, very adroitly, avoided doing so. They were (as everyone unofficially knew) committed to Xerxes; but there was just a possibility that the defence of Thermopylae might prove successful. In any case, a Spartan king on the warpath had to be treated with some circumspection. They therefore decided to hedge their bets: as Herodotus pleasantly puts it, 'they did send troops, but their secret sympathy was nevertheless with the enemy'. Leonidas was given a token force of 400 anti-Persian troublemakers, a gesture which benefited no one to any great extent except the Theban government. He did considerably better from the states in the immediate vicinity of Thermopylae. Trachis offered alliance, while Phocis, Malis,

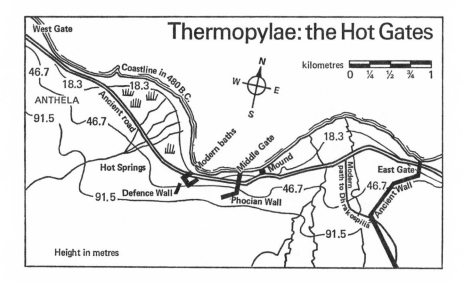

and the Locrians each sent him about a thousand volunteers to help hold the pass – the Locrians after having actually given earth and water to Xerxes. (Leonidas seems to have been adept at rousingly optimistic recruiting speeches.) By the end of the first week in August, at the very latest, the Spartans and their various allies were solidly dug in, with a rebuilt wall to protect them, at what is known today as the Middle Gate of Thermopylae.

It looked, on the face of it, a perfect defensive position. As Leonidas and his men faced north-west, towards Lamia and the Spercheius Valley, they had the rugged heights of Mt Kallidromos [Saromata] protecting their left flank – 'a lofty and precipitous ascent,' as Herodotus rightly observed, 'running up to Mt Oeta, while on the other side of the roadway is the sea, full of banks and shoals'. Owing to the silting up of the Malian Gulf, the coastline today has retreated several miles from the Hot Gates, making it hard for a visitor to visualise the pass as Leonidas found it in 480 BC. Where the Spartans set up their defences it was less than twenty yards wide, and at two other points east and west of Thermopylae, near Anthela and Alpeni respectively, it narrowed still further, to the breadth of a single waggon track. The reason why Leonidas did not occupy either of these positions was that the slopes above them rose less sheer, and he might, in consequence, have been outflanked by a determined assault. Gushing out from the foot of the mountain – then as today – were the hot and sulphurous springs from which the pass derived its name. They appear to have been sacred to Heracles, who had an altar here, and whose latter end was grimly associated with Trachis and Mt Oeta. The springs smell faintly of copper and rotten eggs: on a May morning this odour lends somewhat disconcerting overtones to the ubiquitous heavy scent of broom. A little east of the Middle Gate, behind the wall, is a mound some 150 feet high. In antiquity the road through to central Greece ran between this mound and the Kallidromos massif.

Leonidas had two immediate tasks facing him. The first, and most obvious, was to organise his sources of supply. For commissariat he relied mainly on the nearest village behind the Spartan lines, Alpeni. He also, however, conducted a large-scale night raid into the plain between Thermopylae and Lamia. While some of his troops set fire to farmsteads and cut down trees, others were busy raiding granaries or driving off cattle. They encountered no opposition. The Great King's army had not yet materialised, and until it did, local opinion felt that the Spartans were best left severely alone. This raid, of course, served a double purpose. Besides securing the allied advance force provisions and to spare, it correspondingly reduced the amount available to the enemy. It also established Leonidas, from the very beginning, in a position of moral and psychological strength. Nothing succeeds like success: it was now that Phocis and the Locrians sent their contingents in answer to the Spartan king's exhortations.

Leonidas's second problem was one which has to be faced by any commander undertaking the defence of a pass: to make sure his position could not be turned. There were two known and obvious routes by which troops could circumvent the Kallidromos massif: neither of these, however, constituted a real danger. The first ran from Alpeni, by way of modern Mendhenitza and Kalothroni, to a point on the Lamia-Levadhia highway near the upper valley of the Cephisus River. Since it lay to the rear of Leonidas's position, it could be safely ignored. (After Thermopylae had fallen, Xerxes seems to have sent some of his troops this way into Doris.) The second route followed the bed of the Asopus gorge, debouching in a high valley on the eastern slopes of the Oeta massif: from here it descended, somewhat circuitously, to the Dorian plain. The chances of Xerxes sending troops this way were very slim. The gorge itself is over three miles long, and less than five yards wide in many places, with vertical rock walls a hundred feet and more high. The river-bed is a litter of giant boulders, washed down by seasonal flooding; even after extensive deforestation, the summer visitor has to struggle knee-deep, on occasion, against the current. (Professor Pritchett found it tough going in July, impossible in April.) The dangers of such a route for a large army, complete with baggage-train, scarcely need emphasising. The citadel of Trachis, high on the western cliffs above the entrance to the gorge, effectively controlled all traffic through it; and the Trachinians had declared for Leonidas. At several points – particularly by Kastro Oriás, the hill-fort just beyond the modern railway viaduct – it would be all too easy to roll an avalanche of boulders down on advancing troops. Any task force which successfully overcame these very considerable hazards would still be isolated in hostile territory for several days: to get back to Thermopylae would mean a lengthy detour through Phocis.

The two remaining routes present a fundamentally different problem. Neither was obvious to Xerxes' or Leonidas's reconnaissance patrols, who in this respect were very much at the mercy of local guides. One, indeed, may not have existed at all in 480 BC. This is the road – roughly identical with the pre-autobahn highway linking Thebes and Lamia – which climbs from the Asopus gorge bridge across the Pournaraki Pass, debouching on the southern side of the massif at Brállos. Hignett suggests that the ridge it crossed 'was so thickly wooded in antiquity that no route existed at this point' [XIG p. 139]. If a route *did* exist, clearly it was neither well known nor easily negotiable: otherwise Xerxes would undoubtedly have taken advantage of it.

The remaining path over Kallidromos is that by which the Persians finally succeeded in outflanking Leonidas. There has been considerable debate as to its exact course; but Burn and Pritchett between them have established as convincing a case as the evidence will allow, and the present account (reinforced by personal exploration of Kallidromos) largely follows in their tireless and ingenious footsteps.[2] The path begins, says Herodotus, at the Asopus, and 'running along the ridge of the mountain . . . ends at Alpeni, the first Locrian settlement as one comes from Malis, near the rock known as Black-Buttocks' Stone and the seats of the Cercopes [monkey-like gnomes connected with Heracles in myth and legend]'. He also asserts that during their night march the Persians had the mountains of the Oetaeans on their right, those of the Trachinians on their left. There is only one route which adequately fulfils all these conditions. It begins half a mile or so east of the Asopus bridge, from the modern village of Koutseki [Damasta], skirts up the lower slopes of the mountain past an ancient fort [Kastráki] and the Chalcomata fountain, climbing thence to Palaio Eleftherochori, where it turns east along the mountain ride known today as Nevropolis [see map, p. 125]. The summit of Kallidromos has not one but *two* ridges, between which there stretches a narrow, fertile, well-watered upland plateau: lush meadows ringed by high oak forests. Towards the eastern end of this plateau the path divides. One track zigzags down the southern side of Kallidromos (giving the traveller a marvellous glimpse of snow-capped Parnassus and Oeta *en route*) to join the Lamia-Levadhia highway at Palaiochori. The other follows a circuitous route by Palaio-dhrakospiliá and the Zástano massif, swinging from north-east to north, and finally emerging quite close to ancient Alpeni. It was this latter track which concerned Xerxes and Leonidas. Even today it is an easy proposition for the average walker, and an army of ten thousand men could easily traverse it during a single night.*

Leonidas first learnt of this crucial weakness in his position from the people of Trachis, with whom he made contact soon after reaching Thermopylae. He could not abandon the League's chosen defence-line, since it was inextricably bound up with their naval dispositions at Artemisium. His only alternative was to plug this dangerous gap as effectively as possible, sit tight, and hope for the best. The Phocian contingent, a thousand strong, volunteered to guard the path for him. They did, it is true, have local knowledge of the terrain, and Leonidas – perhaps with some private misgivings – accepted their offer. This was his one error of judgement, and it proved fatal. The Phocians were far too few for so vitally responsible a task. Leonidas should have stiffened their ranks with tougher and more experienced troops; at the very least he should have placed them under a reliable Spartan officer. He did neither of these things. Presumably he calculated that the odds against such a flank attack were long enough to take a chance, especially since he needed every good man he had available to withstand Xerxes' expected frontal assault.

So the Phocians were sent off up Kallidromos, and bivouacked on a little hill in open ground, somewhere west of the point where the

* Further points of confirmation: the territory of Trachis extended eastward beyond the Asopus at least as far as Thermopylae, since Leonidas's position was on Trachinian soil. Its southern border seems to have run along the Kallidromos ridge: see Yves Béquignon, *La Vallée du Spercheios* (Paris 1937) pp. 243–63. Thus anyone following this route would, as Herodotus says, have the Trachinian mountains on their left, those of Oeta on their right. Pritchett (*op. cit.*, pp. 210–11) even claims to have found the Black-Buttocks' Stone, on a spur (or butt) north of the modern high-way identified as the site of Alpeni.

mountain track forks off down to Dhrakospiliá. It is a drowsy, summer-scented place, hay-warm in the meadows, the forest rides dappled with sunlight. After a few days it would not be surprising if the Phocians' vigilance, like that of hundred-eyed Argus, relaxed a little, and the *genius loci* lulled them into a sense of false security. Down below, meanwhile, between sun-scorched rocks and steamy marshland, Leonidas's sentries stared out in boredom across the dusty, shimmering, empty landscape towards Lamia. Day followed day, and still nothing happened. Then, at last, on 12 August, the tension was broken. Beacons flared from the heights of Skiathos and Euboea: Themistocles' fleet had made contact with the enemy. The little garrison fingered their weapons, licked sweat-salt lips, and waited. It could not be long now.

Xerxes marched from Therma at the beginning of August, very soon after the League's forces began to move north from the Isthmus. His exact route is a matter for topographical conjecture, but we know he avoided the Tempe gorge. As before, he almost certainly divided his army into two, if not three, separate columns, to avoid congestion and make the most of all available water-supplies. In that case the bulk of his troops must have advanced through the Petra and Volustana passes, following the same route from Oloösson onwards. One recent theory[3] has the Persians marching south-east from Veroia through Katerini, and thence round Lake Nezero to Gonnus. This was the route by which, in 1941, a German armoured column outflanked the New Zealanders guarding Tempe and Platamon: it also agrees in substance with the (generally discredited) testimony of Herodotus. It is, however, extremely rough going [see above, p. 92], and while Xerxes *may* have sent a commando force that way, he did not enjoy the special advantages conferred by tanks and half-track vehicles. South of Larissa the picture becomes much clearer. There were only two roads available, and it is virtually certain that his unwieldy force used both of them. One went by way of Crannon, and then over the Thaumaki Pass. The other, which Xerxes himself followed, linked Larissa with Pherae, Pagasae, and the west coast of the Gulf: since it avoided the mountains altogether, it was far easier going. These two roads met on the Malian Gulf at Lamia, some ten miles north of Thermopylae [see map, p. 90].

The overland march to the Hot Gates, Xerxes estimated, would take him about a fortnight. The fleet, on the other hand, with a fair north-easter blowing, could reach southern Magnesia in two to three days at most. Since close liaison formed the keystone of Xerxes' strategy no less than of Themistocles', the Great King ordered his admirals to move their advance squadrons into position eleven days after the army's departure: thus, he calculated, land and sea forces would reach central Greece more or less simultaneously. Xerxes was not, it would seem, pressed for time. In Thessaly he held horse-races, matching his own Iranian bloodstock against the local breeds. These Thessalian mares may (as he was informed) have been the finest Greece could produce; but they were, nevertheless, all decisively beaten – which suggests tact on the part of their jockeys. At Halus in Achaea, where three short months previously a Greek army had disembarked [see above, p. 86] the guides now hastened to regale Xerxes with choice bits of local folklore.

While the army was advancing through Macedonia and Thessaly, a fast detachment of ten Phoenician triremes, with Persian marines aboard, sailed from Therma to reconnoitre the Skiathos channel and the anchorages of southern Magnesia. They left before news of the Greeks' arrival at Thermopylae and Artemisium could have reached the Persian High Command: indeed, one of their main tasks was to find out whether the sea-lanes were defended, and if so how strongly. Apart from this, they had orders to mark the channel for the main fleet – a refinement no Greek would have thought of – and to find a suitable harbour for a naval base. They would appear to have set out at the same time as Xerxes' main force: that is, on or about 1 August. Two days later, just as dawn was breaking, they swept down on Skiathos and surprised a Greek patrol in harbour there. It is worth noting that they laid a direct course across open water, presumably steering by the stars: Phoenician seamanship and navigation were both highly sophisticated. This also explains why the Greeks were caught napping. Since their own practice was to island-hop by daylight, the last thing they would have expected was an attack from the open sea before sunrise.

Skiathos harbour lies on the east side of the island, in the Skopelos channel. The three Greek triremes – from Troezen, Athens and Aegina respectively – sighted their attackers just in time to cast off and make for Artemisium. But the fast Phoenician galleys out-sailed and intercepted them south of the Magnesian promontory. The first to fall into their hands was the Troezenian vessel: they took the best fighting man aboard, dragged him to the prow, and there cut his throat. Human sacrifice was not uncommon among the Phoenicians: on this occasion they were probably offering up the first-fruits of victory. The Aeginetan trireme, true to that island's fighting tradition, put up a heroic resistance. One marine named Pytheas fought with all the fury and panache of Sir Richard Grenville aboard the *Revenge*, and when he fell at last, covered with wounds, excited a similar admiration and compassion in his captors. They brought out the ship's medicine-chest (again, a novelty to the Greeks), gave Pytheas first-aid treatment, and afterwards showed him off with some pride to the rest of the Persian fleet. His fellow-prisoners, however, were treated as slaves, in the normal manner – which perhaps somewhat lessened their appreciation of the hero in their midst.

Meanwhile the Athenian trireme had beaten a hasty retreat, slipping away northwards by the only available escape-route, between Skiathos and the mainland. When the Phoenicians at last resumed the chase, she had a good head start on them. It is unlikely that the whole squadron took off after one solitary vessel. Part of it at least must have stayed behind to guard the prisoners and – more important – to reconnoitre the Greek position at Artemisium. Three of the pursuing triremes ran aground on a semi-submerged reef in the Skiathos channel, known then as Myrmex, 'the Ant', and today as Leftari (a corruption of *lithari*, 'rock'). The remainder kept on: they were so much faster in the water than their quarry that the Athenian crew barely escaped with their lives. They ran aground in the Peneus estuary, abandoned ship, and straggled back home by the overland route. This is a revealing incident. That two hundred Athenians could march, without interference, through nominally pro-Persian territory, shows how fluid the situation in central Greece still remained. Besides, this new defence-line made a Greek victory, if not likely, at least possible: no one, now, was going to risk eventual reprisals over a bunch of penniless Athenian sailors.

With methodical efficiency – and unhampered by any hint of enemy interference – the Phoenicians fetched stone blocks from the mainland, and built a navigational marker on the Myrmex reef. They also surveyed the harbours along the coast, and decided that Aphetae [probably Plataniá] offered the best facilities for establishing a naval base.* As they sailed up and down the channel, they had ample opportunity to observe the Greek fleet, drawn up opposite them in Pevki Bay and along the beach immediately west of it. Then, their task accomplished, they set course back to Therma. On receipt of the news they brought, Xerxes' admirals took immediate action. Squadron after squadron moved southward, occupying every available anchorage along the coast of Macedonia and the Pallene peninsula. By 12 August, eleven days after the army's departure – in accordance with Xerxes' instructions – advance units of the fleet were strung out between Casthanea

---

* Herodotus [7.193] seems to suggest that Aphetae was *inside* the Gulf of Pagasae, perhaps at modern Trikeri; but elsewhere he remarks that the harbour was eighty stades, or ten miles, from Artemisium, and the sum of our evidence suggests an anchorage somewhere on the southern Magnesian promontory, in sight of Artemisium itself. See Hignett, XIG, pp. 176–7, and evidence there cited. The other possible site, Olizon, is less satisfactory on all counts.

[Choreftón] and Cape Sepias [Aghios Georgios], the promontory opposite Skiathos. Since beaches in Magnesia were few and small, only the first-comers could be hauled up. The rest had to ride off-shore, eight deep in places. During the still, starry nights of an Aegean August this must have struck the crews as no great hardship. The weather-wise Delphic priests knew better. To a panic-stricken group of local enquirers they now issued one of their pithiest, and most eminently practical injunctions: 'Pray to the winds.'

Far away in Sicily, another side of the great Mediterranean-wide conflict between Occident and Orient was moving towards its climax. The timing was not coincidental: Carthage's treaty with Xerxes [see above, p. 83] provided for synchronisation of attack. While the Great King descended on Old Greece, the Carthaginians and their allies were to destroy the now dangerously powerful Greek tyrants of Sicily. Hamilcar, the leading Carthaginian general – his name was actually Abd-Melkarth, 'Servant of the Lord': Greeks had little aptitude for accurate transliteration – was by no means a stranger to the island. His mother came from Syracuse; his Sicilian guest-friends included not only Terillus, the deposed ruler of Himera, but also Leophron, who now governed Zancle [Messina]. He was on equally good terms with Anaxilas of Rhegium [Reggio], just across the Straits: Anaxilas, we recall, was Terillus's son-in-law. The powerful military *bloc* established by Syracuse and Acragas in conjunction was, from the Carthaginian viewpoint, a most dangerous development: this group of Graeco-Punic alliances might prove strong enough to break it up. Theron's capture of Himera provided a plausible excuse for invasion. Anaxilas, we are told, gave Hamilcar his own children as hostages to persuade him to undertake the expedition. He could have spared himself the trouble. Carthage had weighty enough reasons of her own for invading Sicily: Xerxes may have determined when this attack took place, but the impulse towards invasion was there already.

The force which Hamilcar mustered in the high summer of 480 was certainly impressive enough: a fleet of some two hundred warships, and perhaps up to 200,000 men, with countless transports and freighters. He did not make directly for Selinus, the nearest friendly landfall, but instead coasted round by Eryx and the Castellammare Gulf to Panormus [Palermo]. It was Terillus of Himera who had invoked Carthaginian aid: this suited Hamilcar's plans very well. West and north-west Sicily was controlled by colonies of Carthage or other non-Greek communities (such as Elymite Segesta), ready to support and supply the invading armada. Hamilcar was particularly anxious to avoid tangling at the outset with Gelon's powerful fleet. The latter was based on Syracuse, but its patrols reached westward at least as far as Theron's naval base of Acragas. The Carthaginians' route therefore largely dictated itself. Unfortunately, it also exposed his ships to the first of those late-summer storms – *meltemi* or *mistral* – which all Mediterranean sailors know and dread. Most of the heavy transports carrying horses and chariots were wrecked or sunk. The rest Hamilcar brought safely into the spacious reaches of Panormus Harbour, observing when he landed that their worst enemy (i.e. the sea) had now been beaten, and the war was therefore as good as won. This remark was pure bravado: throughout the campaign that followed the Carthaginians' biggest handicap was shortage of cavalry.

Hamilcar stayed at Panormus for three days, to repair storm damage and give his troops a rest (most of them, one suspects, had been incapacitated by acute seasickness). He also sent off an urgent message to his allies in Selinus, asking for all the horses and cavalrymen they could spare, as soon as possible. Then he marched eastward along the coast towards Himera, while his fleet (like that of Xerxes) kept pace with him offshore. He made no attempt, at this point, to join forces with his allies round the Straits: wisely, since between Messina and Himera the terrain is extremely difficult, as Allied troops found to their cost in 1943. He was, we may assume, relying on Leophron and Anaxilas to hold the Straits if Gelon tried to force his way through by sea: it is possible that some such naval battle in fact took place.[4] Besides, he had the advantage of initiative – unlike Xerxes – and meant to exploit it. Though Theron and Gelon knew very well that a Carthaginian attack was inevitable, they could not be sure precisely when or where it would come. Hamilcar's descent on Panormus left Theron only just enough time to get a strong defence force into Himera before the Carthaginians arrived outside the walls.

Himera (the modern Términi Imerese) lies some 49 km. east of Palermo, on rising ground above the coast road to Cefalú, and immediately beside a shoal-filled river known today as the Fiume Grande. A couple of miles to the west, perhaps marking the original extent of Himera's territories, there runs a second river, the Fiume Torto. Between the city and the sea there lies a flat plain. It was on this plain that Hamilcar established his lines. The ships – except for twenty triremes kept on patrol duties – were hauled up along the shore, and protected by a ditch and palisade. The main camp, says Diodorus, Hamilcar 'placed so that it fronted the city, and prolonged so that it took in the area from the wall extending along the naval camp as far as the hills which overhung the city'. In other words, he now controlled all the western approaches. Having off-loaded his cargo boats, he at once sent them out again to fetch grain supplies from Libya and Sardinia. Next he took some of his best troops, marched boldly up to the walls, and completely routed a defence force which sallied forth against him, inflicting heavy casualties. Theron thereupon bricked up the western gates of the city, and sent an emergency appeal for help to Syracuse. Hamilcar had not established a complete blockade, since the east and south sides of the city were still open; but he had certainly got himself into a very strong position.

Gelon's army was fully mobilised when this SOS arrived (which suggests, again, that no one really knew in advance what Hamilcar's plans were) and marched without delay. The tyrant of Syracuse had raised a force of 50,000 foot-soldiers – a large proportion of them hoplites – and 5,000 cavalry. Sicilian ranchers were practically born in the saddle (horsebreeding formed one of the island's major industries), and even the ordinary farmer was able, without overmuch sacrifice, to meet the cost of heavy body-armour. Gelon 'covered the distance swiftly', we are told: this must mean that he marched across country, by the old road via Enna, reaching Himera from the south-east, along the broad winding river-valley. He saw at once that his first task was to forestall any chance of a complete Carthaginian investment, and therefore set up his own camp on the east bank of the Fiume Grande, fortifying it (just as Hamilcar had protected his ships) with a deep ditch and palisade. Autocrats both, Gelon and Hamilcar imposed far higher standards of military discipline and efficiency than the average amateur city-state general. From this position, moreover, it would be easy to maintain close contact with the beleaguered garrison.

However, Gelon had no intention of merely digging himself in: he, if anyone, believed in the old adage of attack being the best defence. The question was, where and how should the attack be launched? Hamilcar had the advantage of numbers and position. To surprise him now seemed impossible, and a straight pitched battle stood perilously little chance of success. The more Gelon studied the situation facing him, the less he can have liked it. However, one thing he could and did do. Large numbers of Carthaginians, confident now that no one would dare to molest them, were scattered over the surrounding countryside in search of forage and booty. Gelon's crack cavalry squadrons swept down on them in a mass *razzia*, netting thousands of prisoners. Amongst these was a messenger from Selinus. The dispatch he carried was brought to Gelon, who, reading it, at once grasped the fact that here – if anyone had the skill and courage to exploit it – lay the potential instrument of Hamilcar's destruction.

When the Greeks at Artemisium learnt that Xerxes' armada was approaching, says Herodotus, they fell into a great panic. Leaving only their mountain-top look-outs *in situ*, they withdrew as far as Chalcis, some ninety miles away to the south, at the narrowest point of the Euboea channel. This explicit statement has been dismissed as arrant nonsense by most modern historians, who point out, *inter alia*, that such a move would fatally expose Leonidas's position at Thermopylae. What vitiates this argument is the fact that Xerxes and the main body of his army were still three days' march away. It looks very much as though Themistocles made an attempt – this time without success – to employ the tactics which afterwards brought him victory at Salamis. He had two precious days during which the holding force at Thermopylae could safely be left to its own devices. Why not tempt Xerxes' best Phoenician squadrons to give battle in the narrow bottleneck of the Euboea channel, where their superiority in speed and numbers would go for nothing against Greek naval expertise?

Besides, experts had noted a number of signs indicating bad weather on the way. The date was 12 August; Hesiod had prescribed fifty days after the summer solstice as the period during which sailors could safely put to sea between the spring and autumn gales, and his limit was now past. (Modern Greek folklore associates the first bad storms with the Feast of the Assumption, 15 August: I have observed instances myself at least a month earlier.) If a real north-easter blew up, the Persians along the harbourless Magnesian coast would be the first to suffer, it is true; but Artemisium, too, lay on a lee-shore [see above, p. 110] and the Greek fleet would be well advised to move station temporarily in any case. Themistocles had calculated the odds to a nicety. Whether Xerxes' admirals took the bait or not made very little difference: if they stayed clear of the Greeks, they would still have to reckon with the *meltemi*. The Athenians at Chalcis watched the sky hopefully, and offered up prayers to Boreas, the god of the North Wind who had married into a distinguished Attica family: surely one's own son-in-law could be relied on in a moment of crisis?

Sure enough, at dawn next morning, 13 August, the *meltemi* – a 'Hellesponter', Herodotus calls it – began to blow out of a clear sky, and 'raised a confused sea like a pot on the boil'. (No one who has ever travelled by caique in rough weather is likely to read those words without a certain queasy nostalgia.) The Persian fleet, strung out along a series of small beaches from Meliboea [Thanátou], below Mt Ossa, to the Sepias promontory, had a very rough time indeed. Some of the weather-wise Phoenicians, together with those captains stationed close in-shore, managed to beach their vessels; but nearly all who tried, *faute de mieux*, to ride the storm out at anchor were driven on the rocks and had their triremes smashed up under them. Almost a third of Xerxes' entire fleet perished during this three-day blow, 'and the loss of life and treasure was beyond reckoning'. Those who got ashore still had to contend with possible attacks by local bandits or Thessalian nightriders, and barricaded themselves miserably behind the wreckage of their ships. The beachcombers of Magnesia did very well out of the disaster. All along the coast gold and silver cups, treasure-chests, and other valuable flotsam were washed ashore; one enterprising local character made a fortune overnight by snapping them up – though Herodotus takes care to point out that he came to a bad end afterwards.

Late on 14 August messengers from Northern Euboea reached Chalcis with the good news. They also reported that Xerxes' advance guard had been sighted entering the Malian plain. On both counts it was imperative to re-establish the Thermopylae-Artemisium line without delay. So, after offering prayers and libations to Poseidon the Saviour,* the Greek allied squadrons sailed north again, probably at dawn on 15 August. Until they rounded Cape Cenaeum [Litháalha], on the northwest tip of Euboea, they were in comparatively sheltered waters; yet even so they must have been rowing against a heavy cross-wind. It is hard to believe that they entered the Artemisium channel until the following morning [16 August], by which time the gale had more or less blown itself out. Xerxes' Magi had been busy making placatory offerings and putting spells on the wind: eventually their incantations worked – 'or of course,' says Herodotus, with demure cynicism, 'it may be that the wind just dropped naturally'.

On 13 August Xerxes' reconnaissance units were marching along the coast road to Lamia, the waters of the Malian Gulf on their left, white caps flurrying under the north-east gale, Euboea crouching across the straits like an old lion, and away to the south the eastern spurs and ramparts of the Pindus. Next day they advanced from Lamia towards the Hot Gates themselves, across a steadily narrowing plain scoured by sudden dust-storms. Two rivers, the Spercheius and the Asopus, flowed thin and sluggish now in wide, parched channels, scant ration for thirsty camel or cavalryman. Mountains reared in a dark quadrant against their front and right flank, split only by the dark slanting fissure of the Asopus gorge, with hostile Trachis perched perilously above it. Ahead lay Thermopylae, between a towering forest-clad mountainside and the haze-grey sea. Somewhere in that pass a Spartan king stood

---

* The Athenians did not forget Boreas: when they returned to Athens they built him a shrine by the River Ilissus, not far from where the Fix brewery used to stand.

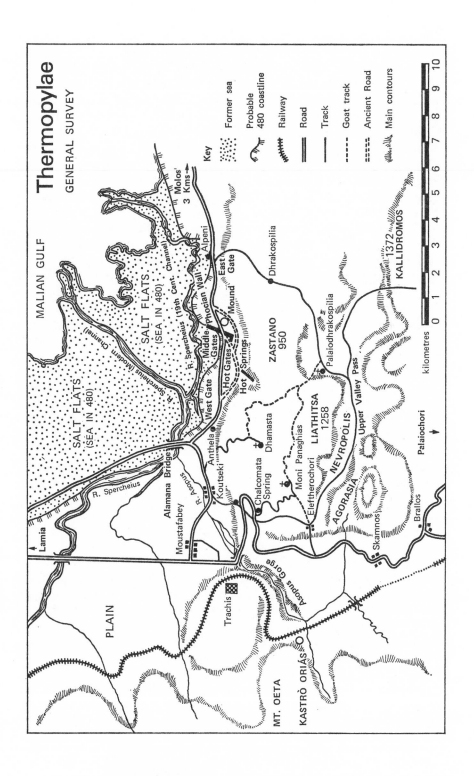

ready to do battle. This intelligence – including the Spartan's name – had reached Xerxes' staff officers while they were still in Thessaly. It must have produced strangely mixed feelings in that other Spartan king, Demaratus, exiled through no fault of his own, no enemy to Leonidas, yet still dreaming of restoration to his rightful throne – as Xerxes' vassal if this was the only possible way. The oracle which Delphi had given the Spartans [see above, pp. 67–8] hinted, crab-wise, at such a solution to their problems. The Persian invasion, like the German invasion of Europe in 1939–40, produced some odd dilemmas of loyalty and conscience.

The Persians pitched camp near Trachis, between the Spercheius and the Asopus rivers, probably occupying Anthela at the same time [see map, p. 125]. Xerxes' first move – as one might expect – was to reconnoitre his opponents' position. A single Persian horseman rode quietly forward towards the Hot Gates. No one tried to interfere with his movements, or gave any sign of noticing that he was there. He saw very little of the main Greek camp, since it was hidden behind Leonidas's defence wall; thus he could not estimate, with any degree of accuracy, how large a force the Persians were up against. What he did see, however, filled him with astonishment. A number of Spartans were gathered in front of the wall. Some of them had stripped off ready to take exercise; others – like modern Masai or Zulu warriors – were busy combing and dressing their hair. The Persian spy had never seen anything like it; such behaviour struck him as merely absurd, a view which Xerxes, on hearing his report, fully endorsed. On the other hand, no man bred on the high plateaux of Iran could fail to recognise a virtually impregnable mountain position when he saw one. This was the real news which he brought back, and it put Xerxes in something of a quandary. His obvious course was to use the fleet: if he could force a victory at sea, Leonidas would have no option but to retreat – or die. The fleet, however, had not yet appeared, and to judge by the violent storm now raging, it would be in no condition for an immediate engagement when it did. What else could be tried? The most promising alternative, clearly, was an outflanking movement; but here, to begin with any any rate, the Persian patrols drew a blank. Xerxes had no intention of getting his army massacred in the Asopus gorge [see above, pp. 114–15], and the secret of Kallidromos still eluded him. Could the Greeks be bribed into surrender by a promise of preferential treatment? A long shot indeed, but still worth trying: anything rather than the final test of a direct frontal assault.

Heralds were accordingly dispatched to parley with Leonidas, and gauge the general state of Greek morale. (It would also be useful to gain admission to that well-hidden camp, and observe what was going on there.) Diodorus, probably drawing on Ephorus, purports to give the text of their proclamation [11.5.4–5]: 'King Xerxes orders all to give up their arms, to depart unharmed to their native lands, and to be allies of the Persians; and to all Greeks who do this he will give more and better lands than they now possess.' The formula had worked to perfection in every state throughout Northern Greece: might it not work again? That the proclamation caused a split among the Greek allies seems clear enough. Many, Herodotus reports, felt sudden doubts about their ability to hold the pass, and a meeting was held 'to consider the advisability of retreat'. The Peloponnesians, as usual, came out with their old *idée fixe* yet again: abandon Northern Greece, fall back on the Isthmus. This proposal, not surprisingly, drew howls of protest from the Phocians and Locrians, who would be left to face Xerxes' wrath on their own; had there been any Athenians in the defence force, they would, no doubt, have objected with equal vigour. Leonidas himself, to his eternal credit, came out flatly against any suggestion of a withdrawal, and it was his opinion that carried the day. At the same time, he sent back an emergency appeal for immediate reinforcements, 'as their numbers were inadequate to cope with the Persians'. Then he delivered his answer to the Great King's waiting envoys. 'If we should be allies of the king,' he told them, 'we should be more useful if we kept our arms, and if we should have to wage war against him, we should fight the better for our freedom if we kept them; and as for the lands which he promises to give, the Greeks have learnt from their fathers to gain lands, not by cowardice, but by valour.' Rhetorical fiction perhaps: but not unworthy of the occasion.

When he received this uncompromising reply, Xerxes once again did the obvious and sensible thing: he summoned his adviser on Greek affairs, Demaratus, and interrogated him closely as to the fighting spirit and military skills of the men holding the pass. The reply, if we can trust Herodotus, was a resounding tribute to Sparta's legendary prowess in war: Demaratus, after all, had good reason to pile it on thick. More drily convincing is the remark put in his mouth by Diodorus: 'You yourself,' he tells Xerxes, 'are not unacquainted with the courage of the Greeks, since you use Greek forces to quell such barbarians as revolt' – a cool gibe too near the truth for comfort. Both accounts, however, represent Xerxes as unconvinced by Demaratus's arguments, and incredulous that so small a force (the heralds, it seems, had duly kept their eyes open) should hold out against his huge army. If this is the truth, then the Great King's subsequent behaviour must be accounted very odd: for at least three days he did nothing at all. But Xerxes' supposed *hubris* was a theme that tended to blind the judgement even of

Herodotus, not least on the present occasion. When we discount such propaganda-inspired motivation, and simply look at the facts, this delay makes very good sense. Xerxes was by no means the rash half-wit Greek historians liked to make him out: he took Demaratus's estimate of the Spartans very seriously indeed. If they were *that* tough, then all the more reason for holding back until the fleet could be brought into action – or an alternative route over the mountain came to light. On the other hand, too long a delay would produce its own problems, above all those of supply. Leonidas had raided the plain with some thoroughness; after four or five days at most the Persians would begin to feel the pinch.

For the second day in succession [15 August] all was quiet at Thermopylae, with each side cagily watching the other. The disaster incurred by Xerxes' fleet had temporarily neutralised the absence of the Greek squadrons from their station at Artemisium: even so, Leonidas must have breathed a sigh of relief when at last, the following morning [16 August], the fleet came thrusting back up the narrows from Chalcis, and swung away eastward into the choppy waters of the Magnesian channel. The last of the gale had now blown itself out, and they had a comparatively easy passage. On the other hand, they missed, by several hours, a unique chance of catching the Persians at a severe disadvantage. As soon as the wind dropped, Xerxes' commanders relaunched their vessels – or those of them that were still seaworthy* – and sailed south round Cape Sepias to their new naval base at Aphetae [Platania]. Strung out in line-ahead formation, still disheartened and disorganised by the storm, they would have fallen easy victims to a determined attack. However, by the time the Greeks reached Artemisium, most of these battered Persian squadrons had limped safely into harbour, and all Themistocles picked up was one late-straggling detachment of fifteen vessels, whose commander unluckily mistook the Greeks for his own side. (With Ionian and Hellespontine squadrons serving the Great King, this confusion must have been all too easy.) After close interrogation – one captain, it transpired, had lost eleven out of twelve ships in the storm – all prisoners taken were sent off under escort to base headquarters at Corinth.

By the evening of 16 August Xerxes must have known that it would

---

* Herodotus (7.190) estimates Persian storm-losses at 400; but this figure probably represents a percentage of his (pre-Doriscus) total of 1,207, and what he was actually *told* may have been 'Up to one-third of the fleet destroyed'. If the post-Doriscus figure of 650± holds good [see above, pp. 60–2], then storm-losses will have been in the region of 200, not counting auxiliary vessels. Perhaps up to 50 of these were subsequently refitted, leaving a net total of rather less than 500. For a discussion of recent scholarship see Hignett, XIG, p. 345 ff.

take anything up to forty-eight hours, working flat out, to repair all storm-damage and make the fleet battle-worthy once more. The strategy he now devised took this enforced delay into account, and turned it to good advantage. During the night of 16–17 August, while the ship-wrights were still busy, a task-force of 200 vessels – a number of them, in all likelihood, supply-ships* – set out on a bold and hazardous mission. They first set course north-east through the Skiathos channel, in order to deceive Greek patrols as to their ultimate destination. But when they had rounded Skiathos they turned south again, sailing down the east coast of Euboea. Their orders were to enter the Euripus [the channel between island and mainland] from the south, and make for Chalcis. 'In this way,' says Herodotus, 'they hoped to catch the Greeks in a trap, one squadron taking them in the rear and blocking their retreat, the rest of the fleet pressing upon them from in front'. The attack was to be simultaneous, and its timing determined by a signal showing that the detached squadron was in position – presumably at the narrow neck of the Euripus. This involved a voyage of nearly two hundred miles, and would take forty or more sailing hours. The Persians cannot have hoped to spring their trap before the morning of 19 August, at the earliest.

Despite its heavy losses, the Persian fleet at this point still probably outnumbered the Greek by about five to three. During 16 and 17 August both sides carried out intensive reconnaissance patrols: an easy task, since Artemisium and Aphetae lay in plain view of one another across the straits. The Persians expressed open contempt for their opponents' paltry numbers: according to Herodotus, one reason for their bottle-stopping tactics in the Euripus was to prevent the Greeks from scuttling away under cover of darkness. Not one enemy ship, not a single marine must be allowed to escape: such was the Great King's pleasure. The Greeks themselves – Eurybiades and the Peloponnesian contingents in particular – were appalled by the size of the armada they now watched assembling against them. The storm had been neither hard nor long enough: *Deus flavit, sed non omnes dissipati sunt.* Once again, there was serious talk of abandoning Artemisium (and presumably Thermopylae too, at the same time) and retreating to 'the inner parts of Greece'.

* It has often been argued (most recently by Hignett, XIG, pp. 173–4, 386–92) that this whole episode is a fiction, concocted partially with the aim of reducing Xerxes' fleet to manageable proportions. One main point made by such ingenious critics is that the Persians would never have sent 200 triremes – normally dependent on a friendly coast for water and supplies – round hostile Euboea, where for four days at least they would be cut off from base. I prefer to assume that Herodotus did not invent recent history in quite so wanton a fashion, and that the Persians were sensible enough to take adequate supplies with them. In this case the actual *fighting strength* may have been no more than 150 triremes.

Early the next day [17 August] there arrived in Artemisium a professional diver named Scyllias, who had either swum or rowed across from Aphetae under cover of darkness. Scyllias was one of those Munchausen-like characters who sedulously promote themselves by a series of charming if outrageous tall stories. He had been doing salvage work for the Persians, and salting away a good deal of loot on his own account in the process. To ingratiate himself with the Greek commanders he let it be known that he and his daughter had been a fathom or two down during the storm, busy cutting Persian anchor-cables – a tale which Themistocles doubtless took with a good pinch of Attic salt, but no more startling than the diver's claim to have swum the ten miles from Aphetae without once surfacing. On the other hand, Scyllias did bring some vital intelligence with him. He gave the Greeks a fairly accurate breakdown of Persian numbers and losses; far more important, he knew all about that elusive squadron now beating southward from Skiathos. When Eurybiades learnt of its existence, 'his immediate impulse,' says Plutarch, 'was to take the shortest way back into Greece, reach the Peloponnese and there use his land forces to screen the fleet, for he regarded the Persians as invincible at sea' – not, perhaps, the best qualification for a Greek admiral.

Ancient notions of security were lax to the point of non-existence, and Eurybiades' intentions soon became known among the local population. This caused something of a panic, and small wonder: if the Greeks pulled out, Euboea would be left wide open to Xerxes' vengeful troops. A deputation of leading citizens called on the Spartan commander, begging him at least not to evacuate Artemisium until they had removed their women and children to some place of safety. Eurybiades would give them no guarantee whatsoever, so in despair they turned to Themistocles. One of their number, Pelagon, was entrusted with a massive sum of money – thirty talents, or over £7,000 – and privately offered it all to the Athenian commander if he would, somehow keep the Greek fleet *in situ*, and stave off the threat of a Persian invasion. As this was precisely what Themistocles meant to do in any case, he heard the Euboeans out sympathetically, took their money, and promised them his full support. He seems, with characteristically cynical insight, to have gauged each man's price to a nicety. Five talents – passed on as though it were a personal gift from Themistocles himself – sufficed to bring Eurybiades round; and most of the other commanders then fell into line as well.

Some, however, still remained obdurate, among them the Corinthian admiral Adeimantus, who threatened to withdraw whether the others did or not. Themistocles thereupon announced that he would pay

Adeimantus more to stay and fight than Xerxes would ever give him for deserting. The passage in Herodotus (8.5) suggests that this *argumentum ad hominem* was given careful publicity. Three talents, delivered aboard Adeimantus's flagship, duly secured his cooperation. One further incident, inimitably recorded by Plutarch (*Them.* 7.5) deserves to be quoted *verbatim*:

Among his own countrymen the bitterest opposition [Themistocles] encountered came from Architeles, the captain of the sacred state galley, who was anxious to sail back to Athens because he did not have enough money to pay his crew. So Themistocles stirred up the feelings of Architeles' men against him to such a pitch that they made a rush at him and snatched away his dinner. Then while Architeles was still nursing his indignation and chagrin at this, Themistocles sent him a box containing a dinner of bread and meat and under it a talent of silver. He told Architeles to eat his dinner at once and look after his crew in the morning, otherwise he would denounce him publicly for accepting money from the enemy.

There are several interesting details here. The lack of financial foresight or provision at which the anecdote hints, so incredible to the citizen of a modern bureaucratic state, was the rule rather than the exception in fifth-century Greece: we come up against it throughout this period [see below, p. 160]. Economic naïvety is a fundamental element of the Greek historical scene. Nor need we doubt that the threats which Themistocles used to persuade this recalcitrant Athenian were also employed against Adeimantus and Eurybiades – and had their effect. Slanders of that particular kind are singularly hard to disprove: some of the mud was bound to stick. At all events, Themistocles got his way, and for a very small outlay. There remained a net surplus of twenty-one talents, the very existence of which was unknown to his fellow-commanders. Having fulfilled his part of the bargain, he now blandly pocketed this windfall himself.*

Once the decision to stand firm at Artemisium had been taken (independently, we may note, of Leonidas: the fastest racing cutter

---

* The general attitude of British, American and German scholars to this episode is instructive. Most of them dismiss it as an outrageous libel: if Adeimantus fought bravely at Salamis, they argue, why should he play the coward before Artemisium? Mistaken strategical convictions, however, do not necessarily imply cowardice. Eurybiades and Adeimantus may honestly have believed, on balance, that an Isthmus defence-line would be preferable. Here modern hindsight can be misleading. But what really lies at the root of the matter, I suspect, is the Anglo-Saxon's fundamental (and very un-Mediterranean) distaste for palm-greasing as such. French, Italian and modern Greek historians seem to take Themistocles' backstairs activities far more in their stride; nor do they expect him and his fellow-commanders to display either a stiff upper lip, puritan moral rectitude, or team spirit in a crisis.

could hardly have made that double journey in much under twelve hours) a council of war at once took place. Scyllias's information made speedy action of some sort imperative. A long debate ensued, of which we know tantalisingly little; and what details we do possess are generally regarded as confused and unreliable. In the circumstances it is, perhaps, wiser to begin by redefining the strategical dilemma which actually confronted the Greek commanders, and then to consider the likeliest way in which they would have dealt with it. They were in serious danger of having their retreat cut off from the south; an enemy fleet which considerably outnumbered them lay across the straits ready to give battle. Given these two factors, the one thing they had to avoid at all costs was being manoeuvred into a double-front engagement. One door of the trap must always remain open. They had to deal with Xerxes' main fleet and his outflanking squadron independently; as far as possible they had to conceal their movements – and their superior military intelligence – from both. They *knew* a Persian squadron had sailed to cut them off, whereas the Persians still supposed they had the advantage of surprise. The moment it became apparent that Themistocles was forestalling his opponents' movements, he lost his trump card. Given these considerations, his obvious defence against being taken in the rear was a strong blockade of the Euripus at Chalcis, which would cost him very little in men and ships – a vital point. Meanwhile anything he could do to disrupt the main Persian fleet at Aphetae was worth trying. What kind of action to take, where and how to engage, were matters for tactical discussion; but the points outlined above *must* have formed the basis of any debate at command level. Bearing them in mind, we may find our sources not quite so hopeless after all.

As regards the threat from the south, the Greeks' decision, according to Herodotus, was 'to stay where they were until after midnight, and then put to sea to meet the Persians who were coming up the Euripus'. It was now about midday on 17 August, and Xerxes' outflanking squadron, as we have seen [above, p. 129], would find it hard to make Chalcis before the morning of the 19th. Scholars often assume that Herodotus says *the whole fleet* was sent south to blockade the narrows; but there is nothing in the relevant passage which warrants so unlikely an assumption. Nor is there any difficulty about the provision for delaying this vital movement until after midnight. Within the next forty-eight hours the moon would be full. It was the merest common sense to wait until moonset before embarking on an operation which required total secrecy if it was to stand any chance of success. On a clear moonlit night every movement at Artemisium would be plainly visible to watchers across the straits. Nor need we doubt that a fast dispatch-boat was sent off at once, well in advance of the holding force, to alert the Athenian squadron patrolling off the coast of Attica. One vessel going south would not attract suspicion: indeed, general communications with Athens and the Isthmus must have ensured fairly regular traffic by this route.

There now remained the more immediate problem of what action, if any, to take against the main Persian fleet. Every Greek commander except Themistocles, with surprising unanimity, came out strongly in favour of doing nothing at all. Stay on the defensive, they urged. Let Xerxes' admirals make the first move. Themistocles alone argued for an immediate attack. Scyllias's report had revealed a sorry tale of storm-damage and demoralisation: why give the enemy time to get his wind back? Besides, the Greek fleet had the advantage of unity and a single base, whereas the Persian squadrons were strung out along the coast in numerous anchorages. If they sailed out in close formation, they could attack the Persians piecemeal, and probably snatch a quick victory over one squadron before the rest came up to relieve it. In any case, it was high time they made trial of the enemy's seamanship and naval tactics, especially of that Ionian manoeuvre the *diekplous*, well described [Morrison and Williams, p. 137] as 'the passage of a squadron of ships in line ahead . . . through a gap . . . in an enemy fleet drawn up opposite in line abreast'. As might be expected, his proposals were not popular; but finally a compromise solution was reached. The Greeks would do nothing until late the following afternoon. If by that time there had been no enemy offensive, Themistocles could put his plan into action. The onset of darkness would provide a convenient *terminus ante quem* for such an operation, and protect the Greek fleet from pursuit in the event of failure.[5]

The Persians made no move towards Artemisium: time enough to demolish this trifling opposition when they had carried out all repairs and reorganised their squadrons for active service. So, about four or five o'clock on the afternoon of 18 August, the Greek fleet put out across the straits in close battle formation: probably the last thing on earth Xerxes' admirals had been expecting. 'And since the barbarians put out from many harbours,' says Ephorus, 'at the outset Themistocles, engaging with the scattered Persians, sank many ships and not a few he forced to turn in flight and pursued as far as the land'. However, his advantage lasted only until the various Persian squadrons had time to assemble under a unified command. Indeed, so crushing was their superiority in numbers, so obvious the disparity between Xerxes' light, fast-sailing Phoenician triremes and the heavier Greek vessels, that the Persians thought Themistocles must have taken leave of his senses. They now attempted, not the *diekplous* – Themistocles had packed his squadrons too closely for that – but the *periplous*, an encircling movement, This the Greeks, relying on their superior expertise, countered by a 'hedgehog' manoeuvre known as the *kyklos* (circle). Vessel after vessel peeled off radially, until the fleet resembled a giant wheel, in which the triremes were the spokes – bows-on to the enemy, sterns converging inwards. From this position they moved out to the attack. It was a hard-fought and indecisive engagement, each side having the better of it in one part of the line, but neither Greeks nor Persians forcing a decisive victory. When gathering dusk broke off the action, the Greeks had captured thirty enemy vessels: probably from the Cypriot squadrons, since among the prisoners they took was the brother of the King of Salamis.* At least one Greek serving with the Great King, Antidorus of Lemnos, changed sides after the battle – an encouraging straw in the wind.

Early that same day [18 August] Xerxes finally decided to launch a frontal assault on Leonidas's position at the Hot Gates. The Great King had waited four days now, and all in vain. The fleet had failed to make its expected breakthrough. Intensive reconnaissance had still not found the alternative route over Kallidromos. The storms and rain which played such havoc with Persia's navy must also have seriously hampered operations on land. All the time, too, as unit after unit of Persia's huge expeditionary force came straggling across the plain from Lamia, the number of mouths to be fed was steadily increasing. Food had begun to run short, and in all likelihood water too, if the modern summer state of the Spercheius and the Asopus is anything to go by. Xerxes had, in every sense of the word, reached an *impasse*. The Hot Gates had to be forced; and there was, unfortunately, only one method, now, by which Xerxes could attempt to force them. Attacking Leonidas head-on was a brutal, messy, and fundamentally inefficient manoeuvre, which neutralised the Persians' one great advantage, overwhelming numerical superiority. Despite Herodotus's propaganda, Xerxes must have hated having to order such an attack. Ephorus makes a revealing comment on his initial choice of shock-troops:

> ... He put the Medes in front of all the other peoples, either because he preferred them by reason of their courage or because he wished to destroy them in a body; for the Medes still retained a proud spirit, the supremacy which their ancestors had exercised having only recently been overthrown.

* A city on the east coast of Cyprus: not to be confused with the island of that name in the Saronic Gulf.

And he also designated together with the Medes the brothers and sons of those who had fallen at Marathon, believing that they would wreak vengeance upon the Greeks with the greatest fury [Diod. 11.6.3–4].

Yet however determined Xerxes' troops might be, they laboured under one insuperable handicap when it came to close-quarters combat: inferiority of weapons and armour. Their spears – javelins, rather – were shorter than those of the Greeks; their large wicker targets, which gave them added mobility over open country, were no protection in a tight-packed, narrow-fronted battle-line. Here the Greeks, with their great body-shields and heavy protective armour, enjoyed every possible advantage.

So, in the cool of that August morning, the struggle for Thermopylae began. The Medes charged, to break like waves against the Spartan shield-wall. Persian casualties were enormous, and had been antici-pated: the moment one man fell, another pressed forward to take his place, and 'in spite of terrible losses [the Medes] refused to be beaten off'. (So Herodotus, thus refuting his own cheap comment that Xerxes 'had in his army many men indeed, but few soldiers'.) At last, after a severe mauling, this battered division was pulled out of the front line, and replaced by contingents of Cissians and Sacae tribesmen. These, says Ephorus, 'joining the struggle fresh as they were against men who were worn out, withstood the hazard of combat for a short while'. After that, it was the same story as before. Leonidas's grim veterans, muscles cracking with fatigue, still maintained that awesome parade-ground discipline which had made them a byword throughout Greece. At one point they even carried out, successfully, that most hazardous of all manoeuvres, a feigned retreat, wheeling about the moment their pursuers broke ranks, and slaughtering them in vast numbers. Three times, it is said, Xerxes, watching the progress of the battle, leapt up from his throne in anguish. The whole of the pass was now littered with corpses, and the Spartans showed no sign of cracking. Finally, the Great King sent up his famous Guards Division, the Ten Thousand Immortals, under their general Hydarnes. These too, after a short and savage engagement, were hurled back in disorder. Dusk was now falling, and Xerxes, for that day at least, abandoned the struggle.

Shortly after dark another violent storm broke out – not the *meltemi* this time, but a south-east *sirocco* – with torrential driving rain, and loud peals of thunder from the direction of Mt Pelion. Corpses, spars, and other flotsam were washed up-channel towards Aphetae, drifting athwart the bows of those Persian vessels anchored off-shore, and fouling the oar-blades of the guardships patrolling the straits. What with this, and the thunder and rain, all coming so soon after a hard-fought sea-battle, the Persian sailors fell into something of a panic. To cap their other troubles, the *sirocco* caught a number of vessels riding in open water, blew them on the rocks, and wrecked them. A similar fate befell the squadron circumnavigating Euboea. At the time when the storm broke, it was rounding the southern extremity of the island (presumably the crews had been ordered to row in shifts, night and day) and had reached that part of the coast, near Carystus, known as the Hollows. The *sirocco* came roaring up out of the south, and the Persians could do nothing but run blind before it, their vision obscured by lashing rain. Many vessels piled up; others drove on before the gale into the Euboea channel. Herodotus claims that the whole squadron was destroyed. 'Heaven', he notes, piously, 'was indeed doing everything possible to reduce the superiority of the Persian fleet and bring it down to the size of the Greek', but this is really too much of a good thing. It seems far more likely that a good proportion of the squadron found haven at pro-Persian Carystus (won over during the 490 campaign), and rejoined the main fleet during the latter's voyage south.

Those Persian vessels carried on into the Euripus found more trouble awaiting them. Alerted earlier that day [see above, pp. 132–3], the Athenian squadron guarding Attica had at once sailed north to help defend the narrows of Chalcis:* a sensible decision, since with only fifty-three vessels at their disposal they could hardly hope to hold off a force at least twice as large in open water. It was this squadron which must have picked up some of the stray Persian triremes, and whose commander, after interrogating his prisoners, at once realised the full significance of what had happened. By now it was about midnight: nothing daunted, the entire squadron at once set off north on the eighty-mile haul to Artemisium. With the *sirocco* behind them, and forcing the pace, they made record time. By noon on 19 August Themistocles and Eurybiades knew that the threat to their southern lines of communication had been virtually eliminated. Much encouraged by this intelligence, and with fifty-three extra front-line triremes at their disposal, they proceeded to repeat the previous day's hit-and-run raiding tactics. Towards evening they swooped down on Xerxes' Cilician squadrons,

---

* We can deduce this from Hdt 8.13–14 in conjunction with the general 'war-diary': Xerxes' Euboean squadron was wrecked not earlier than 8–9 p.m. on the night of 18 August, and by about noon the next day the Attica squadron had reached Artemisium with the news. From Chalcis the distance is about 75–80 miles: with a following wind, and rowing all night, they could have done it. But 130+ miles from the Andros strait is a flat impossibility.

put a number of vessels out of action, and then withdrew to Artemisium – this time without waiting for a full-scale engagement to develop. Two such quasi-victories on successive days gave a much-needed general boost to Greek naval morale; and their sense of urgency was sharpened by the news that Leonidas's troops were now under heavy attack at Thermopylae.

On the morning of 19 August Xerxes mounted his second assault on the Hot Gates. This time he formed a special brigade, consisting of 'such men as were reputed to be of outstanding bravery and daring'. His formal exhortation to them was a classic blend of stick and carrot: if they stormed the pass they would obtain rich rewards, if they broke ranks and fled they would be executed. The Great King also seems to have calculated that the Greeks, as Herodotus says, 'being so few in number might be badly enough disabled by wounds to prevent further resistance'. This assumption proved disastrously mistaken. The Greek territorial divisions continued to take their turn in the front line with a will – all except the Phocians, still guarding the all-important hill track over Kallidromos. Some, according to Ephorus, were so fired by patriotic zeal that they refused to withdraw: I see no reason why this detail should be a mere rhetorical embellishment. When Xerxes' crack troops turned in flight, the 'barbarians who were stationed in reserve' blocked their way and forced them back into the breach: there are parallels here with Hemingway's account of military police activities during the Italian retreat from Caporetto. Eventually Xerxes was forced to call off his attack once more. Persian morale was by now, clearly, at a very low ebb indeed, while Xerxes himself was 'in a state of dismay, believing that no man would have the courage to go into battle again'. The *impasse*, unresolved, continued to baffle him; he had no idea what his next move should be.

It was at this crucial point that there appeared a man from Malis named Ephialtes, seeking audience of the Great King: a *diabolus ex machina* as pat on his cue as Coleridge's Person from Porlock. 'He had come', says Herodotus, 'in hope of a rich reward, to tell the king about the track which led over the hills to Thermopylae'. Tradition associates several other names with this act of betrayal: one man from Carystus, another from nearby Anticyra, and two Trachinians. It is more than likely that any of these volunteered *information* concerning the route over Kallidromos; but only Ephialtes was prepared to guide an outflanking force along it at night (aided, nevertheless, by the full moon), and, like Herodotus, 'I leave his name on record as the guilty one'. Xerxes was delighted, and small wonder: here at last, when he was almost at his wits' end, was the opening he had sought so long, and at such enormous cost.*

He at once sent for Hydarnes, the commander of the Immortals. After the events of the past two days, and with so hazardous an operation in view, only seasoned professional troops could be trusted: demoralised conscript levies, or wild undisciplined tribesmen, would be worse than useless. Xerxes carefully briefed Hydarnes on Ephialtes' information, and ordered him to set out at dusk, 'about the time the lamps are lit'. Crossing the mountain would be an all-night task, and there was always the risk of encountering opposition *en route* – though Persian intelligence does not, in fact, appear to have known about the presence of the Phocian brigade above Palaiodhrakospiliá. If all went well, Hydarnes would come down near Alpeni about mid-morning, and at once attack Leonidas from the rear, when his front was already engaged. Both ancient sources and modern scholars differ sharply as to the number of men Hydarnes actually took with him, the former exaggerating their total, the latter depreciating it. The simplest and most plausible theory is that the Ten Thousand were detailed for this expedition *en bloc*. By now Xerxes must have had a pretty accurate notion of Leonidas's total strength, and he is unlikely to have dispatched a force that did not out-number these formidable warriors by a very comfortable margin.

The Persians climbed steadily all night. About dawn they were marching along the mountain-ride of Nevropolis [see map, p. 125], through thick oak-woods. The recent storms had shaken down a large number of dry leaves from the trees, and as they advanced Hydarnes' Ten Thousand made a great crackling and rustling. The air was abso-lutely still, with not a breath of wind stirring, and this noise of boots kicking up leaves seems to have been the first intimation the Phocians had that a large enemy force was approaching. (What, one wonders, had happened to their sentries and outposts?) They were still struggling into their armour when Hydarnes descended on them. At first he thought, in some alarm, that they might be Spartans. On learning the truth, he ordered up his archers – the Phocians had bivouacked in an open meadow – and, with one well-concentrated fusillade of arrows, sent them scuttling ignominiously for the safety of a nearby hill-top. Having thus cleared his line of march, Hydarnes took no further notice of the Phocians, but pressed on along the track to Palaiodhrakospiliá. This was an exceptional piece of luck for him. Had the approaches to

* I cannot accept Hignett's thesis [XIG, p. 145] that Xerxes knew about the Anopaea path well in advance, but only used it when his direct assault had failed: this is to stand reasonable strategy on its head, and the Great King was not a man to waste troops unnecessarily.

Nevropolis been held in force, his chances of breaking through would have been minimal.

The Spartans learnt of Hydarnes' outflanking movement while it was still dark, though probably not long before his fatal dawn encounter with the Phocians, since otherwise Leonidas would surely have rushed reinforcements to the summit of Kallidromos. The information reached them from deserters, Ionian Greeks who developed sudden ethnic qualms in a crisis.* Even at the time, it must have seemed highly unlikely that a scratch force of local levies, outnumbered by ten to one, would be able to hold off the Immortals. Megistias, the Acarnanian seer said to be descended from Melampus, not surprisingly saw death in the sacrificial victims. Leonidas ordered him to leave Thermopylae – another instance of genuine Spartan piety – but he refused, and instead sent away his only son, who was serving with the defence force. Several sources[6] claim that Leonidas, while it was still dark, carried out a suicidal commando raid on Xerxes' headquarters, and so died. This anecdote, though ridiculed by historians and without doubt preposterous nonsense as it stands, may nevertheless contain a substratum of truth. If Leonidas knew that the pass was sold, he could well have sent a group of determined men to attempt the assassination of the Great King, and so perhaps bring the war to a premature end. They had nothing to lose except their lives, which – if the deserters could be trusted – were forfeit in any case. To dismiss the tradition out of hand is perhaps a little rash. How credible are historians a thousand years hence likely to find the Long Range Desert Group's attempt on Rommel's life in 1942?

Soon after dawn Leonidas's look-outs came hurrying down the mountainside. Hydarnes had broken through: in a few hours the Thermopylae line would become a death-trap. The Greek commanders at once held a council of war. Opinions, Herodotus records, 'were divided, some urging that they must on no account abandon their post, others taking the opposite view. *The result was that the army split: some dispersed, the men returning to their various homes*, while others made ready to stand by Leonidas.' This version of events is seldom quoted, and indeed Herodotus himself at once gives the alternative canonical tradition (caustically labelled by one modern historian the 'Thermopylae Legend') which, today as in antiquity, has all but eclipsed it. According to the Legend, Leonidas *dismissed* his Peloponnesian and local allies before the final battle, not wishing to waste the lives of good fighting men unnecessarily, and himself 'remained behind with his bodyguard of 300 Spartans to fight and die as an act of *devotio*, performed in fulfilment of a Delphic

---

* Ephorus (Diod. 11.8.5) names Tyrrhastiadas of Cyme; since Cyme was Ephorus's birthplace, the detail may well be genuine, and culled from a local tradition.

oracle' [see above, pp. 67–8].[7] In that case, we may well ask, why did he keep the Thebans and Thespians with him to the bitter end, in defiance of his own order? The former, it is alleged, stayed against their will: Leonidas was keeping them as hostages. This nasty libel on a group of very gallant men was long ago refuted by Plutarch. He pointed out, tartly, that had such been the case, Leonidas would have done better to send them away, under escort, with his departing Peloponnesian contingents. (They were also, we may recall, political opponents of the Theban régime, and thus had little to gain by going home.) As for the Thespians, we are asked to believe that they simply insisted, against orders, on sharing Leonidas's fate.

The truth, surely, is far simpler, and no whit less creditable to Leonidas himself, however it may reflect on the reputation of his allies. Both the Thespian and the Theban contingents stayed to the bitter end *because they alone had volunteered to do so*; and at this point, faced with a mass defection, Leonidas needed all the volunteers he could get. One can imagine, all too easily, that contemptuous 'Go, then!' which the dour, grizzled Spartan king flung at the men who had failed him in his hour of crisis – and which they, to save their own honour, would afterwards represent as an unchallengeable military order. So his confederate troops, unit by unit – Tegeans, Locrians, Mantineans, the men of Corinth and Orchomenus and Mycenae – marched aways southwards to safety, along that narrow, dust-laden road between the mountains and the sea, leaving the fate and the honour of Greece in Leonidas's hands. There could be no question of total withdrawal: the pass must, at all costs, be held for as long as possible. If Thermopylae was abandoned, Xerxes' cavalry would cut the retreating Greek army to ribbons. The position of the fleet at Artemisium would be seriously jeopardised. Perhaps most important of all, if central and Southern Greece did not rally now, did not prepare for a last-ditch stand against the invader, Xerxes had won, irrevocably and perhaps for ever. There must be a gesture, a symbol. So, knowing his position hopeless, Leonidas – without fuss or heroics – prepared to sacrifice himself and his men for the better saving of Greece. In that sense, those who see the last stand at Thermopylae as an act of *devotio* are undoubtedly right.

After the departure of the allies a great silence fell. Xerxes had ordered his synchronised attack to be launched 'about the time of the filling of the market-place' – that is, between nine and ten in the morning. Leonidas and his tiny army, now reduced to about two thousand men,*

---

* Their paper strength was: 300 Spartans, ?900 Helots, 700 Thespians, 400 Thebans. This gives a total of 2,300: if we deduct 300 for absentees and casualties incurred during the previous two days' fighting, we shall probably not be far out.

took a hearty breakfast, with the object of giving themselves stomach and energy for the coming struggle: the King told them to make the most of it, 'since they would dine in Hades'. A native of Trachis, who came into camp with the latest news about Xerxes' dispositions, warned his listeners that the Persians shot their arrows in such enormous volleys as to blot out the sun. 'Excellent,' retorted one well-known Spartan wit, 'then we shall fight in the shade'. The honour of participating in this last stand – and the complementary disgrace which attached itself to those who missed it – gave rise to some odd incidents. When Leonidas asked two members of the Three Hundred, in turn, to carry a dispatch back to Sparta for him, both refused. The first said: 'I came with you to fight, not to carry messages.' The second asserted: 'I shall do my duty better if I stay here, and the news will be better if I stay here.' With that they picked up their shields and took their place in the ranks. Of two men recovering from acute eye-inflammation, one insisted – all but blind though he was – on being placed in the forefront of the battle. The other, however, stayed behind, and was cruelly boy-cotted by his fellow-Spartans until he wiped out his disgrace at Plataea. Yet another Spartiate, Pantites, unavoidably absent on liaison duties with the Thessalian loyalists, found himself in such bad odour when he got back home that he committed suicide.

So Leonidas and his men stood to arms for the last time, silent because there was nothing left to say, waiting patiently as the August sun climbed the sky, and their shadows shortened, and the air filled with that odd blended scent of thyme and sulphur and the brackish tang of the sea-marshes. Many of them were wounded; hardly a shield or helmet but bore witness to the fearful battering they had taken during the past forty-eight hours. Then, about nine o'clock, Xerxes' battalions began to advance towards the neck of the pass. Leonidas, determined to make this final engagement a costly one for the Persians, now moved his line forward, well beyond the wall, and deployed it on wider ground, where there would be more elbow-room for slaughter. Once Hydarnes and the Immortals came down that tree-clad mountainside, it would all very soon be over. Watching for the ominous glint of metal among the pines, Leonidas knew how short his time was. Then the first waves of attackers were on them, and all else was forgotten as they flung themselves, with furious desperation, into that harsh, bloody, and immortal struggle. 'Many of the invaders fell,' Herodotus notes, with appropriately laconic concision – and then adds, never able to resist the freedom-slavery antithesis, 'Behind them the company commanders plied their whips, driving the men remorselessly on'. Some were drowned in the shallows; others fell and were trampled to death, by friends or enemies without distinction. When Leonidas himself died, the Spartans fought savagely over his corpse, and at last succeeded in dragging it away. By now most of the defenders' spears were broken, and they had only their swords or daggers. Then, at last, the long-awaited message was passed from mouth to mouth: 'They are coming.' No need to ask who *they* were. The survivors now withdrew, still in good order, to a little mound just behind the wall, at the narrowest part of the Hot Gates. 'Here they resisted to the last, with their swords, if they had them, and, if not, with their hands and teeth, until the Persians, coming on from the front over the ruins of the wall and closing in from behind, finally overwhelmed them' – with *missiles*, be it noted (*ballontes*); even Spartan hands and teeth were things they preferred to stay clear of.

It was all over by midday: at the last possible moment, Habronichus, Leonidas's liaison officer, slipped the anchor of his fast thirty-oared cutter and set out for Artemisium with the grim news. Meanwhile those few prisoners who surrendered (all Thebans, according to Herodotus, but his anti-Theban bias needs watching) were branded with the 'King's mark' – an honourable disfigurement, as Plutarch justly points out. Xerxes and his staff officers inspected the battlefield that afternoon. When the body of Leonidas was discovered, the Great King had his head cut off and fixed on a pole – a barbarous and uncharacteristic gesture, but then the Spartans had given Xerxes more trouble than he bargained for. At the same time, mindful as ever of his public image, he gave orders for all the Persian dead, save a thousand or so, to be shovelled out of sight into hastily dug trenches and covered over with leaves and packed earth. Though naturally anxious to show off his victory, he shrank from revealing its phenomenally high cost.

In a way this gesture was otiose, since not all the glory of Leonidas's last stand could obliterate the fact that the Greek cause had suffered a major setback. (In modern times the evacuation of Dunkirk provides an illuminating parallel.) The pass of Thermopylae had been forced after only three days' fighting – mainly because Sparta's too-cautious leaders failed to send reinforcements when they were desperately needed – and the road into central Greece lay wide open. Themistocles' northern defence-line had been irreparably breached: once Thermopylae fell, the fleet's position at Artemisium became untenable too. A Spartan king lay dead on the field of battle: scant comfort that his death had been foreseen by Delphi [see above, pp. 67–8]. A great deal of face-saving had to be done, and quickly. The most obvious line to take was that Leonidas's end had been inevitable – here the oracle, or part of it, came in handy – and that his last stand had in fact been an act of *devotio* which won Sparta divine reprieve from annihilation. The encomium composed by Simonides is characteristic, and perhaps set the pattern:

> Of those who died in the Hot Gates
> Glorious is the fortune, noble the end –
> Their grave's an altar, in place of grief they know
> Undying remembrance, their fate is praise.
> Such a winding-shroud as this neither mould
> Nor all-devouring time shall ever consume.
> This sepulchre of brave warriors has taken the good renown
> Of Hellas to dwell therein – bear witness Leonidas,
> The Spartan king, who leaves behind him a great
> Crown of valour, and undying renown.

None of the awkward questions are asked: manhood and *virtú* eclipse all else. Yet the propagandists at Sparta who minimised their own inefficiency by concentrating on the glorious self-sacrifice of Leonidas and his men were, paradoxically, much nearer the mark than they knew. Dismay very soon gave way to a sudden upsurge of ethnic pride. The example of Leonidas cut clean across mere parochial allegiances: it belonged to all Greece. The ultimate victories of Salamis and Plataea became possible, in a sense, only through that splendid and inspiring defeat, its spirit crystallised for ever by the classic – and classically simple – epitaph on Leonidas and his three hundred fellow-Spartans:

> Tell them in Lacedaemon, passer-by,
> That here obedient to their word we lie.

On the same day as the final assault against Leonidas [20 August], Xerxes' admirals took the offensive against the Greek fleet at Artemisium. Such well-timed action is unlikely to have been a mere coincidence. Xerxes, confident that he now held the key to victory at the Hot Gates, must already have been planning his further advance south. To ensure smooth cooperation between fleet and army, as before, it was vital that the Euboea channel should be in Persian hands, and Greek naval opposition there eliminated: hence the abortive attempt to get an outflanking squadron through the Euripus. When this strategy failed, Xerxes at once ordered the only possible alternative – a straightforward naval engagement, relying on Persia's still considerable (if reduced) superiority in numbers.* Herodotus is at his worst here: vague, inaccu-

* By now some at least of those vessels disabled by the storm must have been refitted: it is even possible that refugees from the 'Euboea squadron' got back via Skyros and the Sporades. The total figure, losses of all sorts allowed for, was perhaps 450. The original Greek fleet of 271 vessels had been reinforced by the Attica squadron, 53 strong: this makes a total of 324, but, again, we must make allowance for enemy action and storm-damage: say a round 300. In other words, the Persians outnumbered the Greeks by something like three to two.

143

rate, and tendentious, with a generally dismissive attitude to the very real achievements of the Greek fleet. The motives he ascribes to the Persian commanders are purely personal. They were, he claims, 'humiliated at receiving such rough treatment from so small a fleet', which could be true, but is hardly adequate as an explanation. Rather more convincing – though, again, irrelevant to strategical considerations – is his belief that they were beginning to dread the Great King's wrath-to-come. Xerxes, it is true, had a very short way with subordinates who lost ships and failed to take objectives. Even so, it would need more than fear to mount a full-scale sea-battle, which – simply to judge by the numbers involved on both sides – must be regarded as one of the most important actions yet fought in the Mediterranean.[8]

All that morning, while Leonidas's rearguard fought and died in the Hot Gates, the squadrons of Xerxes' fleet – Cilicians, Egyptians, Phoenicians; Greeks from Ionia and Caria and the Hellespont – were moving in to Aphetae from their various anchorages along the coast. These preparations took place in full view of Artemisium: there could be no question of a surprise attack, and the Greeks had ample time to man their own battle-stations. One thing which Herodotus *does* make clear is that the point at issue was control of the Euboea channel – 'the fleet was fighting for the Euripus just as the army with Leonidas was fighting for the pass'. He goes on to say that the Greek fleet took up a position 'off Artemisium', a phrase so vague as to be all but meaningless; but in the circumstances there was virtually one order only which Themistocles and his fellow-commanders could adopt – a cross-channel formation in line-abreast, angled out towards the Gulf of Pagasae [see map, p. 90]. It was midday before the Persians had completed their preparations; all this time the Greeks in the channel made no move against them, but 'quietly awaited their approach'. Then, at last, the great armada put out from Aphetae, and made across the strait in a wide-flung crescent formation, wings curving forward to outflank and envelop the Greek line[9] – 'whereupon,' says Herodotus, with infuriating lack of tactical detail, 'the Greeks advanced to meet them and the fight began'.

Since the Persian ships tended to foul one another – which caused, Herodotus tells us, 'constant confusion' – it looks as though they adopted a *converging* crescent formation; which suggests, again, that the Greeks opposed them with a *kyklos*, or half-*kyklos*, as in their earlier engagement [see above, p. 134]. After the initial collision, with a great crashing and grinding of rams, the front lines had no scope for manoeuvre: what developed here was a battle between marine boarding parties. The Greek marines were fewer in number – fourteen per vessel as opposed to thirty – but on the whole far better armed, which gave them a considerable compensating advantage.* It is noteworthy that the greatest success scored on the other side was by the Egyptians, who 'wore reticulated helmets and were armed with concave, broadrimmed shields, boarding-spears, and heavy axes'. Most of their rowers, too, possessed corslets and carried long dirks, whereas the average Greek on the rowing-bench was near-naked and virtually defenceless once his protecting marines had been overwhelmed. We can see what this meant from Herodotus's casual aside that the Egyptians captured five Greek triremes 'together with their crews'. So the struggle went on all afternoon, under a blazing August sun, with neither side gaining a clear-cut advantage. Casualties were heavy: the Athenians, who bore the brunt of the fighting, had half their vessels disabled. Not until sunset did this crude and protracted slugging-match run its course. Then both sides, disengaging, 'made all speed back to their moorings, and were not sorry to get there' – though the Greeks spent some time picking up their dead from the water and salvaging wrecked triremes, which suggests that, on balance, they had had the better of it.† On that long, melancholy strand by Artemisium, in the gathering dusk, flames licked up from burning wreckage and hastily improvised funeral pyres: centuries later the ash-layer could still be found, deep under drifts of shifting sand. It was now, about eight in the evening, that Habronichus's cutter arrived, with the news that Thermopylae had fallen.

It is not hard to imagine the effect which this catastrophic announcement must have had on the weary – but justifiably elated – sailors of the Greek fleet. With supreme courage, and at heavy cost in both lives and ships, they had held their own against Xerxes' hitherto invincible armada. Now it seemed that their endurance and sacrifice had been so much wasted labour. With Thermopylae lost, and Xerxes in command of the passes, the fleet's station at Artemisium could no longer be held. After fighting something better than a drawn engagement, they now found themselves abruptly faced with the inevitable prospect of immediate, and humiliating, evacuation. This was a bitter pill to swallow, and

* The total *non-rowing* complement of a trireme during the Persian Wars, including petty officers, sailors and officers, was about fifty: it may well be that *all* these, not the marines alone, would join in the fighting during an engagement. Cf. Burn, PG pp. 400–1, whose account of this battle is both full and sensible.

† An inscription set up outside the temple of Artemis-facing-eastward, and recorded by Plutarch [*Them.* 8.3] states, unequivocally, that the Greeks 'conquered in the sea battle', a conclusion confirmed by Pindar, fr. 77 Bergk. Only Herodotus [8.18] implies that this engagement was a quasi-defeat, which left the Greek command 'determined to quit their station and withdraw further south': a libel well refuted by Hignett, XIG, pp. 190–2.

we may doubt whether anyone – even Themistocles – realised for some while to come just how much the events of the past few days had, in fact, achieved for the Greek cause. Psychologically, the sea-battle off Artemisium had proved an invaluable experience. It dented the myth of Persian naval superiority; it acclimatised the Greeks to facing an unfamiliar – and therefore frightening – enemy on equal terms:

> They learned from their own behaviour in the face of danger that men who know how to come to close quarters and are determined to give battle have nothing to fear from mere numbers of ships, gaudily decorated figure-heads, boastful shouts, or barbaric war-songs: they have simply to show their contempt for these distractions, engage the enemy hand to hand and fight it out to the bitter end. [Plut. *Them.* 8.1]

It was Artemisium, not Salamis, which Pindar had in mind when he spoke of 'that great fight where the brave sons of Athens planted the shining corner-stone of their freedom': nor was he thinking merely in terms of a boost to Greek morale. Naval operations in the straits, aided by two highly obliging storms, had destroyed so many Persian ships and men that Xerxes henceforth carefully avoided the one strategy almost guaranteed to win him the campaign: a division of his forces.

This was precisely the advice which Demaratus, the Spartan king-in-exile, gave him after the death of Leonidas – when that empty throne must have seemed particularly alluring and attainable. Demaratus suggested the dispatch of a strong naval task-force to the southern Peloponnese, with its base on the island of Cythera. From here commando raids could be carried out into the very heart of Laconian territory; a determined thrust up the Eurotas valley – led, we need not doubt, by Demaratus himself – might even capture unwalled Sparta. Meanwhile Xerxes' main army could continue the advance into central Greece. This two-pronged divide-and-rule strategy had everything in its favour. It would enable the Persians, for once, to deploy their superior numbers to good advantage, instead of wasting them. It would guarantee that no further reinforcements moved north of the Isthmus, to Athens or anywhere else. The speech which Herodotus puts in Demaratus's mouth is very much to the point: 'With a war of their own, on their own doorstep, as it were, you need not fear that [the Spartans] will help the other Greeks while your army is engaged in conquering them. Thus the rest of Greece will be crushed first and Lacedaemon will be left alone and helpless.' At best, the Greeks would be forced to fight on two fronts when they barely had the men or supplies to defend one. Yet Xerxes' brother Achaemenes, admiral of the Egyptian fleet, instantly vetoed such a project. Hundreds of ships, he reminded the

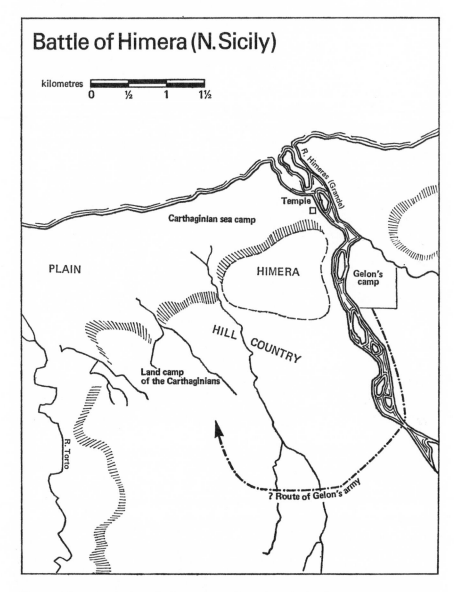

Great King, had already been lost. The Greeks had proved singularly quick to master the complexities of naval warfare. He warned Xerxes, bluntly, that the detachment of such a task force to Cythera would, now, deplete the main armada to a point where 'the enemy will be a match for us'. There, in one sentence, is the justification for Artemisium, and perhaps for Thermopylae too: Xerxes had won a battle, but in doing so he had substantially reduced his chances of winning the war.

While the Greeks of the homeland were thus struggling for their very survival, those of the West – on the same day, according to one tradition, as the loss of Thermopylae – scored a brilliant, crushing, and final victory at Himera. Gelon, at something of a loss when confronted by Hamilcar's strongly entrenched forces, had been contemplating a diversionary fire-raid against the beached Carthaginian fleet. An intercepted dispatch from Selinus [see above, p. 122] suggested something better and more original. In this dispatch, the Selinuntines promised to send Hamilcar cavalry reinforcements on the day for which he had requested them – which was also when the Carthaginian general, himself half Greek by birth, planned a magnificent sacrifice to Poseidon. Gelon, knowing that to these foreign troops all Greek cavalry would look much alike, ordered his own crack Syracusan squadrons to approach Hamilcar's naval stockade early on the appointed day (after making a quick detour out of town to camouflage their movements) and present themselves as the expected contingent from Selinus. Once inside the palisade, they were to fire the tents and ships, and, if possible, to kill Hamilcar in person. Scouts, posted on the hills above the town, were to signal back as soon as this breakthrough had been made, and Gelon would thereupon launch a major frontal assault. At the same time, Theron's troops, standing to arms inside the walls of Himera, would also sally forth against the enemy. No prisoners were to be taken. It was a daring stratagem, and one which afterwards excited the admiration of the whole Greek-speaking world. Better still, it succeeded.

At first dawn a large body of Syracusan horsemen duly appeared at the main gate of Hamilcar's camp, and with cool effrontery called on the guards to admit them – which they did. This part of the operation went off so smoothly that we must assume the captured dispatch to have contained some secret password, which the impostors could produce on demand. As soon as they were all within the lines, they set about their work with swift and lethal efficiency. Flaring pitch-torches sent flames licking across tents and sun-dry hulls. To find Hamilcar was no problem: he must have been about the most conspicuous figure in camp at that moment, having already begun to make sacrifice before a huge fire-altar, on which whole carcasses were roasting. The cavalrymen swept down on this Frazerian priest-king, sabred him to death, and, it would seem, then tossed his corpse in among the flames, one more sizzling sacrifice to add to the sheep and oxen. Gelon is said to have searched high and low for Hamilcar after the battle, 'but there was no trace of him, alive or dead'. As Burn says, when it became known that Gelon wanted his body, those who had destroyed it would hardly publicise their act. The result was a spate of extraordinary fabrications concerning the Suffete's end, most impressive being the one (probably put about by his family) in which he immolated himself as a last desperate bid to secure victory.

For a while the issue of the battle remained doubtful. Some of Theron's conscript militiamen, thinking – wrongly – that their first charge through the Carthaginian palisade had settled matters, broke ranks and began to loot the camp, while Gelon's and Hamilcar's more professional troops were still fighting it out. Some Spanish mercenaries serving with Hamilcar counter-attacked; Theron saved the situation by firing more tents on the landward side, and this, together with the news of Hamilcar's death, made the main Carthaginian defence line waver and break. Gelon's veterans pressed home their advantage, cheering wildly, while flames streamed skywards through the burning camp. The 'no prisoners' rule made a vast slaughter inevitable – though we need not credit Diodorus's picture of 150,000 corpses scattered across the battlefield. Some of the fugitives struggled aboard Hamilcar's twenty-ship duty squadron, riding off-shore, and got clear before anyone thought of pursuing them; but these vessels, heavily over-crowded, presently ran into a storm, and were almost all lost. Other survivors retreated westward, still in good order, to Mt Calogero,[10] and dug themselves in there. It was a strong position, but unfortunately – as Gelon knew – without any source of water; so all he had to do was wait, and in due course raging thirst among the defence force won him an easy surrender. No more than a handful of Carthaginians at last got home, in one small boat, to report the total loss of their Sicilian expedition. Carthage at once sent envoys to sue for peace; and Gelon, very much the master of the situation, dictated his own terms. Some of the marvellous temples, baths and water-conduits which afterwards embellished so many Sicilian cities – Syracuse and Acragas in particular – were built with the spoils, and the inexhaustible slave-labour, acquired at Himera. In the West at least, the 'barbarian threat' had been destroyed for years to come.

PART FIVE

THE WOODEN
WALL

WHEN the news of Leonidas's defeat and death reached Artemisium, Themistocles – who in the emergency seems to have taken over command *de jure* as well as *de facto* – summoned his staff-officers to a conference on the beach. By now night had fallen. They assembled quickly, faces haggard in the lurid glow of the corpse-fires, while all around the local islanders – quick to scent disaster – were driving their cattle down to the water's edge, ready for evacuation. On the main issue no argument was possible: the fleet had to pull out at once, under cover of darkness. Nor was this any time for pandering to civilians. Themistocles gave orders to seize and slaughter the islanders' herds, 'as it was better that their own troops should have them than the enemy'. Numerous camp-fires were built up, probably from salvaged wreckage, and with two objects in view: to roast the cattle, thus providing each ship's crew with a solid meal before the long night's work ahead, and to deceive the enemy by suggesting a general bivouac. As soon as supper was over, the weary, bloodstained Greek sailors clambered aboard their triremes again, and 'got under way at once, one after another, the Corinthians leading, the Athenians bringing up the rear'. Silently they rowed away southward through the straits: we are told that the Athenians were still cock-a-hoop because of their recent exploits, but for the most part morale must have been at very low ebb. Many of the ships – and their crews – were clearly in no condition to fight. Gaps in oar-banks and on rowing-benches testified to the ordeal they had so lately undergone. Rams were cracked and sprung from their timbers. Hulls, stove-in dangerously near the water-line, had been roughly plugged with sail-cloth. A mess of blood and tangled cordage still littered the decks. The wounded lay wherever they could find an empty space.

Themistocles himself took a group of the fastest galleys, and went ahead on an *ad hoc* propaganda mission. He put in briefly at every anchorage or watering-place which the Persians were likely to use, and left messages chalked on the rocks, to be read by the Ionians serving with the Great King's fleet – 'as they did,' says Herodotus, 'when they moved up on the following day', though not (we may surmise) in the discursive and rhetorical version which he records. Themistocles appealed to their ethnic sense as fellow-Greeks: why did they not come over and join the Athenians, 'who were their ancestors and who were risking everything for their liberty'? Otherwise, let them remain neutral, and persuade the Carians to do likewise – or, if there was too much pressure on them, simply refuse to fight next time battle was joined, and by such acts of sabotage damage the barbarian war-effort. Even if the Ionians ignored this somewhat naïve appeal (as in fact they seem to have done) Themistocles hoped that the messages, duly reported to Xerxes, might raise doubts in that suspicious autocrat's mind as to their loyalty, and perhaps induce him to pull their experienced squadrons out of the front line. (No smoke without fire.) It was not one of Themistocles' most brilliant ideas, but at least it was something. What more, in the circumstances, could anyone have done?

The news of the Greek withdrawal was brought to Aphetae by a native of Histiaea, who sailed over immediately after the fleet had gone – presumably in the hope of securing lenient treatment for his city. At first the Persians refused to believe him: one strong argument against the recent sea-battle having ended in a Greek defeat. Obviously suspecting that their informant was an agent of Themistocles, they detained him under guard, and sent out a fast reconnaissance squadron to see what was really going on at Artemisium. Sure enough, all they found was an abandoned site, some dying fires, and large quantities of half-gnawed bones. At dawn next morning [21 August] the whole Persian fleet moved across to the Greek station, where they remained till midday. They then moved on west to Histiaea, which they occupied, together with a number of villages along the coast. No attempt was made to overtake the Greeks in the Euripus; the mauling they had received the previous day had given Xerxes' admirals a healthy respect for their opponents' fighting abilities.

It was at Histiaea that a royal messenger from Xerxes' headquarters presently reached them. On his arrival the entire expeditionary force was paraded to hear the Great King's word. This turned out to be a general invitation to come over and inspect the Thermopylae battlefield. 'Friends and fellow-soldiers,' the messenger announced, 'the king grants leave for anyone who wants it to go and see with his own eyes how he fights against the madmen who thought they could beat him'. There was an immediate rush to take advantage of this offer – so much so that the supply of boats ran out, which suggests that only small craft and transports were being used. All next day [22 August] parties of sailors and marines, from every quarter of the Eastern Mediterranean, pottered about in the Hot Gates, prodding corpses and being lectured by Xerxes' officers. They were not overimpressed. To mistake dead Helots for Spartiates was the kind of error any tourist might make; but, says Herodotus, with visible relish, 'Xerxes' ludicrous attempt to conceal the number of his own dead [see above, p. 142] deceived nobody'. One wonders how he obtained his information: it is hard to imagine even the brashest Levantine sailor voicing open incredulity at the time.

Next day [23 August] these boatloads of visitors returned to Histiaea, and the main body of the army began its march from Thermopylae down into central Greece. An advance force of crack troops and cavalry was sent on ahead to occupy Athens and Phaleron; by now Xerxes' intelligence officers must have known all about the general – if still incomplete – evacuation of Attica. The fleet was sent orders to delay its advance until the 26th. Xerxes' strategy, when proceeding through hostile terrain, was, it seems, to let his land-forces lead the way, securing essential harbours and watering-places for the fleet. A three-day gap was just about right, provided no unforeseen delays took place: ancient tradition allowed a day and a half for the journey from Thermopylae to Thebes [Plut. *Moral.* 864F], and roughly the same for that between Thebes and Athens. Before he set out, Xerxes was anxious to collect what information he could about the state of enemy morale in the south. Accordingly he sent for some Arcadian deserters who had reached his camp, looking for employment as mercenaries, and questioned them, through an interpreter, 'about what the Greeks were doing'. The answer he got proved a trifle disconcerting. The Greeks, his informants said, 'were celebrating the Olympic festival, where they were watching athletic contests and chariot-races' – hardly the behaviour of men about to be steamrollered by an irresistible invasion. Further enquiry elicited the fact that they competed, not for some rich cash prize, but for a simple wreath. This incident is perhaps mere fictional propaganda, designed (like so much else in Herodotus) to point up the contrast between slavish, money-grubbing barbarians and cool, idealistic Greeks. Yet it could well be true; and the contrast, up to a point, remains valid.

While his baggage-train advanced by the coast road through Locris, some of Xerxes' infantry units cut across westward into Dorian territory, probably proceeding – now all opposition had been crushed – up the Asopus gorge [see above, pp. 114–15]. Doris itself collaborated, and was spared – at the Thessalians' request, Herodotus claims; but this may be no more than a convenient contrast to his excursus on the rape of Phocis, the next state along Xerxes' line of march [see map, p. 90].

Immediately after the collapse of the Thermopylae-Artemisium line, Thessaly had tried to blackmail Phocis for the equivalent of about £12,000 in protection money. The Thessalian leaders made much of their influence with Xerxes ('a word from us would get you turned out of your country, and sold as slaves into the bargain') but promised, if paid off, to 'divert the danger': just how, is never made clear. The Phocians, with considerable spirit, refused this proposal point-blank. Had they wanted to go pro-Persian, they said, nastily, they could have done so just as easily as Thessaly. The difference between them was that *they* 'would never willingly prove traitors to Greece'. Herodotus rather spoils the effect of this gesture (the Phocians were, in fact, the only people from this area who failed to medise) by suggesting that it was dictated simply and solely by hatred of Thessaly. 'If Thessaly had remained loyal,' he asserts, 'no doubt the Phocians would have deserted to Persia.'[1]

Nevertheless, their defiance cost them dear, and must have been inspired, in the last resort, by something more than mere border feuding. Xerxes decided, with calculated ruthlessness, to make a public example of Phocis: let the Greeks learn, once and for all, what lay in store for any obstinately non-cooperative state. Actual loss of life was small, since the Phocians, like their modern wartime descendants, promptly took to the mountains: Parnassus has always made an admirable hide-out for guerilla fighters. (Even so, a few stragglers were caught in the foothills, and some unlucky women were 'raped successively by so many Persian soldiers that they died': atrocity stories change very little down the ages.) Xerxes, baulked of human victims, vented his spleen on the rich countryside. The whole of Phocis was systematically devastated by fire and sword – with the more-than-willing assistance of the Thessalians, who 'did not let the Persian army miss a bit of it'. Towns and country estates went up in flames, temples were looted of all their treasures and then razed to the ground. Along the beautiful Cephisus Valley not one single village survived. Watchers across the eastern frontier, in Boeotian Orchomenus, saw that heavy pall of black smoke darken the sky, and gave thanks for the palpable blessings of collaboration: at least their lives and property would be spared, though Xerxes' locust horde might leave them little else [see above, p. 88].

Less than fifty miles beyond Orchomenus, along the Parnes-Cithaeron range, lay the northern outposts of Attica.

The news of Thermopylae can scarcely have reached Athens before 22 August, even by special courier. When it did, it caused something of a panic, and small wonder. Themistocles' evacuation order in June [see above, p. 97 ff.] had siphoned off most of the civilian population –

though some preferred to 'wait and see', and many herdsmen (ignoring Athenian conscription orders) simply vanished into the hills. Almost every able-bodied man in the lower property orders or the resident alien class – not to mention a good many slaves – was on active service with the fleet at Artemisium. If Cimon's example is anything to go by [see above, pp. 103–4], numerous aristocrats and hoplites were also aboard the triremes, fighting as marines. What remained was a small but influential body of middle-aged, conservative farmers and land-owners. Their views – which always carried disproportionate weight – seem now to have overridden the Assembly-backed policy laid down by Themistocles: not surprisingly, since Themistocles himself, together with almost all his supporters, was still away in the north. An emergency appeal was at once sent off to the League's headquarters. In it the Athenians called on their dilatory Peloponnesian allies 'to make a stand in Boeotia and protect Attica, just as they themselves had gone out by sea to fight in defence of the rest of Greece at Artemisium' [Plut. *Them.* 9.3]. Strategically, such a plea made little sense. There were half a dozen routes over or round the Parnes-Cithaeron range, so that any attempt to defend it would entail a dangerous division of forces. Worse, close liaison between fleet and army would become virtually impossible – though this was not a consideration likely to carry much weight with the 'men of Marathon'.

Yet even discounting these grave drawbacks, there was small likelihood – once Thermopylae had fallen – of the Peloponnesians committing a large army in Northern Attica. Previous guarantees of reinforcements in strength now meant nothing: the situation had changed overnight. Athenian aristocrats, with their gentlemanly tradition of pro-Spartan *philoxenia*, never seem to have realised that these friendly ties were entirely dependent on the harsh demands of strategy. Perhaps on 23 August, a general staff conference was held at Corinth, with all-too-predictable results. The delegates turned down Athens' appeal, and voted instead to consolidate a new defence-line at the Isthmus. A wall, or reinforced earthwork, was to be thrown up between the ports of Cenchreae and Lechaeum, more or less along the line of Periander's naval slipway. This work was to be carried out, and the Isthmus defences manned, by the already-mobilised Peloponnesian field army – about 30,000 strong, according to the latest modern estimate – under Leonidas's youngest brother, Cleombrotus. Cleombrotus also had orders to destroy the narrow and precipitous 'Scironian Way' (known by modern Greeks as Kaké Skala, the 'Bad Descent') which ran through to Megara along the sheer corniche of the Geranean Mountains, some 6–700 feet above the sea, a primitive ancestor of the modern Athens-

Corinth highway. This would effectively block the only land approach to the Isthmus, apart from one difficult hill-track through Tripodiscus, more or less identical with the minor road which today links Megara and Loutraki. What role, if any, the fleet was allotted in this scheme our sources do not relate; the most likely supposition is that it would protect the army's flank from a base at Cenchreae.

The news of the delegates' decision – one motive for it was said to have been 'the unrest of the masses', a revealing detail – reached both Athens and Sparta on 24 August. Cleombrotus and his Lacedaemonians at once left for the Isthmus, where they were soon joined by other Peloponnesian contingents,* and work on the wall began in earnest. 'Stones, bricks, timbers, sand-baskets – all were used in the building, and the labour went on continuously day and night.' With something like 30,000 men to fortify a five-mile stretch, their task was soon accomplished: not, perhaps, in a very permanent form, since little more than a century later military operations at the Isthmus were carried out without apparent reference to it. Pessimistic about their chances in a war at sea, and fearing an imminent Helot revolt, the Peloponnesians can hardly be blamed, in retrospect, for the choice they made; but in Athenian eyes it was an act of sheer betrayal, which deliberately abandoned Attica to her fate. Furious, disheartened, powerless to take effective action, Athens' conservatives still, at this eleventh hour, could not face the harsh realities of Themistoclean strategy:

They could not seriously think of engaging so vast an army by themselves, but the only choice which was now left them – namely to give up their city and entrust their very existence to the fleet – seemed utterly repugnant. The majority felt that *they did not want victory on these terms* [my italics] and that safety meant nothing to them if it required that they should abandon the temples of their gods and the tombs of their forefathers to the enemy. [Plut. *Them.* 9.4]

It was *their* estates, *their* investments, *their* beliefs and prejudices which the iconoclast from Phrearri wanted thrown to the hungry Persian wolves; small wonder that reason, even now, tended to be eclipsed by personal prejudice and traditional sentiment. Such was the situation in Athens when, shortly after the League's decision was announced, Themistocles and his battered squadrons limped into Phaleron Bay, to be greeted by the news that the Peloponnesians 'were fortifying the Isthmus, and letting all else go'.

* Herodotus [8.72.1] lists them: Sparta, all the towns of Arcadia, Elis, Corinth, Sicyon, Epidaurus, Phlius, Troezen, and Hermione. Then he adds: 'The other Peloponnesian communities (though the Olympic and Carneian festivals were now over) remained indifferent.' Most prominent among them were Argos and Achaea.

Themistocles seems to have anticipated some such self-defeating *démarche* by the League. After the collapse of the Thermopylae-Artemisium line, normal procedure would have been for surviving Allied units to reassemble at the Isthmus, and there await new orders. Such had been the case after the withdrawal from Tempe, and we have no reason to suppose that things had changed substantially since then. Individual commanders might take voting-instructions *en route* from their own governments, but the League's majority decisions were final and binding [see above, p. 100]. It did not require Themistoclean genius to foresee that a disaster such as Thermopylae, involving the loss of three hundred élite warriors together with a king of the realm, was liable to make Sparta's latent isolationism run riot; and where Sparta led, the Peloponnesian *bloc* would follow. Themistocles had long since determined that Salamis would – must – be the scene of his final challenge to the Persian fleet, and did not intend to let a mere League vote stand in his way. Wisely, he persuaded Eurybiades to put in at Salamis (rather than proceed to the Isthmus) before the League's decision became known. Once the allied squadrons were there, he could, and did, find means to keep them there; whereas the chances of getting them to *originate* independent action in defiance of the League were clearly minimal. Yet the truth came out soon enough; and Themistocles' subsequent relations with his fellow-commanders only make real sense if we bear in mind that *he had talked them into disobeying top-level orders*, and that therefore the entire Salamis campaign was, in strict terms, an unauthorised operation. The attitude of those officers who continued, at every staff-conference, to advocate a retreat to the Isthmus was neither motivated by cowardice nor invented for purposes of propaganda; it simply indicates a tidy belief in the need to obey one's superiors.[2]

While the rest of the allied fleet made directly for Salamis, Themistocles and his much-reduced Athenian squadron – perhaps no more than 110 serviceable vessels in all* – put in at Phaleron. There was much

* The original total of 147 had been brought up to 200, on paper, by the transfer of the Attica squadron (53 strong) to Artemisium: it must, however, have suffered losses prior to this reinforcement. In the final battle about half the Athenian triremes were put out of commission, many permanently, leaving 100± available. The Plataeans who crewed 20 of these were put off, during the retreat, opposite Chalcis [Hdt 8.44], and their vessels probably left there, to be manned by Euboeans, as a guard over the Euripus. Since the Athenians had born the brunt of the fighting, it would be only reasonable for them to take over the 30 enemy vessels captured during the first day's engagement [Hdt 8.11]: 100−20+30 = 110. Add the undamaged Salamis squadron of 57 vessels [see above, p. 109], and we obtain a figure of 167, thirteen less than the canonical battle-strength at Salamis (180). It is reasonable to assume that the balance consisted of post-Artemisium refits, towed home and patched up in the Piraeus shipyards.

to be done, and all too little time in which to do it: they could count, with luck, on forty-eight hours' grace before the first Persian troops reached Athens. The moment he reached Athens, Themistocles issued an Order in Council [*kerygma*] for the immediate and compulsory evacuation of all remaining citizens to Salamis or Aegina (at this late stage, as Burn rightly observes, Troezen would have been too long a haul). Many sailors had run out of cash, and the treasury itself was empty: since troops purchased their own provisions, this called for drastic emergency action. Wealthy members of the Areopagus Council, all former Archons – more evidence, incidentally, as to what type of person still remained in Athens – either volunteered, or were gently persuaded, to make a whip-round. This raised about sixty talents, enough to provide each man in the fleet with eight drachmas, the equivalent of up to a month's rations. According to another account, during the transfer of property down to Piraeus the valuable Gorgon-mask which adorned the breastplate of Athena's statue disappeared. Themistocles made this an excuse to search various evacuees' luggage (presumably he picked his victims with some care: it is hard to believe that Callias the millionaire escaped scrutiny) and to impound the 'excessive' sums in hoarded cash which came to light as a result.

Despite everything, the evacuation was not total. Several thousand country folk, as we have seen, preferred to take their chance in the mountains: Xerxes' troops captured about five hundred of them during the advance through Attica. Two categories deserve special mention, because they stayed behind at the government's express command. The very old and infirm, together with all domestic pets, were treated as expendable: a grim but realistic decision when one considers the amount of shipping space available. (One of the earliest 'faithful hound' anecdotes known to history relates how the dog owned by Pericles' father Xanthippus swam across the Salamis strait after its master – a by no means impossible feat – staggered ashore, and promptly expired: an ingenious, and characteristically Greek, attempt to explain the place-name Cynossema, or the Dog's Tomb.) Secondly, under the provisions of Themistocles' original decree [see above, p. 98], the treasurers and the priestesses were 'to remain behind on the Acropolis guarding the property of the gods'. It seems a reasonable assumption that the old folk were given temple-sanctuary with them – the least they could expect on humanitarian grounds. This clause in the evacuation-decree has been condemned as 'incredibly callous'[3] – and rightly so, had it involved any notion of deliberate sacrifice; but the treasurers and the priestesses were there *to protect temple-property*, not commit *hara-kiri*, and they could hardly carry out such a task without adequate military backing. On all counts it is clear, not only that a strong garrison was posted on the Acropolis, but that those who left it there believed it stood every chance of survival during a not-too-prolonged Persian occupation.

That such a garrison existed we know from Herodotus, though he is at some pains to minimise its size and importance. It consisted, he says, of a few needy folk, who could not afford to provision themselves for the journey to Salamis, and were, moreover, convinced that the 'wooden wall' of the oracle, identified by Themistocles with Athens' fleet, in fact referred to an ancient fence round the summit of the Acropolis. They therefore 'barricaded the Acropolis against the invaders with planks and timbers', secure in their conviction that 'the wooden wall would not be taken'. Here, again, we see the dangers of hindsight. After Salamis, everyone took it for granted that Themistocles had been right all along the line: on the eve of the great invasion this was far less obvious. Herodotus, writing some forty years later, makes the defenders of the Acropolis sound like a group of indigent crackpots, thus effectively dismissing them from the reader's mind. At the time, however, most pious conservatives and *bien-pensants* in Athens were staunchly behind the scheme. They had fought Themistocles' evacuation proposals tooth and nail; they demanded – and got – substantial concessions as the price of their ultimate support. One such concession was the garrisoning of the Acropolis ('safety meant nothing to them if it required that they should abandon the temple of their gods', etc.). Since the whole project proved an embarrassing failure, those who had promoted it would be only too eager to have it forgotten – or at least reduced to a marginal incident, in which they played no part – when the war was over. In the oracular world as elsewhere, nothing succeeds like success.

'In this way,' Plutarch writes, 'the whole city of Athens put out to sea'. Ancient rhetoricians never wearied of embroidering the scene: dogs howling at being left behind, the uncertainty of the future, agonised partings of fathers from children and husbands from wives, as the men sternly sent off their families to Aegina 'and themselves crossed over to Salamis, unmoved by the cries and tears and embraces of their own kin'. No one could foresee how the war would turn out. 'What was actual,' says Aelius Aristeides, with an unwonted flash of psychological insight, 'was the loss of their city and possessions and all familiar things'. Walking today along the shore by Perama it is not hard to picture the scene: rows of triremes and merchantmen lying inshore, many still bearing the scars of battle, each with its swearing crew and close-clustering horde of evacuees; pathetic household goods piled high on rickety hand-carts; endless arguments as to what could, or could not, be taken aboard: fear, urgency, confusion everywhere. Greek sea-travel, even under optimum conditions, has always kept its share of drama and hysteria (as countless popular songs testify), and this final evacuation must have produced scenes of quite indescribable chaos. The urgency at least was well-justified: they had cut it very fine indeed. The last over-loaded boat pulled across to Salamis on 26 August – the same day, incidentally, as the Persian fleet set sail from Histiaea – and less than twenty-four hours later Xerxes' first outriders came clattering through the deserted streets of Athens.

When news came through that the squadrons from Artemisium had put in at Salamis, the commanders of the allied reserve fleet found them-selves faced with a crucial decision. Their own orders were to establish a new base at Pogon, the harbour for Troezen [now Galatás, opposite the island of Poros: see map, p. 90] – exactly what one might expect after the League had voted to establish a defence-line south of the Isthmus. Now Themistocles, it was clear, had decided to implement his own strategy, without reference to the League: the question was, should they, too, ignore the League's explicit instructions, and join him? It is not clear whether all of them in fact did so; but for the largest squadron, Athens' Salamis-based reserve, the choice was never in doubt, and over forty other triremes (from the Peloponnese, the Western colonies, and the islands) followed suit. The total strength of these reinforcements was about a hundred ($57 + 42 = 99$), and would have been a good deal more if the squadron promised by Corcyra had ever materialised. The Corcyraean vessels, sixty in number, did, in fact, after much delay, actually put to sea, but never got further than the southern Peloponnese. Here they lay harbour-bound until the crisis was over: ostensibly held up by the *meltemi* (which would, indeed, have made rounding Cape Malea something of a problem), in fact cautiously waiting on events, convinced as they were that the Persians 'would gain a resounding victory and make themselves masters of all Greece'.

The combined fleet which now [27 August] assembled in the three eastern inlets of Salamis 'was larger than it had been at the battle of Artemisium, and made up of ships from more towns'. The question is, how much larger? This remains a matter for dispute, since ancient estimates of the Greeks' fighting strength at Salamis vary considerably. Aeschylus [*Pers.* 339–40] puts the figure at 310. Herodotus [8.48] makes it 380 – though somewhere along the line in his calculations he has left out a twelve-ship squadron, probably belonging to Aegina, so that his accountable figures only total 368. Thucydides [1.74.1] opts for a round 400, of which – or so he makes his speaker claim – the Athenian quota

was something under two-thirds.* Of the three, Aeschylus is most likely
to be correct, and that not merely because he was a contemporary
witness, who fought in the battle himself. The Athenians at Artemisium
had half of their triremes put out of action, and it is improbable that
in so hard-fought an engagement allied losses would be proportionately
less. This would, on paper, reduce the fleet's *effective* strength from 324
to 162. If we add to this latter figure 30 for captured vessels, and
perhaps another net 20 for refits – few of these can actually have been
made seaworthy in time; and how many, one wonders, were actually
towed home on the retreat through the Euripus? – we obtain a total
of 212, and an overall combined strength of 311, which agrees very well
with Aeschylus's estimate. Herodotus and Thucydides, here as elsewhere, appear to give us 'paper strength' figures, which take no account
of battle-casualties.

When the reserve squadrons were in, and the whole effective strength
of the allied Greek navy was concentrated at Salamis, Eurybiades, as
commander-in-chief, at once summoned his senior officers to a staff
conference – the first of many such meetings to be held during the next
three weeks. By the very nature of the case, we can know little of what
was discussed – no minutes were preserved, or, in all likelihood, ever
taken – and that little is highly tendentious. Such veterans as Herodotus
could still interrogate in the 440s had been young recruits at the time of
Salamis, and not privy to the counsels of their elders. What they had
was a worm's-eye view of strategy, compounded from half-understood
orders, the occasional public *bon mot*, and those garbled rumours which
circulate in any camp during a major campaign. Later, their reminis-
cences would have been still further distorted by political prejudice and
local civic pride. To read our sources, one might suppose that the
entire three weeks were spent arguing over whether to fight at Salamis
or the Isthmus; and though this may have been a more fundamental
issue than most modern historians will allow, it is only the actual
conduct of the battle itself which reveals meticulous staff-planning at
every stage. Events can often speak for themselves more eloquently than
their commentators: Salamis is a classic case in point. If we had no other
witness but Herodotus, for example, we might be forgiven for supposing
that Adeimantus, the young, brilliant, quick-tempered Corinthian
admiral, was a fool at the conference table and a pusillanimous coward

* If we take this in reference to the paper strength *at Artemisium*, before casualties,
it is a justified claim. The overall strength of the Artemisium and reserve fleets, 271 +
53 + 57 + an estimated 20 for the original non-Athenian guardships (? mostly Aeginetan) would give a figure of 401. Two-thirds of 400 is 266+, and the total Athenian
contribution (147 + 53 + 57) was 257.

in battle. Yet, curiously, the *facts* are all there; as so often, Herodotus does not so much falsify a man's record of action as damn him with discreditable motives.

On the other hand, his account of that first staff conference may well be substantially accurate (even though he runs it straight into another one which must have taken place eight or nine days later: detailed chronology is never his strong point). As so often, the bald narrative hints at more than it actually states:

... Eurybiades called for suggestions, from anyone who wished to speak, on the most suitable place for engaging the enemy fleet: this, he said, would have to be in some part of Greece which was still under their control – Attica was excluded, as it had already been given up. The general feeling of the council was in favour of sailing to the Isthmus and fighting in defence of the Peloponnese, on the grounds that if they were beaten at Salamis they would find themselves blocked up in an island, where no help could reach them, whereas if disaster overtook them at the Isthmus, they could at least find refuge amongst their own people. This view was, *of course* [my italics], most strongly held by the Peloponnesian officers. [8.49]

Two important points emerge from this passage. In the first place, the atmosphere is one of profound defeatism. Strategical considerations are based on the lacklustre belief that any battle is more likely to be lost than not: this initial premiss granted, they make very good sense. Themistocles, as we shall see, was the only commander at Salamis who worked from the unquestioning assumption of *a Greek victory*: the distinction is based on something more than mere Athenian propaganda, and explains the risks he was always willing to take in pursuit of his goal. He had gained an initial advantage by getting the whole fleet where he wanted it, in defiance of the League; but there were bound to be some commanders, even now, who would argue that, strategically speaking, the League knew its own business best. Shortsighted self-interest – that endemic plague of Greek city-state politics – was undoubtedly the driving motive here: this is the second point which Herodotus's narrative brings out. The meeting split between Athens, Aegina and Megara on the one hand – all with excellent reasons for wanting to hold Salamis – and on the other the Peloponnesian *bloc*, ever prone to embrace an isolationist policy at the expense of allies beyond the Isthmus [cf. Hdt. 8.49.2]. If the Peloponnesians controlled a majority of the votes, Athens and her supporters contributed something like three-quarters of the fleet: it is only too easy to see how a complete deadlock might arise. Appeals to patriotism fell on deaf ears; the most promising line would be one where patriotism and self-interest appeared to coincide. For this, patience and diplomacy were essential. Yet time, the Greeks' most precious commodity, was running perilously short. Themistocles had an unenviable task to perform: small wonder if, on occasion, his temper in debate got the better of him.

At Panopeus, on the frontier between Phocis and Boeotia, Xerxes divided his forces. While the main body advanced on Orchomenus, and thence across the Boeotian plain towards Attica, one division struck west through Daulis and carried out an abortive raid on Delphi. This whole episode bristles with improbabilities, and may even be a fiction invented by the Delphic priests, anxious to rehabilitate their somewhat tarnished reputation after the war was won. According to our sources [Hdt. 8.34–9; Diod. 11.14.2–4; Justin 2.12.8–10] Xerxes detached 4,000 men for the specific purpose of plundering Apollo's shrine, having conceived a lively interest in the accumulated treasures which it contained. However, after burning several towns along the way, these raiders were repulsed from Delphi itself by a series of supernatural manifestations – a 'divine shout' from within the shrine, opportune showers of thunderbolts, gigantic warriors who materialised from nowhere and created havoc in the Persian ranks, and two great rocks which, miraculously, broke loose from Parnassus and came crashing down on them (Ephorus attributes this last phenomenon, more prosaically, to the thunderstorm). Apollo, it was clear, had looked after his own; the men of Delphi duly commemorated the fact with a monument and an inscription:

As a memorial of man-repelling [i.e. defensive] war and a testament to victory
The Delphians set me up, giving thanks to Zeus, who
With Phoebus Apollo thrust back the city-sacking column of Medes
And protected the bronze-crowned sanctuary.

What are we to make of all this? Tradition places responsibility for the raid squarely on Xerxes' shoulders. Yet Delphi's defeatism had served Persia well before the invasion, and some sort of working agreement with the priesthood would be essential on a long-term view. The Great King was neither an iconoclast nor a fool; why should he gratuitously antagonise his Greek allies by so barbaric a gesture? On the other hand, if he *did* intend to plunder the shrine, would he have given up quite so tamely after a single reverse? Some scholars have supposed that the attack was unauthorised (which argues an incredible lack of discipline in the Persian army) and that Xerxes had a secret agreement with Delphi (for which there is no evidence whatsoever). Others, more radically, argue that the entire episode is a fabrication; and in default of other evidence this would seem the likeliest hypothesis.

About the main advance, however, there are no such problems or doubts. All Boeotia had gone over to the enemy. Terms were negotiated partly through King Demaratus, the Great King's Spartan aide, who happened to be a close friend of the Theban oligarchic leader Attaginus; and partly through yet another royal intermediary, the pliable Alexander of Macedon, who placed liaison officers of his own in the various cities 'to make it clear to Xerxes' – but did Xerxes need convincing? – 'that the people of Boeotia were friendly to him'. The Thebans, never averse to making political capital out of national disaster, took care that the stubborn hostility displayed by Thespiae and Plataea, enemies both of Thebes, was brought to the Great King's attention. Their inhabitants, however, had already fled to the Peloponnese, and Xerxes' troops merely destroyed both empty towns. Loyalist Haliartus, south of the great Copaic lake, received similar treatment. The Persians spent about three days in Boeotia; then [? 31 August] they took the road south from Thebes, crossed Cithaeron by the Eleutherae pass (some units may have travelled by way of Oropus and Decelea) and came swarming down, unopposed, into Northern Attica. Two days previously [29 August] the Persian fleet, reinforced by fresh quisling contingents from central Greece and the islands, had anchored in Phaleron Bay – leaving a trail of smoke-blackened coastal villages behind it as far as Sunium – and linked up with Xerxes' advance guard. The Great King would have been less than human had he not felt a sense of triumphant anticipation at this moment. His march from the Dardanelles to Athens had taken him only three months.

The advance through Attica was marked by a policy of wholesale devastation: crops and farms went up in flames, temples and altars were destroyed, statues of the gods overthrown. Xerxes, it seemed, knew only two formulae for dealing with an occupied country, conciliation and terrorism: when one failed, he would try the other. A late fugitive slipped across to Salamis with the news that 'the whole country was ablaze'. One point of resistance, more symbolical than strategic, still remained: the garrison on the Acropolis had, so far, defied all attempts to dislodge it. When the main body of the Persian army entered Athens, Xerxes' officers at once set about dealing with this obstinate and impertinent anomaly. So long as Athena Polias still ruled over her rock, an inspiration and a rallying-point for those across the water, Xerxes could not in all conscience claim Attica as Persian territory. The western end of the rock (later surmounted by the Propylaea) was the only point at which an assault could be made without climbing-irons, and it was here that the defenders had erected their 'wooden wall'. A brigade of archers was posted on the Areopagus rock opposite, and instructed to pepper this barricade with flaming arrows. Their technique proved highly effective: the 'wooden wall' went up in smoke, along with much hopeful oracular exegesis. At this point the Persians sent over a group of Peisistratid *collabos* with truce proposals (curious how that persistent clan never gave up hope of restoration, even after thirty years in the post-Cleisthenic wilderness), but the defenders would not so much as listen to them.

Xerxes now tried tougher methods, at first with little success. A direct assault on the western gate was driven back by skilfully directed boulders and column-drums, which came rolling down the rocky slope, to skittle the attackers like ninepins. Finally [about 5 September] a commando group managed to scale the sheer rock-face, near the sanctuary of Aglaurus, and broke open the gates. Some of the garrison, seeing further resistance was hopeless, threw themselves off the rock, and so perished. Others took sanctuary in the inner shrine of the temple; but the Persians were in no mood, by now, to respect foreign religious scruples. Every suppliant, every living creature – including the priests and priestesses – was butchered.* After carrying out this pogrom, the attackers looted the temple of its valuables (one hardly imagines they found any cash) and then 'destroyed the whole Acropolis by fire'. Absolute master of Athens at last, the Great King proudly sent off a dispatch-rider to announce his triumph in Susa. Yet perhaps he was still not wholly devoid of religious qualms, because next day he summoned the Peisistratids, together with other Athenian exiles who were serving him as liaison officers, and commanded them 'to go up into the Acropolis and offer sacrifice there according to Athenian usage'. This gesture was, I suspect, made in response to shocked protests by the Athenian *ultras* themselves. Of all people, they were the least likely to stomach this shocking piece of Oriental vandalism: it was, after all, their ancestor Peisistratus who had done so much to make the Acropolis a centre of civic and religious pride. Anti-tyrannical propaganda might paint them as monsters or toadies, but in their own eyes they were patriots. After they had offered sacrifice, they could not resist informing Xerxes that the blackened stump of Erechtheus's sacred olive-tree had, overnight, put out a new green shoot eighteen inches long.

Across the straits, in the three main eastern anchorages of Salamis,† the

---

* Ctesias, the Greek doctor at Artaxerxes' court, claimed [§26, Henry p. 31] that a number of the defenders escaped by night: if they did so, it must have been prior to the final assault, concerning which the explicit and detailed testimony of Herodotus [8.53] is hard to gainsay.

† Ambelaki, Paloukia, and the modern naval base: see map, p. 173.

allied fleet lay at readiness. Morale was shaky, to say the least, and seems to have deteriorated still further as time went on. The withdrawal from Artemisium did not exactly provide grounds for optimism. Like Churchill in 1940, Themistocles had little to offer his men at this point but 'blood, toil, tears and sweat', with the additional disadvantage that what we now term the 'Dunkirk spirit' was something quite unknown

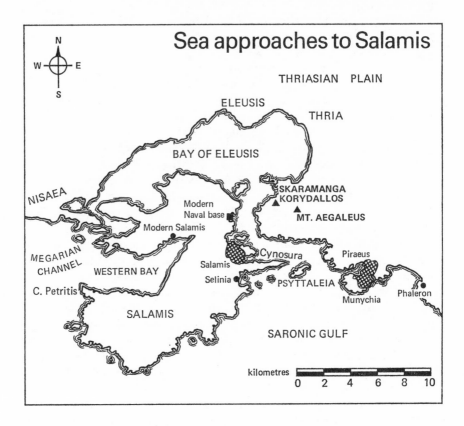

to the Greeks of 480. The appearance of the Persian fleet off Phaleron on 29 August, though long anticipated, caused further alarm and despondency, so that 'the Peloponnesians once more cast their eyes longingly towards the Isthmus'. But nothing, it is safe to say, had so profound a psychological effect on the sailors of the fleet as the burning of Athens and the Acropolis. That lurid glow against the night sky brought their predicament home to them with humiliating clarity. It also encouraged just those centrifugal, *sauve qui peut* instincts which were liable to disrupt even the firmest city-state alliances in a real crisis. When the news came through, some commanders (it would be interesting to know which) did not even wait to discuss it, but 'hurried on board and hoisted sail for immediate flight'. A quorum of those who remained hastily passed a resolution 'to fight in defence of the Isthmus' – which, as Themistocles for one saw, came to very much the same thing: 'Once the fleet leaves Salamis, it will no longer be one country that you'll be fighting for. Everyone will go home, and neither Eurybiades nor anybody else will be able to prevent the total dissolution of our forces.'[4] Cornelius Nepos [*Them.* 4.2], with characteristic Roman bluntness, asserts that 'the greater number recommended withdrawing to their homes and taking refuge within their walls'. We may doubt if this was what they *recommended* – unblushing self-interest has its limits – but it was undoubtedly what most of them had in mind.

Themistocles, anxious at all costs to get this disastrous decision reversed before it was too late, sent a private message to Eurybiades' flagship, saying he had something of great importance to discuss. Eurybiades invited him aboard, and, says Herodotus, 'gave him permission to speak his mind' – a tactful bowing to the inevitable, one feels, since quite clearly nothing short of a universal cataclysm would silence Themistocles once he had committed himself. In any case, he knew Eurybiades' weak points, and played on them. The mere suggestion that a return to the Isthmus would mean the dissolution of the fleet – a risk which Themistocles may well have exaggerated for his own ends – was enough to make the Spartan take very prompt action indeed. He at once summoned his deputy commanders to a second staff conference, with the object of reconsidering the decision taken at the first. This, of course, was exactly what Themistocles wanted. As soon as the meeting assembled – indeed, before Eurybiades had time to announce what it was all about – the Athenian burst into a long and impassioned speech. This violation of protocol drew a sharp rebuke from Adeimantus, the Corinthian admiral, who interrupted to remind Themistocles that 'in the races, the man who starts before the signal is whipped'. 'Yes,' came the lightning retort, 'but those who get off the mark late win no prizes'. For the moment, at least, Adeimantus was silenced, and Themistocles had the floor.

Tact, if nothing else, required him to forget the unflattering arguments he had used on Eurybiades; as Herodotus puts it, in a more than usually charming understatement, 'it would have been unbecoming to accuse any of the confederates actually to their faces'. Instead, he delivered a sharp and cogent lecture on strategy, which shot the whole concept of an 'Isthmus line' to pieces – and, incidentally, disposes of the erroneous notion that Herodotus knew little or nothing of the fundamental issues involved.[5] The speech he puts in Themistocles' mouth is so important that it must be quoted at length:

Take the Isthmus first: if you fight there, it will have to be in the open sea, and that will be greatly to our disadvantage, with our smaller numbers and slower ships. Moreover, even if everything else goes well, you will lose Salamis, Megara, and Aegina. Again, if the enemy fleet comes south, the army will follow it; so you will yourself be responsible for drawing it to the Peloponnese, thus putting the whole of Greece in peril.

Now for my plan: it will bring, if you adopt it, the following advantages: first, we shall be fighting in narrow waters, and that, with our inferior numbers, will ensure our success, provided things go as we may reasonably expect. The open sea is bound to help the enemy, just as fighting in a confined space is bound to help us. Secondly, Salamis, where we have put our women and children, will be preserved; and thirdly – for you the most important points of all – you will be fighting in defence of the Peloponnese by remaining here just as much as by withdrawing to the Isthmus – nor, if you have the sense to follow my advice, will you draw the Persian army to the Peloponnese. If we beat them at sea, as I expect we shall, they will not advance to attack you on the Isthmus, or come any further than Attica; they will retreat in disorder, and we shall gain by the preservation of Megara, Aegina and Salamis – where an oracle has already foretold our victory . . . [8.60].

That this speech also represents Herodotus's own beliefs is shown by his uncompromising comment, in another context [7.139]: 'I cannot myself see what possible use there could have been in fortifying the Isthmus, if the Persians had command of the sea.'

Whether Eurybiades and the Peloponnesian *bloc* were as strategically enlightened is another matter altogether. The constant interruptions, the angry gibes and sneers to which Themistocles was exposed throughout his speech hardly lead one to suppose so. One commander, for example, 'told him to hold his tongue because [since the capture of Attica] he was a man without a country, and tried to prevent Eurybiades from putting any question to the vote at the instance of a mere refugee'. So Herodotus; Plutarch rationalises the objection by explaining that 'a man without a city had no right to press those who still possessed one to abandon it and forsake their country'. The level of discussion is neither more irrational nor more childish than much parliamentary debate in any age; but it has singularly little to do with strategy. What we are dealing with here are the emotional reactions of old-fashioned militarists whose *idées fixes* have been exposed to the winds of change. The simple truth may be that Themistocles was a genius ahead of his time, forced to deal with the normal ruck of stupid and hidebound second-raters – who had, in addition, the endorsement of elected authority for their views. Certainly it was not his display of

strategical expertise which finally won them over – at least in Hero-
tus's opinion – but a desperate threat (brought in when all else failed)
to pull out the entire Athenian contingent and emigrate *en masse* to
southern Italy.* 'Where will you be without the Athenian fleet?' he
asked Eurybiades. Where indeed? The Spartan, however reluctantly,
had seen the writing on the wall. So, preserving the shreds of his
authority as best he could, 'he took the decision to stay where they were
and fight it out at Salamis' – a more momentous choice for the future
of Europe than that dull, well-meaning nonentity can ever have
dreamed when he made it.

This debate had consumed most of the night [5–6 September] and
ended just before dawn. As the sun rose, an earthquake was felt 'both
on land and sea', which the Greeks must surely have taken as an omen
of their decision. They offered up prayers to the gods, and called upon
the tutelary heroes of Salamis and Aegina – Ajax, Telamon, Aeacus and
his sons – to fight by their side. Then, just as modern Greeks are liable,
in times of crisis, to send for the miracle-working ikon of Tenos, they
dispatched a ship to Aegina to fetch the sacred images of Aeacus himself
'and the other Aeacidae'. Nothing could better have symbolised their
new resolve – or, indeed, its fundamentally irrational genesis. This is a
side of the Salamis campaign which, for obvious reasons, gets less attention from modern writers than perhaps it should. When Aeschylus, in
The Persians, makes the Messenger declare to Atossa: 'Some avenging
spirit or evil demon, my lady, began our whole undoing', he is not
indulging in a mere literary figure of speech. For him, as for Herodotus,
gods took the most vigorous and partisan – not to say arbitrary – interest
in human affairs. It was, viewed retrospectively, so brilliant an age that
we tend to forget the naïvety which characterised it. This emerges from
the strategical *niaiseries* of men like Eurybiades no less than the divine
motivation which keeps cropping up in our historical sources. Thucydides and Periclean rationalism are still a whole world away.

Xerxes, meanwhile, had his own problems to contend with. Before he
could force the Isthmus line, he had to neutralise the Greek fleet. His
own land forces were heavily dependent on sea-borne supplies, and the
risk of these supplies being cut off by enemy action was one he could not
afford to take. This being so, either he had to stake everything on a

* The actual place he named was Siris, in the Gulf of Taranto – 'it has long been
ours, and the oracles have foretold that Athenians must live there some day'. Was it?
Had they? The claim is more than doubtful. J. Perret, *Siris* (1941) pp. 128–30,
suggests that Herodotus invented it on behalf of the Ionians of Thurii, who wanted
(*c.* 430) to establish Athenian rights to it in the face of Tarentine aggression.

major battle, or else leave behind a holding squadron strong enough to limit Themistocles' movements at sea. The second of these considerations was automatically ruled out by one simple fact: the Persian navy had been so reduced in size that to divide it now would lose Xerxes numerical superiority [see above, pp. 146–8]. On the other hand, no land-force could ever hope to turn the Greek position at the Isthmus without close naval support. Furthermore, autumn was now coming on, with its equinoctial gales and storms; very soon all naval campaigning would have to stop. This provided a *terminus ante quem* for rapid action of some sort: to let the situation drift on unresolved all winter was out of the question. Everything pointed in one direction: Xerxes would have to fight. If he by-passed Salamis and made straight for the Isthmus, he would be fatally vulnerable to a crushing flank attack. It is clear, however, that he and his admirals had no desire to fight where Themistocles hoped they would – that is, in the narrows of the Salamis strait. They were far from blind to the severe disadvantages this would impose on them; whatever made them take that fatal chance in the end, it was *not* mere strategical obtuseness. Perhaps they hoped that dissension among the Greek leaders would, after all, produce a withdrawal from Salamis (which in fact it well might have done) and break the *impasse* without any need for drastic action on their part. At all events, not until the very last moment, and then only after at least one alternative plan had been tried and found wanting, did they finally commit themselves to a direct trial of strength at sea.

This alternative project, on which Xerxes' engineers busied themselves for about a fortnight [5–17 September][6] was a causeway, or causeways – Plutarch's use of the plural is significant – designed to span the Salamis channel at its narrowest point, and thus provide a bridgehead from which Persian troops could strike directly at allied HQ without confronting the fleet. As Burn well observes, 'the island ... crowded with Athenians, including Athenian troops and the magistrates and councils, represented an important military objective, the capture of which might end the resistance of Athens and bring within sight the end of the war'. Nor is there anything inherently improbable about such an undertaking. The Achaemenids, with unlimited supplies of cheap labour at their disposal, were always partial to large-scale engineering schemes, both civil and military. (Cyrus's damming of the Tigris, Xerxes' own ship-canal through Mt Athos – examples come readily to mind.) Here the Great King was probably influenced by his earlier bridging of the Dardanelles: the Salamis channel must have seemed child's play by comparison. If we accept Pritchett's contention [*Topography* pp. 98–100] that the sea-level in this area has risen by about a fathom since 480, it is not hard to work out how the causeway was planned [see map below]. There were to be three sections. The first would run from Perama (starting near the departure-point of the modern ferry-service) to the smaller of the Pharmakoussae Islands, today a semi-submerged reef, then something approaching a hundred yards in length. The middle link would span the channel between this

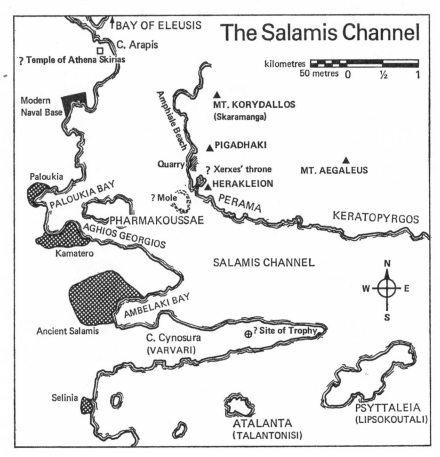

and the larger of the Pharmakoussae, now Aghios Georgios, where Circe was traditionally supposed to be buried. The third section would run from Aghios Georgios to Salamis itself, probably southward across the Kamatero channel, which offers shallower soundings than does Paloukia Bay.

One glance at an Admiralty chart shows us just where the Great King's engineers were liable to encounter real trouble – in the second, mid-channel span, where the depth, even allowing for subsequent changes in sea-level, was nowhere less than 5–6 metres, or nearly twenty feet.[7] The first stage, built as a normal mole or pier, with rocks and a rough stone 'fill', presented no particular problem – though, ironically enough, it must have later contributed to Xerxes' own discomfiture [see below, p. 193]. The central channel, however, as a few preliminary soundings will soon have made clear, demanded radically different methods. Here the Persians seem to have adopted a modified version of their technique at the Dardanelles, 'lashing together a number of Phoenician merchantmen to serve at once for bridge and breakwater'. During this difficult stage in their operation the Greeks – who, it is safe to assume, had occupied Aghios Georgios the moment they reached Salamis – brought up a regiment of Cretan archers, with instructions to harass the construction-team by continual sniping. This device proved so successful (similar tactics later gave Alexander the Great immense trouble at Tyre) that in the end Xerxes was forced to abandon the project altogether. Even now, however, he still shrank from ordering a full-dress confrontation with the Greek fleet. Perhaps on the morning of 16 or 17 September,* he came down to Phaleron and held a general naval conference. According to Herodotus, there was one subject, and one only, on the agenda, 'the propriety of risking a battle at sea'. Subsequent events, however, suggest that Xerxes was still actively canvassing for some alternative to this 'ultimate solution' – and not only found one, but implemented it.

Herodotus's account of what took place at this conference looks, on the face of it, straightforward enough. There sat the Great King's commanders, in strict order of precedence, while Mardonius went round them individually, soliciting their views on the advisability of a naval engagement. All except one, Queen Artemisia of Halicarnassus, were 'unanimously in favour of engaging the Greek fleet'. We are not told their reasons: many, no doubt, simply said what they thought Xerxes wanted them to say. But we *do* hear Artemisia's views, at some length; and very interesting they are. Starting from the premiss of Greek superiority in naval tactics (which would argue against giving battle to

* The chronology of the last week or two before Salamis is very difficult: what does seem clear is that at several vital points Herodotus has, as Hignett says (XIG, pp. 211–12, cf. 215) 'deliberately or unconsciously accelerated the march of events', perhaps in the interests of dramatic unity. (For a notable instance see below, pp. 191–2 and note.) In particular, many of the events which he compresses into the twenty-four hours preceding the battle itself – beginning with the naval conference referred to above – must have been spread over several days: only then do they make any kind of sense (see Hignett, p. 217). For the timing of Sicinnus's mission into the Persian lines see Burn, PG p. 450.

top Xerxes as Crown Prince: detail from the Treasury Frieze at Persepolis. Xerxes stands behind his father Darius, who is holding audience during the New Year Festival.

bottom Persepolis: the east stairway of the Apadana. Sacae or Chorasmians bearing tribute. Their leader is being escorted by a Crown usher in ceremonial attire.

top The 'Serpent Column': originally a memorial consisting of three entwined serpents supporting a golden tripod. Dedicated at Delphi, now in the Hippodrome at Constantinople (see p. 273).

centre The city-walls of ancient Plataea, looking northward across the Theban plain from the lower slopes of Cithaeron. On the skyline, left, Pyrgos Hill.

bottom Aerial view of the Tempe gorge from the south, looking towards the Olympus massif. The line of the road (and the modern railway) is clearly discernible.

them on their own chosen ground) she went on to emphasise that Xerxes in fact had a won game *provided he could control his impatience*. He had already captured Athens ('the main objective of the war'), and the rest of Greece was within his grasp: an exaggeration, but not so great a one as is generally supposed. Then came the Queen's clinching argument, which, again, must be quoted *in extenso*:

... If only you are not in too great a hurry to fight at sea – if you keep the fleet on the coast where it now is – then, whether you stay here or advance into the Peloponnese, you will easily accomplish your purpose. The Greeks will not be able to hold out against you for long: you will soon cause their forces to disperse – they will soon break up and go home. I hear they have no supplies in the island where they now are; and the Peloponnesian contingents, at least, are not likely to be very easy in their minds if you march with the army towards their country – they will hardly like the idea of fighting in defence of Athens. [8.68]

Artemisia wound up her speech with a well-considered strategical warning ('If you rush into a naval action, my fear is that the defeat of your fleet may involve the army too') and a scornful aside on the uneven quality of some of Xerxes' confederate squadrons – not without point, this, though tactless (to say the least of it), and manifestly unfair, as events had already proved [see above, p. 145], in the case of the Egyptians.

What effect did this plain speaking have on Xerxes? Despite the fears of the Queen's friends, who thought she would be executed for speaking out against an attack, the Great King declared himself well pleased: 'He had always considered her an admirable person, but now he esteemed her more than ever.' So indeed he might: she had presented him with the key to an easy and inexpensive victory. Yet (if we are to believe Herodotus) he rejected her advice in favour of the majority verdict, convinced that now he himself was there to supervise operations, his men would no longer shirk their duty as they had done off Euboea. This not only flies in the face of common sense, but is at direct variance with the events – as told by Herodotus himself – which immediately followed. What Xerxes in fact seems to have adopted was a compromise solution. He gave orders for a large army corps – perhaps 30,000 men strong[8] – to set out, that very night, on the road which runs, by way of Eleusis and Megara, to the Isthmus. At the same time he brought up advance squadrons of the fleet from Phaleron, and stationed them in readiness off Salamis. If Artemisia had calculated correctly, this move would either force the Greeks to give battle in the open waters of the Saronic Gulf (where their opponents would enjoy every advantage) or else result in a break-away by the Peloponnesian *bloc*, whose ships could then be mopped up piecemeal as they left the shelter of the Salamis channel.[9]

If Xerxes had hoped to create alarm and dissension in the Greek camp, he undoubtedly succeeded. The Peloponnesians were 'in a state of acute alarm . . . for there they were, waiting at Salamis to fight for Athenian territory, and certain, in the event of defeat, to be caught and blocked up in an island, while their own country was left without defence'. The well-publicised movement of Persian troops towards the Isthmus – they seem to have had orders to carry torches and sing marching-songs as loudly as they could – caused more panic than anything else. Who on Salamis would keep a cool enough head to realise that this *must* be a feint, that without the fleet Xerxes' entire host could accomplish nothing? As Artemisia had pointed out, they were short of provisions. Salamis could not feed them all for more than a very limited period, and one obvious task for that Persian advance corps was to cut their supply-line from Megara. What would happen if Xerxes then blocked all the channels, and waited? Better to pull out while they still could, and fight at the Isthmus, rather than sit there on Salamis, trapped and helpless, until they were starved into ignominious surrender. Some of their fears were groundless; but others – in particular those to do with essential supplies – deserve more serious attention than they normally get from modern scholars.

It was on the evening of 17 September that Xerxes had put his new plan into operation; throughout the following day the Greek camp seethed with rumours and desperate discussion among the rank-and-file:

At first there was whispered criticism of the incredible folly of Eurybiades; then the smothered feeling broke out into open resentment, and another meeting was held. All the old ground was gone over again, one side urging that it was useless to stay and fight for a country which was already in enemy hands, and that the fleet should sail and risk an action in defence of the Peloponnese, while the Athenians, Aeginetans and Megarians still maintained that they should stay and fight at Salamis. [Hdt. 8.74]

Themistocles saw all his well-laid plans in danger of total disruption. With such a line-up in debate there was every likelihood that the Peloponnesian *bloc* would outvote him and his supporters. Plutarch [*Them.* 12.3] pictures him as 'enraged at the prospect that the Greeks might throw away all the advantages of their position in these narrow waters', which we may well believe: if he dismissed the wretched Eretrian admiral as a cuttlefish ('all sword and no guts') who can blame him? Yet even if he somehow contrived to secure a majority of the votes, that did not necessarily mean he would get the crews to obey him. If we can believe Ephorus, they were by now in a near-mutinous mood, and, understandably, hell-bent on getting away to the Isthmus as soon as possible. Eurybiades and Themistocles gave them a pep-talk, and were hooted down for their pains [Diod. 11.16.1]. At the same time, Xerxes' strategy had taken a dangerous turn which no one seems to have anticipated.

Themistocles therefore had two urgent and simultaneous problems to solve. He must take *effective* action, not only to block any projected withdrawal by the Peloponnesian contingents, but also to ensure that they fought where and when he planned that they should; and he must somehow tempt Xerxes into making the one move which might lead to a Greek victory – that is, ordering his fleet to attack *in the Salamis channel*. It has been suggested (e.g. by Hignett, XIG p. 406) that when the Greeks refused to come out and fight in the open waters of the Saronic Gulf, Xerxes, finally, had no option but to extract them from their sheltered position by main force. This ignores the fact (undoubtedly uppermost in many Greek sailors' minds) that the Persians could get what they wanted far more easily by blockading the land and sea approaches to Salamis, and then waiting for starvation to put their opponents in a more reasonable frame of mind.

The device Themistocles finally adopted – what Plutarch calls 'his celebrated trick with Sicinnus' – is one of the most enigmatic episodes in all Greek history. Evidence for it goes back as far as Aeschylus's *Persians*, performed only eight years after Salamis. Yet at least three reputable scholars[10] have argued that 'the whole story was unhistorical, a legend without foundation', and many more, while accepting it as fact, have found it, as did Macan, 'the most highly problematic of all the antecedents of the battle'. What seems to have happened was this. At some point during the long argument over final strategy, Themistocles, anticipating defeat, slipped away from the conference and sent for his children's tutor, 'the most faithful of his slaves', an Asiatic Greek named Sicinnus.[11] This man was given a carefully prepared message, or letter, to deliver to Xerxes, and sent off across the straits in a small boat, probably just before dawn on 19 September. He does not appear to have had audience with the Great King in person: Herodotus's narrative suggests that he contacted some responsible officer, without even leaving his boat – a wise precaution – and then, 'his message delivered . . . lost no time in getting away', vanishing into the dawn mists as swiftly and silently as he had come. It was a daring exploit; Sicinnus well deserved the riches and – for him, perhaps, more important – the citizenship of Thespiae which Themistocles afterwards obtained on his behalf.

The substance of the message was as follows. Themistocles sent it under his own name, as commander of the Athenian contingent: he had, he told Xerxes, changed sides, and was now ardently desirous of a Persian victory. (No reason is given for this *volte-face*, though disgust at the attitude of the Peloponnesian contingents would provide a strong enough motive to carry conviction.) The Greek allies were at each others' throats, and would offer no serious opposition – 'on the contrary, you will see the pro-Persians amongst them fighting the rest'. Furthermore, they were planning a general withdrawal from Salamis under cover of darkness, to be carried out the following night. *Sauve qui peut* panic was the main motive for this operation, but it also had a sound strategical purpose: to link up with the Peloponnesian land-forces at the Isthmus. If Xerxes struck at once, on the divide-and-rule principle, he could forestall such a move. 'Attack them and destroy their naval power, while they are still disorganised and before they have joined forces with their land army' [Plut. *Them.* 12.4]. The conquest of the Peloponnese would then become a comparatively simple matter. On the other hand, if Xerxes allowed the various Greek contingents to slip through his fingers and disperse homewards, the war might drag on indefinitely, since he would have to deal with each separate city-state in turn. Sicinnus's arguments impressed the Persian admirals, and they duly passed them on to the Great King himself. Xerxes, we are told, believed the report because it 'was in itself plausible' – and also because it was just what he *wanted* to hear: there was trouble brewing in Ionia and the empire, and the sooner this Greek expedition was wound up, the better. Themistocles, always a shrewd judge of human nature, knew very well that after so many days of delay and frustration, the Great King would grasp at anything which seemed to offer a quick solution to his problem.

Such is the traditional story; and though it may well be true in essence, there are some very odd features about it. Was the dispatch of Sicinnus *really* a spur-of-the-moment device, put into operation by Themistocles without reference to the Greek High Command? The man in the ranks may have thought so; Themistocles' fellow-commanders almost certainly knew better. Like many other details of the Salamis campaign, this hints at most carefully concerted strategy – which, in turn, has been thought to discredit the whole tradition of a would-be Peloponnesian retreat to the Isthmus. (Burn suggests that the rumours of dissension and cowardice were carefully prepared propaganda: a more convincing argument than Hignett's blunt assertion that men who were ready to retreat one day would not fight bravely the next.) But intelligent staff-work, at operational level, by no means always implies strategic agreement among the top brass, and I am inclined to accept this fundamental split between the allies as historical fact. Themistocles' opponents could, after all, appeal to the authority of the League: trumping *that* ace must have really taxed his ingenuity. On the other hand his message to Xerxes, as reported, is remarkable for one quite extraordinary omission. The whole success of such a ruse depended on getting Xerxes' fleet into the narrows: *yet nowhere is it suggested that the Great King should order this crucial move.* Indeed, positive strategical recommendations of any kind are conspicuous by their absence. Aeschylus and Ephorus dispense with them altogether. Herodotus's version of the message merely urges Xerxes not to let the Greeks slip through his fingers; Justin's asserts that he 'should be able to capture the Greek forces very readily now they were all concentrated in one spot'. In Plutarch (*v.supr.*) and Nepos an attack is advised, *tout court*, but without the barest suggestion as to *how* it should be carried out. Perhaps Themistocles went on the assumption that any direct prescriptive advice would be automatically suspect; but to give battle within the straits was a far from obvious decision – a blockade would have served the Persians' purpose far better – and the chances of Xerxes doing so unprompted must have seemed minimal.

Other *a priori* objections are perhaps more apparent than real. Herodotus gives a fuller version of the incident than Aeschylus, but this does not necessarily mean that Aeschylus wrote down all he knew: the two accounts can be reconciled without undue trouble. It has also been argued that Xerxes would never have stopped a Greek withdrawal to the Isthmus, since the fleet (as Themistocles had foreseen) would almost certainly disperse after such a move: why not let the enemy do your work for you?* This theory, so attractive at first sight, can only be maintained by ignoring the direct testimony of our later sources, which emphasise the dangers of a link-up between the Greek fleet and the Greek army. It also disregards the element of vainglory in Xerxes' character. 'Like the Czar Alexander at Austerlitz, he threw away the advantages gained by sound and cautious strategy in the vain hope of a brilliant victory' [HWComm, vol. 2, p. 381]. More puzzling, certainly, is the apparent readiness with which Xerxes accepted Athens' supposed change of allegiance. As Hignett says, the Persians 'knew that the Athenians were their bitterest enemies and that their enmity must have been intensified by the recent devastation of their land and the destruction of their temples'. Yet they accepted Sicinnus's story at once, without checking it, and did not even detain him for close interrogation. Even if

---

* That Xerxes was not in principle averse to such methods we know from his treatment of grain ships passing through the Dardanelles: see Hdt. 7.147, and above, p. 78.

later Greek history does provide some striking parallels, this kind of *simpliste* credulity arouses one's suspicions, especially when contrasted with Persian canniness at Artemisium. Yet such an attitude may, in the last resort, have been induced by cynicism rather than naïvety. Xerxes' experience during this campaign, not least in Phocis and Boeotia, might well have convinced him that any Greek state's resentment against Persia ran a very poor second to the implacable hatred it reserved for its own neighbours and rivals: why should Athens be any kind of exception to this rule?

If Sicinnus's message reached the Persian lines shortly before dawn on 19 September, Xerxes is unlikely to have made up his mind what to do about it until mid-morning, at the earliest. An intelligence bonanza of this magnitude demanded, and doubtless got, top-level analysis by the Persian High Command. Was the information genuine? And if so, what should be done about it? On the first question, Xerxes' reaction is clear: he believed Sicinnus. Why should he not have done? Northern Greece had been full of venal and cowardly trimmers; Salamis, it now appeared, was about to repeat the same pattern. Once again Xerxes' enemies were more concerned with knifing each other than holding a united front against the barbarian. Strategically, too, the situation must have looked very tempting. The Greeks did indeed appear unwilling to give battle – at any rate outside the straits. When Xerxes had pushed his squadrons forward the day before there was no attempt at interception. A withdrawal by night was, therefore, entirely plausible. Indeed, given the element of surprise, it might well have succeeded. Xerxes' squadrons – surprising though this may be to a modern reader – did *not* normally patrol all night (when they do, it is a matter for special comment), but put back into Phaleron during the hours of darkness. Any attempt to pull out was bound to rely heavily on this omission. The average speed of a trireme at night did not, in all likelihood, exceed four knots,* especially if secrecy was to be observed: the noise of oars – nearly two hundred to a ship – moving in unison must have been considerable. For the Greeks to get well clear of Salamis into the Saronic Gulf, and beyond reach of pursuit (whether through the Bay of Eleusis or down past Psyttáleia) would, therefore, take a good six hours. They could not set out before dusk – say about 9 p.m. – without betraying their movements. By midnight they were unlikely to have got further than the mouth of the Megarian channel or the southern tip of Salamis itself; and their

* N. G. L. Hammond, JHS 76 (1956) 51–2, would put the figure even lower, at three knots, which seems excessively cautious: even a merchantman made as good an average speed. In general Hammond's nautical and topographical data are of the greatest value.

situation then would be doubly vulnerable because of the moon, which had risen some time earlier, and on 19–20 September was at the full.

In other words, the success of such a withdrawal was wholly dependent on maintaining perfect security: the slightest leakage of information would turn it, literally, into a death-trap. The prospect of springing this trap was so delectable that Xerxes and his officers never (it would seem) asked themselves whether the leak might not have been deliberate. Even so, discussion seems to have gone on well into the afternoon, while an overall battle-strategy was worked out. At last Xerxes issued his fleet orders.[12] Four crack squadrons were already cruising off the eastern channel, for the second day in succession, in case the Greek fleet should, after all, risk an engagement. One of these squadrons, the Egyptian, was now ordered to peel off westward, round Cape Petritis, and block the Megara channel, while two more were to close up on either side of Psyttáleia, guarding, as Aeschylus says, 'the exits and narrow sea-races'. Yet another was to patrol off the southern coast. Herodotus is quite specific about the object of these movements: it was 'to prevent the escape of the Greek fleet from the narrow waters of Salamis, and there to take revenge upon it for the battles at Artemisium'. Whether the Egyptians set out immediately, or, like the rest, waited for nightfall is uncertain. If they had been patrolling off south-east Salamis when they got their new orders, they could have made the fifteen-mile journey in about four hours. Since midnight was Xerxes' deadline [Hdt. 8.76], they probably took off at some point between seven and eight. At the same time, just before dusk, an infantry force four hundred strong was landed on Psyttáleia, 'because,' as Herodotus says, 'it lay right in the path of the impending action, and once the fighting began, most of the men and damaged vessels would be carried on to it'. This is the first indication we get that Xerxes meant to force a battle in the narrows.

All these manoeuvres were carried out in complete silence. Once the blockade was complete, the main Persian fleet could, as Plutarch says, be 'manned at leisure'; but meanwhile it was vital that the Greeks should not be alarmed by any unusual activity at sea. The slightest hint of a 'leak', and they were liable (or so Xerxes' staff-officers assumed) to cancel the entire operation at short notice. It was equally important that the blockade should be one hundred per cent effective. When Xerxes' commanders received their orders, they learnt that

> if the Greeks should contrive
> To slip their ships through the cordon, and so escape
> Their evil doom, each captain would lose his head

– a provision which doubtless led to considerable stringency in the posting of lookouts. There are grounds for supposing [Hdt. 8.76, cf. Rados, p. 282] that these squadrons actually withdrew from Salamis to Phaleron before dusk, in accordance with normal usage; it was perhaps now that the Egyptians unobtrusively slipped away on their long haul towards Nisaea [see map, p. 168]. Aeschylus gives us a graphic picture of the crews going ashore for dinner that evening, each man leaving his oar 'clewed by its thong to the well-trimmed thole' (Greek practice, no doubt, but probably just as true of Persians).

> But when the sunlight faded, and night came on,
> Then every oarsman hastened back
> To his ship, and the men-at-arms went aboard as well,
> And crew cheered crew in the long ships of war –

the squadrons having been carefully posted, as Ephorus reveals, on a territorial basis, so that 'speaking the same language and knowing one another, the several contingents might assist each other with alacrity'.

> Each vessel sailed as soon as it was manned,
> And hour by hour the fleet patrolled the night.

By midnight at the latest the Persians had sealed off the western entrance to the Bay of Eleusis, established their patrols in the Saronic Gulf, and 'blocked the whole [eastern] channel as far as Munychia'. Now it was merely a matter of waiting until the Greeks – demoralised, anarchic, at loggerheads with one another: ripe for surrender or betrayal – came straggling out into the superbly efficient ambush that had been laid for them.

What, meanwhile, was happening in the Greek camp on Salamis? According to Herodotus (whose account is contaminated with the most blatant anti-Themistoclean bias) the admirals were 'still at loggerheads'. In other words, on the very night before Salamis, they were *still* debating whether or not they should retreat to the Isthmus. This may have remained a hot topic for lower-deck strategists, but by now the High Command had surely settled it to their own satisfaction. Apart from the intrinsic unlikeliness of Herodotus's assertion, what nails it as pure romance is the disciplined tactical coordination which these supposedly dissentient commanders displayed a few hours later. The battle of Salamis was *planned*, down to the last detail; its complex strategy could never have been put through without long and painstaking preparation. Once again, our record would seem to be compounded from the fanciful anecdotes of young rankers, and spiteful conservative propaganda – the latter designed to exaggerate (whether by puff or smear) the not very glorious role which Athens' landed gentry played at this crisis in her history. Their record since Marathon had been worse than reactionary, it had been demonstrably *wrong*, all along the line: flat opposition to naval development, unswerving support for a land-based defence policy. One name which we find closely associated with this movement is that of Aristeides. When Themistocles and the naval party proposed appropriating funds from the Laurium silver-strike to build new triremes [see above, p. 55], it was Aristeides who led the opposition – and was ostracised for his pains. No group, especially one so influential and upper-crust, cares to be remembered solely as a collective repository of error. In the decades which followed, the conservatives worked hard – and successfully – both to denigrate Themistocles' achievements, and, *per contra*, to glorify the role which they themselves (symbolised, as it were, by Aristeides) played at Salamis. This is the tradition which Herodotus was carefully fed in Athens, and which passed into most of our sources. Disentangling the truth from this web of fiction is a well-nigh impossible job; the best we can do is eliminate the more patent fabrications.

The determined effort to present Aristeides as a 'hero of Salamis' begins (quite literally) very early in the day. At some point after midnight, we are told,[13] he reached Greek headquarters from Aegina, having slipped through the Persian patrols with a single trireme, and sent a private message to Themistocles (who was still in conference) asking for a word with him. When the Athenian admiral came out, Aristeides at once embarked on a sanctimonious speech about the need for them to drop their personal feud at this moment of crisis. Themistocles (who, one might suppose, had more urgent things to do at such a time than listen to third-rate rhetoric) heard Aristeides out with patience. His reply, as recorded by Plutarch, has that special oily humility characteristic of the Buchmanite convert: 'I would not have chosen to be outdone by you, Aristeides. But I admire the example you have set me and I shall try to follow it and to do better still in future.' After this Aristeides got down to business. The Greeks, he said, were entirely surrounded. Themistocles greeted the news with evident delight, at the same time taking care to explain that 'it was I who was responsible for this move of the enemy'. He then asked Aristeides to pass on his information to the other commanders in person – 'if I tell them, they will think I have invented it and will not believe me'. Aristeides duly obliged, but even so his audience remained incredulous 'until a Tenian warship, commanded by Panaetius, the son of Sosimenes, deserted from the Persian navy and came in with a full account of what had occurred'.

The first point that must strike anyone about this anecdote is that

Aristeides' part in it could be eliminated altogether without disturbing the historical record. Even on Herodotus's showing, what forced the Greeks into action was full and circumstantial intelligence supplied by a deserter from the enemy, who was surely in a far better position to assess Xerxes' strategy than a mere casual blockade-runner. If Aristeides *did* arrive with such a tale, the Greek admirals could hardly be blamed for doubting his word. How did he *know*? If he had sailed up past Cape Petritis, and turned into Western Bay (travelling thence across the neck of the island on foot) he *might* have observed the Egyptian squadron off Nisaea, by moonlight; but that would hardly make him an authority on conditions in the eastern channel. Besides, it has been calculated [Hammond, *op. cit.*, pp. 51–2] that if he took this route, he could hardly have reached Greek HQ before 4 a.m. It is incredible that Themistocles – with or without the connivance of his fellow-commanders – should only have learnt about the success of this carefully planned deception through casual informants, and at so late an hour. In fact the whole coastline, from Cynosura to Cape Petritis, must have been swarming with look-outs: one imagines a constant stream of messages being relayed throughout the night. It was essential to pin-point the Persian fleet's movements; in particular, to have early warning of any nocturnal infiltration into the Salamis strait.* In this connection it is safe to say that the Persians were *not* the only people (as is generally assumed) to be up and at the oar all night. At least two guard-squadrons must have been posted by the Greeks, off Ambelaki and in the eastern end of the Megarian channel.

What really shows up the Aristeides episode as an Athenian fabrication, however, promoted *ad maiorem nobilitatis gloriam*, is the alternative, and equally fictitious, version provided by Ephorus [Diod. 11.17.3–4]. Clearly, the identity of 'the man who told Themistocles' was a convenient blank, to be filled in according to local preference. In Ephorus, the commanders of the Ionian contingents send over a Samian swimmer with the good news – and a promise that 'in the course of the battle they were going to desert from the barbarian' [see below, p. 194], which is supposed to have improved Greek morale enormously. Here we can detect the grinding of a different propaganda axe. Ephorus – that loyal

* I do not subscribe to the once-popular view (demolished by Goodwin, revived by Beloch and, most recently, Hignett, XIG p. 219 ff.) that the Persians successfully entered the straits during the night, their main object being to 'cut the exit into the Bay of Eleusis'. Apart from the manifest improbabilities of such a scheme – it could only succeed if the Greeks posted no patrols, and in any case the obvious point at which to block the Bay of Eleusis was its western channel – it clashes with the evidence of Aeschylus, *Pers.* 398 ff. For further arguments and a brief survey of literature see Burn, PG pp. 456–7 and n. 13.

Cymaean – is anxious, in retrospect, to exculpate the Eastern Greeks who fought with Xerxes. Both stories have an identical motivation; both are equally worthless as history. But the prize for sheer gratuitous malice must undoubtedly go to that anonymous Athenian propagandist who accused Themistocles of sacrificing three of Xerxes' nephews, just before the fleets engaged, to Dionysus the Flesh-Eater [Plut. *Arist.* 9; *Them.* 13; *Pelop.* 21]. This *canard*, picked up and perpetuated by Phaenias of Lesbos – 'who was', says Plutarch defensively, 'a philosopher and well-read in history besides' – shows to what lengths a smear-campaign could be carried by the aristocracy when it felt its funda-mental beliefs were in danger. It also illustrates the hazards attendant upon slapdash historical libel. Where were suitable prisoner-victims to be found? With superb insouciance, our propagandist solved his problem by transferring the capture of Psyttáleia [see below, p. 196] from its proper context at the climax of the battle to a point well before it. This is just as well, since otherwise some ultra-conservative historian would be sure to argue, sooner or later, that Themistocles was, in fact, the murderous ogre his enemies made him out to be.

Hour after hour, weary but vigilant, the Persians held their stations off Salamis, watching and waiting for the mass break-out that never came. As Burn says, 'long before dawn the Persian admirals must have had an uneasy suspicion that they had been fooled; but it was impossible now to call off the operation'. It was indeed. Communication, in the dark, between several widely scattered squadrons could be achieved neither quickly nor effectively; even after sunrise it would take at least an hour, probably longer, to pass countermanding orders throughout the entire fleet. Furthermore, such orders must, ultimately, originate from Xerxes himself, as Commander-in-Chief; and the Great King, having conceived a grandiose vision of destroying his opponents' navy in a single engagement, was unlikely to abandon it without a blow being struck. The Persian admirals, knowing this, were – if forced to make up their own minds in a sudden emergency – more likely to attack and damn the consequences rather than face their imperial master's wrath for refusing battle. What Themistocles was banking on was Xerxes' vanity and impatience, coupled with his officers' serf-like fear of him, and his determination that the information Sicinnus brought *must* be true. In such circumstances, after the strung-up expectancy of a night at sea – but at no other time – an apparent break-away by the Greeks, *in broad daylight*, far from being ignored as the trap it so obviously was, would precipitate a hysterical, eleventh-hour assault. Themistocles had to time his crucial movement for that dawn hour of depression and uncertainty: too soon, and Xerxes' strategy would go through as planned; too late, and the entire operation was liable to be called off.

Shortly before first light the Greek crews were assembled, and given the customary exhortation by their respective commanders. By far the most memorable speech, we are told, was that which Themistocles made to the Athenians, in which 'the whole burden of what he said was a comparison of the nobler and baser parts of human nature, and an exhortation to the men to follow the former in the coming ordeal'. Though his actual words are not extant they became legendary: they caught and fired his listeners' hearts as surely as Churchill's great 'Blood, toil, tears and sweat' speech fired Britain in the dark days of 1940. It is a guess – but a plausible guess – that the 'great shout' of encouragement described by Aeschylus's Persian messenger in fact enshrines the peroration of that famous address:

> On, sons of Greece! Strike for the honour and freedom
> Of country, children, wives, graves of your forefathers,
> Ancestral gods: all, all are now at stake.

Themistocles did not, as is often assumed, address the entire Greek fleet, nor does Herodotus say he did; this would, in any case, have raised practical difficulties, since the squadrons were at some distance from one another [see map, p. 173]. The Corinthians held a detached station towards the northern end of the narrows, where the modern naval base is now situated, while the Megarians and Aeginetans lay in Ambelaki Bay. Between, along the Paloukia beaches, and sheltered by Aghios Georgios Island, were ranged the squadrons of the main fleet: Athenians on the left of the line, with contingents from the Peloponnese and the islands beyond them, and Eurybiades, as admiral-in-chief, holding the 'station of honour' on the right. When the speeches were over, the crews went aboard, fiercely elated and determined, and the Greek fleet at last stood out to sea.[14]

Just what happened during those first few crucial moments of the engagement is a matter for conjecture. Paradoxically enough, and despite its momentous importance, Salamis must be regarded as one of the worst-documented battles in the whole history of naval warfare. Aeschylus gives us the invaluable personal impressions of a participant who also happens to be a superb dramatist. Herodotus and Plutarch make do with a series of *pointilliste* combat anecdotes. Strabo and Pausanias supply a few topographical details. The only coherent tactical narrative is provided by the late (and generally despised) scissors-and-paste historian Diodorus, who, most scholars agree, based his account on that of Ephorus (c. 405–330 BC). Polybius, with some experience in such matters, went on record as saying that Ephorus 'seems to understand naval tactics' [12.25, cf. Burn PG, p. 10]. On Salamis, at least, his evidence must carry weight; at least he makes some attempt to understand the rationale of what was going on. Yet neither he nor our earlier sources fully clarify the way in which battle came to be joined. Since, on the face of it, Xerxes had excellent reasons not to engage at all, this problem demands close scrutiny. We *know* that the Persians were lured forward into the narrows between Aghios Georgios and Perama; their decision to attack has been variously criticised by modern scholars (though always along the same lines) as anything from 'a somewhat risky movement' to 'an act of stark lunacy'. Though the wisdom of hindsight can often be detected in such pronouncements, Xerxes' decision – so perfectly calculated to give the Greeks every possible advantage – is undoubtedly baffling. How did it come about?

Let us briefly review the Persian position. They had been given to understand, by a false message which they eagerly accepted, that the Greeks were demoralised and bent only on flight: better still, that some contingents would switch sides when it came to a showdown. The Megarian channel was effectively blocked, a move which in all likelihood was not yet known to the Greek High Command. Greek inactivity during the night could be interpreted as one more sign of low morale; we know from Aeschylus [*Pers.* 390 ff.] how taken aback the Persians were when they discovered, too late, the true mettle of their adversaries:

> Then fear gripped hold of us: our expectations
> Faded away –

but by then, of course, they were irrevocably committed, as squadron after squadron came crowding into the narrows: to call off the attack was a sheer physical impossibility. To begin with, however, the deception had to be maintained: on this the whole hope of a Greek victory depended. There was one way, and one only, in which the Persians could be confirmed in their disastrously mistaken beliefs, and that was by a simulated flight on the part of the Greeks. There is, in fact, evidence that such a movement took place – and was duly misinterpreted, not only by the Persians, but by a good many Greeks as well (evidence of good security?). Herodotus states, without any explanatory comment, that at the beginning of the action the Greek triremes 'checked their way and began to back astern'. Even more suggestive is the libellous story he recounts, at some length, concerning the Corinthian admiral Adeimantus.

Adeimantus was afterwards accused, by Athenian ill-wishers, of hoisting sail, right at the beginning of the battle, and making off north, with his squadron, towards the Bay of Eleusis. When they were near the temple of Athena Skiras (that is, off the north-east quarter of the island, beyond Cape Arapis, and more or less opposite Skaramanga) they were hailed by a strange boat. Those aboard her called out: 'Adeimantus, while you are playing the traitor by running away with your squadron, the prayers of Greece are being answered, and she is victorious over her enemies.' After some initial show of incredulity, the tale goes on, Adeimantus and his squadron put about to rejoin the main fleet, but arrived after the battle was over. Even Herodotus found this Athenian libel a little hard to swallow; and small wonder. It was not merely that the Corinthians themselves dismissed it as a lie, asserting that their ships 'played a most distinguished part in the battle'; the rest of Greece, as Herodotus admitted, gave evidence in their favour, while the epitaphs on those Corinthians who died at Salamis, and, latterly, on Adeimantus himself, do not sound like whitewashing jobs designed to hush up notorious cowardice. How did such a grotesque story ever get started? Burn [PG, p. 445] almost certainly has the correct answer: 'Adeimantus and his men, on the day of battle and in the face of the enemy, carried out a very peculiar manoeuvre, which probably not only deceived the enemy to his ruin, but was open to misunderstanding by the Athenian rank and file.'

It is not hard to deduce the nature of that manoeuvre. We have to make a clear distinction here (as so often in Herodotus) between the observed facts, which are seldom in dispute, and the causes or motives attributed to them. What some Athenians actually *saw*, from their position towards the left of the Greek line, was that Corinth's fifty triremes had hoisted sail (which was only done in panic flight or for long journeys, never before joining battle) and were bearing away northward as fast as they could go. So much was known: misinterpretation soon followed, to become ever more elaborate as time went on. Many veterans present that day – on both sides – must have recalled, instantly, what started the defeat at Lade in 494: the defection of the Samians, who 'abandoned their place in the line, *got sail on their vessels*, and made for home' [Hdt. 6.14]. The behaviour of the main Greek fleet at Salamis did not, on the face of it, belie such a notion. Something over two hundred strong, it needed space in which to deploy for action, and this it could only find across the mile-wide section of the strait between Paloukia and Amphiale beach, north of the Pharmakoussae. The number of triremes to a mile in close-order line abreast formation has been variously calculated;* seventy, with intervals of 35–50 feet, would

---

* See Rados, p. 325 ff., followed by Hignett, XIG p. 227 (80 to the mile), cf. Tarn, JHS 28 (1908) 219; Grundy p. 396 (20 yds frontage per trireme); Keil, *Antike Schlachtfelder*, vol. 4, p. 103, n. 1 (15 metres frontage); Custance, *War at Sea* (1919) p. 13 (100 yds frontage); Hammond, *op. cit.*, p. 50 with notes (50 ft intervals, or 63 to the mile); Burn, PG p. 457 (66–70 to the mile; cf. n. 15).

seem a fair estimate. Since the southern channel between Aghios Georgios Island and Salamis was too shallow for efficient navigation [see above, pp. 172-3] these Athenian and Peloponnesian squadrons would move out from Paloukia Bay in a north-easternly direction, *as though following the Corinthians.* The line they finally took up, according to Ephorus, ran from Salamis (i.e. the northern end of Paloukia) across to the Herak-leion, a shrine situated near Xerxes' mole [see map, p. 173]. But before they could do so they had to redeploy from perhaps nine columns in line ahead to three in line abreast. Under optimum conditions this was a tricky movement to execute, and doubtless the expert Athenian crews could give it a convincing air of confusion and inefficiency. If the Aeginetans and Megarians emerged from the shelter of Ambelaki Bay at this early stage (which is a debatable point) we may guess that they, too, swung away northwards during those first few crucial moments.

To the Persians already at sea, resting on their oars off Psyttáleia and Cynosura and all along the Attica coast towards Piraeus, these enemy movements can have meant very little. Indeed, few of Xerxes' captains were in a position to see them at all. Only those holding a station immediately east of Psyttáleia can have had the faintest idea what was happening, and even then their angle of vision was severely limited by the two Pharmakoussae Islands. The remainder had nothing more exciting in view than Cynosura Point, Aghios Georgios Island, and the dull coastline of Perama. Wherever the decision to attack originated, it was certainly not (as Burn for one apparently thinks) with some nervous admiral in the fleet. Because all our sources (except Ephorus) approach Salamis at what one may term petty-officer level is no reason why we should do the same. This does less than justice to Xerxes and his High Command, who at least realised that no one could adequately control such an operation unless they were in a position to see what was going on. They therefore established a general command-post on the lower slopes of Mt Aegaleus, above the mole and the Herakleion [see map, p. 173], which, says Plutarch [*Them.* 13.1] enabled Xerxes *to overlook his fleet and its order of battle.* Precisely: the fact that our sources portray this scene in subtly comic terms should not blind us to its fundamental significance. The golden throne, set on Byron's 'rocky brow', may have been a mere touch of typical Oriental flamboyance; but the crowds of busy aides and secretaries ('whose duty it was to record the events of the battle' – and, we may guess, to keep operational HQ in constant touch with the fleet) sound efficient as well as authentic. From here – and from nowhere else, except a point midway along Cynosura – one can survey the whole panoramic sweep of the Salamis channel; and it was from here, soon after dawn on 20 September, that Xerxes and his staff-officers saw the Greek fleet, in apparent disorders, streaming northward towards the Bay of Eleusis. *Why northward?* Why towards a cul-de-sac from which there was no escape? We can imagine the sudden exhilaration among that tense, exhausted group of men as some excited officer jumped to the obvious conclusion, the conclusion that Themistocles had meant him to draw – 'They don't know the Megara channel's blocked' – while like an electric current the thought ran through every mind: '*We've got them*'. No time for sober reflection now; amid a flurry of near-hysterical excitement Xerxes himself, as Commander-in-Chief, issued the fatal fleet-order to his High Admiral: 'Advance against the enemy.'

From Xerxes' command-post a messenger rode off along the coast (perhaps as far as Keratopyrgos) where the advance units of the fleet lay waiting. Squadron by squadron, the Persians deployed into line-abreast battle formation: Phoenicians on the right wing, Ionians and Hellespontine Greeks on the left, with contingents from Caria, Pamphylia, Lycia, Cilicia and Cyprus holding the centre. Their vessels – unlike the triremes of the mainland Greeks – were decked throughout, with high prows and sterns. This enabled them to carry a large complement of *epibatae* [marines] and archers: thirty or forty, as against a mere fourteen (with four archers) for the Athenians. Since we know from Herodotus [6.15.1] that the Chians, too, carried forty *epibatae*, it is likely that Xerxes' whole Ionian contingent was similarly equipped. Whatever advantage in manpower such top-heavy overloading may have given the Persians, it made their vessels dangerously unmanageable in bad weather. At present there was no more than a light south breeze blowing (of which the Corinthian squadron must have taken advantage); but in an hour or two – as local weather-experts could well have predicted from cloud formations – a heavy cross-channel swell would come rolling in northward past Psyttáleia, only dying out in the bend of the strait beyond the Pharmakoussae.[15] One good reason for Themistocles to refuse battle until the last possible moment was his foreknowledge of this swell, and of the disastrous effect that a choppy sea might well have on Xerxes' warships.

So the entire Persian fleet surged forward to the attack, moving up-channel on a mile-wide front between Perama and the Cynosura promontory, under the vigilant eye of Xerxes and his staff. As each squadron entered the strait, others moved up behind them from Munychia and the Saronic Gulf, crowding the narrow channels on either side of Psyttáleia: a peculiarly disastrous manoeuvre, since it at once precluded any chance of an organised withdrawal. But withdrawal, it is safe to say, was the last thing Xerxes had in mind at that moment: he sat there on his golden throne, monarch – as he thought – of all he surveyed, complacently awaiting the kill. What happened next has been described with brilliant panache by Aeschylus, from the viewpoint of a combatant aboard one of Xerxes' front-line vessels. As they approached the narrows, with Ambelaki Bay ahead on the port quarter, their quarry – hitherto so elusive and disorganised – abruptly dropped all pretence of flight and, with lethal speed and competence, deployed for immediate action:

> An echoing shout of battle, like some triumph-song
> Went up from each Greek throat, and shrilly rang
> Reverberating from the island crags.
> Then fear gripped hold of us: our expectations
> Faded away. This sacred battle-hymn
> Did not betoken flight, but stubborn courage
> Impetuous for attack. A trumpet sounded,
> And at that note their men were fired to action –
> With measured beat the oars fell all together,
> Sweeping the foam back at the one command,
> And soon they all were clearly visible.
> First their right wing, advancing in close order
> And well-aligned, led on; next the main fleet
> Stood out against us.
>
> [*Pers.* 388–401]

This is just as we would expect. While the Athenian and Peloponnesian squadrons were still moving into position north of the Pharmakoussae, the Aeginetans and Megarians came thrusting out from Ambelaki* at full speed, great bronze rams agleam in the morning sunlight, ready to close on the Ionians' exposed left flank as they advanced past the Salamis headland. This detached contingent, reasonably described by Aeschylus as the Greeks' right wing, was the first real sight Xerxes' sailors had of their opponents.

The Aeginetans insisted, after the battle, that they had been the first to engage the enemy: this honour, they said, belonged to the crew of the trireme which had earlier fetched the sacred images of Aeacus and his sons from Aegina to Salamis.† Their claim, on the face of it, looks

* If they had taken part in the northern decoy movement, on the other hand, they would simply have redeployed from line-ahead column into line-abreast, facing squarely across the channel. In either case the final result would have been the same: a perfect ramming position.

† Hdt 8.84. We have here another instance of Herodotus's telescoping chronology during these final weeks. The trireme left Salamis to collect the images [8.64] after a conference which can be dated, with reasonable assurance, to September 5–6th [see

plausible: certainly the flank attack was more likely to begin before the main engagement developed. The Athenians, however, had two rival candidates of their own, Lycomedes, and Ameinias of Pallene. Lycomedes was said to have sheared the figurehead clean off a Phoenician vessel (afterwards dedicating it to Apollo the Laurel-bearer at Phlya). Ameinias's story was even more dramatic. His trireme – like that of his rival – had pressed on far ahead of the rest, and found itself bearing down on the Phoenician admiral's flagship, which was likewise well out in front of the line. (Their meeting must have taken place in the channel between the Pharmakoussae.) Plutarch's description of this huge vessel, from which archers and javelin-men discharged a constant hail of missiles 'as though on the wall of a fortress', recalls the great *San Felipe*, against which Sir Richard Grenville pitted himself in the *Revenge*. Ameinias held his course, at full speed; the two vessels smashed into each other bows on, with a great grinding of bronze beaks, and lay there inextricably entangled. The admiral, Ariabignes – 'a man of great courage, who was both the most stalwart and the most high-principled of the king's brothers' – now led a boarding-charge against his assailant, only to be killed by Ameinias and his lieutenant, Socles, who ran their spears through him and tossed his body overboard. Plutarch adds that Queen Artemisia of Halicarnassus recognised the corpse as it floated among broken spars and cordage, and had it conveyed to Xerxes; but this sounds like a late embellishment. It is just the kind of detail which Herodotus found irresistible; had it been known to him – and he was, after all, from Halicarnassus – he would surely have mentioned it during his excursus on Artemisia.

By now the engagement had become general: the third captain to close with the enemy, Democritus of Naxos, was, as an islander, stationed at the centre of the Greek line. But the real damage had already been done. Ameinias, if anyone, deserved his accolade: the death of Ariabignes proved peculiarly disastrous to the Phoenicians. Had they forced right through into more open water this battle might have had a very different ending. As it was, there seems to have been no accredited second-in-command who could at once take over – a tell-tale detail suggestive of extreme over-confidence. The inevitable results, as

above, p. 171]. Yet according to Herodotus [8.83] it only returned on the morning of the battle. How, we may well ask, did it get through the Persian blockade after sunrise? (Cf. Hignett XIG pp. 233–4, and HW Comm., vol. 2, pp. 262–4). And what had it been doing at Aegina for the past fortnight? The answer would seem to be that it in fact returned much earlier, and was only dragged in, fictitiously, on the night of September 19–20th to provide transport for Aristeides [see above, p. 183] – another good reason for disbelieving *that* anecdote.

Ephorus says, was that 'disorder seized the barbarian fleet, for there were many now to give orders, but each man did not issue the same commands'. So the attack ground to a halt, and the leading Phoenician vessels began to back off – while they still could – to more open water: which, again, suggests that the first clash took place in the deep narrow channel between Aghios Georgios Island and the smaller of the Pharmakoussae, now a sunken reef. The width of this channel is generally given as 1,300 yards, measuring from the coastline at Perama; but if Pritchett is right, and we must allow for a one-fathom rise in the water-level since 480, such an estimate will have to be drastically reduced. If the reef was then an island, and the island still linked to the mainland by Xerxes' abortive mole, the central channel can have been no more than 800 yards across. This would automatically cut down any advancing force to a bare 16–20 triremes in line-abreast – a fact which in itself had already produced much confusion, since as they approached the narrows, it became necessary for the Persians to pull over half their squadrons out of the front line. Meanwhile more and more contingents came crowding up from Psyttáleia; this, inevitably, led to severe congestion. The situation, though dangerous, was not in itself irremediable; but then, once again, the weather – Greek weather – made a decisive intervention.

By now it was about nine o'clock in the morning. Suddenly Themistocles' rowers felt a sharpening southern breeze blow strong in their faces, saw the surface of the channel begin to chop and heave as that long-awaited deep-sea swell came rolling up it. The crowded Phoenician galleys, with their high decks and sterncastles, began to roll and yaw. Some swung broadside on to the Greek line; others – already packed too close for safety – began to jostle and foul each other. The Athenians, who had been anticipating just such a *contretemps*, and whose long, narrow, low-lying triremes* rode the swell far more effectively, at once swept forward into the attack, ramming those galleys which lay broadside on to them, shearing the oar-banks off the rest – 'and when the men at the oars could no longer do their work, many Persian triremes, getting sideways to the enemy, were time and again severely damaged by the beaks of the ships' [Diod. 11.18.6]. Aeschylus completes the picture:

* Research on the trireme-sheds in Zea Harbour (Pacha Limani) suggests that an Athenian trireme was about 120–40 ft long, by 18–20 ft in the beam (a classic 1:7 racing ratio) with a 4–6 ft draught: the most recent study is that by D. J. Blackman, *ap.* Morrison and Williams, pp. 181–92. Fewer marines on deck [see above p. 190] also must have made an appreciable difference to the Themistoclean trireme's stability.

At first the Persian line withstood this shock; but soon
Our crowding vessels choked the channel, and none
Could help each other; soon their armoured prows
Smashed inward on their allies, and broke off short
The banks of oars, while the Greek ships skilfully
Encircled and attacked them from all sides.

[*Pers.* 412–18]

The Greek line, in fact, had become a noose; and the Persians were now energetically hanging themselves in it. At last the Phoenician squadron ceased backing water, and turned to flight. This produced the most unutterable chaos, since, as Herodotus says, 'those astern fell foul of them in their attempt to press forward and do some service for their king'. Some of these Phoenician vessels – those on the right of the line, nearest to the reef and the mole – ran aground, and their crews struggled to safety. Haled before Xerxes (whose temper by now, we may surmise, was none of the best) they tried to throw the blame for their defeat on the Ionians, whom they accused of deliberate treachery. The Great King, having seen for himself the splendid fight the Ionians were putting up, had these Phoenician survivors beheaded on the spot, and began threatening dire reprisals against the rest of them; which, in the circumstances, though understandable was nevertheless a little tactless. Xerxes did not have so many first-class naval contingents that he could afford to antagonise the best of them in a crisis.

In one sense, however, his wrath was fully justified. The Phoenicians, under that relentless assault, had broken and run for it. By so doing, they had exposed the Persian centre and imperilled the entire line. Through that fatal gap Athens' victorious triremes went thrusting shorewards, in pursuit of their now totally disorganised Phoenician and Cypriot opponents. Hitherto the Cilician and allied squadrons of the centre had been holding their own well enough; but now their right flank was laid bare, and 'when they saw the strongest ships [i.e. the Phoenicians] taking to flight they likewise abandoned the fight' – though not before their admiral, Syennesis, had met a glorious death. That left only the Ionians and East Greek islanders, on the Persian left, where, says Ephorus, 'the battle was stubbornly fought and for some time the struggle was evenly balanced'. The Athenians, however, with cool Themistoclean discipline, now proceeded to execute a manoeuvre which marked the true clinching-point of the battle. Quickly disengaging from their pursuit, they put about and charged back into the fray, taking the Ionians in flank and rear. To counter this new threat, the East Greeks were forced to pull several of their best squadrons out of line. Battered on one flank by the Athenians, on the other by the

Aeginetans, they still put up a magnificent last-ditch defence: Herodotus records one vivid episode in it. An Ionian trireme from Samothrace charged and sank an Athenian vessel, only to be rammed herself, a moment later, by an Aeginetan. 'Just before she was gone, the Samothracian crew, who were armed with javelins, cleared the deck of the attacking vessel, leapt aboard, and captured her.'

But such individual feats of bravery could not save the day. After a while the Ionians, too, gave up their unequal struggle and put about. The log-jam broke, and a vast mass of Persian ships – many of them badly crippled, with trailing spars and cordage, oars broken off short, timbers sheared or sprung by those terrible bronze-sheathed rams, went streaming away past Psyttáleia towards Phaleron. The water was thick with corpses and wreckage. Those Greeks who had their vessels rammed under them, and survived the hand-to-hand fighting on deck which followed, for the most part managed to struggle ashore on Salamis. But few of the Persians (unlike the Greeks) could swim, and they suffered heavy casualties by drowning. This must have been particularly true of the Iranian or Scythian marines, from regions far inland, who would be further hampered by their heavy armour. The retreating vessels were harried relentlessly, not only by the main pursuing force, but also by the Aeginetans and Megarians, who made havoc of them from their flank position at the mouth of Ambelaki Bay:

> Crushed hulls lay upturned on the sea so thick
> You could not see the water, choked with wrecks
> And slaughtered men; while all the shores and reefs
> Were strewn with corpses. Soon in wild disorder
> All that was left of our fleet turned tail and fled.
> But the Greeks pursued us, and with oars or broken
> Fragments of wreckage split the survivors' heads
> As if they were tunneys or a haul of fish:
> And shrieks and wailing rang across the water
> Till nightfall hid us from them.
>
> [Aesch. *Pers.* 418–28]

The pursuit now degenerated into a *sauve qui peut* rout, from which our sources salvage one or two famous individual episodes. We glimpse a pair of erstwhile rivals turned allies, Polycritus of Aegina and Themistocles, the latter aboard his emblazoned admiral's galley, racing neck-and-neck down-channel, while Polycritus – having just scuppered an enemy vessel – yells across, half-cocky, half-defensive: 'Who said Aegina was pro-Persian?'[16] We see Queen Artemisia of Halicarnassus, hotly pursued by a trireme from the Attica squadron, cram on all speed and ruthlessly run down one of her own side, a vessel commanded by some Carian princeling from nearby Calynda. 'I cannot say', Herodotus observes demurely, 'if she did this deliberately because of some quarrel she had with this man . . . or if it was just chance that that particular vessel was in the way'. At all events, she did doubly well out of the error. Her assailant – that same Ameinias of Pallene who had attacked the Phoenician admiral's flagship at the onset of the engagement – observing what had happened, came to the conclusion that his quarry was either a Greek or a deserter fighting on the Greek side, and turned off in search of some other victim. (Xerxes, in the mistaken belief that she had actually sunk an enemy ship, now made his celebrated *mot*: 'My men have turned into women, my women into men.') Ameinias was out of his mind with rage and frustration when he learnt the truth, since the Athenians (who disliked the idea of a woman taking up arms against them) had put a 10,000-drachma price on Artemisia's head, and given their captains special instructions to capture her at all costs.

There still remained that body of four hundred Persians on Psyttáleia. Stationed there by Xerxes to deal suitably with friend or foe as they came ashore during the battle – and also, in all likelihood, to form the spearhead of an invasion force after the Great King's presumptive naval victory – they were now cut off and helpless. When the pursuit slackened somewhat, a heterogeneous group of Greek marines, archers, slingers and hoplites left their ships, landed on the island, hunted this wretched holding force down, and carried out a wholesale massacre:

> Our men were trapped. Showers of stones rattled about them,
> Arrows leapt from the bowstring and struck them down:
> In the end the Greeks bore down on them like a wave
> Of the sea, hacking and carving at their wretched limbs
> Until they had ripped the life from each last one of them.
>
> [Aesch. *Pers.* 458–64]

Both Aeschylus and Herodotus vastly exaggerate the importance of this trifling action, and one can see why. It was, after all, the first land victory of any sort scored by Greek troops against Persians during Xerxes' invasion. Far more important, however, was the fact that the hoplites – as opposed to the despised 'sailor rabble', now metamorphosed into Athens' all-glorious navy – had so far done nothing at Salamis except man the shore defences and serve aboard ship as men-at-arms. Honour demanded that they had their own independent victory, and Psyttáleia happened to be the only place where they went ashore and fought. The propagandists had to make what they could of this somewhat unpromising material. Aeschylus gave a reasonably trustworthy account of the battle itself – eight years after the event he could scarcely do otherwise – but he represented the Persians as all aristocrats, the flower of Xerxes' army, and made the Great King order an immediate retreat when he heard of their loss. Both statements are flagrant and obvious lies, though of the flattering kind which no veteran was liable to challenge in retrospect. Herodotus, predictably, drags in Aristeides as the leader of the Greek commando force (giving him a tremendous personal plug at the same time) and claims that it was composed *exclusively* of shore-based hoplites. Plutarch embroiders this theme. Seldom does one get the chance to observe a myth-in-the-making quite so clearly.[17]

At sea, the pursuit seems to have been kept up, in a scattered and sporadic form, until sunset. 'Such Persian ships as escaped destruction', says Herodotus, 'made their way back to Phaleron, and brought up there under the protection of the army'. Losses, according to Ephorus – our sole informant – were about two hundred vessels, or half the entire surviving fleet, as against forty Greek triremes sunk or disabled. Some of the wrecks left adrift in the channel were towed over to Salamis by the Greeks; but during the afternoon a fresh west wind sprang up – the 'Ponendis' of modern Greek sailors, which often follows on a few hours after a sirocco – and blew the remaining hulks down-channel as far as Cape Colias, a narrow headland between two and three miles south of Phaleron. Persian corpses were washed up 'on the shores of Salamis and all the country round', Aeschylus reports: dashed among hard black rocks by the thrash and surge of the sea, their flesh torn by kites or, worse, by impatient looters, eager to strip off the gold torques and rings and bracelets which they wore. Themistocles, according to one faintly hostile story, went strolling along the beach that evening, and saw many such bodies lying there. He told his companion to take anything he wanted – 'You are not Themistocles!' – but himself held aloof. One would like to believe that such an attitude was dictated, not so much by mere vainglory (which the anecdote does its best to imply), as by civilised fastidiousness and a natural generosity of spirit.

In any case, at this juncture Themistocles had more urgent problems on his mind. The Greeks do not seem to have understood the full magnitude of their victory for at least forty-eight hours after the actual battle was over: a not uncommon phenomenon in such circumstances. All next day [21 September] they laboured to get their battered squadrons seaworthy again, carrying out what makeshift repairs they could, and all the time 'fully expecting that Xerxes would use his remaining ships to make another attack'. But the Great King's fleet, now reduced to a point where it could no longer even achieve parity with its opponents, was finally *hors de combat*, its morale broken, and fit for nothing but the long voyage home. Despite some desultory work on the half-finished mole, no attack materialised that day; and when the Greeks awoke on 22 September they found – to their great astonishment – that the Persian fleet, or what was left of it, had silently vanished away during the night. Then, at last, realisation of the full truth began to dawn on them. They were by no means out of the wood yet; Xerxes' unconquered field-army was still encamped opposite them on the shores of Attica. But their freedom no longer stood (as that anonymous Isthmus epitaph phrased it*) on the razor's edge. At the eleventh hour, and against all expectation, Greece had been saved; and not even his bitterest enemies – of whom there were many, both at home and abroad – could deny that it was Themistocles who had saved her.

* The distich, preserved by Plutarch [MH. §39] was for the Corinthians, who were credited with saving Greece at the cost of their own lives. Where and how this feat was performed remains obscure: we cannot really account for their movements after they hoisted sail for the Bay of Eleusis. They *may* have gone on and engaged the Egyptian squadron (Aeschylus, *Pers.* 311–13, mentions several Egyptian casualties), or they may, after their diversionary activities, have got back in time to participate in the main battle, despite the conflicting evidence of Herodotus (8.94). This absence of evidence is a remarkable testimony to the way in which propaganda can permanently vitiate a historical tradition.

PART SIX

 # THE DOORS
OF THE
PELOPONNESE

XERXES and the Persian High Command realised the full extent of their defeat much sooner than the Greeks did: it may be that the wind which blew away so many wrecked vessels led Themistocles to underestimate his opponents' losses. He was also, one suspects, taken in by the Great King's calculatedly misleading activities on the morning after the battle. A great show of reorganisation went on among the Persian squadrons, as though for another naval engagement, while a large working-party was observed swarming over the still unfinished mole. It is sometimes assumed that these operations were genuine in intent; that Xerxes only gave up when he saw that (as Burn says) 'the heart had gone out of his sailors'. But there could have been no doubt about their demoralisation from the moment of defeat; and in any case Herodotus is quite specific as to Xerxes' motives. These ostentatious preparations were intended as camouflage all along – in which aim, one may add, they succeeded to perfection. Xerxes saw, all too well, that while he still might have a fighting army, he could no longer rely on his fleet. Some of the Phoenicians, alarmed by the summary execution of their captains, had deserted under cover of darkness; those who stayed on were understandably jittery and in no condition to fight. Every consideration pointed towards an immediate withdrawal. First-class fighters such as the Egyptian marines were taken off their ships and drafted into army units. Then, during the night of 21–22 September, the remainder of the fleet sailed from Phaleron, 'the commander of every vessel making the best speed he could across to the Hellespont, in order to guard the bridges for Xerxes' use on his return' [Hdt. 8.107]. They set course, first, for Phocaea and Cyme, on the coast just north of Chios; from here it was an easy run to the Dardanelles. The state of their morale can be gauged by the fact that when they were off Cape Zoster [Vouliagméni], a few miles south of Phaleron, they mistook the rocky point for an enemy squadron, and stood out to sea to avoid it. As anyone who has swum off Vouliagméni by moonlight can testify, this represents a most remarkable feat of the imagination.

What were Xerxes' motives in acting as he did? Here, again, Herodotus shows himself shrewder than many modern scholars will allow. The Great King, he says [8.97], having realised the full extent of the disaster, 'was afraid that the Greeks, either on their own initiative or at the suggestion of the Ionians, might sail to the Hellespont and break the bridges there. If this happened, he would be cut off in Europe and in danger of destruction.' As things turned out [see below, pp. 205–7], the Spartan-dominated High Command felt, on balance, that the sooner this uncomfortably large Persian army got out of Europe (preferably by its own volition) the better; the last thing Eurybiades, for one, wanted was to cut off their retreat and lend them the courage of despair. Xerxes, however, could hardly gamble his entire expedition on a hopeful reading of Spartan psychology. Doubtless he remembered how Darius had faced a very similar predicament on the Danube, during his unsuccessful Scythian foray (513); then, too, the Persians' escape-route had been controlled by potentially treacherous Ionians. Xerxes' strategic position after Salamis was perilous in the extreme. The Greek allies – whether they knew it yet or not – had won absolute naval supremacy in the Aegean. If Themistocles chose to lead his squadrons across into Ionian waters, and pursue the war from there, the whole East Greek littoral, from Caria to the Dardanelles, might well rise in revolt – especially when the news of Salamis became widely known. In such a case, Xerxes would have no option but to withdraw his entire field-army from Greece as fast as possible, without risking a further battle.[1] Better, surely, to anticipate trouble, and return home at once: after such a setback the Great King's place was undoubtedly at Sardis or Susa, where he could keep a watchful eye – and if need be a heavy hand – on the restless provinces of the empire. Besides, the Persian army had been largely dependent on the fleet for its provisioning [see above, p. 91]; with the collapse of his naval arm, Xerxes could no longer depend on a seaborne commissariat. The Greeks were now in a position to intercept his ration-convoys or sever his lines of communication more or less as and when they chose.

At the same time, it was unthinkable (if only for reasons of face-saving and public propaganda) that Xerxes should admit by his actions that the Greek expedition had been a near-total fiasco. His victorious advance into Attica was, after all, undisputed fact; news of it had so excited the Persians at home that they 'strewed the roads with myrtle-boughs, burned incense, and gave themselves up to every sort of pleasure and merrymaking'. Xerxes' official dispatch reporting the naval defeat at Salamis put something of a damper on these festivities, but it was still possible, by concentrating on the land forces' achievements, to represent the campaign as at least a qualified success. The verbatim discussions which Herodotus records [8.100–2] between Xerxes, his cousin Mardonius, and Queen Artemisia must be regarded, in their present form, as mere *ex post facto* rationalisation. Nevertheless, they do contain several interesting and plausible details. One comment attributed to Mardonius sheds a good deal of light on the propaganda line at Susa: 'Why should we care if the Egyptians and Phoenicians and Cypriots and Cilicians have disgraced themselves? Persia is not involved in their disgrace.' In other words, defeat at Salamis had been due entirely to the craven spirit of Xerxes' foreign subjects: Persian ethnic prestige was still undimmed.

This transfer of emphasis from naval to military operations made one decision inevitable: a holding force had to be left in Greece after the main army was withdrawn. The idea of such a force, in Herodotus's narrative, came from Mardonius. This could be true, but is more probably an inference drawn from the fact that he was appointed its commander: an unenviable responsibility, and one which he is unlikely to have sought out. Such a force would labour under several grave disadvantages. Stripped of all naval support, it could not mount a successful attack on the Isthmus line, and would thus be condemned (short of tempting its opponents away from their fortress) to remain permanently on the defensive. If it was too large, it would run short of supplies – here, again, the loss of the fleet proved crippling. On the other hand, if it was too small, its margin of security vanished, and it might well find itself beaten in fair fight. Nevertheless, these risks had to be taken. It is an ironic paradox that Xerxes found himself driven, on political grounds, into actions which made no kind of sense as strategy. One function of this force may have been, as Plutarch suggests [*Them.* 4.4], to cover the main army's line of retreat; but the central truth surely lies elsewhere. Hignett [XIG p. 266] puts it in a nutshell: 'The Persian Empire had sustained a severe shock in the decisive defeat of its great armada at Salamis; the ignominious retirement of its army from Europe without any further attempt to force a battle on land with the main Greek army would have meant a loss of face that would have fatally compromised the prestige of the ruling race.' Even if Xerxes no longer felt inclined to linger in Greece himself once the chance of a quick and showy victory had been lost, the honour and security of the Achaemenid throne demanded that *someone* did – and who better suited for the task than his ambitious, fire-eating cousin? Once chosen, Mardonius could hardly show himself anything but an eager and loyal subject.

Having assessed the situation with his advisers, Xerxes acted at once.

His prompt dispatch of the fleet, by night, was a shrewd move on several counts. The smell of defeat is contagious; to have kept those shattered squadrons at Phaleron would have been extremely bad for army morale, and their continued presence would have constituted an embarrassing reminder of his own personal humiliation. At least they could, with luck, be relied upon to protect the Dardanelles bridges:* Xerxes was understandably anxious about safeguarding his now all-too-vulnerable lines of communication. At the same time he must have foreseen that one effect of this withdrawal would be to lure the Greek fleet away from Salamis in pursuit. With a good night's start, there was little fear of the Persians being overtaken: defeated or not, they could still outsail Themistocles' heavier triremes across open water [see above, p. 119]. From Xerxes' point of view, however, their main function was diversionary. He intended, within the next few days, to evacuate his whole field army from Attica – a task more easily accomplished if the Greeks were occupied elsewhere, beyond the Isthmus wall or, as now, among the Aegean islands. The Great King had no wish to find them harrying his column on the march with hit-and-run commando attacks, or threatening his (by now somewhat problematical) supply-lines. Since he planned to evacuate Euboea *en route* – how could he hold that strategically vital island without a fleet? – this was no idle fear. Nor could he rely absolutely on the continued support of the northern Greek states: Salamis was bound to produce some hard rethinking all round. Perhaps he had, after all, gauged the attitude of the Peloponnesians well enough; Demaratus will doubtless have told him of the old Spartan tradition 'not to pursue a retreating foe *à outrance*, but to "thank God they were rid of a knave"' [Burn, PG p. 468].

Everything, in the event, went as planned. On the morning of 22 September the Greeks awoke, saw Xerxes' battalions still encamped along the opposite shore, and – very reasonably – deduced from this that the fleet would likewise still be lying at Phaleron. After all, close liaison between fleet and army had been the mainstay of Xerxes' strategy throughout. Once again they made ready to meet a second attack by sea. Then patrols came in with the incredible news: Phaleron roadstead was empty, the Persians had pulled out. The decision to give chase was taken immediately. Perhaps leaving a single guard-squadron at Salamis (there was little point in Xerxes assaulting the island now, even if he had had the ships to do it), the Greeks manned their triremes,

---

* Artemisia's squadron (Hdt 8.103, 107) appears to have proceeded independently: the Queen laid a course, not for Cyme or Phocaea, but for Ephesus, taking several of Xerxes' illegitimate sons with her as passengers.

hoisted sail, and rowed away in a south-easterly direction, hugging the coast of Attica. The Great King must have heaved a sigh of relief when the last of them vanished hull-down beyond Sunium. Then he and Mardonius set to work. The army corps that had set out for the Isthmus on the evening of 19 September (and must probably be held responsible for a 'miraculous' dust-cloud blown from Eleusis towards Salamis during the battle itself – the winds seem to have been variable that day) was recalled before it had got as far as Megara. Unit after unit made ready to strike camp and march. Before September was out Xerxes' advance column had crossed the Cithaeron-Parnes range and was well on its way to Thessaly.

The Greeks kept up their pursuit of the retreating Persian squadrons as far as Andros. Themistocles, for one, must have had a pretty shrewd idea as to his quarry's immediate destination, and probably followed the regular route for vessels sailing to the Dardanelles, then or now – that is, north-east by Sunium head, leaving Kea on the starboard bow, and so through the channel between Andros and Euboea into the central Aegean. Even to this point is a haul of about ninety-five miles. If the Greeks rowed in relays, day and night – as they surely must have done – they could have cleared Euboea by sun-up on the morning of 23 September. But when dawn broke, and still no Persian sail was visible above the horizon, they abandoned the chase as hopeless, and changed course south-east, past Cape Kambanós. Some five or six hours later, weary and frustrated, they dropped anchor in Andros roads. The local inhabitants were cautiously polite, but (as subsequent events proved) far from submissive. Like most Cycladic islanders, they had collaborated with the Persians, and are unlikely to have forgotten Miltiades' punitive expedition against nearby Paros after Marathon [see above, pp. 44–5]. On the other hand they could not, at this early stage, appreciate the overwhelming nature of the Greek victory at Salamis; it is doubtful whether the victors themselves understood, as yet, that they now enjoyed complete naval superiority throughout the Aegean.

Since they had failed to overtake Xerxes' retreating squadrons, Eurybiades now summoned a council of war to decide on their next move. Our sources for this debate, and its immediate aftermath,[2] are riddled with internal contradictions – mostly, it would appear, the result of deliberate tampering for purposes of propaganda – but the main points come through clearly enough. The debate opened with a proposal that 'they should carry on through the islands direct for the Hellespont, and break down the bridges'. Only one late epitomist, Justin, takes the trouble to adduce any arguments quoted in favour of this strategy. Its advocates* hoped, first and foremost, to cut Xerxes' army off and destroy it: in Plutarch's memorable phrase, to 'take Asia without stirring out of Europe'. Failing this, they expected him to recognise the hopelessness of his situation, and sue for peace. There were several grave objections to such a plan, not all of which seem to have been appreciated by those who opposed it. Above all, unless we assume that one preliminary to demolishing the bridges was the final hunting down and elimination of the Persian fleet, Xerxes could afford to snap his fingers at such a threat. If the bridges were down, he would use a naval ferry-service; and if the Greeks controlled the Abydos crossing, he would simply embark elsewhere (at Eion, say, or Byzantium) and set course for Ephesus instead, secure in the knowledge that a suitable welcome awaited him from his satrap at Sardis. The point urged in debate – an equally cogent one – was that such a policy, if successfully enforced (i.e. after the neutralisation of the fleet), would merely give Xerxes and his army the courage of despair. If driven on by hunger and isolation, they would live off the land and fight to a finish. This vast force was a very real and present danger, still well capable of reversing the victory achieved at Salamis. Why tempt Providence by provoking a show-down? Far better to let Xerxes withdraw unimpeded, and good riddance. The majority approved this view. Greece had quite enough enemies on her soil already without adding to them.

'Very well, then,' said Themistocles, with his usual robust common sense, 'if we agree on that, it is high time we were considering and contriving some means to get him out of Greece as quickly as we can'. The question was, would he go? On 23 September, to a group of naval commanders over a hundred miles distant from Attica, this must have seemed highly problematical. Only Themistocles, with his strategical insight and brilliant flair for logistics, is likely to have recognised that Xerxes must *inevitably* withdraw the bulk of his army from Greece once

* According to Herodotus (8.108) and Plutarch (*Them.* 16.1, *Arist.* 9.3) the scheme originated in the fertile brain of Themistocles, and was opposed by Eurybiades and the Peloponnesians, or, alternatively, by Aristeides (an automatically suspicious discrepancy). Justin (2.13.5–8) and Nepos (*Them.* 5.1–2) reverse these roles, making 'the Greeks' advocate a Hellespont policy, to be *opposed* by Themistocles (cf. Diodorus, 11.19.5–6, where Ephorus seems to draw on a similar tradition). The dubious rule-of-thumb whereby Herodotus's testimony is *by definition* preferred to that of later sources when they differ (see e.g. Hignett XIG p. 229) breaks down badly here, since Herodotus's prejudice (or that of his informants) against Themistocles is so blatant as to be embarrassing. On the other hand, it would be a mistake always to credit Themistocles with strategical infallibility. The verdict must remain open; but since all our sources agree that Themistocles was brought round to the 'opposition view' during debate, whether he held it *ab initio* is a more or less academic point.

Two of the *ostraka* used in the potsherd vote, or ostracism: each bears Themistocles' name. Until recent fresh finds, he was easily the highest scorer.

Olympias under sail and oar, from Frank Welsh's *Building the Trireme*, London (Constable) 1988.

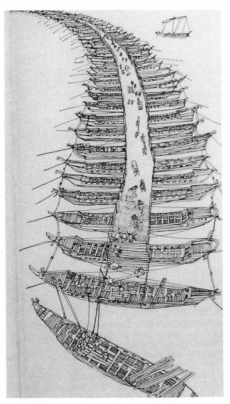

A modern bridge of boats, on the Kabul River, from Vol. 4 (Δ, Ὁ Μεγαλέξανδρος καὶ οἱ Ἑλληνιστικοὶ χρόνοι) of the *Historia tou Hellenikou Ethnous* (Ἱστορία τοῦ Ἑλληνικοῦ Ἔθνους), Athens, *Ekdotike Athenon* (Ἐκδοτικὴ Ἀθηνῶν), 1973.

Sketch of the bridge of boats over the Hellespont, from C. M. Bowra's *Classical Greece,* New York (Time-Life) 1965.

the Persian fleet, or what was left of it, had sailed for Ionia. Eurybiades and the other Peloponnesian admirals were more or less whistling in the dark. What we would expect *them* to do, given so unpredictable a situation, is to sit tight and spin out time until they got some decisive news from home; and that, in the event, is precisely what they did. Having been dissuaded from pressing on to the Dardanelles, they showed no immediate signs of sailing back home either, but settled down to besiege the Andrians, who were proving unexpectedly sticky about paying protection-money. Meanwhile Themistocles, tongue in cheek, had devised a ruse which, he claimed, was guaranteed to speed Xerxes on his way out of Europe. Some trusted agent was to take the Great King another private message, saying that the Greeks had decided to destroy the bridges; were, indeed, already embarked for the Dardanelles. (In some variants of this episode Themistocles merely sends a tip-off, and leaves it at that; in others he claims to have dissuaded – or at least promises to dissuade – the Greeks from any such course of action: a claim which Thucydides, for one, regarded as false.) Finding his all-important lines of communication thus threatened, Xerxes would at once strike camp and make for home.

On the face of it, this is a preposterous scheme, which many scholars understandably regard as fiction. For the second time in a week, we are asked to believe, Themistocles sent a deliberately misleading message to Xerxes; for the second time in a week, the Great King and his staff officers acted on it with the same gullibility and guilelessness as before, though it came from precisely the same source. In some versions (to strain credulity further) the agent is once again the faithful Sicinnus, tutor to Themistocles' children; Herodotus even has him deliver his warning to the Great King in person. As Burn pleasantly observes, 'it would certainly have been more than rash for Sikinnos to put his head in the lion's mouth again, after his first message had turned out to offer mere bait for a trap' – and, one may add, would have substantially reduced the already minimal chances of such a ruse succeeding. (Plutarch, more convincingly, makes Themistocles' messenger a eunuch named Arnaces, a prisoner of war released specially for this mission.) The entire story, in fact, has often been taken as an unintelligent *ex post facto* doublet of the earlier – and I believe genuine – message delivered by Sicinnus on the eve of Salamis [see above, pp. 177–9]. This surely, is to miss its real significance altogether. Whether such a message was actually sent or not scarcely matters. Xerxes had recognised the need for evacuation immediately after Salamis, and needed no advice from Themistocles to help make up his mind. The important thing for us is the use Themistocles made of his own shrewd foresight. If he knew that

Xerxes was bound to pull out anyway, it must have been a great temptation to claim the credit for making him do so. Themistocles' somewhat transparent cover-story may raise eyebrows among modern scholars, but it was probably quite convincing enough for most of his contemporaries. If he actually sent an anonymous message to Xerxes before the latter left Attica, it can have caused no harm, and at least added a convincing touch of local colour to some fairly thin propaganda.

Meanwhile, victory or no, there was the unromantic but ever-pressing problem of finance to be considered. Crews needed pay, the machinery of government must continue to function. Unlike many great battles, Salamis appears to have yielded comparatively little booty. There were no cash reserves left in the public treasury, and most of the sacred temple reserve funds had likewise fallen into Persian hands. Xerxes' invasion had lost Athens the best part of one harvest already, and was to lose her another before the danger finally receded. It is clear that the Greek squadrons now stationed off Andros had not been sent out exclusively on a wild-goose chase after the Persian fleet. Like Miltiades in 489 [see above, pp. 44–5], Themistocles and his fellow-commanders were sizing up the Cycladic islands for cash contributions. Agents went round from one to another, ostensibly raising funds for the war-effort, but in fact extorting a mixture of guilt-payment and protec-tion-money. Paros and the southern Euboean port of Carystus, uneasily aware that their pro-Persian record hitherto would take some explaining away, both paid up without demur: not that this did the Carystians much good, since the Greeks subsequently devastated their land any-way. Themistocles also seems to have made a brisk profit out of restoring anti-Persian exiles to their native cities. The exiles, naturally, paid him well for this service. Sometimes, however, the civic authorities paid him even more to keep them away, especially if they happened to be political rivals. We have the protest of one such victim, preserved by Plutarch [*Them.* 21.2–3]:

> We know that Leto,
> Who loves the truth, detests Themistocles,
> That liar, cheat, and traitor, who broke his word
> And, for a sordid bribe, refused to restore
> His host Timocreon to his native Rhodes,
> But pocketed three silver talents, no less,
> And then sailed off.

By and large it seems to have been a successful operation, considered financially; only on Andros itself did the prospective contributors flatly refuse to pay up.

At first Themistocles treated their attitude as a joke. They would have to make a contribution in the end, he told them, because the Athenians were backed by two powerful deities, Persuasion and Compulsion – the implication being that if the first fell on deaf ears, they proceeded to invoke the second. The men of Andros, entering into the spirit of the thing, congratulated Athens on the possession of two such handy gods, 'who were obviously responsible for wealth and greatness'. Unfortunately, they went on, their small and unproductive island had two deities of its own in permanent residence – Poverty and Shiftlessness. It followed that no money would be forthcoming, since, try as they might, the Athenians could never make their power triumph over the islanders' sheer inability to pay. Seeing he would get nowhere by jokey diplomacy, Themistocles now placed Andros under siege. If he expected a quick surrender he was, once again, in for a disappointment. The Andrians, having shrewdly worked out that their assailants had little leisure for a prolonged operation of this sort, simply dug themselves in and waited. After about a fortnight the Greeks saw that they had embarked on a hopeless venture. However, by then news must have reached the fleet that Xerxes had indeed withdrawn from Attica, and Themistocles' reputation now stood even higher in consequence. Relying on this, the victor of Salamis now* proposed that they abandon the siege and return to base. 'At the moment,' he said, 'all is well with us; so let us stay where we are, in our own country, and look after ourselves and our families. The Persians are gone – flung out, once for all; so repair your houses, every one of you, and attend to the sowing of your land. We can sail for Ionia and the Hellespont next spring.'

This was to make a virtue of necessity. The campaigning season was over, and raging autumnal gales had begun to sweep down through the Dardanelles from the Black Sea. Ironically enough, within a week or two both Xerxes' bridges were to be swept away by a violent storm: for once Themistocles' prescience – or persuasiveness – failed him. So the Greeks, after a little desultory raiding on Euboea, returned to Salamis, about the beginning of October. Here, before doing anything else, they duly shared out the plunder taken in battle, and chose 'first-fruits' to be offered up as a token of gratitude to the gods. At Olympia they set up a bronze Zeus. From the gold and silver objects sent to Delphi – no hard feelings against *that* oracle for its wartime record – was fashioned a male statue eighteen feet high, with a ship's figurehead in its hand: the Greeks dedicating their spoils to the god. The admirals also set aside three

* Not, as Herodotus (8.109) oddly suggests, during the first council of war, held on 23 September, at a time when Xerxes had not yet left Attica, and even if he had, Themistocles could not possibly have known it.

Phoenician triremes, to be consecrated respectively on Sunium, at the Isthmus, and on Salamis itself. (Herodotus remarks, *en passant*, that the one at the Isthmus was still there in his day, a mere forty years later: what had happened to the other two meanwhile?) As a memorial of the battle itself, the Greeks set up a free-standing marble column on a circular base, slightly more than half-way along the Cynosura peninsula – an appropriate site, since from here alone on Salamis the entire length of the straits is visible. As late as the eighteenth century fragments of this column could be discerned from Athens; but by 1819, though the site was still identifiable, dilapidation had all but destroyed the trophy itself. 'Many of the marbles', Gell reported, 'are in the sea'. Today only a slight flattening of the rocky surface indicates where the base may have stood. *Sic transit.*[3]

Salamis had keyed the Greek allies up to unprecedented heights of cooperation and self-sacrifice; now victory was won, and the immediate threat removed, reaction swiftly set in. All the old inter-state and inter-class rivalries, suspended for the duration of the emergency, began to raise their heads once more – somewhat prematurely, as things turned out. Modern parallels are not hard to find. Wartime heroes became politically expendable: at Athens in particular a tremendous upsurge of reactionary conservative-agrarian feeling sabotaged Themistocles' plans for further large-scale naval operations, and denied him any part in the campaigns of 479. Before Xerxes and Mardonius had got as far as Thessaly, the Greeks were once more bickering jealously among themselves; in particular, acute tension began to develop between Athens and Sparta. The Athenians, who had borne the brunt of all naval campaigning while the Peloponnesian army sat inactive behind its Isthmus wall, now understandably expected some sort of *quid pro quo* for all their labour and sacrifice. They had followed up the triumph of Salamis with a very effective punitive expedition in the Cyclades: as Herodotus says [8.132], the seas were now clear as far east as Delos. Was it too much to hope that Sparta and her allies would now return the compliment, send an army north over the Cithaeron-Parnes range, and cow the quislings of Boeotia into decent subservience? Apparently it was. The commander at the Isthmus, Leonidas's younger brother Cleombrotus, got as far as 'making sacrifice against the Persian'; but while he was thus occupied (2 October) a solar eclipse took place – could the Ephors, whose original function was to 'watch the heavens', predict such phenomena? – and the whole Peloponnesian army, suitably deterred by this bad omen, marched back home for the winter. They, no less than the Athenians, had the autumn ploughing and sowing to think about. If pressed, Cleombrotus might have argued that far too many potential hoplites were still serving with the fleet, and that he had no intention of risking a clash with Xerxes' land-forces until he had brought his own numbers up to full strength. To the Athenians, however, (and indeed to Herodotus) this simply looked like yet another instance of self-seeking Spartan isolationism; and they may well have been right.

That the Spartans themselves felt some qualms of conscience on this score we can, perhaps, infer from the following rather curious anecdote. While the men of Athens took oxen, ploughs and seed-corn across to the mainland, and grimly set to work in their devastated fields, the Spartans enquired of the Delphic Oracle whether they should demand justice from Xerxes for the slaying of their king Leonidas. Since they traditionally never pursued a beaten foe (perhaps because they were not equipped for such operations) they may have hoped that even a token admission of defeat on Xerxes' part would absolve them from further responsibility in the matter.[4] Delphi, diplomatic as always, endorsed their proposal, and a herald duly made his way north to Xerxes' camp in Thessaly. Here he delivered himself of the following message: 'My lord King of the Medes, the Lacedaemonians and the house of Heracles in Sparta demand satisfaction for murder, because you killed their king while he was fighting in defence of Greece.' The response was not quite what had been hoped for. Xerxes exploded into unceremonious laughter, and for a while made no answer. At last, however, he pointed to his cousin and said: 'They will get all the satisfaction they deserve from Mardonius here.' If the herald kept his eyes open and his wits about him, he must very soon have realised the full significance of that remark. Mardonius was busy selecting a streamlined task-force, perhaps 30,000 strong,* from the Persian army's toughest front-line regiments – Iranians, Medes, Bactrians, Sacae, Indians – to carry on the war in mainland Greece.

This must have come as cold comfort to the Spartans; it also seems, in a rather cynical fashion, to have dictated the change which now becomes apparent in their general attitude to defence policy. Mardonius had a strong army but no fleet; so long as the Peloponnesian states sat tight behind their Isthmus wall he could not get at them. He might well reoccupy Athens, and ravage the Megarid: that (they argued privately) was no concern of theirs. In public, however, they began to

---

* Accepting the theory (cited by Hignett, XIG p. 351) that the Greeks misinterpreted a Persian chiliad (1,000) as a myriad (10,000), so that 'all figures derived from Persian official sources were automatically multiplied by ten' [see above, pp. 58–9]. This also produces a more reasonable figure (6,000) for the escort which Artabazus provided for Xerxes as far as the Hellespont (Hdt. 8.126.1, and below, p. 217].

veer round towards the idea of a predominantly naval campaign – the one thing the Peloponnesian *bloc* had hitherto opposed throughout. It is not hard to see why. While they supplied a commander-in-chief and a few ships, Athens and Aegina could go on doing all the real work – and taking, in their exposed position, all the real risks. The Spartan army need not be heavily committed beyond its frontiers; the Helots – restless as always – could be kept under proper control. In the event this scheme, as we shall see, considerably underestimated Athenian shrewdness and self-interest; but to the Spartans, whose dourness was only matched by their weakness for crabbed Machiavellian diplomacy, it must have looked singularly attractive. During the months that followed they went out of their way, as was only natural, to cultivate and flatter Themistocles, the prime exponent of Greek naval strategy. This gambit hardly improved Themistocles' popularity in Athens. The topsy-turvy irony of the situation was that the Athenians, too, had performed a sudden *volte-face* – but in precisely the opposite direction. Themistocles and his naval activists were rapidly losing ground to the conservative-agrarian alignment of farmers and aristocrats, headed by Aristeides; the predominantly sea-based strategy of 480 was soon to be replaced – not surprisingly, with Mardonius at large in central Greece – by a demand for some kind of land-based, Marathon-style campaign. Athens and Sparta had, in effect, exchanged their natural roles, a state of affairs which could have extremely dangerous consequences.

Meanwhile the allied fleet sailed back from Salamis to its dispersal-point at the Isthmus, and the various commanders assembled to award individual and civic prizes for valour during the campaign which had just ended. Anything more calculated to promote envy, spite, and ill-will at such a juncture it would be hard to imagine. The backstairs lobbying and intrigue reached an apogee of competitive bloody-mindedness. It all sounds, from what little evidence we possess, rather like the wrong sort of major film festival, where the same cult (or anti-cult) of personality tends to be matched by a very similar political indifference to the claims of pure merit. If the Spartans had already worked out their new policy in detail (which is by no means certain) they signally failed to impose it on their allies. The Peloponnesian admirals, jealous of Athens' overwhelming success, and irritated by Themistocles' cocky arrogance, saw to it that the civic prize went to Aegina, while the individual crown seems not to have been awarded at all.* The Athenians were proclaimed runners-up. Piqued by this

---

* Herodotus (8.123) followed by Plutarch (*Them.* 17.1) alleges that all the commanders, when it came to a ballot, voted for themselves first but Themistocles second, a story which, though *ben trovato*, is surely fictional. If it was a private ballot, who would

deliberate snub, they now began circulating a slander which at least had the merit of originality. When the Greeks enquired of Apollo whether their Delphic offerings were to his satisfaction (they said) the god replied 'that he was satisfied with what everyone had given, except the Aeginetans'. Since they had been awarded the prize of valour, they could afford to be more generous. This, says Herodotus – leaning heavily, as usual, on Athenian informants – is what made the Aeginetans commission the bronze mast with three gold stars which still stood there in his day – 'near the bowl which was dedicated by Croesus'. The Corinthians, who got no prizes (despite the fine service commemorated in their various memorial epitaphs) and were also the target for some choice Athenian libels, sourly declared that the Persians had been beaten chiefly through their own errors, a view which we still find them propagating half a century later.[5] As a demonstration of Panhellenic unity this prize-giving can hardly be accounted an unqualified success.

Themistocles must have felt such a rebuff more sharply than most. He had gone to Corinth as the acknowledged hero of the hour, and – to judge from the various anecdotes told about him – probably played his new role for all it was worth. It may well have been this occasion which Timocreon of Ialysus had in mind when he wrote [Plut. *Them.* 21.3]:

> But always he lines his purse, and at the Isthmus
> Plays the great host – and the great laughing-stock –
> With that cold banquet he gave, where all the guests
> Ate, and then prayed he would come to no good end.

The Spartan government, informed of these events, saw its opportunity. A caucus of jealous admirals might be beyond its competence to control; but at least it could make prompt amends to their principal victim – and perhaps score a diplomatic victory in the process. So Themistocles was invited to Sparta as an official guest, and received such honours there as no other foreigner had known. When the Spartans held their own prize-giving, Eurybiades (properly enough) won the olive-leaf crown for valour, but a similar wreath was bestowed, *honoris causa*, on the victor of Salamis, in recognition of his pre-eminence as strategist and tactician. He was also given, as a present, the finest chariot in all Sparta; and when his state visit ended, he was escorted, as far as the Tegean frontier, by three hundred horsemen of the Royal Household

have told? And if public, who would have done it? Ephorus (Diod. 11.27.2) states that the prize went to Ameinias of Pallene (cf. above, p. 192), but this may be no more than rationalisation from Hdt. 8.93, where an Aeginetan and two Athenians (including Ameinias) are named as having fought with the greatest distinction.

Cavalry – the first, and last, non-Spartan to be accorded such a privilege. Themistocles, in fact, got what is known nowadays as full VIP treatment; and the price of this, for a visiting statesman, is generally some hard political bargaining in private. What Themistocles and his hosts discussed we do not know (though we may guess that it was now he first struck up his friendship with Cleombrotus's son Pausanias, soon to become Regent of Sparta and Captain-General of the Hellenes[6]). What we *do* know – and what, surely, has great significance – is that his visit to Sparta did him no good at all with his own countrymen.

When he returned to Athens, Themistocles very soon learnt the truth of the old adage that, in politics, gratitude is a lively sense of favours to come. He had served his purpose; now he was expendable. He afterwards said of the Athenians that 'they did not admire or honour him for himself, but treated him like a plane-tree; when it was stormy, they ran under his branches for shelter, but as soon as it was fine, they plucked his leaves and lopped his branches' [Plut. *Them.* 18.3]. There is a great deal of truth in this; yet one can only ask, what else did he ever expect? His father had warned him, years before, about the harsh realities of Athenian political life [see above, p. 26]; yet he still, like any modern romantic, seems to have felt he should be loved for himself alone – without, one might add, taking any noticeable pains to make himself lovable. To a great extent his eclipse was his own fault. He badly misjudged the political situation in the winter of 480–79, and hardly improved matters by displays of quite incredibly brash tactlessness. After Salamis, he seems to have felt himself invulnerable to criticism, on a higher plane than mere common mortals; yet his power rested, in the last resort, on nothing more solid than a temporary upsurge of public emotion. He could turn off, with a cutting personal gibe, the charge brought by Timodemus of Aphidnae, that he had arrogated to himself honours which more properly belonged to Athens (an early example of 'the cult of personality'). But the present he had accepted from the Spartan government left him dangerously exposed to accusations of political bribery, while his own conceit and intransigence proved godsends to those who were working for his removal. When he built a temple for Artemis, he gave offence to many by dedicating it under the name Artemis-of-good-Counsel (a fairly blatant piece of self-advertisement, and taken as such); he compounded the *bêtise* by choosing a site just opposite his own house. When one of his fellow-generals began comparing their achievements, he snapped dismissively: 'If Themistocles had not been there on the day of Salamis, where would all the rest of you be now?'

This, of course, was the kind of ill-advised remark that no one, least of all an elected Greek politician, could hope to get away with for long. Themistocles' most fatal error, however, was not to realise how strongly the tide had turned against him – or, indeed, how radically the strategic situation had changed, almost overnight. To a good-looking youth who had formerly disdained his attentions, but now cultivated him because of his fame, he remarked, blandly: 'Well, my boy, time has taught both of us a lesson, even if we have left it late.' From the political viewpoint it was too late already. Effective power had largely passed into the hands of Aristeides and his associates, a swing that was to be confirmed by the spring elections of 479. Most of these men were aristocrats or landowners who detested Themistocles personally (all the more, we may surmise, since Salamis), had opposed his 'wooden wall' strategy throughout, and on both counts would stick at nothing to get him out of office. *They* were pinning their hopes on some sort of military *entente cordiale* with the Peloponnesian *bloc*, leading to a joint land-based campaign against Mardonius; yet here was Themistocles, lording it at Sparta, falsely assuming the authority of an accredited government spokesman, and doubtless selling his all-too-receptive hosts a comprehensive *naval* policy for the coming year. (The Spartans, as everyone knew, would seize any excuse to keep their superb army safely south of the Isthmus.) Both on public and on personal grounds, he had to be eased out of power, and the sooner the better: as things stood he was a direct threat to national security. If the Spartans accepted the idea of a renewed naval offensive (and the subsequent replacement of Eurybiades as High Admiral by King Leotychidas in person lends much support to such an assumption) then two consequences would follow, neither of them acceptable in Athens. The Greek land forces would be reduced to a merely defensive role; and Mardonius would find little or nothing to stop him carrying out a second invasion of Attica.*

At all events, during that winter Themistocles' political enemies worked hard to turn public opinion against him – with remarkably successful results. A rumour was started that Apollo of Delphi had refused his offering, and his alone, after Salamis (one would like to think that this *canard* originated with some disgruntled Aeginetan). It was probably now, too, that the story of his supposedly sacrificing three noble Persian youths before the battle [see above, p. 185] first got into

* E. Meyer, *Geschichte des Altertums* (Stuttgart 1901) vol. 3, p. 402 ff., followed by Hignett, XIG pp. 275–6. This kind of fish-and-fox campaign could straggle on inconclusively for a very long time. Mardonius's small, flexible army was specially designed to live off the land, and Thessaly provided him with an excellent base. The fleet might cut his communications, but was unlikely to achieve much else in one season. To that extent the anti-naval group had a strong case.

circulation: the second libel may even have been used to explain, or justify, the first. Circumstantial anecdotes of his arrogance, greed and dishonesty were promoted with sedulous care. All this sniping inevitably whittled away his support in the Assembly. When the new Board of Generals was elected, in February 479 (for the period July 479–June 478) Themistocles either failed to secure a place on it, or, if he did, was kept very much in the background throughout his term of office. Ephorus [Diod. 11.27.3] claims that he was debarred because he had taken gifts from the Spartans: this may be no more than speculation, as most scholars assume, but it is the only positive evidence we have.

What cannot be gainsaid, however, is that in office or out of it, he played no part at all – certainly none befitting his status – in the last great campaign of the Persian Wars, the campaign which finally and for ever destroyed the threat of Persian domination over Greece. Other men reaped the final harvest of victory which he had sown. Aristeides, predictably, took over the command of Athens' land forces, while the fleet that had virtually been Themistocles' personal creation was now placed under Xanthippus, the father of Pericles. Personal vindictiveness may well have played some part in these appointments. Both men had been sent into political exile largely through Themistocles' machinations [see above, pp. 55–6 and 57], while Xanthippus, whose new appointment was probably a sop to the 'sailor rabble', had been one of his own colleagues, and thus perhaps bore a more than usually bitter grudge against him. Though Themistocles contrived to recover some of his lost influence by 478, he took no further part in the war; and Herodotus – having introduced him at the last possible moment – now drops him from his narrative with an almost audible sigh of relief.

Late in October Xerxes handed over to Mardonius, and led the bulk of his great army back, along the road he had come, to the Dardanelles. Greek tradition – never averse to exulting over the downfall of the ungodly – made this retreat a highly imaginative essay in horror and deprivation. Where disasters did not exist, they were invented: every generation added its own rhetorical embellishment to the saga. This process began very early, with Aeschylus, who has a vivid and circumstantial account of how Xerxes' troops rashly attempted to cross the frozen Strymon, but fell through and were drowned when its thin ice gave way at the centre after a morning's sunshine [*Pers.* 495–507]. In fact, as we know from Herodotus, the Persians had bridged the Strymon before their march into Greece [see above, p. 53]; though it is just possible that some units, impatient of congestion at the bridgehead, decided to risk a quick dash across the ice. Herodotus himself draws a stark picture of starvation and disease, with the Great King's troops reduced to eating grass and bark and leaves, while plague and dysentery decimate their ranks. So many corpses were left by the wayside, says Justin [2.13.12], that a whole host of vultures, hyenas and other scavengers followed the army throughout its retreat. One curious anecdote (refuted by Herodotus) shows Xerxes taking ship at Eion, getting caught in a storm, and forcing dozens of his Persian noblemen to jump overboard – a drastic but effective way of shedding top-heavy ballast.

When we strip off all these dramatic accretions, we are left with a less romantic and not particularly disastrous story. Xerxes marched from Thessaly to Sestos in a brisk forty-five days, arriving shortly before mid-December. The bridges, as we have seen, were down, but the fleet had duly arrived, and now ferried the entire force across to Abydos – without mishap, unless we count the illnesses which resulted from over-eating (after a lean march, supplies were now plentiful) and the change of water. From here Xerxes marched to Sardis, where he spent the winter. All this hardly suggests a chronic breakdown of health, discipline, or the commissariat. The Great King was escorted to the Dardanelles not only by Hydarnes, but also by a force of some six thousand picked troops under Artabazus: this body subsequently made its way back to Chalcidice without noticeable deprivation or mishap.[7] If his troops suffered from hunger or disease – and they may well have done – it was not to an extent that incapacitated them. Nor did they have to contend with any sort of military opposition. Despite the crushing defeat which Persia had sustained at Salamis, Thessaly, Macedonia and Thrace still remained loyal to Xerxes: his march was through friendly territory from start to finish. It was said that only when he reached Abdera in Thrace did he feel safe enough to undo his girdle (as a token of his relief and gratitude he presented the citizens with a golden sword and a gilt tiara) but this was through fear of pursuit rather than any suspicion of local treachery. Besides, Persian garrisons were placed at strategic points (such as Eion and Doriscus) all along his route. Those troops who fell sick were left behind in the nearest Greek city, with instructions as to their care and maintenance – a revealing detail. Whatever they may have felt about Xerxes in Athens or Sparta, up north, clearly, he was a far from unpopular taskmaster.

Nevertheless, once he and the larger part of his expeditionary force had withdrawn into Asia Minor, the odds against any city defecting shortened considerably. The first open revolt seems to have broken out about mid-December, when Artabazus, having seen Xerxes across the Dardanelles, was on his way back to rejoin Mardonius in Thessaly. As so often throughout the course of Greek history, it was a Chalcidic city which gave the lead. Potidaea, astride the narrow neck of the Pallene peninsula, was admirably placed to withstand any assault from the landward side; and Mardonius (as the Potidaeans knew very well) had no fleet. The other towns of Pallene joined Potidaea in her rebellion; so – rather more rashly – did Olynthus, which lay north of the Isthmus and was thus far more exposed to attack. Mardonius and his main task-force were wintering in Thessaly – another point the rebels surely took into consideration when planning their *coup*. It has been suggested by several scholars[8] that this revolt owed its inception to the Peloponnesian *bloc* (in particular to Potidaea's mother-city Corinth) and was encouraged as an inexpensive way of cutting Mardonius's lines of communication. Since this theory is rapidly acquiring canonical status, it may be as well to remind the reader that not one shred of evidence can be adduced in support of it. Potidaea never received any help or reinforcements from the League, which she surely would have done had her rising formed part of a deliberately concerted plan. Furthermore, the defection of Pallene (as one glance at a map should suffice to make clear) did not in any way threaten Mardonius. The revolt was a genuine symptom of resurgent Greek independence, and should never have been taken as anything else. In itself it achieved little; but for the Persians it was an ominous forerunner of things to come.

Artabazus, his original corps of six thousand Parthians and Chorasmians now augmented by strong local levies from Macedonia, took prompt action against the rebels. He first blockaded the Pallene Isthmus, after which (having thus sealed off Potidaea) he was free to besiege Olynthus at his leisure. When the city fell, which it seems to have done soon afterwards (through treachery within the walls, one suspects: in the fifth century a well-placed bribe came cheaper, and worked faster, than total investment), he took its revolutionary leaders out to a nearby lake, where their throats were cut *pour décourager les autres*. Artabazus had nothing to learn about the divide-and-rule technique when dealing with Greeks. The accomplished way in which he now proceeded to exploit local jealousies was not lost on Xerxes, who three years later appointed him satrap of Dascylium. He seems to have secured the cooperation of various Chalcidic cities during his punitive expedition, all anxious to cash in on the discomfiture of some hated rival. When Olynthus fell, he turned it over to a garrison from Torone, whose citizens seem to have been granted possession of the site in perpetuity. At the same time he was privately intriguing with one of the generals defending Potidaea, a Scionian named Timoxenus, to bring about another quick victory through betrayal. Why waste time and money on extended siege operations?

The two men communicated in a somewhat novel manner. They 'wrote the message on a strip of paper, which they rolled round the grooved end of an arrow; the feathers were then put on over the paper, and the arrow was shot to some predetermined place' [Hdt. 8.128]. However, after a while Artabazus's archer grew careless, and one of his loaded shafts hit a Potidaean in the shoulder. A typical Greek crowd gathered round ('as usually happens in war' says Herodotus, and indeed after any untoward public incident): the arrow was extracted, its message brought to light. Some patriotic citizen at once took it to the allied commanders (of Potidaea and the towns on Pallene who had come to her assistance); they, anxious to save Scione's good name, hushed up the scandal and brought no charges against Timoxenus – uncharac-teristically quixotic behaviour, which suggests that others may have been implicated in the plot. Despite their forbearance, Artabazus's cover was, as they say, blown, and his plan had to be abandoned. Regretfully, he settled down to besiege Potidaea in earnest. After three months of this stultifying non-activity he was ready to grasp at any chance, however remote, of penetrating the city's defences. One day an exceptionally low ebb-tide (probably, as Burn suggests, caused by an earth-tremor: the normal Aegean tide is measured in inches) left a negotiable if water-logged channel beside the exposed end of the city-wall across the isthmus. Artabazus at once decided to send part of his force through this gap, and consolidate a position in rear of the city. Unfortunately, while they were still less than half-way across, the sea came flooding back, and most of those who did not drown were slaughtered by the Potidaeans, who ran them down in small boats.* Artabazus extricated the remainder of his corps as best he could, raised the siege of Potidaea, and marched away westward to join Mardonius.

The latter found himself in a somewhat paradoxical position. Persia might have suffered a major naval defeat, but the Great King, either directly or through his loyal subject-allies, still controlled all northern and central Greece east of the Pindus. Mardonius was, in effect, the satrap of a new province stretching from Thrace to Attica. Nor could he be regarded as barely holding his own under heavy pressure from the enemy. The Greek fleet represented far less fundamental a threat to his

---

* Hdt. 8.128. The historian adds, piously: 'This excessive tide and the consequent disaster to the Persians are put down by the people of Potidaea to the fact that the men who met their deaths were the same ones as had previously desecrated the shrine of Poseidon, and the statue of him which stands just outside the town. Personally, I think their explanation is the true one.' If the phenomenon was in fact due to an earth-tremor, Poseidon, as the god of earthquakes, might indeed be regarded as responsible. See Burn, PG p. 499.

communications than is usually supposed. His small army could survive perfectly well without sea-borne supplies, and until Xerxes' own squadrons were finally destroyed or disbanded, there was no real chance of his being cut off in mainland Greece. Even if denied the Dardanelles, he could still reach home safely by way of Thrace and the Bosporus. This, it is safe to say, was the least of his worries: the real problem lay elsewhere. If Xerxes had left a crack army corps in Greece, it was not merely to show the flag and police occupied territory. The Isthmus line still held firm; Sparta and her allies still stood out against Persian overlordship. Mardonius had a clear brief: to mop up this anomalous pocket of resistance. There were two ways, and two only, in which his object could be achieved. He must either outflank the Isthmus defences, and open a wide door (as Chileus the Tegean later put it) into the Peloponnese; or else he must tempt his opponents out from behind their wall to fight on terrain of his own choosing – preferably where the Persian cavalry arm would have room to operate. The first scheme was by definition impossible without a strong fleet, which Mardonius signally lacked; the second required that the Spartans should wantonly throw away every strategical advantage they possessed.

At this point Plutarch [*Arist.* 10.2] represents Mardonius as sending a primitive kind of challenge to the Greek High Command: 'With that fleet of yours you have managed to defeat men who are used to dry land and know nothing about handling an oar. But now the land of Thessaly is wide, and the plains of Boeotia are fair ground for good cavalry and infantry to fight on.' This piece of late rhetorical fiction may state the case correctly, but it very much underestimates Mardonius's subtlety and resourcefulness. So naïve a challenge, if ever dispatched, would have caused considerable amusement at the Isthmus. Mardonius, however, had his own devious way of going about things, which the Spartans, in the event, did not find amusing at all. He maintained an active fifth-column, and kept himself well abreast of the various dissensions among his opponents. In particular, he studied the deepening rift between Athens and Sparta. Here, if he could find the right way to exploit it, was the most promising *apertura* of them all. In the Peloponnese itself his agents worked hard, with bribes and diplomacy, to soften up those cities traditionally hostile to Sparta: Argos, Elis, Mantinea. The Argives agreed, in private, 'to prevent Spartan troops from taking the field', presumably by blocking their exit-routes through the northern Peloponnese. Mardonius, however, is unlikely to have placed much reliance on so nebulous an undertaking, well described by Hignett [XIG, p. 279] as 'a kind of insurance against the faint possibility that the Persians might win after all, as insincere as the messages of good will sent by some Whig politicians in England to James II when he was in exile'. After Salamis, the Argives were hedging their bets with extreme caution, and had no intention of committing themselves irrevocably to what might well prove the losing side. Elis and Mantinea were similarly unpredictable. With that shrewd if cynical realism which was the hall-mark of all Achaemenid politics, Mardonius found his thoughts turning more and more towards Athens.

If – and it was a large if – Athens could be detached from her Peloponnesian allegiance, and brought over to the Great King's side, this would at once provide Mardonius with the first-class fleet he needed to by-pass the Isthmus defences. Sparta's downfall would then be simply a matter of time. Even if the Athenians held out against his advances (which considering their record to date seemed more than likely) the mere knowledge that such advances had been made was liable to scare the Spartans into a far more accommodating mood where Athens was concerned. Mardonius knew all about the change which had taken place in the Athenian political climate since Salamis; it had not escaped his notice that what the conservative-agrarian group now in power wanted was a direct military show-down, preferably north of the Cithaeron-Parnes line.[9] Since this was precisely what he hoped for himself, he at least had a ready-made *point d'appui*. Either he got his 'wide door' into the Peloponnese, or, failing that, the Athenians, with luck, would put enough pressure on Sparta to make her send a strong army into central Greece. The gamble was well worth trying. On the other hand, Athens would never even consider so staggering a *volte-face* unless the terms offered her were generous enough to outweigh every other consideration. Mardonius consulted with Xerxes (perhaps the plan had been worked out between them before the Great King finally left for Sardis) and they agreed on the following proposals: (1) a blanket amnesty for all past Athenian acts of aggression against Persia, (2) guaranteed internal autonomy of government, (3) the establishment of Athens as *de facto* mistress of Greece, with *carte blanche* to extend her present frontiers, (4) the restoration of all temples and city-walls destroyed during Xerxes' invasion, (5) massive financial assistance. In return for these remarkable concessions, the Athenians were to ally themselves formally with Persia, and support Xerxes in any war he undertook – which, of course, meant primarily the campaign against Sparta.

How far these grandiloquent undertakings would ever have been honoured, when it came to the point, is a matter for speculation. Mardonius must have known perfectly well that by promising Athens such extraordinary privileges he was all too liable to provoke an explosion among Persia's existing Greek allies, most of whom – Boeotia above all – regarded the violet-crowned city with cordial detestation, liberally tinged with envy. Perhaps this is why we now find him sending a confidential agent to consult all the leading oracles in central Greece: indeed, if we exclude the shrine at Abae in Phocis, the list is exclusively Boeotian – the cave of Trophonius at Lebadea, the precinct of Ptoan Apollo above Lake Copais, and, in Thebes itself, the oracle of Ismenian Apollo and the shrine of Amphiaraus. The omission of Delphi is remarkable, and perhaps significant. One unacknowledged function of oracles in Greece was to serve as diplomatic clearing-houses; it is legitimate to suppose that Mardonius was taking the political temperature among his allies without overtly committing himself. This is what Herodotus seems to be hinting at when he observes: 'Presumably [Mardonius] sent for information and advice on the business he had at the moment in hand, and not for any other purpose.' Doubtless he also, by the same circuitous method, satisfied Boeotian concern as to Athens' eventual position in a Persian-dominated Greece (though it is hard to see what adequate guarantees he could have furnished of Xerxes' good intentions, to Thebes or, indeed, to Athens herself). Having thus prepared the ground to the best of his ability, Mardonius was left with one last delicate problem: to find a convincing and acceptable envoy, who would make the best possible job of selling this package deal to a highly critical Athenian audience. His choice fell on King Alexander of Macedon, whose Persian family connections had not prevented his receiving high civic honours at Athens: like his son and grandson after him, Alexander probably sold shipbuilding lumber impartially to both sides. He had, moreover, already carried out a somewhat similar mission during the Greeks' brief occupation of Tempe [see above, p. 87]. It was this plausible and mercurially ambivalent character who now appeared in war-ruined Athens as Mardonius's special ambassador.

It took the Athenian government very little time to realise that here was an unprecedented and probably unique opportunity to get their recalcitrant Spartan allies over a barrel. Normal diplomatic procedure on such occasions, then as now, was to hold a series of preliminary discussions behind closed doors, during which any major differences of opinion could be explored, and all the real bargaining or compromises took place. The Athenians deliberately spun out these talks as long as possible, 'in the conviction', says Herodotus, 'that the Spartans would hear that someone had arrived in Athens to represent Persia in peace negotiations, and that the news would induce them to send representatives of their own without delay'. In other words, the shrewd conservative caucus now responsible for Athenian foreign policy had decided to play Mardonius and the Spartans off against each other. Whether they were prepared, if necessary, to follow this policy to its logical conclusion, and sell out to the highest bidder, is another matter entirely. Even in the cut-throat world of fifth-century Greek politics, it is hard to believe that they seriously contemplated a step which would have made macabre nonsense of every ideal they had professed and fought for hitherto. Yet both Mardonius and the Spartans regarded such a switch of allegiance as well within the bounds of possibility. If they finally turned it down, their motives for doing so were at least as much practical as moral. The benefits they would get from such a deal were exclusively short-term, and unlikely long to outlast the departure of Mardonius and his army. As Persia's collaborator, Athens would incur the lasting obloquy and hatred of every free state in Greece. Better to have medised *ab initio* than to turn your coat for profit at the eleventh hour. Worst of all, Athens had no adequate guarantee that Xerxes would honour his side of the bargain: its essence, after all, was that the Athenians should commit themselves and their fleet to the Persian cause, and be duly rewarded afterwards. Once Mardonius was established as satrap of all Greece, the Great King's fine promises might well be conveniently forgotten – and who, then, could hold him to his word?

The truth is that Mardonius seems seriously to have underrated the men with whom he had to deal. The Athenians had learnt their politics in a hard school: heirs to the century which had thrown up in turn Solon, Peisistratus and Cleisthenes, they were subtle and hard-headed enough to take on any Persian grandee or Macedonian trimmer. It must have become apparent to them, long before the first round of negotiations was over, that Mardonius's offer stank in every possible way, and not merely to high heaven. On the other hand, as a weapon with which to blackmail the Spartans (whose opinion of Athenian integrity was by no means high enough to ignore the threat of a mass sell-out) it came as an absolute godsend. While the talks dragged on, day after day, news of Alexander's mission duly filtered through to Sparta, and caused a sizable panic there. The Spartans, doubly alarmed because of a prophecy 'that the Dorians would one day be expelled from the Peloponnese by the Persians and Athenians' – unusually specific for oracular material, and one wonders who put it into circula-tion – at once sent representatives of their own to Athens. The Council, whose procrastinating tactics had had just this end in view, now arranged for both sides to make their formal address to the Assembly during the same session, 'in order that the Spartans might be present when they declared their views'.

Alexander spoke first. He began by outlining the Great King's five-point programme (which must have caused something of a sensation) and then added a personal message from Mardonius. The gist of this message was that continued resistance against the Great King must prove, ultimately, self-defeating. 'Stop imagining yourselves a match for Xerxes: it can only end in the loss of your country and the continual peril of your lives.' Xerxes, Mardonius pointed out, was in a generous mood at the moment, but who could tell when his mood might change? Then came the clinching exhortation: 'Make an alliance with us, frankly and openly, and so keep your freedom.' Having passed on all this, Alexander – assuming the role dictated by his position as Athenian *proxenos* and titular benefactor – added a few words of personal advice. 'It is clear to me', he told his listeners – how sceptical were they by now? – 'that you will not be able to maintain your struggle with Xerxes for ever – had I thought you could, I should never have come to Athens on this mission'. Having thus cleared his own conscience for the record, he went on to emphasise the limitless nature of Xerxes' resources, the folly of passing up 'such excellent terms', which might never be offered them again. He reminded the Athenians (not that they can have needed much reminding) of their nakedly exposed position: 'Your country, being a sort of no-man's-land, is bound to be the scene of constant fighting, and again and again you will have to suffer alone.' Having thus played on the theme of self-interest, Alexander wound up his speech with an appeal to Athenian vainglory: surely it was no mean compliment that the Great King should bestow his favours on *them*, alone of all the Greek city-states, and not only forgive the past, but actually extend the hand of friendship towards them?

The Spartans, no mean diplomats themselves, seem to have had a fairly shrewd idea of what the Athenians were up to. Their brief speech was contemptuous rather than persuasive in tone, and made surprisingly few concessions to Athenian interests. They were quite capable of working out for themselves the stand which Athens would, in the last resort, take against Mardonius's offer: once on the spot, in fact, they seem to have sized up everyone's position with remarkable speed and accuracy. Have done so, they coolly proceeded to cash in on their own foresight. Alexander was cut down to size with one dismissive phrase ('a despot himself, of course he works in another despot's interest') and the Athenians were given a broad hint as to what they might expect if they were ill-advised enough to believe Mardonius's promises ('surely you know that in foreigners there is neither truth nor honour'). How inconsistent with decency and honour it would be if Athens, a city whose devotion to freedom went back hundreds of years, now became the instrument through which slavery descended on Greece! All this covered familiar ground: more disconcerting was an attempt to make Athens alone responsible for the present crisis: 'It was you, in the first place, who started this war – our wishes were not considered. It began by being a war for your territories only – now all Greece is involved.' Up to a point this was true enough. While Athens was helping the Ionians to burn Sardis [see above, pp. 20–1], Sparta, one canny eye on Argos, had prudently stayed neutral; and the Great King's declared motive for invasion was, as everyone knew, to take reprisals against Athens. Nevertheless, it stood out a mile that this gambit simply provided a handy excuse for avoiding military commitments north of the Isthmus. All doubts on the matter were removed when the Spartan envoys, with many expressions of sympathy, wound up their speech by offering – superb anticlimax – 'to provide support for all the women and other non-combatant members of your households, for as long as the war lasts'.

This was, in itself, a generous enough proposal (it included not only provisions, but also temporary living-quarters). Most of Athens' evacuated families had by now returned home from Salamis, and were having an extremely hard time of it 'as a result of their city and their territory having both been overrun at once' [Plut. *Arist.* 10.3]. Such a concession, however, was a far cry from what Athens' leaders had been confidently expecting to obtain – that is, massive and unqualified military support against Mardonius. Far from blackmailing the Spartans, they were now in a very pretty cleft stick themselves. Whatever happened, they dared not accept the Great King's proposals, even though to refuse them would, inevitably, precipitate a second invasion of Attica. (That the Spartans realised all this when they called Athens' bluff was made insultingly clear by the offer to support her evacuees.) All they could do now was grin and bear it: squeeze out every last drop of moral credit, in public, for their nobly altruistic stand, while applying all the pressure they could, in private, to Sparta's blandly elusive ambassadors. Their speech of refusal in the Assembly (traditionally said to have been drafted by Aristeides: the sanctimonious note is certainly in character) must have caused Alexander, who was nobody's fool, some moments of wry amusement, even though it spelt failure for his mission:

We know as well as you do that the Persian strength is many times greater than our own: that, at least, is a fact which you need not have troubled to rub in. Nevertheless, such is our love of freedom, that we will defend ourselves in whatever way we can. As for making terms with Persia, it is useless to try to persuade us; for we shall never consent. You may tell Mardonius, therefore, that so long as the sun keeps his present course in the sky, we Athenians will never make peace with Xerxes. On the contrary, we shall oppose him unremittingly, putting our trust in the help of the gods and heroes whom he despised, whose temples and statues he destroyed with fire. Never come to us again with a proposal like this, and never think you are doing us good service when you urge us to a course which is contrary to all the dictates of religion and honour . . . [Hdt. 8.143]

By so uncompromising a declaration the Athenians had indeed, as Macan once said, given away their diplomatic weapons; but whether it was altogether 'in a fit of pan-Hellenic generosity' seems rather more open to doubt.

It is sometimes alleged that they still managed to extort some concessions from Sparta; but what pressure could they put on their allies after a *démarche* of this sort? Their subsequent assertion that Sparta had, in fact, promised to send an army into Boeotia sounds like pure wishful thinking – though a Spartan ambassador, no less than Sir Henry Wotton, was quite capable of 'lying abroad for the good of his country'. The evidence of Plutarch [*Arist.* 10.4–5] and Herodotus [8.144] suggests, what we could have deduced for ourselves, that they fell back on holier-than-thou moral righteousness – about the only line open to them in the circumstances – and rather overdid it. 'Were we offered all the gold in the world', they are reported as saying, 'and the fairest and richest country the earth contains, we should never consent to join the common enemy and bring Greece into subjection'. The priests of Athens were solemnly enjoined to lay a curse on any man who entered into negotiations with Xerxes. Sparta's offer to look after civilian evacuees provoked the Athenians, not surprisingly, to a certain waspishness: they refused such aid, declaring (in Plutarch's words) that 'they were offended with the Spartans . . . for so far forgetting the bravery and the spirit of the Athenians as to appeal to them to fight for Greece by offering rations.' Herodotus gives a more diplomatic version of this refusal, but makes it even clearer what the real point at issue was. The Athenians would rather carry on as they were, they said, without imposing any extra burden on their allies. Then came the punch-line:

That being our resolve, *get your army into the field with the least possible delay* [my italics]; for unless we are much mistaken, it will not be long before the enemy invades Attica – he will do it the instant he gets the news that our answer has been an absolute refusal of all his requests. This, then, is the moment for you to send a force to meet him in Boeotia, before he can appear in Attica.

Doubtless the Spartan ambassadors promised to do what they could, safe in the knowledge that they had no plenipotentiary powers; and with that crumb of comfort the Athenians had to be content.

It is just possible (though the evidence for such a theory[10] is flimsy, to say the least) that Athens did, after all, have a bargaining-counter which could be brought to bear against the Spartans at this point, and with some effectiveness. If Sparta persisted in withholding her army from Boeotia, Athens could, with equal intransigence, withhold her fleet from the Aegean. In early spring 479 (about the same time as the final failure of Artabazus's campaign against Potidaea) Xerxes' squadrons, having lain low all winter, were reported to be once more making ready for action. Those ships which had wintered at Cyme now moved down to the great naval base on Samos. A corps of predominantly Iranian marines joined them there, and the whole fleet – which with the inclusion of some fresh Ionian contingents now totalled about three hundred vessels – was placed under the joint command of three new high-ranking Achaemenid admirals: Mardontes, Artaÿntes, and the latter's nephew Ithamitres.* Their morale, according to Herodotus, was so low that they shrank from sailing farther west than Samos – a sneer somewhat at variance with their vigorous preparations, and convincingly refuted by Ephorus. Their immediate task, Ephorus says, was to keep a close watch on the cities of the Ionians, 'who were suspected of hostile sentiments' (true or not, by now such suspicions were virtually inevitable). So far the nearest thing to real trouble had been an abortive plot on Chios. A seven-man junta had planned the ruling tyrant's assassination, but one of their number betrayed them; the remaining six fled to Sparta, and thence to Aegina, where the allied fleet was now assembling.

Here they approached King Leotychidas, the new commander-in-chief, urging him to sail at once for Ionia. Their tale of imminent revolt doubtless bore much resemblance to those highly-coloured promises which GHQ Cairo became accustomed to receiving, in 1942-3, from hopeful Greek partisan leaders. Leotychidas sized this group up with an expert eye, saw that – at best – they represented a small and ineffectual minority, and fobbed them off with vague assurances. He was in no position, as yet, to do anything else, even had he so desired. At present he had a mere 110 vessels assembled in Aegina roadstead; if Munro is right, he was waiting for the Athenians, and the Athenians had no intention of showing up except on their own terms. Finally he could

---

* Artaÿntes was the son of Artachaeës, Xerxes' giant and Stentorian overseer during the construction of the ship-canal through the Athos peninsula [see above, p. 89]. Ephorus (Diod. 11.27.1) estimates the total numbers of this new fleet as 400; the lower figure is preferable, not simply because it is vouched for by Herodotus (8.130.2) but because it suggests a tripartite command with each admiral responsible for two fifty-vessel squadrons.

delay no longer, and put to sea regardless; but as things were he found himself so heavily outnumbered that he dared advance no farther east than Delos. For some while the two fleets seem to have taken little, if any, effective action against each other. While the Persians were acting as uneasy watchdogs over Ionia, Leotychidas sat tight and hoped for reinforcements (not perhaps an adequate term, since Athens could, if she so chose, more than double the present size of his fleet). During those early months in 479 naval operations remained conspicuous by their absence.

It was late spring, after the first rains, when Alexander returned to Thessaly, and acquainted Mardonius with the Athenians' flat rejection of his offer. Mardonius (as the Athenians themselves had predicted) at once struck camp and marched south, collecting fresh levies as he went. He was given every encouragement by the leading Thessalian dynasties (now so far committed to Xerxes' cause that any reappraisal was out of the question for them) and in particular by the Aleuadae of Larissa, the continuance of whose régime had become largely dependent on a quasi-permanent occupation. When he reached Boeotia, however, he found the Thebans far less ready to endorse his policy of straightforward aggression. Instead, they advised him to set up his headquarters in Thebes, and from there break up the Peloponnesian *bloc* by fifth-column techniques, playing off one city against the other. 'Send money to the leading men in the various towns,' they told him. 'By doing that you will destroy the unity of the country, after which you will easily be able, with the help of those who take your part, to crush such others as still offer resistance.' This was shrewd advice – Philip II of Macedon, Alexander the Great's father, afterwards took it as his main political maxim for dealing with Greeks – but Mardonius, a vain man, wanted the glory of recapturing Athens, of sending the news to Sardis by means of a special beacon-chain he had organised across the Aegean. He also calculated that after Attica had been invaded for a second time, the Athenians might prove more amenable to his proposals. As so often during this campaign, in terms of logical *Machtpolitik* he should have been right; once again, it was their obstinate and irrational passion for freedom at all costs which proved his undoing.

At first the Athenians seem to have convinced themselves that a Peloponnesian army was, in fact, marching to their relief. Whether the Spartans had actually given them any such assurance remains quite uncertain. In any case, as day followed day, and no troops appeared from the Isthmus, it became all too clear that Athens would, once again, have to fend for herself. When Mardonius reached Northern

Boeotia, the Athenians 'waited no longer, but crossed to Salamis with all their movable property' – the second total evacuation they had carried out in less than a year. At the same time an emergency diplomatic mission, headed by Cimon and including envoys from Megara and Plataea, was sent off to Sparta. These ambassadors were instructed

to reproach the Spartans for allowing the enemy to invade Attica instead of marching with them to meet him in Boeotia, and to remind them, besides, of the offers they had received from Persia in the event of their deserting the Greek confederacy – not to mention the obvious fact that, if they got no help from Sparta, they would have to find some means of helping themselves [Hdt. 9.6].

So much for their flowery protestations of never making peace with Xerxes so long as a single Athenian remained alive! At the same time (by way of offsetting this rather desperate threat) they may have conveyed the news that Athens had at last released her naval squadrons for service with the Aegean fleet. When Mardonius reached Attica, says Herodotus, 'once again there were no Athenians to be found; for nearly all of them, as he learnt, *were either with the fleet or at Salamis*' [9.3] – clear indication that the squadrons had already put to sea. A hundred and forty triremes were now sailing east to join Leotychidas at Delos, thus bringing the allied Greek fleet up to an operational total of two hundred and fifty.*

Meanwhile Mardonius, his forces now swelled to something over 50,000 by the addition of contingents from Thrace, Macedonia, and the medising Greek states, had marched through Attica without encountering any opposition. Towards the end of June 479 he established himself in the empty, half-burnt ghost-town that was Athens. From here he sent an ambassador across to Salamis, a Hellespontine Greek named Murychides, with instructions to offer the Athenians exactly the same terms as Alexander had done. The chances of an eleventh-hour acceptance were very slim, even allowing for the psychological effect which the reoccupation of Athens must surely have produced. Now, if ever, Mardonius felt the lack of a fleet. But one way or another he had to

---

* Hdt. 9.3; Diod. 11.34.2; Munro, *loc. cit.* The main objection to Munro's theory, well summarised by Hignett (XIG p. 250), is that Athens in 479 lacked the manpower to mobilise both her fleet and a field-army (cf. Burn p. 500, n. 34). This is simply untrue. Athens contributed 8,000 hoplites at Plataea; she also, at the same time, put forty fewer triremes into commission than she had done at Salamis (180−40 = 140). By what seems to me no coincidence, the total saving of manpower at sea exactly matches the new military commitment on land (200 × 40 = 8,000). It is reasonable to infer from this that all hoplite marines were drafted out of the fleet before it sailed, and replaced by thetes, metics, or slaves.

break the deadlock. If he could not win over Athens, and use her squadrons to strike at the soft underbelly of the Peloponnese, he had, somehow, to tempt an allied army into central Greece. Put enough pressure on Athens' loyalty to the Greek alliance, and there was just a chance that – even if the Athenians themselves stood firm – Sparta might crack rather than take the fearful risk of presuming indefinitely on her ally's altruism.

Mardonius was, in his own way, a shrewd and sophisticated diplomat. For once he had judged the situation with uncommon perceptiveness. The Athenians were near the end of their tether: how near, we see from the way in which they reacted to Murychides' offer. When he addressed the Council, a certain Lycidas was in favour of admitting the Great King's proposals, and bringing them before the Assembly for ratification. The other councillors, in hysterical fury, made a bodily assault on Lycidas. When people outside heard what had happened, they tore the wretched man from the council-chamber and lynched him. A mob of screeching women then broke into his lodgings, and stoned his wife and children. Murychides himself was allowed to depart unharmed, and in due course made a report of this nasty episode to Mardonius. The Persian commander, though doubtless disappointed by so uncompromising a rejection of his terms, may well have consoled himself with the thought that civilised men who abandoned their standards in this barbaric fashion had come perilously close to breaking-point. As yet, however, he held his hand, and took no immediate action. What most concerned him now was the behaviour of the Peloponnesian *bloc*.

The same might be said of the allied embassy which had been sent to Sparta. Some days later it arrived back in Salamis, seething with resentment and frustration.* The envoys, by what one can only regard as a masterpiece of mistiming, had arrived during the Hyacinthia, an Adonis-type festival which the Spartans took about as seriously as their modern descendants do Easter or the Feast of the Assumption. The people, as Herodotus says, without irony, 'were on holiday and thinking of nothing so much as giving the God his due'. Work on the Isthmus wall, the envoys noted, was almost complete: nothing remained to be added but the upper battlements. The atmosphere, in short, did not on

---

* I am developing here a tentative suggestion advanced by Hignett [XIG p. 284] that there were in fact *two* embassies to Sparta during June 479: the first, conducted by Cimon, Xanthippus (the archon for 479–8, not Ariphron's son, who was with the fleet), and Myronides, at the time of Athens' re-evacuation [Hdt. 9.7; Plut. *Arist.* 10.8; Diod. 11.28.5]; the second perhaps ten days or a fortnight later, under Aristeides [Plut. *Arist.* 10.7]. The crucial Spartan decision to march will have been taken at some point between them. For a general discussion of the difficulties in the tradition see Hignett, *ibid.*, pp. 281–5, and reff. there cited.

the face of it suggest imminent mobilisation, least of all for a campaign in central Greece. Nor had the Ephors, in interview, proved any more satisfactory (at least, so one gathers from Herodotus, whose account seems to have been based exclusively on Athenian sources). Accused of cashing in on Athens' loyalty for their own purposes, and of going back on the agreement they had made (when?) 'to oppose the invader in Boeotia', they shuffled and prevaricated. 'Your immediate duty', the ambassadors told them, bluntly, 'is to accede to our present request: put your army in the field, that you and we together may meet Mardonius in Attica'. Now that Boeotia was lost, they added, the best site for an engagement would be the Thriasian plain. This challenge got no definite answer at the time. The Ephors promised a decision within twenty-four hours, but kept postponing it. After some days of these delaying tactics, the envoys gave up and went home.

The Athenian government, now thoroughly alarmed, at once sent off a second mission, this time under Aristeides, who was supposed to have a good deal of influence at Sparta. They could, as things turned out, have spared themselves the trouble. After the departure of Cimon and his colleagues, the Ephors, for whatever reason, had made a serious reappraisal of the situation. There must (despite the current policy of isolationism) have been a strong 'war-party' in Lacedaemon – perhaps led by Pausanias, now Regent for his young cousin Pleistarchus, Leonidas's son – which wanted nothing better than to seek out and destroy Mardonius. This group got some useful backing from the Tegean diplomat Chileus – 'a man with more influence in Sparta than anyone else who was not a native'. Chileus pointed out (what might have seemed obvious enough already) that if the Athenians *did* switch sides, 'the doors will be wide open for the Persian invasion of the Peloponnese'. This is said to have been the decisive argument – though it probably gained extra strength from Athens' last-minute dispatch of her naval squadrons to Delos. A campaign which would take the cream of Sparta's troops abroad automatically increased the risk of trouble at home from the Helots: this problem was solved by drafting an unprecedented number of Helots into the ranks as light-armed troops – 35,000, according to Herodotus. By the time Aristeides reached Sparta, the Lacedaemonian army was already on the road: had, in fact, got as far as the Arcadian frontier, by way of Orestheion. In addition to the Helots, 5,000 full Spartiate warriors (about two-thirds of the total reserve) had been mustered for active service. When the Ephors told Aristeides this news he was, at first, flatly incredulous, and 'retorted that it was a particularly ill-timed joke to deceive their allies instead of their enemies'.

One can sympathise with his attitude. These events form one of the most enigmatic (and, historically speaking, least satisfactory) episodes in the whole of Xerxes' invasion. The evidence is one-sided where not downright suspect; motives often appear inadequate, actions inexplicable. Sparta's sudden military *volte-face* is hardly less baffling than the diplomatic tergiversations which had preceded it. Did the Ephors in fact ever promise Athens a task-force to help drive 'the strangers' from Boeotia? If they did, why, having promised it, did they then go back on their word – surely the one move designed to produce the Athenian betrayal which they most feared? Were they (to borrow a neat phrase of Burn's) quite as 'short-sighted, isolationist, even Maginot-minded' as Athenian propaganda afterwards made them out? Is it conceivable that they mounted, and won, a major campaign for no better reason than that they were blackmailed into doing so? Their large-scale and efficient mobilisation suggests long-term planning. Yet all their actions hitherto had been based on a firm determination to avoid expensive military commitments north of the Isthmus. They had enough worries of their own, far nearer home. Argos was perennially hostile, and Arcadia, at best, unreliable: perhaps Chileus furnished the Ephors, *inter alia*, with a guarantee of Arcadian neutrality for the duration [so Burn, PG p. 505]. Trouble was stirring among the sullen serf-population of Messenia – trouble which would, within a very few years, reach its climax with a full-scale nationalist revolt. Then what, finally, brought the Spartans round to the idea of a strong offensive against Mardonius? Perhaps, in the last resort, the realisation that isolationism would not work; that even if Mardonius failed to secure the Athenian fleet, he was bound, sooner rather than later, to get a fleet from *somewhere* – after which it would only be a matter of time before Persian shock-troops came riding up the Eurotas valley to unwalled Sparta. Better to crush 'the stranger' now, while he still lacked adequate naval support. Besides, so long as his army remained on Greek soil, the freedom for which Greece had fought so hard and so long would be, at best, problematical.

As we have seen, once the decision to march had been taken, no time was lost. Pausanias, appointed Captain-General of all allied land forces (which would seem to imply some sort of prior consultation between member-states of the League) set out for the Isthmus forthwith, at the head of his 5,000 Spartiates and 35,000 Helots. For a young man still in his twenties[11] he bore a heavy responsibility, which, however, he did not allow to overawe him. Picking up the contingents of Tegea and Orchomenus *en route*, he reached the Isthmus assembly-point before most of his own allies – let alone the enemy – knew that he had marched from Sparta. Here he encamped, and waited for the remaining Peloponnesian contingents to join him. First came another force from Lacedaemon itself, which had taken somewhat longer to mobilise: 5,000 hoplites mustered by the outlying townships, each man with one Helot in attendance on him. These arrived twenty-four hours after Pausanias, and Aristeides – his mission now brought to an unexpectedly successful conclusion – came with them. He is unlikely to have lingered at the Isthmus: as commander-in-chief of Athens' land forces, he had to get back home as fast as possible. What he did do before his departure was to arrange a rendezvous-point with Pausanias. The Athenians, he said, would meet him at Eleusis, where the road to Thebes turns inland from the coast.

The speed and secrecy of Sparta's mobilisation had been designed, in part, to deceive Mardonius's fair-weather friends the Argives, which it may very well have done. Conceivably, though, they turned a diplomatic blind eye to Pausanias's preparations until it was too late. Despite their undertaking to block the advance of any Peloponnesian force making for the Isthmus, one cannot really see them, in 479, as a willing match for the whole embattled might of the Spartan army. They were nothing if not discreet. The moment news came in that Pausanias was on the march, they sent off their fastest long-distance runner to Attica, with a message for Mardonius which has a certain disingenuous charm about it: 'Mardonius, I am sent by the Argives to inform you that the young men have sallied forth from Lacedaemon, and the Argives are powerless to prevent them. Wherefore, may fortune grant you good counsel.'[12] The warning was not untimely, since a quick advance by Pausanias might well have blocked at least the westernmost pass over Cithaeron, that followed by the main road to Eleutherae and Thebes. Such a move seems, in fact, to have been attempted: Mardonius heard that an advance force of one thousand Lacedaemonians had got as far as Megara, and sent out his cavalry to hold them in check. He saw at once that he would have to evacuate Attica. It was bad cavalry terrain, and, as Herodotus says, 'had he been beaten in an engagement, his only way of retreat would have been by a narrow defile [this may refer to any of the Cithaeron-Parnes passes] which could have been held by a very small force'. He therefore decided to fall back on Thebes. Beyond the Asopus lay first-class cavalry country, with the additional advantage of a friendly base in his rear.

Before he withdrew, however, he carried out a thorough and ruthless scorched-earth devastation. Athens itself was burnt, and those few smoke-blackened houses, walls or temples which survived the holocaust his men now systematically razed to the ground. Even so, the destruction was not complete. To obliterate any built-up site *in toto* is a surprisingly difficult business. Parts of the city-walls proved too tough for Mardonius's demolition-workers, and for some reason the old temples of Dionysus and the Dioscuri seem to have been left standing. Mardonius also ravaged the whole of the Attica countryside as far west as Eleusis, burning off crops, rounding up livestock, and setting fire to every inhabitable building. Our sources[13] regard this primarily as an act of vengeance or reprisal, provoked by anger at Athenian uncooperativeness. It is true that Mardonius had been at some pains to behave well in Attica so long as there was the slightest chance of doing a deal with its inhabitants: he even went so far as to repair some of the war-damage done by Xerxes a few months earlier. But to destroy city and countryside now, with a hostile army gathering at the Isthmus, made good strategic sense as well. Why gratuitously help the enemy by leaving him food-supplies or comfortable billets? Just how effective this *razzia* was we can see from a later casual reference by Herodotus [9.39]: during the campaign which followed the Greeks had to bring in the greater part of their commissariat by waggon-convoy from the Peloponnese.

By now Mardonius had received fuller and more accurate intelligence reports concerning Pausanias's field army – relayed back, in all likelihood, by his reconnaissance force of cavalry and mounted archers in the Megarid. It was increasingly obvious that the Captain-General of the Hellenes meant business: so large an assault-group could be intended for nothing less than a full-scale invasion. Mardonius accordingly began the withdrawal of his own units into Boeotia, while he could still do so in relative peace. Why he chose the easternmost pass, over the Parnes hills by way of Decelea, has never been satisfactorily explained. Of the five other routes available, the so-called 'Gyphtokastro Pass' – followed, for much of its course, by the modern road linking Eleusis with Thebes – offered a far easier and more convenient crossing-point. Perhaps Mardonius moved away eastward because he was scared of being ambushed during his retreat. Any column moving through a defile is appallingly vulnerable, and Pausanias, knowing this, might well send a commando force over Cithaeron by way of Aegosthena and Villia [see map, p. 242]. One function of Mardonius's own reconnaissance group was, clearly, to anticipate such a move by covering the road from Tripodiscus to Aegosthena. Half-way along it, at Pagae, a detachment of Persian archers was, in fact, intercepted by the Megarians, and the arrows they shot off in their panic were still shown, as a tourist attraction, in Pausanias's day, protruding from some fissured rocks by the roadside [Paus. 1.40.2, 44.4]. Perhaps a loyalist garrison

was already established in the commanding hill-fortress above Eleutherae, thus blocking Mardonius's line of advance through the pass.
Alternatively, he may have chosen to leave the easiest route open and
undefended, his object being to lure Pausanias on towards that 'good
cavalry country' which he had selected as an ideal Persian battle-
ground. On the other hand, to deduce from his route that 'Aristeides
held the Thriasian plain and all the western passes of Cithaeron' [Parke
and Wormell, vol. 1, p. 175] is to enter the realm of pure speculative
fantasy.

From Decelea, escorted by local guides, Mardonius made his way
down into the plain. Leaving the Attic deme of Sphendale behind him,
he crossed over to the northern bank of the Asopus, and followed the
Oropus-Thebes road westward as far as Tanagra, where he bivouacked
for the night. Next day he continued his march to Scolus, 'and so found
himself in Theban territory'. The exact site of Scolus is still uncertain.
Our evidence suggests that it may have been slightly less than five miles
downstream from the Morea bridge [see map, p. 242], and probably
on the south bank of the river.* What seems quite clear, however –
though the matter has provoked much argument – is that Mardonius,
having once taken the trouble to get himself and his army north of the
Asopus, never crossed back to the Cithaeron side again. As Pritchett
rightly points out, 'no army would be drawn up with its back to the
river'. What is more, there seems to have been no east-west road running
through the southern part of the Asopus valley, nor any major bridge
between Mardonius's original crossing-point near Oropus, and the
Morea bridge on the main road to Thebes. Had the Persians meant to
take up a position on the Cithaeron side, they would never have gone
near Tanagra in the first place. Our main ancient sources [Hdt. 9.36;
Diod. 11.30.1] both locate Mardonius north of the river later; there
would have been no problem at all had not Herodotus described the
position he took up to begin with as 'along the Asopus, from Erythrae,
past Hysiae, to the territory of Plataea'. [9.15.3]. Though the exact
location of these sites has given rise to much discussion, they all undoubtedly lay south of the river. Most scholars assume, sensibly, that
Herodotus employed them as 'markers', to indicate the extent and
position of the Persian line. Hignett, who calls this explanation 'very

* Paus. 9.4.4; Strabo 9.2.23, C. 408; cf. Xen. *Hell.* 5.4.49. Leake, *Travels in Northern
Greece*, vol. 2, p. 330, followed by Pritchett, AJA 61 (1957) 13 and *Topography*, pp.
107–8, 110, place the site 'on a little rocky table-height, overlooking the river', at
the edge of a *metóchi*, or priory farm, belonging to the monastery of St Meletius,
about three-quarters of a mile west of Darimári village. Theirs seems the most likely
identification. Cf. Hignett, XIG pp. 426–7, with reff. there cited.

artificial', conveniently forgets that, as far as we know, there was not a single ancient town on the *northern* bank between Tanagra and Thebes.

Mardonius, then, took up a defensive position along the northern bank of the Asopus, squarely astride the main roads leading into Thebes. His front was about five miles long, with its right flank pushed out westward as far as Plataea. Farther east – perhaps near the modern bridge – he built a large military stockade, 'to protect his troops and to have somewhere to retreat in the event of the battle going against him'. The construction material for this enclosure (a square with sides ten *stadia* in length, and thus containing an area of about 900 acres*) he acquired by clearing off all standing timber and *maquis* in the Scolus region. Herodotus emphasises that he did this, not through hostility to Thebes, but out of sheer military necessity – which suggests that even by 479 BC deforestation, afterwards the curse of Greece, had already become a serious problem. In fact Mardonius appears to have been on excellent terms with the Thebans, and to have received every kind of help from them throughout. They maintained an excellent liaison system: it was due to Theban forethought that local guides were laid on for the Persian army during its first advance from Decelea into the Asopus valley. When the Persians had dug themselves in, a leading Theban statesman, Attaginus son of Phrynon [see above, p. 166], arranged a state banquet for Mardonius and fifty of his senior officers. On each couch a Theban and a Persian were placed together. Herodotus tells this story to indicate the resigned pessimism and low morale which at least one Persian colonel revealed in his cups; but it also gives a glimpse into the kind of top-level fraternising which seems to have been *de rigueur* under a Persian occupation. When Alexander the Great embarked on his schemes of Graeco-Persian integration he was exploring familiar ground.

---

* By a most ingenious comparison with Roman legionary camps, Burn [PG p. 511] obtains a cross-check from the dimensions of this stockade on the actual size of Mardonius's army. The stockade was about 12–14 times as large as a camp for one legion. Allowing for Roman 'superior orderliness', which would economise the available space, Burn posits an army of 60–70,000 men, of whom not more than 10,000 were cavalry. Any increase in the cavalry figure would sharply reduce the overall total. This estimate is not much higher than that obtained above by quite different methods: see pp. 211 and 229. The gap can perhaps be narrowed still further by the inclusion of auxiliaries and pack-animals: though not reckoned among the main fighting force, these undoubtedly took up space inside the stockade.

PART SEVEN

THE
LAST ENEMY

WHILE Mardonius was setting up his command headquarters on the Asopus, Pausanias, with exemplary Spartan *pietas*, was taking the sacrificial omens at the Isthmus. They proved favourable (what, one wonders, would have happened had they not?) and those Peloponnesian contingents so far assembled at once set out for their rendezvous at Eleusis, leaving late arrivals to follow on as and when they could. (Units were still streaming in when the Greeks took up their position on the northern slopes of Cithaeron; the contingents from Elis and Mantinea arrived when the battle was actually over, like Blücher after Waterloo.) If Pausanias's father Cleombrotus did, in fact, break down the 'Scironian Way' as a defence-measure after the fall of Thermopylae [see above, pp. 157–8], it is clear that he – or his son – had made it fit for military traffic again during the winter. At Eleusis Pausanias and his men were joined by eight thousand Athenian hoplites under Aristeides: this force had crossed over from Salamis after the Persian evacuation. The events of the past few months must have left considerable distrust, and perhaps some open friction, between Athens and the Peloponnesian *bloc*: the former's anxiety concerning Spartan intentions was probably shared by other 'exposed' states such as Megara and Aegina. This was the atmosphere which brought about the famous 'Oath of Plataea', sworn by all member-states of the League before Pausanias led them across the Boeotian frontier to do battle with Mardonius. Discussion of textual variants (no version is earlier than the fourth century BC; all have undergone extensive embellishment and editing) tends to obscure the most interesting point about the Oath: that it should have been thought necessary at all. Far from being, as is generally held, a great patriotic gesture – or, for some, a late patriotic forgery, cooked up during the brief Theban hegemony of 371–62 – it stands on record as a formal insurance against inter-state feuding, rivalry, distrust, and bad faith. Only on these terms do some of its very curious clauses even begin to make sense.[1]

There is some doubt as to where the Oath was actually administered:

Eleusis seems the most logical point, when Pausanias and Aristeides first joined forces. Ephorus plumps for the Isthmus, and Lycurgus for Plataea itself, but of these the first is surely too early, and the second dangerously late. What the League's Peloponnesian representatives did at the Isthmus was vote '*to make common cause with the Athenians* [my italics] and, advancing to Plataea in a body, to fight to a finish for liberty'. This does no more than confirm what we already knew: that up till then relations between Sparta and Athens had been (to put it mildly) under a severe strain. What both sides badly needed after all their diplomatic in-fighting and threatened betrayals was some mutual guarantee of good will. This the Oath provided. The version which follows here is that preserved and dedicated in Acharnae by Dion, son of Dion, a priest of Ares and Athena the War-goddess:

I will fight to the death, and I will not count my life more precious than freedom. I will not leave my officer, the commander of my Regiment or Company, either alive or dead. I will not withdraw unless my commanders lead me back, and I will do whatsoever the Generals order. I will bury the dead of those who have fought as my allies, on the field, and will not leave one of them unburied. After defeating the barbarians in battle, I will tithe the city of the Thebans; and I will never destroy Athens or Sparta or Plataea or any of the cities which have fought as our allies, nor will I consent to their being starved, nor cut them off from running water, whether we be friends or at war.

And if I keep well the oath, as it is written, may my city have good health; but if not, may it have sickness; and may my city never be sacked; but if not, may it be sacked; and may my land give increase; but if not, may it be barren; and may the women bring forth children like their fathers; but if not, monsters; and may the cattle bring forth after their kind; but if not, monsters.

Lycurgus and Ephorus record some minor (but significant) variations from the text presented here. Ephorus makes no mention whatsoever of reprisals against the medising states; Lycurgus preserves the clause, but tactfully omits to specify any city by name. Both add an odd rider at the end, which does not figure on the Acharnae stele: 'I will restore none of the temples which have been burned and cast down, but will leave them to remain as a memorial to men hereafter, of the impiety of the barbarians.' Odd, but not all *that* odd; men do make extravagant claims and promises under the stress of emotion in wartime. Much patriotic propaganda issued between 1939 and 1945 would look equally fustian today. Nor is it hard to explain the omission of this clause in a sacerdotal context. Its provisions had generally fallen into abeyance, at Acharnae as elsewhere, and no priest – however well-intentioned – would wish to perpetuate the memory of his ancestors' broken vows.

By far the most disconcerting aspect of the Plataean Oath, however, is the low level of discipline, patriotism and morale which it presupposes. Oaths, like laws, are called into being only if there is a genuine need for more than usually binding sanctions. Where no crime attracts, declarations of virtue become meaningless. To judge from our text, a Greek soldier's characteristics in 479 included cowardice on the battlefield, gross insubordination, impiety, lack of elementary hygiene, and an alarming tendency to turn and rend his allies-in-arms the moment victory was won. Greek and Roman history, one fears, can supply all too many instances of such behaviour (though exceptions, as this book should by now have made clear, are numerous and dazzling). When Wellington called his Peninsula army 'the scum of the earth' he was up against considerable competition from the ancient world. The mere fact that Pausanias and his fellow-commanders were forced to impose such an oath – one can only imagine how a Spartiate warrior felt when he took it – hints, all too eloquently, at the precarious nature of the Greek alliance. It was, in fact, little more than a year before Athens broke away from Sparta and formed her own maritime league – thus embarking on an imperial career which led, within half a century, to the tragedy of the Peloponnesian War. Small wonder that nostalgic fourth-century Panhellenists romanticised the Oath. Having got a confederate army to fight at Plataea at all was in itself something of a miracle.

Pausanias took the sacrificial omens a second time. Once more they were favourable. The whole Greek army now set out northward from Eleusis on the road to Thebes: first across flat open country, bare and parched under a late July sun, then climbing steadily from the lower to the higher ranges of Cithaeron, the smell of thyme sharp in their nostrils as they wound their way across the upland plateau, to enter the last rocky defile above Eleutherae, under the towering crags of Gyphtokastro. They reached the head of the pass at last, and saw all southern Boeotia spread out beneath them like a chequerboard, humping into a broken range of low rolling hills between the Asopus and the lowest spurs of the Cithaeron-Pastra massif. They had an unrivalled view of Mardonius's army, encamped along the river on either side of that mile-square headquarters stockade; and beyond, gleaming in white unearthly splendour away towards the distant north-west horizon, lay Helicon and Parnassus. From here the Greeks began their descent to the plain. The modern highway, with its wide banked loops, very soon diverges from the ancient road – steeper, more direct – which one can

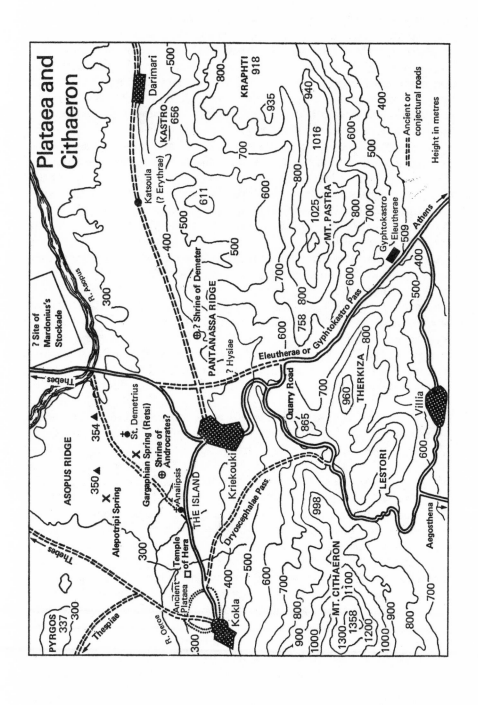

Plataea and Cithaeron

PYRGOS 337

Thespiae →

R. Oeroe

Thebes →

ASOPUS RIDGE

Alepotripi Spring ✕

350 ▲   354 ▲   ✕

✕

St. Demetrius ☩
Gargaphian Spring (Retsi)

Shrine of Androcrates? ⊕

Analipsis ✕

Ancient
Plataea ▯

Temple
of Hera ▯

Kokla

THE ISLAND

Kriekouki

Dryoscephalae Pass

300

400

500

600

700

800

900

1000

MT. CITHAERON

1358   1300   1100   1200   1000   900   800

700

R. Asopus

? Site of Mardonius's Stockade

Thebes →

300

300

PANTANASSA RIDGE

? Shrine of Demeter ⊕

? Hysiae

611

Eleutherae or Gyphtokastro Pass

Quarry Road

865

998

960

THERKIZA   800

LESTORI

Aegosthena →

700

600

500

400

300

500

Katsoula ●
(? Erythrae)

(KASTRO) 656

Darimari

500

500

600

700

800

KRAPHTI
918

935

940

1016

1025   MT. PASTRA

758   600

700   800

600

Gyphtokastro
Eleutherae
509

Villia

Athens →

400

500

600

400

━━━ Ancient or
conjectural roads

──── Height in metres

still follow on foot or in a jeep, and which debouches a little east of modern Kriekouki (now, as though to confuse the amateur topographer, wrongly renamed Erythrae). Pausanias now deployed his troops in a strong defensive position along the lower slopes of Cithaeron, roughly opposite Mardonius's lines.* Modern strategists argue that Mardonius ought to have attacked them before they were clear of the pass, and some scholars (by virtually ignoring all the evidence) have convinced themselves that he actually did so. In fact his plan was simpler, and arguably more effective: to lure Pausanias across the river, where he would – it was hoped – fall an easy victim to the Persian cavalry.

There are signs that Mardonius's decision to withdraw beyond the Cithaeron-Parnes line came as something of a surprise to his opponents, and that at first they were undecided as to how they should react. The Athenian ambassadors to Sparta had been talking hopefully of fighting in the Thriasian plain, above Eleusis (which would have suited them a good deal better than it did Mardonius). Aristeides consulted Delphi, and the Oracle duly replied that 'the Athenians would overcome their adversaries on condition that ... they risked a battle on their own territory in the plain of the Eleusinian goddesses Demeter and Kore'. Here we have a nice instance of the strategic situation changing a little too fast for Apollo to keep up with it.[2] From our main source for this episode [Plut. Arist. 11.2–4] it is clear that Aristeides solicited Delphi's advice while Mardonius was still in Attica, but only got a reply after the Greek army had crossed Cithaeron. He is said to have found the oracle 'bewildering in the extreme', and his irresolution plainly reflects a lack of strategic flexibility on the part of the High Command. Various compromises were now suggested. A seer named Teisamenus of Elis 'foretold that they would win a victory provided that they did not advance to the attack, but stayed on the defensive' – advice which, to begin with at any rate, Pausanias duly followed.

Meanwhile the Plataeans (who now saw their chances of a triumphant return home rapidly dwindling) decided that the situation called for drastic remedies. Their general Arimnestus had (or so he claimed) a dream in which 'the god declared that they had missed the whole meaning of the oracle, for the places which it mentioned were all in the

---

* Herodotus [9.19.3, cf. 15.3] locates them near Erythrae, which suggests a position, or command-post, well east of the main road. But the precise location of Erythrae remains a puzzle: the only thing on which all scholars agree is that it is *not* Kriekouki. Leake's identification of Erythrae with Katsoula, some 2½ km. east of the Pantanassa Ridge, followed by Pritchett and, tentatively, by Hignett (XIG p. 426) is perhaps the most plausible guess; but a guess it remains. It would be unwise to build too much on so shaky a foundation.

neighbourhood of Plataea'. Frantic searching revealed an ancient temple of Eleusinian Demeter and Kore near Hysiae.* Arimnestus took Aristeides on a tour of this position, emphasising its excellent natural defences – 'since the spurs of Cithaeron, where they adjoin the temple and run down into the plain, make the ground impassable for cavalry' [Plut. *Arist.* 11]. To explain how the Athenians were to fight 'on their own territory' was more difficult. In the end the Plataeans put up, and ratified, an emergency motion 'that they should remove their boundary stones on the side facing Attica', and make an *ad hoc* gift of all this land to Athens. It would be interesting to know if they ever got it back again.

At present Pausanias had every intention of letting the Persians take the initiative. His rear was well-protected by the Helots and other light-armed troops, who seem to have been guarding not only the main Gyphtokastro pass, but also the far less precipitous, if somewhat more leisurely, crossing from Plataea to Eleutherae by way of modern Villia. Waggon-convoys would find the second of these two routes – known by the Athenians as Dryoscephalae, or the Oakheads, and as Three Heads by the Boeotians – a good deal easier than the first. We may note that throughout this campaign Mardonius never attempted to cut the Greeks' communications in the mountains (though he did so with some success down on the plain). The obvious explanation is that the passes were held in strength. As we hear nothing of light-armed operations at Plataea, it is logical to assume that a large proportion of the Helots (stiffened by brigades of more reliable troops) were posted at strategic points in and below the passes.[3] Pausanias had not the slightest intention of being drawn across the Asopus. On the contrary, if he stayed firmly where he was, sooner or later Mardonius would have no option but to take the offensive. In one respect at least Arimnestus had been quite right: the terrain between Cithaeron and the low foot-hills some two miles further north towards the river was – is – a horse-man's nightmare. Unlike most Greek lowland terrain, far from being level, it consists of abrupt ridges and hummocks and hollows, full of

* Hysiae lay west of Erythrae [Hdt. 9.15, 19, 25] and just to the right of the Eleutherae-Plataea road [Paus. 9.2.1, 9.1.6]. Pritchett, AJA 61 (1957) 22, places it on the Pantanassa ridge; Burn (PG p.518) suggests, more convincingly, that it may under-lie modern Kriekouki. The temple of Demeter [see also below, p. 248] stood near the Gargaphia spring, on the site of the modern chapel of St Demetrius (Grundy, GPW p. 496; Ufer, *Ant. Schlachtf.*, vol. 4, pp. 136 ff.). It is not to be confused with the shrine of Demeter to which the Spartans retreated (Hdt. 9.57.2; see below, pp. 263–4], convincingly located by Pritchett (*op. cit.*, p. 27) close to a well between Kriekouki and the Pantanassa ridge. On the other hand it is possible (though not certain) that Plutarch (*Arist.* 11), cited here, may have confused features from both.

concealed potholes, and in places rolling like the Cotswolds. Let the Persian cavalry make what they could of *that*.

When the Greeks showed no sign of advancing further into the plain, Mardonius sent for Masistius, his newly appointed cavalry general, and told him to try a massed frontal attack on their positions. He had chosen the right man for such a job. Masistius was tall, dashing, handsome, and something of a dandy. Like most Iranian aristocrats, he was never happier than when in the saddle, and must have chafed during his previous command, over a dull Caucasian infantry brigade. For Mardonius, this raid was something of an experiment: he wanted to see how his cavalry would shape up, over rough ground, against a disciplined line of Greek spearmen. Its only real chance of success was through surprise, and Masistius was therefore ordered to launch his attack before dawn. If the Greek outposts gave the alarm, and their defences were manned in time, he was to try harassing tactics, with the object of luring them out into more open ground. Mardonius's ulterior aim (not, one would suppose, revealed to Masistius) was to give his opponents a false sense of confidence. He knew perfectly well that the chances of a cavalry charge succeeding under such conditions were minimal. On the other hand, if the Greeks came off best in a brush with the enemy's strongest arm, might they not be tempted to advance their own lines somewhat – perhaps at least to that low range of hills facing the Asopus? The gamble was well worth trying. Mardonius badly needed a decisive battle: the longer he stayed *in situ*, the more acute his supply-problem became. Unlike Xerxes, he could not bring in convoys by sea, and Phocian guerilla bands were seriously threatening his land-communications with the north. Thebes, it is true, had plentiful reserves – but how long would they last an army of over 50,000 men (not counting auxiliaries and animals) if all other sources dried up?[4]

Masistius and his cavalry came thundering in to the attack before first light. The Athenian sentries spotted them while they were still a good way off, and at once raised the alarm. When the Persian horsemen reached their objective, it was to find a grim line of armed hoplites awaiting them, echeloned back in irregular formation among the rocky spurs of Cithaeron. It was an axiom of ancient warfare that cavalry could not successfully charge a phalanx of spearmen head-on; such a task became even more hazardous here, where rough ground inevitably slowed down the charge itself. Since the element of surprise had failed, Masistius turned instead to hit-and-run tactics. He sent in one squadron after another from the flank; his troopers rode swerving down the Greek line, picking off an occasional unwary victim, and calling the rest women when they refused to come out and fight in the plain. By these methods he inflicted a fair number of casualties, but made no decisive impact. His best chance of achieving a real breakthrough, he soon saw, was by concentrating on the Megarian brigade, three thousand strong, which occupied a more exposed position than the other Greek contingents – perhaps, it has been suggested, astride the main road to Thebes, immediately below its exit from the Gyphtokastro pass. Hard-pressed and hemmed in on both flanks, the Megarians sent an appeal for help to Pausanias, threatening to quit their post unless they were relieved at once. Pausanias saw that his own slow-moving, heavy-armed troops would be useless for such a task. Instead, he very sensibly ordered up a special Athenian commando force of three hundred light infantry and archers, which had been posted well ahead of the main line, perhaps as shock-troops.*

The Athenians at once set off, at the double, and a truly Homeric struggle now took place. Masistius himself, a gigantic figure in full armour, his golden fish-scale cuirass covered by a purple surcoat, rode down on them at the head of his squadron: the eternal romantic cavalry leader, recognisable a mile off, apt target for any archer with his wits about him. Athenian archers, however, wasted few arrows on armoured men. It paid off better to shoot their horses from under them. One such shot skewered Masistius's charger, which reared up in agony and threw him. His predicament was now that of a mediaeval French knight: once he had fallen, the sheer weight of his armour made it impossible for him to get up again. He lay there helpless, like a tortoise on its back, while Greek infantrymen carved and prodded ineffectually at his metal-cased body. Finally one of them solved the problem by thrusting his javelin-spike through the eyehole in Masistius's ornate helmet, killing him instantly. When the Persians learnt of their general's death, they charged, not by squadrons as before, but *en masse*, in a furious bid to recover his dead body. The Athenians, overwhelmed by this attack, sent an immediate appeal for strong reinforcements, and, until it was answered, took a terrible beating from Masistius's cavalrymen. However, once Pausanias and his men came up, the Persians were forced to retreat. They had failed to recover Masistius's corpse, and suffered further heavy losses. Two furlongs off, their troop-commanders held a quick conference, and decided to call off the attack altogether.

There was great lamentation in the Persian camp for Masistius, whose reputation in the army stood second only to that of Mardonius

---

* Hdt. 9.21; Plut. *Arist.* 14.3; Diod. 11.30.4. The tradition that Pausanias called for volunteers, and that only the Athenians would go, is surely Athenian propaganda; what mattered to Pausanias was that they were the only unit equipped with archers – a vital point in the battle which followed.

himself. The mourners, says Herodotus [9.24] 'shaved their heads, cut the manes of their horses and mules, and abandoned themselves to such cries of grief that the whole of Boeotia was loud with the noise of them'. The Greeks, on the other hand, were jubilant. They had not only stood Mardonius's cavalry off, but forced them to retreat; best of all, they had killed Masistius. The Persian general's huge body was placed on a cart and paraded along the lines; men broke ranks in their eagerness to get a look at it. Perhaps Mardonius had not expected to pay quite so high a price for his experiment; but he could console himself, a day or two later, with the knowledge that its main object had undoubtedly been achieved. When no further Persian offensive materialised, Pausanias redeployed his forces in a far more advanced position. The general direction of this movement is clear enough, though its details have been fiercely disputed.[5] The Greek centre of gravity, as it were, shifted westward, from Erythrae towards Plataea, one reason apparently being that Plataea offered a more abundant water-supply. This change of front was carried out, insofar as possible, 'along the lower slopes of Cithaeron' – that is, without descending into the open plain, where there was always the risk of a sudden cavalry-charge. Troop movements were also to a great extent concealed by the low line of broken hills, now known as the 'Asopus ridge', which ran parallel with the river [see map, p. 242]. At the same time, Herodotus makes it clear that this redeployment also brought the Greeks, finally, down from high ground into the plain, along a line not far short of the Asopus [9.25, 31.1]. Their march took them into Plataean territory by way of Hysiae, after which 'the contingents of the several confederated towns halted close by the spring and the sacred enclosure of Androcrates, in flat country rising here and there in low hills'. The spring was that known as Gargaphia, and marked the position of the Greek right wing, held by Pausanias and his Spartans [9.49.3]; other units took up their stations further westward, and closer to the river.

This very precise description would help us more if so many of the landmarks to which Herodotus refers had not since vanished or changed their names. Nevertheless we can, with a fair degree of confidence, reconstruct both Pausanias's line of advance, and the final disposition of his troops. Hysiae, as we have seen, stood either on the site of modern Kriekouki, or a little farther east, on the Pantanassa ridge. The Gargaphia water-point has been convincingly identified with a pair of springs now known by the local inhabitants as Rhetsi, and situated about a thousand yards south-west of the chapel of St Demetrius [see map, p. 242]. According to Pritchett[6] 'the natives told us that the water level had never gone down in their memory and that this is regarded as the most copious water supply in the entire Kriekouki area' – a claim which the present writer would, from personal observation, be inclined to confirm. This agrees well with Herodotus's claim [9.49] that the entire Greek army obtained water from Gargaphia. The shrine of Androcrates, according to Herodotus, was situated close by this spring. Plutarch [*Arist.* 11.7–8] adds that it stood 'in the midst of a thick and shady grove', near the temple of Eleusinian Demeter. If the Rhetsi springs are ancient Gargaphia, then the chapel of St Demetrius almost certainly indicates the site of Eleusinian Demeter's temple, and we can place the shrine of Androcrates in the same area. It is noteworthy, as Pritchett says, that 'the one cluster of trees in this part of the Boeotian plain today is at our Gargaphia'. Moist and low-lying ground must have produced very similar physical conditions in antiquity. Thucydides [3.24.1] mentions a road from Plataea to Thebes which had the shrine of Androcrates on its right, and a spur road leading off towards Hysiae and Erythrae rather less than a mile from the city-boundary of Plataea. This spur probably followed a course very similar to that taken by the modern road between the chapel of the Análepsis and Kriekouki. Pritchett reports an ancient waggon-track running seventy-five yards west of Gargaphia towards Thebes: this is surely the road referred to by Thucydides.

Pausanias, then, swung his forces into position, and away from the Cithaeron foothills, when he reached the comparatively open and level ground just west of Kriekouki. It is safe to assume that he made no fundamental changes in the general order of battle given us by Herodotus [9.28.2 ff.], which places the Lacedaemonians and Tegeans on the right wing, and the Athenians and Plataeans on the left. His right wing, perhaps at the suggestion of Arimnestus [see above, pp. 243–4], took up a position by the Gargaphian spring: that is, on the little hill of St Demetrius, where its flank had excellent natural protection against cavalry attacks. Once we know this, it becomes possible to work out the battle-stations of the entire Greek line. The total number of combatants, as reported by Herodotus [9.29], was 38,700. Allowing one yard per man in line, and assuming the usual phalanx formation, eight deep, we get a *minimum* front of 4,837 yards, which should probably be increased to a round three miles. The left wing, we are told [Hdt. 9.49], was stationed near the Asopus, and far more vulnerable to harassment by Mardonius's cavalry. If we now run a three-mile line from the Rhetsi springs to the Asopus it at once reveals the Athenian position: on a slight rise above the river, known today as Pyrgos Hill. With the centre occupying low ground between Pyrgos and St Demetrius, all Herodotus's conditions are faithfully met. This line, facing north-north-east

rather than directly north [see map, p. 242], was indeed supplied with
plentiful water. Apart from the Asopus itself, its minor tributary
(prosaically labelled A1 by Grundy), and the Gargaphia spring,
Pausanias's men also had access to a second, smaller spring, some way
north-west of the first, and known today as Alepotrypi, or the Foxhole.

When this move was reported to Mardonius, he at once brought his
own army up-river, and established a similar battle-line, roughly
opposite Pausanias's position. The relative positions and numbers of the
various contingents on either side [Hdt. 9.28–32 *passim*] can best be set
out, as below, in diagrammatic form. Herodotus gives no individual
figures for Persian units, and his overall totals are highly suspect. The
estimates given here have been worked out on the basis of figures arrived
at earlier in this narrative [see above, pp. 211 and 229], according to
which Mardonius's total *Persian* forces numbered 30,000, and his
various Greek allies a further 20,000 +. Out of this total (50,000 +) the
cavalry, both Persian and Greek, perhaps accounted for one-fifth: say
a round 10,000, equally divided. What follows here is a list of the
infantry divisions alone:

	GREEKS			PERSIANS	
Unit	*Strength*	*Position*	*Strength*	*Unit*	
Lacedaemon	10,000	RW ⎱ LW	? 12,000	Persians	
Tegea	1,500	RW ⎰			
Corinth	5,000	RC ⎤			
Potidaea	300	RC ⎟ LC	? 7,500	Medes	
Orchomenus	600	RC ⎟			
Sicyon	3,000	RC ⎦			
Epidaurus	800	RC ⎤			
Troezen	1,000	RC ⎟			
Lepreum	200	RC ⎟ LC	? 3,000	Bactrians	
Mycenae, Tiryns	400	RC ⎟			
Phlius	1,000	LC ⎦			
Hermione	300	LC ⎤			
Eretria, Styra	600	LC ⎬ RC	? 1,000	Indians	
Chalcis	400	LC ⎦			

[N.B. RW = Right Wing; RC = Right Centre;
LC = Left Centre; LW = Left Wing.]

Ambracia	500	LC ⎫			
Leucas, Anactorium	800	LC ⎬ RC	? 1,500	Sacae	
Pale	200	LC			
Aegina	500	LC ⎭			

Megara	3,000	LC ⎫			Macedonians,
Plataea	600	LW ⎬ RW	? 15,000		Boeotians,
Athens	8,000	LW ⎭			Locrians,
					Malians,
					Thessalians,
					Phocians
					(1,000)

Several points about this order of battle require comment. Firstly, even if we allow no more than 5,000 cavalry to the Iranian divisions, out of a putative total of 30,000, and accept Herodotus's statement that the Persians 'heavily outnumbered' the Lacedaemonians, it follows, inevitably, that in the centre the *Greek* contingents were numerically superior to the Medes, Bactrians, Indians and Sacae combined. On the other hand, a total of 15,000 for the medising Greek states (again, allowing 5,000 for cavalry) so heavily outnumbers the forces of Athens, Megara and Plataea that Mardonius may well have used several thousand of them to stiffen his centre, along with the mixed bag of Phrygians, Mysians, Thracians, Paeonians and reallotted Egyptian marines for whom Herodotus provides no specific station. As far as the Greeks were concerned, the most influential cities undoubtedly obtained the best – and safest – positions, up on high ground. They may also have contributed the most experienced fighting men, but one doubts whether this will have cut much ice with those who were not so lucky. (That the allotment of positions could cause bad blood is made all too clear by a ridiculous quarrel[7] between Athens and Tegea, as to which of them should obtain the secondary place of honour on the left wing. Such an argument may have been grotesquely inopportune, with enemy forces massing just across the river; this, however, is no guarantee – as some suppose – that it never happened.) Neighbouring cities were brigaded together, unless – like Corinth and Sicyon – they happened to be on particularly bad terms [Burn, PG p. 524]. A special exception was made in favour of Potidaea, whose volunteers Pausanias permitted to fight alongside the men of her mother-city Corinth. Otherwise, all minor contingents were lumped unceremoniously in the centre, Peloponnesians to the right, under Sparta's aegis, islanders and other miscellaneous units to the left, where the Athenians could keep a weather eye on them.

The effect of this double redeployment was a complete stalemate. For eight days the two armies lay encamped on either side of the Asopus – no great obstacle, especially in mid-summer – and took very little action against each other. From time to time mounted Persian archers would swoop down on details sent to draw water from the river, and harry them with showers of arrows and javelins; in the end these repeated hit-and-run attacks forced the Athenians in particular to go inland for their water, to the Gargaphian spring or the Foxhole. Greek troops had no adequate defence until Alexander's day against the bow-carrying Oriental horseman, a fact of which Mardonius now took full advantage.[8] But apart from such minor brushes, nothing at all happened: surprising at first sight, yet inevitable when we consider the near-identical aims of the two commanders, and the special advantages in terrain and personnel which each was anxious to exploit. Their main dilemma at this stage is well reflected by the findings of the various seers and diviners – always a useful instrument for reconciling public opinion to essential but unpopular strategy. Hignett [XIG, p. 320] states bluntly that 'the Spartan high command had mastered the art of exploiting unfavourable omens to keep in check the impatience of their troops', which is perhaps an over-rationalised approach: a subconscious adaptation to the requirements of the moment might describe the process more fairly. The fact that Herodotus devotes what must strike the modern reader as a quite disproportionate amount of space to these religious preliminaries [9.33–8 *passim*] merely shows how seriously the Greeks themselves took them. Anyway, on this occasion the priests of both sides were unanimous: Mardonius and Pausanias alike 'would win a victory if they remained on the defensive, but would be defeated if they attacked' [Plut. *Arist.* 15.1].

This crystallises the problem with admirable concision. Mardonius, in the north, had first-class cavalry country and a friendly base; Pausanias, in the south, had terrain ideal for infantry manoeuvres, and strongly held mountains at his back. If either one of them crossed the Asopus, he ran the risk of losing every tactical advantage he possessed. Mardonius had already learnt, the hard way, how tricky it was for cavalry to operate among the lower spurs of Cithaeron. Pausanias, on the other hand, was far too canny a strategist to risk annihilation by taking infantry across the river on a wide, open front, with exposed flanks. It was an almost perfect deadlock. Yet somehow the deadlock had to be broken: one of the two generals must make a decisive move – and, by so doing, perhaps lose the game. Each preliminary gambit had been' a bait, extended and refused. When Mardonius's cavalrymen taunted the Greeks, calling them women,* their main object was to make them lose their tempers, break ranks, and charge headlong into the plain. If the Plataean Oath is anything to go by, this assessment of the average Greek militiaman's reactions was not far wide of the mark; Pausanias's tightly imposed Spartan discipline seems to have come as something of a surprise. Similarly, when Pausanias moved up towards the river, he was hoping to tempt Mardonius across it. Each man's main object throughout was to make his opponent take the offensive.

In this psychological duel, the advantage, ultimately, lay with Pausanias, simply because he was in rather less of a hurry. Mardonius, as we have seen, was having trouble with his commissariat, and the longer he delayed, the more acute this problem would become. Worse still, by now he surely knew that Athens had sent the bulk of her fighting squadrons to join Leotychidas off Delos. He may even have heard rumours – soon to be confirmed – that the Samians were urging Leotychidas to launch an all-out naval offensive in Ionia. No help, then, could be expected from the remnants of Xerxes' fleet, which seemed likely to have its work cut out even maintaining a foothold in the eastern Aegean. Most crucial of all, these new developments threw an extra burden of responsibility on Mardonius himself. Unless really drastic measures were taken, another general revolt of the Asiatic Greeks, from Byzantium to Caria, seemed almost inevitable: one army corps under Tigranes was hardly enough to keep them quiet. If *that* happened, Mardonius's chances of getting back out of Europe alive shrank almost to vanishing-point. The one thing calculated to forestall such an uprising, he saw, was a swift and annihilating Persian land-victory in Greece. Pausanias, on the other hand, had no such dilemma facing him. He could not, it is true, afford to delay indefinitely – if the situation drifted on unresolved till winter his allies would disperse, perhaps for ever – but the pressures operating on him were far less immediate. For the moment he was happy enough to stay on the defensive. His potential hoplite strength stood at something over forty thousand, and with fresh contingents coming in daily he saw no reason why he should not achieve it.

His only worry at this stage (a worry he shared with Miltiades before Marathon) concerned the possibility of treason in the ranks during this enforced period of inactivity. No one enjoys sitting still and being sniped at in hot weather, on short rations, with too little to drink and the

---

* 'Is this the first case recorded', asks Burn parenthetically, 'of badinage between trousered and kilted men?' (PG p. 516, n. 16], to which one might add: Were the Persians specially taught the Greek word for 'woman' before going into action?

constant risk of an arrow through breast or back while drawing water. The Athenians, posted close to the river, must have found this period particularly trying, and it was amongst them – 'while the cause of Greece still hung in the balance and Athens above all was in mortal danger' – that an abortive take-over plot now developed.[9] The conspirators were all 'members of the leading families', previously wealthy but now impoverished through the war: a common enough predicament in 479, one might have thought. They had lost their influence along with their capital – a nice gloss on Theognis's aristocratic sneer that 'Money, and nothing but Money, holds all the power in the world' – and now saw the positions of power and honour going elsewhere. They were the natural heirs of men like Lycidas [see above, p. 230], summarily lynched when he spoke out against the war-party; denied a legitimate platform for their collaborationist views, they turned conspirators instead. Not that their programme could be called idealistic, in any sense of that portmanteau word. Gathering secretly in a house in Plataea,[10] they resolved 'to overthrow the democracy, or if they could not achieve this, to harm the Greek cause in every possible way and betray it to the barbarians'. In other words, what they wanted was power, and it made very little difference to them whether they got it by a *coup* or as puppets of the Persian government.

The plot was betrayed, though not before it had won a considerable number of adherents throughout the camp. Aristeides, who as Athenian commander-in-chief was responsible for its suppression, saw that he would have to walk very warily indeed. If he went by the rule-book, regardless of expediency, there was no knowing what sort of hornet's nest he might uncover. A conservative himself, he would, at best, be in the embarrassing position of having to arrest large numbers of his own more extremist friends. Worse, he might provoke a wholesale mutiny: morale was very uncertain, and tempers more than a little frayed. In the event he acted with considerable circumspection. Eight men only were arrested. Of these, the two ringleaders, Aeschines of Lamptrae and Agesias of Acharnae, 'contrived' (i.e. were allowed) to escape from custody. The remaining six Aristeides then officially released, on probation as it were, 'so as to give those who still believed they were unsuspected a chance to take courage and repent'. A broad hint that they could all clear themselves of the treason charge by conducting themselves as gallant patriots in battle did the rest. Aristeides, once ostracised himself, understood the harsh realities of Greek politics all too well; a veteran soldier, he could appreciate the strains and tensions that had built up during the past twelve months. Now, if ever, was the moment to temper justice with a little pragmatic common sense. Yet the episode went deeper than perhaps he allowed. Surveying the whole course of fifth-century Athenian history, we can see that this was no mere wartime accident, but a symptom of those deep and endemic class-divisions which – increasingly as time went on – shook Athens' social structure to its very foundations, and proved the rock on which all her imperial ambitions came to grief.

After a week spent in largely unconstructive idleness, Mardonius was ready to try almost anything that offered the prospect of decisive action. No favourable omens could, even now, be obtained for an offensive – a tribute, perhaps, to strategic prudence on the diviners' part. On the eighth day, however, a Theban named Timagenidas came to Mardonius and 'advised him to watch the passes of Cithaeron, as he would be able to cut off a great many of the men, who every day were streaming through them to join the Greek army' [Hdt. 9.38]. Mardonius, we are told, jumped at the idea. His subsequent actions, however, suggest that he concentrated on one pass only, and on supply trains rather than combatant troops. That same night, acting on information brought back by Persian or Theban patrols, he sent a strong cavalry force to the northern outlet of the Dryoscephalae pass, near Plataea, and duly intercepted a convoy of five hundred provision-waggons from the Peloponnese. The raid was an unqualified success. Mardonius's rough-riders carried out their ambush with lethal expertise, massacred most of the convoy's escort, and diverted all supplies to the Persian camp. If they had any trouble from Pausanias's light-armed troops during this operation, we do not hear of it. That the hijacking of one Greek convoy was no isolated incident, but part of a carefully worked-out plan, becomes clear from what followed. During the next four days *all* Greek provision-trains coming up from the south were halted on Cithaeron, not daring to leave the shelter of the hills. 'The enemy's horse might at any time sweep down on them if they attempted to cross the open ground between the pass and the Greek position.'[11] Yet during this same period combatant reinforcements continued to reach Pausanias's lines daily, a matter of great annoyance to Mardonius. He might have cut off his opponent's supplies, but clearly he was in no position to affect Greek troop movements. The clear implication is that his cavalry now dominated the approaches to Plataea, where the Dryoscephalae pass debouched into the plain, but could not get near the main road from Eleutherae to Thebes, presumably because Pausanias had it defended in strength.

For three whole days after this raid no further action was taken by either side, except that Mardonius's cavalry 'kept the Greeks on the jump by continual sorties', and rode temptingly along the very brink of the Asopus, hoping, it would seem, even now, to lure Pausanias across and into a general engagement. The young Spartan coolly refused to be drawn; he would not advance – yet he did not retreat, either. Neither side, says Herodotus, actually crossed the river. Presumably he is speaking of hoplites, since at that very moment Persian cavalry squadrons were blockading the entrance to the Dryoscephalae pass. Such all-round lack of initiative is startling – yet perhaps no odder than anything else recorded in this and the preceding paragraph. Questions crowd the mind, and find no adequate answer. Take Pausanias first: a general (it is said) of unassailable military competence, whatever we may feel about his ambivalent politicking in later life. His supply-line over Cithaeron spelt life or death to him; when it was cut, the Greeks ran through their existing food-reserves in four days. Yet he maintained so slack a guard over the crucial two-mile stretch between his command-post and Cithaeron that a Persian cavalry force could sever his communications with impunity – indeed, it would seem, unopposed – and, having done so, continue to hold up his convoys, day after day, while he took no retaliatory action whatsoever. He did not even, so far as we can tell, take the elementary precaution of re-routing supplies by the steeper (but still negotiable) Gyphtokastro pass. When he was finally driven into action, and began withdrawing his forces towards Cithaeron, he planned (says Herodotus) to use *half his entire army*, nearly 20,000 men, on a night operation to relieve the provision trains now immobilised in the mountains above Plataea. This sounds an oddly massive over-reaction to a blockade by a few cavalry squadrons. If Mardonius had cut *all* his lines of communication with the south, and interposed a strong force between him and the passes, it might be more intelligible. But none of our sources suggests such a move.

Mardonius's motives, though not quite so impenetrable, still give one pause for thought. If Pausanias had left his lines of communication wide open after he occupied the Asopus ridge, why was it over a week before the Persian commander took advantage of so obvious an opening – and then only at the instigation of a local well-wisher? When he ordered his raid on the waggon-convoy, what was he hoping to achieve strategically? How could he *know* that Pausanias would behave in so paradoxical and self-defeating a fashion? As several scholars have pointed out,[12] Mardonius was taking a very considerable risk. When Pausanias found his supply-lines threatened by enemy cavalry, his most obvious and predictable move would have been to order the whole Greek army back, under cover of darkness, to its former defensive position along the Cithaeron foothills. Once there – and how could Mardonius have

255

stopped such a movement at night? – he would at once recover control of the passes, and render himself virtually immune to further cavalry attacks. How would Mardonius's prospects of forcing a decisive battle look then? It speaks volumes for the Persian commander's predicament that he authorised a raid of this sort with such alacrity: he may have been short of rations, but he was even shorter of time. Yet what instinct told him that his opponent, far from closing back at once on Cithaeron, would sit obstinately on the Asopus ridge for four long days, increasingly harassed by Persian cavalry attacks, and with his rations dwindling away to nothing?

More important, why, having got such a bonanza, did Mardonius so signally fail to take advantage of it? His obvious course at this point would have been to cross the river in strength at night, come down squarely behind Pausanias's lines of communication – those Theban guides would prove their value here – and thus force the Greeks to fight a reversed-front engagement, cut off from their own reserves, and with a hostile Thebes behind them. One drawback to such a scheme was the fact that Pausanias's troops still held the main pass over Cithaeron. This, however, was not an insuperable disadvantage. Greek control of Dryoscephalae had been destroyed without apparent trouble; might not a well-organised commando raid dislodge them from the Gyphto-kastro pass as well? This, as we shall see, may have been Mardonius's original intention – and if so, all credit to him. Such rational theories, however, will not do for Pausanias, whose conduct remains an enigma throughout. All we can say for certain is that a battle took place, and Pausanias, whether by luck or good judgement, duly won it. He did, it is true, drive Mardonius, at last, into taking the offensive; but how *voulu* were any of his actions? One would like to believe that his long-delayed withdrawal from the Asopus ridge came as the culminating move in some ultra-Machiavellian scheme to make himself appear stupider than in fact he was, and thus to tempt Mardonius on to destruction. Such a theory is not *prima facie* implausible; during the next decade Pausanias showed himself a past master in the art of devious intrigue. But this question – like so many about Plataea – remains tantalisingly open: no final solution is possible. One can only record the facts.

Eleven days after this silent duel of wits had begun, Mardonius's patience, like Hitler's, became exhausted. Both Herodotus and Plutarch [Hdt. 9.41; Plut. *Arist.* 15.1] represent him as vexed and angry, worried by the reinforcements which kept coming in on the Greek side, and desperately short of food – though five hundred waggon-loads of good Peloponnesian beef and barley-bread would (one might have thought) suffice to keep the wolf from the Persian army's door for quite a while.

At all events he had, at last, made up his mind to launch an attack. He may, as Herodotus suggests, have been 'irked by protracted inactivity'; after all, he was only human. He may, too, have had worrying news from the Aegean. It was about this time [see below, p. 277] that the newly-augmented Greek fleet sailed for Samos. But surely his strongest motive was the belief that now, as never before, he had the Greeks at a severe disadvantage. The pusillanimous way in which Pausanias and his supposedly invincible Spartans had lost control of the Dryoscephalae pass, followed by their equally baffling reluctance to abandon an advanced position once their supply-lines had been cut, were two *bêtises* which cried out for swift, effective action. Mardonius therefore summoned a council of war. Among those present were Artabazus, whom we last met at the siege of Potidaea [see above, pp. 217–9], and a group of anonymous Thebans, which must surely have included Timagenidas. Artabazus, on whom the urgency of the situation would appear to have been lost, suggested falling back on Thebes, and pursuing the war from there by fifth-column methods. Why not systematically bribe the most influential citizens in various key towns until this Greek alliance split apart of its own accord? The Thebans, who foresaw rich pickings as well as military protection from the long-term presence of a Persian garrison force, gave Artabazus their enthusiastic support.

If Mardonius had had six months to spare, this divide-and-rule technique might have worked admirably. Few Greek coalitions survived intact much beyond one campaigning season, and this one had already shown more signs of strain than most. But the ominous news from Ionia, if nothing else, meant that Mardonius had to fight, and fight soon: somehow the Persians must pull off a showy major victory. Mardonius, too, was a man under pressure, and his temper was beginning to fray. He therefore wasted no time on diplomatic niceties or strategical explanations, but rode roughshod over Artabazus's proposals and the sacrificial omens alike, dismissing both with the same curt off-hand contempt. What they must do, he said, was take the offensive at once, that same night, before the Greeks could consolidate their forces any further. Mardonius had never been one to suffer fools gladly, and on this occasion he showed himself more than ready, if need be, to pull his rank as Xerxes' viceroy. Not surprisingly, the meeting approved his proposal without a dissentient voice. He at once summoned his company commanders and gave them their orders for a dawn attack the following day. One would dearly love to know just what his battle-plan was, and in particular why, after days of near-total inactivity, he chose to strike precisely when he did. In a day or two, if not sooner, Pausanias's position on the Asopus ridge was bound to become untenable, and the

Greeks would be forced to fall back on Cithaeron. Mardonius, it is clear, had to forestall such a move. But if he simply wanted to attack the Greeks in their exposed forward position, he could have done so at any time during the past week. Why the calculated delay? Two points suggest themselves here. First, the Asopus ridge would be very difficult to take by direct frontal assault, and it is improbable, to say the least, that Mardonius ever contemplated doing so. Both Greek wings commanded a strong position above the river, and no Persian infantryman would fancy his chances fighting uphill against Spartan or Athenian hoplites. Second, the ridge was strategically vulnerable in rear. Mardonius, then, had a straightforward problem: to dislodge his opponents from their forward position without letting them checkmate him by promptly falling back on the hills. The obvious solution, which in fact he adopted, was to strike hard at Pausanias's lines of communication. If he succeeded in cutting off the Greek army altogether, well and good; if he merely disrupted their supplies, they would still be forced to come down off the Asopus ridge and fight.

Even in the second case, however, Mardonius had to be reasonably sure that his opponents would not, or could not, forestall him by a quick withdrawal. Ever since Pausanias moved up to a forward position this risk must have been uppermost in the Persian's mind. If Mardonius was planning a full-dress attack at dawn, it is hard to believe that he meant simply to throw his best troops against the Asopus ridge (where they would be massacred), while at the same time leaving Pausanias every opportunity to pull out and redeploy *his* line on Cithaeron if things got too hot for comfort. The Persian battle-strategy must surely have depended on a massive infiltration of troops across the river during the night, infantry as well as cavalry, and the seizure of all the Cithaeron passes in Pausanias's rear, so that the Greeks were caught in a pincer-movement and cut off from any possible chance of retreat southward. Yet we know that, in the event, despite all Mardonius's careful preparations, no such movement developed, while his actions during the next forty-eight hours all bear the stamp of hasty, not to say desperate, improvisation. Between the decision to attack and the beginning of the actual engagement something, somewhere, went very wrong. Mardonius's battle-plan, to put it crudely, was blown to Pausanias; and once again, the go-between in what sounds like a peculiarly tortuous piece of nocturnal double-dealing was that enigmatic and pliable trimmer, King Alexander of Macedon.

The ascertainable facts are as follows.* About midnight a solitary

* Sources: Hdt. 9.44–5 *passim*; Plut. *Arist.* 15.2–3. The two accounts show some interesting discrepancies of detail – e.g. in Herodotus Alexander asks for his message

horseman crossed the Asopus and rode quietly up to the Athenian outposts. He would not give his name, but demanded a private interview with Aristeides or some other senior officer. A sentry was dispatched to get the generals out of bed, and inform them that some stray horseman from Mardonius's camp wanted to speak to the officers in charge. Aristeides, accompanied by some members of his staff, at once came out, and to them the stranger revealed his identity: he was Alexander the Macedonian. His flowery protestations of sympathy for the cause of Greek freedom were only equalled by his nervous insistence that no one should know about his visit – a decidedly authentic touch. Aristeides dealt with this *prima donna* act in very short time. While Pausanias must be privy to the secret, he said, the remaining commanders could be kept in the dark – 'on the other hand, if the Greeks were victorious, everybody should be told of Alexander's courage and enterprise'. Unabashed by this withering snub, the Macedonian now got down to business. Our sources agree fairly well on what he actually told Aristeides. He revealed Mardonius's intention to attack at dawn, emphasising that the Persian army had supplies for no more than a few days – a statement which has understandably incurred the suspicion of scholars. According to Herodotus, he also gave his listeners one very odd piece of advice. If Mardonius should by any chance postpone his attack, he told them, they ought to hold on where they were. Once again the Persians' shortage of rations was invoked as a motive. Having delivered his message, and made one last plea for favourable treatment if the Greeks secured a victory, Alexander vanished into the darkness again.

If we accept the historical authenticity of Alexander's visit to the Greek camp, can we determine his real, as opposed to his alleged, motives? Was he – this would have been very much in character – simultaneously running with the hare and hunting with the hounds? It looks uncommonly like it. He must, by now, have had a pretty shrewd idea which side was going to win in the long run, but he dared not trust his judgement too far, nor, as yet, commit himself too openly. It was still preferable to hedge one's bets, to play in with both sides, to produce a story that would stand up to investigation *whichever way the battle went*. In this context, nothing is more revealing than his absurd

to be passed on to Pausanias alone, whereas in Plutarch's version he wants Aristeides to keep Pausanias, too, in the dark. The entire episode is often dismissed as mere *ex post facto* propaganda designed to exculpate Alexander, after the war, from the obvious and inevitable charge of medism (see e.g. Legrand on Hdt. 9.42, and HW Comm., vol. 2, p. 307, on 9.44.1). This seems far too sweeping. The best propagandists never invent historical incidents if they can help it; they much prefer to take actual events and give them a favourable slant.

suggestion that the Athenians would be well advised to hold firm on the Asopus ridge. If this idea had been Mardonius's own, it could hardly have been better calculated to produce disaster: which opens up an interesting line of thought. Coupled with those suspect assertions about the continuing low state of the Persian commissariat, it strongly suggests that Alexander was acting, in the first instance, as a Persian *agent provocateur.*

The one thing that Mardonius must have feared was that Pausanias would withdraw from the Asopus ridge before the necessary steps had been taken to cut off his retreat. Why not send Alexander (whose employment on these ambiguous missions was, after all, no novelty) to discourage him from so undesirable a move while posing as a secret well-wisher? What Mardonius never seems to have suspected is that the Macedonian king, devious as always, might intend to play a double game as a means of insuring himself with both sides at once. Over and above handing out false advice on Mardonius's behalf, he seems also to have revealed the entire Persian assault-plan, in detail, to Aristeides. The immediate result of this must have been that Pausanias put his troops on an all-night alert, paying particular attention to the river-fords and the passes over Cithaeron. When Mardonius's assault-group was ready to go into action, at some time during the small hours, patrols will have reported all Greek positions manned in strength. The gamble had failed; the element of surprise was lost. Having mounted his attack, Mardonius would not (and probably could not) abandon it altogether; but the whole original battle-plan had to be scrapped at short notice, and replaced by mere *ad hoc* improvisation. If this, or something like it, is what really happened on that fateful night, then Alexander deserves his title of 'the Philhellene': however ambiguous his motives, he made a Greek victory possible.

When dawn broke, there was a certain amount of troop-redeployment on both sides of the river, as each commander manoeuvred for a position of advantage. Mardonius, it is clear, like Epaminondas at Leuctra a century later, took the sensible view that he would be well-advised to post his best troops opposite the Spartans.* These preliminaries, however, seem to have ended in a stalemate, whereupon Mardonius (knowing where his best advantage lay) ordered up his cavalry in strength. All day long his Persian horse-archers – including a contingent of

---

* Herodotus [9.46–8] and Plutarch [*Arist.* 16.1–6] have elaborated this into a kind of military-cum-rhetorical square-dance, with Pausanias switching his right and left wings back and forth, while Mardonius reshuffles his own troops correspondingly. However, as all participants in the game ended where they originally began, it is an entirely academic point whether the episode was fact or fiction.

Sacae from the eastern steppes – kept circling round Pausanias's positions, galloping in from the flank, squadron by squadron, discharging volleys of arrows and javelins as they passed by, then swerving away again, as elusive and irritating as gadflies. How much actual damage they could inflict on a well-disciplined hoplite phalanx – especially when both its wings were protected by high ground – is debatable. It looks as though the mixed contingents of the Greek centre [see above, p. 249], stationed on low ground between Pyrgos and St Demetrius, bore the brunt of these attacks, which, we are told, inflicted 'heavy losses'. In any case, the psychological and moral effect of this endless hit-and-run sniping must have been very great. The Greeks had no adequate means of retaliation against such tactics. To achieve a victory, they needed to make the enemy stand and fight, which at present Mardonius had no intention of doing. He wanted Pausanias off that ridge; but he knew less expensive ways of achieving his object than by a direct frontal assault. The Greeks were already down to their last day's rations; now Mardonius put the finishing touch on their discomfiture. While the Spartans were busy holding off these tangential assaults from the river, one enterprising Persian squadron, cutting its way through south of Pyrgos Hill and the ridge, 'choked up and spoilt the spring of Gargaphia, from which all the Greek troops got water'.*

Soon after this disaster, the generals from the various Greek contingents made their way up to Pausanias's command-post on the knoll and demanded an emergency staff conference. They had been badly shaken by Mardonius's cavalry tactics, and their men were now without any assured source of food or water. It was, on the face of it, impossible to stay where they were much longer. After some heated discussion, they undertook to stick it out for the rest of that day – not that they had much choice in the matter: a withdrawal now would have been tantamount to suicide. When darkness fell, however, provided Mardonius had not brought on a general engagement meanwhile, they agreed to fall back on Plataea. The various units would converge on a ridge of land known as the Island, a little east of Plataea itself, between two arms of the river Oëroë. Its general position lay somewhere near the site of the Análepsis chapel [see map, p. 242].[13] Here they would have abundant water, and be protected against cavalry attacks by the spurs and foothills of

---

* Hdt. 9.49.3. The practical details of this achievement have not aroused much comment among modern historians: wrongly, I feel. It was an emergency operation, and had to be done fast, presumably with any materials (stones, earth, rubbish) that came to hand. I still cannot see how the Persians managed to block and foul it (? by defecation) so effectively that ten minutes' work by the Greek pioneer corps would not have produced a free flow of water once more.

Cithaeron. The Island, as scholars are fond of pointing out, was not large enough (being less than half a mile wide at its broadest point) to accommodate the entire Greek army. Pausanias, however, never intended that it should; indeed, it is probable that Herodotus's entire account of his plan needs considerable modification [see below, pp. 263–4]. As subsequent events show, what Pausanias envisaged was a new defence-line stretching from Plataea itself to a point slightly west of modern Kriekouki, in which the Island would form the central pivot. That same night, moreover, after its withdrawal from the Asopus ridge, half the army (by which, as we shall see, Herodotus in fact meant the contingents of the centre) was to make an expedition up the Dryos-cephalae pass and escort down the provision-trains still stranded there. The Island, in short, would not be overcrowded.

Pausanias's new strategy was more sensible than Herodotus makes it sound. A planned withdrawal would not only extricate the Greek army from its dangerously exposed position, but also, with any luck, tempt Mardonius into risking a general engagement, on a restricted[14] front where his cavalry could not operate with any real effectiveness. That the execution of this withdrawal went hopelessly adrift in its first phase was not really Pausanias's fault. After the decision to retreat had been taken, it was still necessary to stand off the relentless attacks of the Persian horse-archers until nightfall. Pausanias's thirsty, hard-pressed troops never got a moment's respite while any daylight remained. Only as dusk drew on did Mardonius recall his squadrons to base. The Greeks got what rest and refreshment they could, which (one imagines) was singularly little. Then, soon after 10 p.m., the contingents which made up the centre [see above, p. 249] moved off southwards to take up their new position. They were brigaded from twenty different states, a fact in itself liable to produce confusion, and they were carrying out a night-march, through unfamiliar territory, while nearly dead from fatigue. In the circumstances it is not at all surprising that they lost their way; we can safely disregard Herodotus's malicious assertion [9.52][15] that they chose to disobey orders out of cowardice. They finally found themselves outside the walls of Plataea, by the temple of Hera. At this point, making the best of a bad job, and reluctant to go on stumbling around in the dark, they piled arms and waited on events. 'There was', says Plutarch [*Arist.* 17.1], 'great confusion as they proceeded to scatter and pitch their tents at random'. One can well believe it.

In analysing that night's activities, particularly the motives of the various protagonists involved, Herodotus seems to have relied on camp-gossip at its most tendentious. We must, therefore, make a sharp distinction between the known, public events which he reports, and his explanations as to how or why they came about, most of which are mere semi-rationalised fantasy. To begin with, he asserts that Pausanias – unaware, of course, that the Greek centre was now wandering off towards a position more suitable for the left flank – ordered the Spartan divisions to begin their own withdrawal almost immediately afterwards, at some point before midnight. Yet both the Spartans and the Athenians were still in their old positions when dawn broke the next morning. It seems at least arguable that this was the result of deliberate policy; but since, according to Herodotus, Pausanias meant to move hours earlier, there has to be some other explanation for so long a delay. We are therefore given a circumstantial but highly dubious story[16] concerning one Amompharetus, a Spartan battalion commander, who flatly refused to compromise his honour by retreating: neither persuasion nor threats would budge him. The original order to march was countermanded (or so we are asked to believe) while Pausanias spent hour after hour trying to make this pigheaded fire-eater see that he was imperilling the success of the entire operation. The Athenians – again, according to Herodotus – anxious to learn the reason for this hold-up, sent a messenger across to Pausanias's headquarters, who found 'the Lacedaemonians still in their old position and their officers at loggerheads' – a state of affairs which apparently went on till sunrise.

Could anything be more jejune or implausible? Spartan kings of Pausanias's temper had a very short way with insubordinate officers, in which sweet reason played no part whatsoever. There is only one possible motive for anyone, let alone Herodotus, to concoct so monumentally silly a story, and that is to explain why the Spartans and Athenians delayed so long in evacuating their respective positions (a delay which does, admittedly, call for explanation of some sort). What really happened, however, becomes plain enough when we follow the sequence of events after dawn. Pausanias sent orders for the Athenians, on Pyrgos Hill, to close up towards the Spartan position, and only to retreat when he did. Herodotus says that these instructions were issued in the middle of the night; but what prompted them was surely Pausanias's realisation (only possible after first light) that the Greek centre had gone astray, leaving a dangerous gap in the new Cithaeron line. At all events, Pausanias now began to move his Lacedaemonians and Tegeans southward, along the high broken ground of a watershed which ran between the Oëroë and another tributary of the Asopus, the Moloeis. The Athenians, taking their cue from him, marched down off Pyrgos Hill and set out across the plain in a south-easterly direction, towards Kriekouki, thus closing the gap between the two wings. Amompharetus held his division back on the Asopus ridge while Pausanias withdrew as far as the shrine of Demeter, a distance of ten stades or one and a quarter miles [see above p. 244], and got the troops of the right wing into position just east of Kriekouki, their rear protected by the Cithaeron massif. Then, at last, Amompharetus followed them, in coolly disciplined good order, at the standard marching-pace. There is no mystery about his true function: he commanded the rearguard which covered Pausanias's retreat, and the legend, in all likelihood, arose from his insistence on holding this dangerous and honourable post. What was more, he timed his own withdrawal with amazing judgement: within moments of his rejoining the main body, the Persian cavalry came sweeping down on them.

When first light dawned, Mardonius's scouts saw that Pyrgos Hill and the Asopus ridge had been abandoned. The Persian horse, 'meaning', as Herodotus says, 'to continue their old harassing tactics,' at once saddled up and rode off in pursuit of the retreating columns. Mardonius himself, in his command-post on the left flank, near the Morea bridge, could see only the Lacedaemonians and Tegeans. The Athenians were hidden from him behind low hills (though the medising Greeks who held his right wing must have still had them clear in view). We are told that in his jubilation he summoned the Thessalian quisling, Thorax of Larissa, together with two of his brothers, and made them a bombastic speech, which began: 'Well, gentlemen, what will you say, now that you see that place deserted? You, who are neighbours of the Lacedaemonians, used to tell me that they were grand fighters, and never ran away!' Fictional rhodomontade this may be, but it nevertheless enshrines an important truth. Mardonius *genuinely believed the Greeks were in full flight*, and without a moment's hesitation gave the order to advance. His own Persian troops charged across the Asopus at the double, and the other divisional commanders, seeing this, promptly followed their example: 'Without any attempt to maintain formation they swept forward, a yelling rabble, never doubting that they would make short work of the fugitives' [Hdt. 9.59–60]. Mardonius's own crack division was at least in battle-order, but nevertheless 'bore down on the Spartans with a tremendous shouting and clashing of arms . . . as if it were not a matter of fighting a battle, but merely of sweeping away the Greeks as they fled' [Plut. *Arist.* 17.4].

Now, at last, we can understand exactly how Pausanias planned his final bid for victory. Everything hinged on making Mardonius give battle: by now, with their rations and water-supply both exhausted, the Greeks needed a show-down no less urgently than the Persians did. There was never any question of the whole Greek army evacuating its forward positions under cover of darkness. Only the mixed and mostly inexperienced troops of the centre (though stiffened with a strong leavening of Corinthians and Sicyonians) were sent back the night before the battle, to establish themselves on the Island and escort the provision-convoys down from Cithaeron – neither of which tasks, incidentally, they seem to have carried out. For the hoplites of Athens and Sparta a far more dangerous and exacting role was reserved: to function as bait for Mardonius. They moved off at first light, not because of some lunatic obstinacy on Amompharetus's part, but because that was when they would be visible from the Persian lines. They must, in other words, not only retreat *but be seen to retreat*, by the cold light of day: a movement against every rule in the military hand-book, and almost invariably a sign of genuine and demoralised flight. Only the best-drilled and most experienced troops could hope to expose themselves in such a fashion, as a deliberate lure, and get away with it. The trick was a speciality of the Spartans: Leonidas had used it with striking success at Thermopylae.[17]

Nevertheless, in the initial stages of this engagement Pausanias was very far from having things all his own way. When the first massed Persian cavalry squadrons came thundering down on his spear-line, he sent an immediate urgent appeal to the Athenians, who were still moving in across the plain. Stripped of its Herodotean rhetoric, and reduced to appropriately Laconic brevity, the gist of his message would be as follows: 'Hard-pressed by the enemy. Close up on our left flank. If this impossible, send archers.' Aristeides and his eight thousand hoplites, who were now somewhere near the Island, at once changed direction and set off as fast as they could towards the Spartan position. They had gone only a little way, however, when they were overtaken by the cavalry of the medising Greeks who formed Mardonius's right wing [see above, p. 250], and whose line of advance had been across much easier country than that followed by the Persian centre. This powerful task-force included contingents from Thessaly and Macedonia, together with a strong regiment of Boeotians, fighting on their own soil and for the recovery of their own former frontiers. Aristeides was constrained to halt (probably near the Análepsis chapel) and to form up his troops in battle order. No sooner had he done so than the Boeotian and allied infantry came up in force, and he found himself heavily engaged. Pausanias and his Lacedaemonian division, together with the men of Tegea, were left to face the full onslaught of the Persian left wing unaided.

Herodotus claims that their battle-strength was 53,000; to reach such a figure (which he may have done by pure inference from his muster-lists) he would have to reckon in all the light-armed troops, both Helot and free. It seems highly doubtful whether these actually played any effective part in the battle.[18] Without them, Pausanias had a total force of 11,500 at his disposal, which – allowing for a regular line, eight deep – would give him a front about three-quarters of a mile long, spread out between the eastern edge of Kriekouki and the Pantánassa ridge. A quick survey of the situation can hardly have given him much grounds for optimism. Aristeides and the Athenians had failed to reach him, which meant that they must be engaged against Mardonius's right wing – and that he himself had no archers to cover his left flank. What the lost contingents sent off the night before were doing was anyone's guess; Pausanias can hardly have counted on them for relief in an emergency. The Persian centre, made up of the Median and Eastern divisions under Artabazus, was still uncommitted. All Pausanias could do was hang on and pray; oddly enough, during the crucial first phase of the engagement, this, quite literally, is what he did. While his diviners took the sacrificial omens, and he himself invoked the gods for victory, his disciplined hoplites stood firm behind their shield-line, awaiting the word of command that would launch them against the enemy.

Mardonius, for his part, had no intention of matching the Persian infantry, man for man, against that grim line of fully armoured hoplites without a preliminary softening-up process, if only because of the disparity between them in protective equipment. As at Marathon [see above, p. 36], it was spear against scimitar, metal breastplate against quilted cuirass, bronze helmet against leather cap. So the horse-bowmen rode in again, troop by troop, sweeping down the line with a rattle of arrows and javelins; and after them the foot-archers formed line and kept up a deadly fusillade from behind their tall wicker shields. It was now, before the true engagement began, that Callicrates, 'the handsomest and the tallest man in the Greek army', was struck through the lungs by an arrow, and carried out of the ranks to die. He was still lingering painfully when the battle was over, and told Arimnestus of Plataea, with bitter resentment: 'It is no sorrow to me to die for my country; what grieves me is that I have not used my arm or done anything worthy of myself, such as I longed to do.' Many Spartans and Tegeans must have felt as he did that day; Pausanias tested their self-restraint to the uttermost. But the omens still remained unfavourable; it is possible, too, that Pausanias deliberately held back until Mardonius's rearguard, pressing on from behind, made it impossible for his front line to get away in the event of a rout. At last the Tegeans, men of less iron self-control than the Spartan élite, broke ranks and charged the enemy. It was now or never. An instant before, Pausanias had been praying to Hera of Cithaeron; presumably his prayer was answered, since at this critical juncture the omens obligingly turned favourable. He at once gave the order to prepare for action, 'and suddenly there came over the whole phalanx the look of some ferocious beast, as it wheels at bay, stiffens its bristles and turns to defend itself, so that the barbarians could no longer doubt that they were faced with men who would fight to the death' [Plut. *Arist.* 18.2].

The only commander on either side who had a general view of the battle at this stage would seem to have been Artabazus. While Mardonius's right and left wings swept forward to the attack through easy gaps in the hills, Artabazus, with the Medes, Bactrians, Indians and Sacae who formed the centre,* was forced to slog his way uphill, for a mile and more, towards the summit of the Asopus ridge. This delayed arrival, one suspects, suited him very well; he seems to have been a man whose discretion habitually outran his valour. He had always disliked the idea of Mardonius staying on in Greece, right from the beginning; and no more than forty-eight hours previously he had come out with a markedly non-militaristic plan for dealing with the recalcitrant states of the Peloponnese. Now, as he took in the panoramic scene before him, he saw little reason to change his views. Ahead of him and on his left, astride the Pantánassa ridge, a bitter struggle was developing between Pausanias's troops and the Persians. The Spartan hoplites, shields locked, were grimly advancing on Mardonius's infantry and archers. Mardonius himself, conspicuous on a white charger, and surrounded by his *corps d'élite* of a thousand picked guardsmen, could be seen directing operations in the forefront of the battle. Further west, and on lower ground, the Athenians were locked in a fierce struggle with the troops of Thessaly and Boeotia, and suffering a good deal from their lack of cavalry cover. Artabazus could also see something that Pausanias, at this moment, would have given a good deal to know: the Greek contingents of the centre were, at last, on the move from Plataea. They afterwards excused their tardy appearance by the bland assertion that Pausanias *had forgotten to signal them*: 'For this reason they did not hurry up to his support at once or in regular formation, but came straggling along in small groups after the battle had already begun' [Plut. *Arist.* 17.5].

Nevertheless, their intervention had important consequences. The Megarians and Phliasians, together with the other smaller contingents

---

* Herodotus [9.66, cf. 70] estimates the force under Artabazus at 40,000. This figure, derived in all likelihood not from the muster-roll but from hearsay reports which filtered in during Artabazus's subsequent retreat, is quite certainly a vast exaggeration; 13,000 is about the largest number of troops which the Persian centre could have contained: see above, pp. 249–50, and below, p. 271.

who made up the left-centre – some 7,000 men in all – now came hurrying across the open plain, north of the Island, to bring relief to the hard-pressed Athenian division. This was courageous but foolhardy of them. Their drill, apparently, left much to be desired on the march; Herodotus refers contemptuously, with his usual Athenian bias, to their 'complete lack of order and discipline'. They deserve a better tribute. What they did, at great risk to themselves, was to draw off the formidable Theban cavalry, which hitherto had been concentrating, with some effectiveness, on Aristeides' weary hoplites. The Theban commander, Asopodorus, saw this mob of citizen-volunteers rushing towards him, game but disorganised, and swept down on them in full strength. Six hundred were left dead on the plain, and the remainder driven headlong into the hills: an 'inglorious end', says Herodotus, whose prejudices can on occasion be remarkably tiresome. The truth was that Athens' troops had been granted a badly needed breathing-space; and by the time Asopodorus and his cavalrymen had done with pigsticking fugitives along the road to Plataea, the tide of battle had turned against them. At about the same time a second, larger column, headed by the Corinthians, left the temple of Hera and marched quickly eastward along the lower slopes of Cithaeron, with the clear intention of closing up on Pausanias's flank. Whether they in fact engaged or not has been much disputed; but Simonides (in a poem which Plutarch later quoted to confound Herodotus) specifically claims for them the honour of having 'held the centre', so they very probably did.[19] In any case, their flank movement must have done much to discourage Artabazus from committing his own forces at this critical point. The Athenians (whose gratitude seldom outlived their latest political quarrel) subsequently claimed that neither Corinth nor Megara had sent in their troops until the real battle was over.

The timing was certainly very close. Pausanias and his Spartans, after a desperate struggle, had begun to gain ground against their Persian adversaries, whose undoubted courage was no compensation for their lack of body-armour and coherent discipline. They tended to rush the Spartans individually or in small groups, of ten or less, which were easily isolated and cut down. When the Persian archers were driven back, they threw away their bows and, with the infantry, fought long and fiercely against men who were their superiors both in equipment and in military expertise. Round the shrine of Demeter the battle raged to and fro. With their terrible long spears the Spartans

thrust ... at the faces and breasts of the Persians and slaughtered them in great numbers. In spite of this the Persians fought bravely and skilfully before they fell. They seized the long spears of the Greeks with their bare hands, snapped many of them off, and then closed in to fierce hand-to-hand fighting, using their daggers and scimitars, tearing away their enemies' shields and grappling with them, and in this way they held out for a long time [Plut. *Arist.* 18.3; cf. Hdt. 9.62].

So long as Mardonius and his guardsmen were there, and fighting, the struggle went on; but presently Mardonius fell, his skull crushed in by a stone from the hand of a Spartan named Aeimnestus, just as an oracle at Amphiaraus's shrine had foretold. With his death, and the scattering of his bodyguard which followed, all effective resistance against Pausanias came to an end.

When news of this victory on the Greek right wing reached the Boeotians, they saw the battle was lost, and at once disengaged; by now the Theban cavalry had come back, and was ready to cover their retreat. They had fought well, and suffered few casualties: no more than three hundred of their front-line troops, according to Herodotus. Alone of Mardonius's allied contingents they now withdrew, in good order, to Thebes, where they set about preparing for the inevitable siege that would follow. Their comrades from Thessaly and Macedonia do not appear to have put up nearly so determined a fight; while that wily opportunist Artabazus, like W. S. Gilbert's Duke of Plaza-Toro, put up no fight at all. The instant he saw which way the battle was going, he prudently pulled out his division without striking a blow, and marched away westward into Phocis. From here he made his way to Thessaly, and from Thessaly to Thrace. He never breathed a word of Mardonius's defeat in any country he passed through, but gave out that he was on a special mission, and that Mardonius, together with the main army, would soon be following him. 'When he comes,' Artabazus told his unsuspecting hosts, 'mind you entertain him with the same friendliness as you have shown me – you will never have cause to regret it'. He claimed to be in a great hurry; and this, if nothing else, was the simple truth. By such means he got safely to Byzantium, where he commandeered every available boat, and ferried his troops (somewhat reduced by starvation, illness, and brushes with the Thracians) back across the Bosporus into Asia. Xerxes, who was a pragmatic if demanding taskmaster, far from censuring him for desertion in the face of the enemy (as some British scholars have done) was only too grateful that he had contrived to withdraw a large body of first-class troops without loss. Plataea, if we can trust Herodotus [8.126.1], actually left Artabazus with an enhanced reputation.

As the battle had been divided, so was the pursuit. The Corinthians, the Sicyonians, and various other contingents from the force which had marched from Plataea to relieve Pausanias now gave chase to Artabazus, but seem to have done his retreating column little damage. The Athenians, together with the men of Plataea and Thespiae, followed on doggedly after the Boeotians, who were still capable – aided by some fresh Theban reinforcements from the city – of acquitting themselves well in a final rearguard action. After some sharp fighting, however, with heavy casualties on both sides, the Boeotians got the worst of it, and ran headlong for the sheltering walls of Thebes. Aristeides might have pursued them further, but just at this moment a runner arrived from Pausanias, once again calling for his help. The Spartans and Tegeans had driven Mardonius's shattered right wing back across the Asopus, but then found themselves faced with an unexpected obstacle. Most of the Persians took refuge inside their great military stockade beyond the river, barring the main gates against their pursuers and quickly manning the guard-towers. From here they put up a vigorous last-ditch defence, defying all Pausanias's efforts to dislodge them. The Spartans had little experience of sapping and scaling; hence their appeal to the Athenians, who were experts in every branch of siegecraft.

Aristeides at once led his exhausted men back down the great loop in the river, and set grimly to work. It was by no means an easy business. Cornered, the Persians were desperate. Drifts of arrows and sling-stones came whistling down from every vantage-point; of those Athenians striving to breach the defences many, says Ephorus, were 'slain by the multitude of missiles and met death with stout hearts'. But finally they achieved their object. A gap was battered in the wooden palisade, and thousands of triumphant Greek soldiers, the men of Tegea in the lead, went storming through it. Pausanias had issued an order that they were to take no prisoners. The Persians went to pieces as soon as their stronghold was breached. All discipline lost, and half dead with fright, they huddled there in their thousands like so many sheep, and the stockade became a ghastly abattoir. Of perhaps 10,000 who had taken refuge there, less than 3,000 were left when Pausanias called off his blood-crazed men and began restoring some semblance of order. Seven years later Aeschylus could write:

> So great shall be the toll of butchered blood
> Spilt by Greek spears, that shall clot on Plataea's field,
> And heaped-up dead with voiceless testimony
> Before men's eyes, to the third generation,
> Shall cry the penalty of presumptuous pride,
> Which having flowered, bears a bloody fruit,
> And tears and sorrow are its harvesting.

[*Pers.* 816–22]

At long last the Persian shadow had been lifted from Greece, this time for ever. What Salamis had begun, Plataea brought to a triumphant conclusion. Both by sea and land, Xerxes' defeat was absolute.

Curiously, considering the importance of Plataea, we cannot determine the exact date on which the battle was fought, let alone the battle casualties suffered by either side. The most likely period is about mid-August, some six weeks after Mardonius's occupation of Athens, and very close in time to Leotychidas's victory at Mycale [see below, p. 281], for which the subsequent siege of Sestos provides a *terminus ante quem* some time before the beginning of September.[20] Casualty figures are even more elusive. Herodotus claims that of Mardonius's non-European troops who failed to get away with Artabazus, not 3,000 survived the slaughter in the stockade. This *per se* is a plausible estimate. On the other hand he firmly pegs the number with Artabazus at 40,000 (Ephorus gives confirmation of a sort by making this 400,000) which, as it stands, is nonsensical, being larger than the paper strength of left wing and centre combined. Two explanations are possible. Either this figure represents the *total* number of survivors, including the medising Greeks who got away to Thebes; or else, if it really refers only to Artabazus's column, it has been bulked out with light-armed troops, camp-followers, and perhaps some stray refugees from the stockade. Of these two theories the former is preferable. The medising Greeks had few casualties, the centre (since it did not engage) none. Modern scholars estimate Mardonius's non-European losses, in battle and at the storming of the stockade, as somewhere in the region of 10,000. Allowing 1,000+ for casualties among the medising Greeks (the Boeotians lost 300), this agrees well with a general survival-figure of 40,000, on the basis of an army corps originally 50,000+ strong [see above, p. 229]. Applying the chiliarch-myriarch theory, it also, oddly enough, agrees with Ephorus (over 10,000[0] Persian casualties) and Ctesias (overall losses of 12,000[0] after Salamis). Greek losses are absurdly minimised by Herodotus: he admits only 91 Lacedaemonians, 16 Tegeans, and 52 Athenians in what was, by any standards, a desperately hard-fought battle. Elsewhere he casually alludes to the death of 600 Megarians, Phliasians, and others from the left-centre. Plutarch gives total Greek losses as 1,360. If we assume that this refers only to citizen-hoplites, it is a low, but just conceivable, figure, and again consonant with the estimate of Ephorus (over 1,000[0]). Further than this we cannot go. What does emerge, inescapably, is that Mardonius's best Persian troops were virtually wiped out, along with their commander-in-chief, while the remainder scattered to the four winds. As a fighting force, his army had ceased to exist.[21]

The usual camp-followers soon appeared, eager to make a smooth transition for themselves between the old and the new régimes. One enterprising lady from Cos, the mistress of a high-ranking Persian officer, was quicker off the mark than anyone. The instant news of Mardonius's defeat arrived, she decked out herself and her maids in the finest clothes and jewellery she could lay hands on, ordered up her carriage, and set out for the battlefield. She actually reached the stockade while Pausanias's men were still at their work of slaughter. A quick glance round told her who was giving the orders, and she sank down at the Spartan king's feet, clasping his knees as a suppliant. Thanking him for 'the killing of these men, who reverence neither gods nor angels', she begged him to spare her 'the slavery which awaits the prisoner of war', explaining that she was a Greek of good family who had been forcibly abducted by a wicked Persian nobleman. Pausanias, who, though partial to pretty girls, was nobody's fool, rather took the wind out of her sails by claiming close acquaintance with her alleged father. Despite this he placed her, as a temporary measure, under the protection of the Ephors. Later she asked for safe-conduct, to Aegina: Cos was not yet liberated. Pausanias, amused, let her go. He must have had many such applications during the first difficult days after Mardonius's defeat.

Close behind this elegant *fille de joie*, with her carriage and lady's-maids, arrived the somewhat crestfallen contingents of Elis and Mantinea. 'Such was their indignation and distress when they found that all was over, that they declared they deserved to be punished' – a classic case of over-protestation from men whose Peloponnesian allegiance was something less than well-defined. Besides, the Greek army had been in Boeotia for at least a fortnight: where were they lingering all that time? To begin with they declared their intention of pursuing Artabazus into Thessaly; when the Spartans vetoed this proposal, they marched back home and, as a self-exculpatory gesture which cost them comparatively little, passed sentence of exile on all senior officers involved. Pausanias was also approached, while still on the battlefield, by some sedulous lickspittle from Aegina who, remembering how Xerxes and Mardonius had stuck Leonidas's head on a pole after Thermopylae, now proposed similar treatment for Mardonius as a *quid pro quo*. If he hoped to curry favour in this way, he had badly misjudged his man. Pausanias dismissed him with a scathing rebuke, saying he was lucky to escape punishment for so barbaric and obscene a suggestion. Next day Mardonius's body had mysteriously vanished, and no one knew who took it away; though various people claimed credit (and got rich rewards) for having given Xerxes' brother-in-law proper burial. It seems very likely that the Spartan Regent, in a chivalrous mood after his crushing victory, made a private arrangement with some of the dead man's friends or relatives for the disposal of his corpse.

Over the spoils of war, however, Pausanias had no such scruples; like most upper-class Spartans, he found rich pickings fatally attractive. A good deal of plunder had been captured in the stockade: the Tegeans, for example, made off with a special bronze manger, kept for Mardonius's horses, which they afterwards dedicated to Athena Alea. When the battle was over, however, the Captain-General of the Hellenes set about gathering up Mardonius's loot in a most systematic fashion. Private plundering was forbidden, on pain of death, and squads of Helots set to work to collect all that lay scattered over the banks of the Asopus. The result was fantastic: tents with gold and silver furnishings, inlaid couches, bowls, cups and cauldrons, armlets and torques, daggers and scimitars all of pure gold – 'not to mention richly embroidered clothes which, amongst so much of greater value, seemed of no account'. In addition to this there were concubines, horses, camels, and an infinity of coined money: months afterwards the Plataeans were still turning up hidden strong-boxes and treasure-chests. Later rhetoricians declared that this was when the Greeks first became enamoured of affluence; there may even be something in such an idea. It was a popular Athenian *canard* that the Helots contrived to steal a good deal of gold when carrying out their search, and later sold it to the Aeginetans (not knowing any better) at the price of brass, thus laying the foundation of Aegina's future prosperity.

A tithe of the total plunder collected was set aside for dedication to Apollo at Delphi. From this offering was made a golden tripod, supported on a bronze pillar eighteen feet high, the latter being in the form of three intertwined serpents, The tripod itself long ago vanished (melted down by the Phocians during the Sacred War of 355 BC) but the serpent-column still survives, battered but recognisable, in the Hippodrome at Constantinople. On its coils were inscribed the names of thirty-one Greek states which fought against Xerxes at Salamis or Plataea.[22] The opening words of the inscription, memorable in their brevity, read: 'These fought in the War'. There follows a simple list of names, headed by Lacedaemon, Athens, and Corinth. Pausanias – an ominous foretaste of *hubris* to come – originally prefaced these words with an elegiac couplet (cut either on the stone pedestal or the thirteenth serpent-coil) which ran:

> After destroying the Median host, Pausanias, Captain-General
> Of the Hellenes, set up this memorial to Apollo.

Such a boast gave extreme offence at Sparta, where the cult of personality was frowned on. Pausanias's distich was stricken out, perhaps to be replaced by the following:

> The saviours of wide Hellas set up this memorial
> Having preserved their cities from loathsome slavery –

which at least preserved the semblance of an 'anonymous collective'. Further portions of the spoils were assigned to temples at Olympia and the Isthmus. From these were made, respectively, a fifteen-foot bronze Zeus, and a ten-foot bronze Poseidon.

The remaining spoils were shared out among the troops. Herodotus, though sure that special prizes must have been awarded for valour, found no surviving record of such awards – or perhaps, in the edgy political atmosphere of the 440s, tactfully preferred not to mention them. According to Plutarch [*Arist.* 20.1–3] some very undignified bickering arose on the subject between the Spartans and Athenians, which Cleocritus of Corinth solved, diplomatically enough, by proposing that the prize should go to Plataea, a *tertius gaudens* acceptable all round. Before their victory was more than a day or two old, the Greek allies were already reverting, it seems, to their usual centrifugal state of feuding and separatism. Eighty talents-worth of loot was set aside for the lucky Plataeans, who used it to rebuild their sanctuary of Athena at Delphi, setting up a new shrine and decorating the temple with frescoes – 'which', says Plutarch, himself a Boeotian priest, 'have remained in perfect condition to this day'. Pausanias himself, as Captain-General, was voted ten of everything, including women, horses, and camels. Perhaps to show that he nevertheless remained a homespun soul at heart, he had a Spartan supper served up side by side with a Persian banquet in Mardonius's great marquee, and asked his officer-guests to observe the contrast. The dead were ceremonially buried *in situ*, each state choosing a separate site for its common tomb. Before official thank-offerings could be made, or other religious ceremonies performed, those shrines and temples desecrated by the Barbarian had to be ritually purified. All altar-flames were extinguished, and a fast runner, Euchidas, sent to bring fire 'fresh and pure from the public altar at Delphi' with which to rekindle them. Euchidas left Plataea at dawn and was back before sunset, having covered 125 miles in a single day. Delphi had once again been publicly recognised as the religious centre of Greece; the stigma of medism – if it ever existed – was now forgotten.[23]

The general mood was one of extravagant relief, gratitude, and exultation. Pausanias, after the ceremony of purification had been carried out, made sacrifice to Zeus the Liberator in Plataea's ruined market-place. With all the allies to bear witness, the Captain-General formally guaranteed the Plataeans their territory and independence, while solemn oaths were taken to protect the little city against any future aggression. The Greeks established a new Panhellenic festival, the Eleutheria, to be held every four years at Plataea, with public games, in honour of Greece's final deliverance. If they also, carried away by the solemnity and enthusiasm of the moment, swore 'that they would hand down enmity to the Persians as an inheritance even to their children's children, so long as the rivers run into the sea', that – like their earlier resolution never to repair war-damaged temples – was surely very understandable at such a moment. Further elaborations on this theme, in particular the supposed *ad hoc* creation, under Aristeides' guidance, of a permanent military League against Persia, complete with standing army and fleet, can safely be dismissed as fiction.[24] In return, the Plataeans undertook to care for the graves of those Greek warriors who lay buried on the field of battle, and to offer up sacrifices every year in their honour. Plutarch gives an eyewitness account of this latter ceremony, which was still being observed, with great punctilio, over five hundred years later. Among other ritual acts, the chief magistrate of Plataea, after asperging the tombs with holy water and anointing them with myrrh, slaughtered a black bull and called upon the illustrious dead to drink its blood. Then, mixing wine and water, he raised his cup, saying as he did so: 'I drink to the men who died for the freedom of Greece.'

For ten days, while the dead were interred with due solemnity, and the temples purified, and a bewildering variety of booty was apportioned, and sacrifices of thanksgiving were made to all the gods, Pausanias and his Greek allies lay encamped at the scene of their historic victory. Though the war with Persia was not over yet – peace would only be ratified thirty years later, after innumerable crises and at least one major naval engagement – its shadow had, at last, receded from Greek soil. The champions of a free Hellas were left in possession of the field; but this (as another group of Allies found in 1945) soon posed its own problems. Above all, what action was to be taken against the medising Greeks, who had survived Plataea with few casualties, and whose territories remained virtually intact? In the atmosphere of oath-taking and dedication which had marked the past few days, no one was likely to forget that a year before, when the invasion crisis was at its height, the League had sworn to punish all medisers, once victory was won, by 'tithing' them to the god at Delphi [see above, pp. 70–1]. Now whether this meant destroying their cities *in toto* or merely confiscating one-tenth of their property as war-reparations,* it was a fundamentally unrealistic project, which posed difficult problems for the victors. To carry out their sworn commitment would, in effect, mean declaring war on the whole of Northern and central Greece, a prospect which Pausanias's battle-weary troops can scarcely have regarded with enthusiasm. (Faced with such terms, moreover, any medising state would undoubtedly have fought to the death.) Autumn was coming on; against all expectation, the Barbarian had been driven out of Greece. All now were more concerned to repair their ravaged farms and get on with the sowing than to set out on another major expedition. During the next year or two sporadic attempts were, in fact, made to take reprisals, but only when an urgent political reason presented itself for doing so.

In this respect what happened now set the pattern. The prospect of leaving Boeotia united under a strong central government in Thebes can scarcely have appealed to Athens – much less to Thespiae and Plataea, whose new independence would be worth very little without Allied sanctions to enforce it. On the tenth day after the battle a general war-council was held, and a formal decision taken to march against Thebes 'and demand the surrender of all those who had gone over to the Persians, especially the two men, Timagenidas and Attaginus, who had led the pro-Persian movement'. This could hardly be called, by any stretch of the imagination, tithing Thebes to the god; but then seven-gated Thebes was an immensely strong city, the reduction of which would have called for more effort than Pausanias's levies were prepared to exert. Like post-war veterans anywhere, in any century, they wanted one thing only now: to go home. Besides, the real danger from Boeotia, in political terms, was its close-knit oligarchic system of government. Remove that, and everyone could relax: hence Pausanias's request for the surrender of Thebes' most prominent oligarchic quislings. He probably calculated (with good reason) that their popularity would not long outweigh the average Theban citizen's distaste for being besieged. In the event, nine days sufficed, by which time Timagenidas saw that if he did not surrender voluntarily, he was liable to have little choice in the matter. Attaginus, a cleverer man, agreed to give himself up and then slipped away by night; the rest were duly turned over to Pausanias. The Spartan Regent refused to take action against Attaginus's sons, saying he did not believe in guilt by association. On the other hand, he dealt out very summary justice to Timagenidas and the

* The former view has been argued, very persuasively, by H. W. Parke, *Hermathena* 72 (1948) 92–7, and is followed by Burn, PG p. 345: 'To "give the tithe" to a god was what Greeks did when they sacked a city, or when a state confiscated the property of a convicted malefactor.'

rest, who (as he realised) were confidently expecting to bribe their way to an acquittal if put on trial. After breaking up the Theban hegemony over Boeotia, and installing moderate governments in the various cities, Thebes included, Pausanias dismissed the various allied contingents to their homes. Having done this, he escorted his political prisoners as far as the Isthmus, where they were summarily executed – an object-lesson and warning to extremists everywhere.

One last episode in the drama remains to be told. While Pausanias and the Persians lay watching each others' movements across the Asopus, a group of Samian envoys (unbeknown to the Persian-backed ruler of the island) arrived in Leotychidas's naval headquarters on Delos. Like the Chian junta who had made a similar appeal before the fleet left Aegina [see above, p. 227], these would-be rebels now urged the Greeks 'to save the Ionians, men of the same blood as themselves, from slavery, and expel the foreigner'. Samos itself, they said, was ripe for revolution. The mere appearance of a strong Greek naval force in the eastern Aegean would be enough to make every Ionian city come out against Persia. The Persians themselves were unlikely to put up any serious resistance. Their ships had deteriorated through long service, and were in no condition for a pitched battle; the Persian fleet as a whole would present no real opposition to a determined Greek offensive. This statement strongly suggests that the Persian admirals had *already* dismissed their powerful Phoenician contingent [Hdt. 9.96.1], a piece of news which would doubtless have given Leotychidas considerable encouragement. Various explanations have been advanced for this surprising move. It is just possible that the Phoenicians were detached (with fear of an imminent Ionian rising in the air) to guard the coast of Thrace or the Dardanelles; but what seems more likely is that after Salamis [see above, p. 201] their loyalty had become so doubtful that they were now regarded as a bad security risk, and better out of the way. In either case the Persians can hardly have been sanguine about their prospects for a naval campaign: to that extent Leotychidas's visitors were not exaggerating. The Spartan admiral listened carefully to what they told him, and this time decided it was worth taking a chance. The leading delegate pledged his people to wholehearted support of the Greek cause, and an oath of alliance between Samos and the League was administered there and then. Twenty-four hours later, sped on its way by favourable omens, the Greek fleet left Delos harbour and sailed east.

The moment Artaÿntes and Ithamitres, the Persian admirals on Samos, learnt of this move, they pulled out their squadrons and made for the mainland opposite: not quite so craven a retreat as it might appear, since the channel between Tigani harbour and the Mycale peninsula [Samsun Dag] is only a mile or two wide at its narrowest point. In any case, they had very little alternative. With suspected treachery in the fleet, and a stubbornly hostile population on Samos, they might easily find themselves cut off if they stayed where they were. Besides, after the departure (for whatever reason) of the large Phoenician contingent, they now had little more than a hundred ships in active commission. They therefore decided, after discussion, that 'as they were no match for the Greek fleet, they had better not risk an engagement'. On the Mycale coast they would be able to establish overland communications with Sardis and the interior (not to mention an easy line of retreat if things went badly for them). They would also have the support of Tigranes – 'the tallest and best-looking officer in the Persian army' – who had been specially detached, at Xerxes' orders, with a division about six thousand strong,* to keep watch over Ionia. What they now planned, in effect, was to link up with Tigranes, and convert their useless fleet into an emergency military base. Somewhere along the southern shore of the Mycale promontory, near a temple of Demeter and Kore, and on the east bank of a small river, the Gaeson, they beached their ships. Having done so, they fenced them about with a strong stockade, using stones and tree-trunks in combination, and topping off the whole with a *cheveux-de-frise* of sharpened stakes. They had wooded hills and ravines behind them, and an accessible pass leading away northwards over Mt Mycale: either Domatia or Ak Bogaz offers a very plausible site. With the marines which they took off their remaining galleys, they and Tigranes could muster a combined force of perhaps 10,000 men. They dug themselves in on their narrow beach, prepared, as Herodotus says, either to do battle or stand siege.

Leotychidas, meanwhile, brought his fleet to anchor in the great eastern bay of Samos, near those smoke-blackened ruins which were all that Xerxes' troops had left of the famous Heraeum, unique among

---

* Herodotus [9.96.2] puts this force at 60,000, a manifestly impossible figure (Hignett XIG pp. 254–5, Burn PG p. 549). It was long ago suggested by Tarn [JHS 28 (1908) 228, n. 99] that Tigranes' rank was that of myriarch, and that the forces under his command, an original paper strength of 10,000, had been whittled away by the campaign in Greece and the retreat which followed it. In that case Hignett's myriarch-chiliarch theory gives (as so often) a very plausible total. As Ephorus estimates the *total* Persian forces at Mycale, including those 'from Sardis and the neighbouring cities' (i.e. Tigranes' division), and the naval division from Samos, as 10,000[0] – see Diod. 11.34.3 – we can hazard a guess that some 4,000 marines were serving with the fleet. Allowing 30–40 per ship [see above, p. 190], this would give a total of rather over 100 vessels in commission after the departure of the Phoenicians.

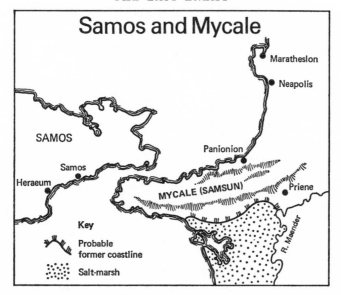

Samos and Mycale

ancient temples. He had sailed in with decks cleared, ready for immediate action; but the Persians were already gone. Pleased though Leotychidas must have been to find himself presented, gratis, with a first-class naval base for future operations in the eastern Aegean, this new move by his opponents left him a trifle disconcerted. He was eager and well-

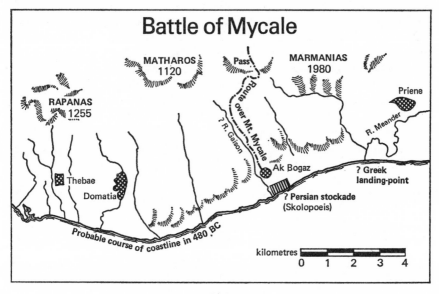

Battle of Mycale

279

equipped to fight at sea – but how well would his force acquit itself if suddenly transferred to dry land? He had no more than 2,500 regular marines with him, and perhaps 1,000 archers (if these had not been drafted to Plataea). It has been argued[25] that some at least of the Peloponnesian states had been forced, through a severe shortage of manpower, to draft hoplites as rowers. If these had brought their armour with them, or could borrow some from the Samians, they might bulk out the available total of heavy-armed troops, but even so the number at Leotychidas's disposal is unlikely to have exceeded a round five thousand, at most. On the other hand, it was by now a well-known fact that, man for man, only the very best Persian infantry could hold its own against trained Greek hoplites. Leotychidas held a staff conference to discuss what they should do next. Some officers advocated returning to base, while others, more adventurous, wanted to by-pass the Persians at Mycale altogether, and make straight for the Dardanelles. No one, oddly, seems to have thought of consolidating their position on Samos. The decision they finally reached – to attack the enemy stockade, and if possible destroy it – was a bold one, but arguably correct. Until this had been done, any further advance ran a risk of leaving the Greek fleet cut off, if and when the Persians decided they would put to sea again.

By now it was about midday. The fleet at once put to sea, and stood across towards the mainland. When Leotychidas saw a strong infantry force drawn up along the beach, and every vessel safely within the shelter of the stockade, he stood close in-shore, taking aboard his flagship a herald 'who had the strongest voice of anyone in the fleet'. This herald now proclaimed that the Greeks were come 'to liberate the Greek cities of Asia', and called on all true Ionians to change sides in the hour of battle, giving them the password for the day, which was 'Hera' – a nice reminder of the vandalism perpetrated against their most famous temple. Leotychidas was, of course, simply borrowing the device which Themistocles had employed after Artemisium: this time it seems to have had rather more effect. Tigranes at once disarmed all Samians serving in his ranks,* and put the men of Miletus on line-of-communication duties, to guard the passes leading over Mycale. This latter move does not suggest that the Milesians had, to date, given any overt signs of disloyalty; but doubtless Tigranes preferred to keep them away from

---

* Since Leotychidas now held Samos, this was a wise precaution anyway; but apparently the islanders had already given evidence of their disaffection by releasing the five hundred prisoners taken by Xerxes' troops during the advance through Attica [see above, p. 160], and sending them home to Athens with provisions for their journey (Hdt. 9.99).

the actual fighting. This attitude is quite understandable: why place unnecessary temptation in their path?

Leotychidas now brought his whole fleet much further eastward along the coast, so that he could get his troops ashore and into battle-formation undisturbed by the enemy. During this period of disembarkation, a persistent rumour spread through the ranks that Pausanias and his forces had just won a great victory over Mardonius in Boeotia. Since both Herodotus and Ephorus state, quite unequivocally, that Plataea and Mycale were fought *on the same day*, Plataea in the morning and Mycale in the afternoon, much ingenious rationalisation has gone on, from that day to this, as to just how such a rumour gained currency, let alone proved correct. Herodotus, of course, took it as manifest proof that 'the hand of God is active in human affairs', a theory less popular nowadays than it used to be. According to Ephorus, Leotychidas *invented* a victory in Boeotia to give his troops extra confidence, and afterwards had the satisfaction of seeing his pious lie vindicated as historic fact. (The Persians, similarly, to encourage *their* troops, announced that Xerxes was on his way from Sardis, at the head of a vast army; but this prediction, unluckily for them, proved less reliable.)

Modern opinion is divided on the matter. Some historians assume that Plataea was fought several days before Mycale, so that news of the earlier battle would have time to get through in the normal course of events. Those who accept the traditional dating – and such odd historical coincidences, though rare, are by no means unknown – tend to explain the rumour in one of two ways. Either they claim that the victory which Leotychidas heard about, and duly passed on to his troops, was not that of the final battle, but some earlier minor success (perhaps the temporary repulse of Masistius's cavalry squadrons); or else, like Hignett, they sturdily dismiss the story altogether as 'a pious fiction for the edification of the faithful'. There may, however, be an alternative solution. When Aeschylus introduced that famous chain of beacons in the *Agamemnon*, he was clearly describing a communications-system familiar to him and to his contemporaries – perhaps, indeed, dating from this very campaign. As has often been pointed out, such a chain would be hard to set up across the north Aegean, from Troy; but a route through Euboea and the central Cyclades presented few difficulties. If Pausanias's look-outs lit the Cithaeron beacon at mid-morning, his news could reach Mycale – by way of Parnes, Styra, Ocha, Andros, Tenos, Myconos, Icaria, and the high peaks of Samos – somewhere about noon. When Leotychidas's men saw that black column of smoke curling up against the blue summer sky, they must have had a very shrewd idea what had happened. At the same time, complete certainty was impossible. These were just the circumstances in which a rumour (as opposed to a circumstantial report) could well have arisen.[26]

Leotychidas is unlikely to have disembarked more than a small proportion of his rowers; apart from any other consideration, he wanted the ships manned and ready in the event of a defeat. He had perhaps 2–3,000 light-armed sailors with him in addition to his heavy-armed infantry, a total fighting force somewhat smaller than that of Tigranes. If the Persians went to ground inside their stockade, moreover, he would find himself at a severe disadvantage. The Greeks had neither the special equipment with which to carry this impromptu fortress by storm, nor sufficient leisure and strength to invest it. Leotychidas's best hope, he saw, lay in convincing Tigranes that he had to deal with an attacking force even smaller than it actually was: a nice case of making a virtue of necessity. The prospect of snatching a quick, easy victory would, with any luck, tempt the Persians into taking the offensive. Leotychidas therefore divided his forces. The larger part, led by the Athenians, and including contingents from Corinth, Sicyon, and Troezen, was to advance directly along the beach and the narrow strip of plain below the mountains, in the hope of engaging the enemy. Meanwhile he himself and the Lacedaemonian division would make a detour inland, well out of sight, working their way up a ravine and then crossing several ridges, to come down eventually on Tigranes' left flank.

It was a bold strategy, and it worked to perfection. When the Greek line came in sight of the stockade, the Persians, 'observing how few the enemy were, disdained them and bore down on them with great shouting'. As at Plataea, the archers set up their great spiked wicker shields in a row, and shot from behind this barrier. After a moment's hesitation – natural enough in the circumstances – the Athenians and their allies, though heavily outnumbered, closed ranks and joined battle. For some while it was an extremely close-run thing. The Sicyonian regiment had particularly heavy casualties, including their commander, Perilaus. But then the disarmed Samians, snatching what weapons they could find, went over to the invaders' side, and many other Ionians fighting for Tigranes soon followed their example. The Greek hoplites, elated by the thought of bringing off a victory on their own, without any assistance from the Spartans, redoubled their efforts. At last they smashed their way through the Persian shield-line, and Tigranes' men broke and fled for the ships, with the Greeks hard on their heels. Organised resistance was now at an end, and most of the defenders promptly took to the hills. As always, it was the Persians themselves who fought with the greatest distinction. Several scattered groups of Tigranes' imperial guardsmen made a savage last-ditch stand inside the stockade, until Leotychidas's Spartans, arriving in the nick of time before it was all over, cut them down and took over what might, euphemistically, be termed mopping-up operations.

By now more and more of the Asiatic Greeks, with the opportunistic valiance of buck-rabbits, were turning openly on their former masters. The Milesians, stationed up in the passes as guides, had a particularly enjoyable time, 'for when the Persians were trying to escape, they led them the wrong way, by tracks which brought them back among the enemy, and finally joined in the slaughter and proved their bitterest enemies'. Tigranes and his deputy commander Mardontes were killed in action; the fleet admirals, Artaÿntes and Ithamitres, escaped. They, together with several thousand other fugitives who escaped both Leotychidas's troops and the wild beasts[27] that roamed Mt Mycale, made their way, by slow stages, northwards to Sardis, where Xerxes, it is said, received their news 'in bewilderment'. (His brother Masistes, more forthright, described Artaÿntes' generalship as 'worse than a woman's'.) About four thousand Persian and allied troops had lost their lives in this battle and the subsequent rout; Greek casualties are unrecorded, but must have been heavy. As dusk drew on, and the pursuit slackened, Leotychidas had all booty and treasure removed from the Persian camp, and assembled on the beach. Then he set fire to the stockade and the empty ships drawn up inside it, and sailed back to Samos. The cornerstone of freedom was securely in place at last.

Victory, however, at Mycale as at Plataea, brought its own problems and responsibilities. The most pressing, of course, was how to protect the newly-liberated cities of Ionia. Leotychidas held an immediate debate on this thorny topic, and the fundamental differences of attitude which it revealed – the next fifty years' history in embryo – were far from reassuring. The Spartans, a self-sufficient and naturally isolationist people, detested all overseas commitments on principle. To accept new members into the League meant guaranteeing them military protection against Persia. Now Sparta's line on Ionia had been clear and consistent since before the first Ionian Revolt: she would give diplomatic protection, but steadfastly refused military assistance.[28] This was quite understandable. How could Sparta, a land-based power and weak in cavalry, undertake to defend this vulnerable coastal strip against the full might of the Achaemenid empire? Leotychidas's arguments were straightforward enough. The League had been formed to drive the Persian invader out of Greece. This task was now fulfilled. Any further commitments in Asia Minor would imply a fundamental change of policy, from defence to aggression. This the Spartans resolutely refused to countenance. They had agreed, before Mycale, to admit

Samos as a member of the League. They were ready to extend similar privileges to Chios, Lesbos, and all other islands that 'had fought for Greece against the foreigner'; but there they drew the line. Economically self-sufficient, and with strictly limited military resources, they had no driving need to establish any kind of control over the Ionian seaboard or the Dardanelles. With Xerxes still no further away than Sardis (and bearing in mind their innate disinclination to pursue a foe) it is easy to see why such a policy was anathema to them. Their own limited objective had been obtained, and they wanted nothing better than to leave it at that.

At the same time, on ethnic and moral grounds alone, *something*, clearly, had to be done about the Ionians. Here we come up against an interesting and significant change in Greek self-awareness. When Athens had been under pressure to secede from the League and join Mardonius [see above, pp. 222–6], her spokesman had reassured the Spartans with a reference to 'the Greek nation – the common blood, the common language; the temples and religious ritual; the whole way of life we understand and share together,' admitting frankly that 'if Athens were to betray all this it would not be well done' [Hdt. 8.144]. It is hard to imagine any Greek talking in this way before Marathon. Common resistance and sacrifice in the face of a profoundly alien invader had begun, however slowly and imperfectly, to forge a sense of what afterwards came to be known as the Panhellenic ideal, of an identifiable and unique Greek spirit which no other race could share. This was perhaps the best and most lasting legacy of the Persian Wars. The Spartan delegates on Samos at least understood and accepted the intangible responsibility they bore for their fellow-countrymen in Ionia, even though the solution they proposed (wildly impractical as it stood) was chosen to suit their own specialised needs and fears, with little regard for its potential impact elsewhere. What they had in mind was a mass transfer of population. Since the League could not guarantee their independence, let the Ionians leave home and migrate to mainland Greece, where they could settle in the commercial or maritime cities of the medising states – a nice way of 'tithing the god' to everyone's advantage. No one made it clear how the present populations were to be evicted, or where they would go: presumably, as zealous pro-Persians, to the vacant cities of Ionia. The idea was a curiously persistent one; Bias of Priene had formulated it long before, and a largely successful attempt to carry it out, on a large scale, was made as recently as 1922.

The most violent and determined opposition to this scheme came, predictably, from the Athenians, though their declared reasons hardly justify so inflexible a stand. They disliked the idea of Peloponnesians determining the fate of Athenian colonies; they feared that 'if the Ionians were given new homes by the Greeks acting in common they would no longer look upon Athens as their mother-city'. So insistent were they that the Ionians should remain *in situ* that they even, according to Ephorus, offered them independent guarantees of support, regardless of whether the other Greek states did so or not. It would have been less than politic to mention hard economic facts; yet they must have been uppermost in the Athenian spokesman's mind throughout. For one thing, there were far more potential Ionian emigrants than cities to accommodate them: the result would be chronic overcrowding, when there was little enough room already. More important, the Ionians were experienced and highly successful maritime traders. The last thing Athens wanted – having, with great difficulty, eliminated Corinth as a major commercial rival – was a new influx of competition for her markets. It was all very well for little Sparta, secure in her isolation, and adequately fed by the serf-tilled wheatfields of Messenia, to advocate such a radical realignment of forces in Greece: she would suffer nothing as a result. Athens, on the other hand, depended for her very life-blood on overseas trade, and therefore preferred to keep these too-clever cousins of hers firmly at a distance. Like every militant state in Greece, Athens had fought Xerxes, first and foremost, on the principle of self-determination. Yet she had other, equally pressing motives, high among them a desperate need to recover access to the vital Black Sea grain-routes. Her wearily triumphant leaders had no wish to see their hard-won independence cut from under them by thrusting and acquisitive colonials. In the face of such adamant hostility, Leotychidas prudently dropped his proposal – with the result that the Ionians, for the moment, got no protective treaty at all.[29]

This basic disparity of purpose between Athens and the Peloponnesian *bloc*, long obscured by common preoccupations and dangers, is even more apparent in the events which followed. After their abortive debate, the allied commanders agreed to sail for the Dardanelles, their primary object being to remove Xerxes' two bridges. (These, presumably, had been repaired since the previous autumn; it is quite incredible that their earlier destruction should have remained unknown to the Greeks for so long.) The Spartans regarded such an expedition in purely military terms. Its only justification, as they saw it, especially with autumn well advanced, was to guarantee Europe against further invasion, a recurrent anxiety which long haunted their minds [see e.g. Thuc. 1.89]. Thus, for them, the whole matter, at present, began and ended with the breaking down of the bridges; once this was done, Persia's European garrisons, in Thrace and elsewhere, could be dealt with piecemeal. To the Athenians, on the other hand, this meant the first essential step in a predominantly *economic* mission: the recovery of Sestos and Byzantium, the securing of key trade-routes and profitable markets too long denied them by the Great King [see above, pp. 24–5]. The war might be over – some would deny even that – but the peace most undoubtedly still remained to be won, and the Athenians had every intention, *ab initio*, of winning it.

At Abydos, to their surprise, they found the bridges down already: an enterprising Persian officer from Cardia had, with considerable fore-thought, dismantled them and carried the great cables across to Sestos for safekeeping. Leotychidas, learning of this, came to the conclusion that their task was over; the Athenians had other ideas on the matter. While the Peloponnesian contingents sailed off home, Xanthippus and his Attic squadrons, aided by various unnamed 'Ionian allies' – a significant straw in the wind – stayed on and methodically laid siege to Sestos. The situation had transformed itself almost overnight. Not only were the Greeks now taking the offensive against Persia – that had started with Mycale – but already parting company among themselves over their basic strategy: the rapid emergence of Athens as an inde-pendent leading power had immense and unforeseeable repercussions. Xanthippus held on right through the winter, till the starving defenders were reduced to boiling and eating their bed-thongs, and the Athenian troops themselves came very close to mutiny. But Sestos fell at last, and Xanthippus (after capturing and crucifying the Persian garrison-commander) sailed back to Athens in triumph, towing Xerxes' bridge-cables behind him – the last, most extravagant, and most symbolically appropriate of all the spoils to be dedicated by a grateful people at Delphi. For Herodotus, as for Thucydides, this was the point at which the Persian Wars ended; as a historian one may challenge their view, but both dramatically and psychologically they were quite right. The crowded half-century ahead was best left severely alone. The nearest Herodotus comes to a judgment on it is in the very last sentence of the *Histories*, when he remarks that the Persians 'chose rather to live in a rugged land and rule than cultivate rich plains and be slaves'; a subtly disturbing comment, and one would like to know how it struck Athens' great imperial leader Pericles.

So the Athenians once more brought wives and children and house-hold goods back to their war-shattered city, and began the long painful task of rebuilding what had been destroyed. The defence of the West had been brought to its splendid and successful conclusion; now it was time for more humdrum but no less necessary tasks. A new world was dawning, a world in which the ideals and loyalties of the League were soon forgotten or lost their meaning. This is understandable in human terms; one cannot live at the highest pitch of sacrifice, courage, and selfless idealism for more than a very little time. Such rare flash-points illuminate, but are unsustainable. Yet something pure and indestructible had been created in the crucible of war, as carbon atoms, under inconceivable pressures, will coalesce to form a diamond. Throughout all the betrayals and failures which followed, that one bright element still shone clear. The ultimate achievement of such a victory is hard to measure in appreciable terms. So fundamental and lasting a debt almost defies our understanding. Perhaps its finest summing-up is that by William Golding. In a most moving and memorable essay[30] he once wrote (of Leonidas, but his words have universal applicability):

> If you were a Persian . . . neither you nor Leonidas nor anyone else could foresee that here thirty years' time was won for shining Athens and all Greece and all humanity . . . A little of Leonidas lies in the fact that I can go where I like and write what I like. He contributed to set us free.

Freedom, in the last resort, implies the privilege and right to abuse freedom, a privilege of which every Greek state availed itself liberally throughout its history. To follow that melancholy yet inspiring story further is not, at present, my concern. As Xenophon said at the end of his *Hellenica*, 'for me, then, let it suffice to have written thus far; and what followed thereafter may be some other man's care'. Let us leave the Greeks in their brief and incandescent moment of triumph over the Barbarian: a timeless instant when – as at the apogee of a successful revolution – all values are simple and clear-cut, every human ideal achievable. Such fragile and perfect revelations cannot long exist in time: for one day only, perhaps – and yet that one day, *sub specie aeternitatis*, continues to irradiate and quicken our whole Western heritage, now and for ever.

Athens – Methymna, 1968–9

287

NOTES

1 I am thinking in particular of Pericles Georges' *Barbarian Asia and the Greek Experience*, Edith Hall's *Inventing the Barbarian*, and François Hartog's *The Mirror of Herodotus* (see Supplementary Bibliography: any work cited in this Introduction will be found there). The first sentence of Oswyn Murray's chapter on the Ionian Revolt in CAH iv² (p. 461), clearly advanced as a truism, is: 'Like the Jews, the Greeks learned to define themselves as a nation in the course of their contacts with the Persians.'

2 The literature is by now immense. See in particular, in addition to the items mentioned above, Briant 1982 and 1989, Cook 1983 and 1985, Cuyler Young 1988, Dandamaev 1989, Elayi 1988, Frye 1983, Gershevitch, Herzfeld. A very handy general update for the period 1962–83 is provided by Lewis, *ap.* Burn 1984, 588–602. Especially useful (as Burn notes on page xv of his Preface to the second edition) is work on 'the prosopography of the Persian nobility and military high command'.

3 I have listed in the Supplementary Bibliography only those volumes most strictly relative to the Persian Wars (i.e. V, VIII, and IX). For the same reason I do not include separate editions of the earlier books such as that of Book I by R. A. McNeal, or Alan B. Lloyd's magisterial three volumes (1975–88) on Book II, useful though I have found them. My inclusion or exclusion of general works on Herodotus is governed by the same principle.

4 It was Gomme's dictum that originally led me to plan what many saw as an impossibly hubristic graduate seminar: i.e., to read and discuss all nine books of Herodotus in Greek in one semester. In fact the experiment proved a great success and (which shows it was not a fluke) has since been repeated, with equal enthusiasm, four or five times. Quite apart from instilling a surprising mastery of Greek (not only Ionic Greek, either) in the victims, it made us realise on just how vast and well-organised a canvas Herodotus presented his material, how masterfully architectonic his overall aim.

5 Despite the evidence of two lost Athenian harvests (presumably those of 480 and 479) reported by Herodotus (8.142.3, cf. Hammond 1988, 560–

1), I do not believe that this requires us to put the date back to the September of 481, as Hammond (1982) argued at length, and Burn (1984, xvi) tentatively accepted. The 480 harvest may have been late that year; modern calculations based on Greek and Persian military manoeuvres may be a trifle early; even if the harvest *was* got in, in whole or part, events almost certainly moved too fast towards evacuation for any real benefit to be got from it. Furthermore, an evacuation *so far* ahead of an immediate crisis, in Athens more than most places, is hard to credit. Even if farmers and citizens had agreed to move, they would very soon have drifted back again. I hope to return to this chronological problem elsewhere.

6 Sometimes I feel that scholars should be banned from invoking forgery as support for their urge to prove themselves superior to their sources until they have taken a basic course in the fundamentals of the practice, beginning with Anthony Grafton's excellent introduction, *Forgers and Critics: Creativity and Duplicity in Western Scholarship* (Princeton 1990), then moving on to the classic work of W. Speyer, *Die literarische Fälschung im heidnischen und christlichen Altertum* (Munich 1971), and the articles collected in *Pseudepigraphie in der heidnischen und jüdische-christlichen Antike*, ed. N. Brox (Darmstadt 1977). Useful material in English includes Gilbert Bagnani's 'On Fakes and Forgeries', *Phoenix* 14 (1960) 228–44, the late Sir Ronald Syme's *Emperors and Biography: Studies in the Historia Augusta* (Oxford 1971): especially chapter xvii, 'Fiction and Credulity', 263–80, but the whole book is loaded with fascinating *aperçus*; and, for a broad survey of forgery in the art-world, *Fake? The Art of Deception*, ed. Mark Jones (Berkeley & London 1990).

7 See in particular this passage: 'We can see from the "constitution of Draco" in Arist. *Ath. Pol.* 4 the inability of a forger to understand the conditions of an earlier period and to envisage the spirit of the past. Moreover, we should expect to find in a forgery matters of interest to a late-fourth-century writer, such as the methods of raising finance or compelling reluctant trierarchs (in the fourth-century sense) to shoulder the financial burden, and not the once-and-for-all methods of manning a navy with army personnel' (p. 91).

8 The reviews I consulted are (listed in no particular order) the following: *Phoenix* 25 (1971) 86–7 (Eliot); *Riv. Stud. Class.* 19 (1971) 95–7 (d'Agostino); CPh 66 (1971) 264–5 (Frost); AHR 76 (1971) 750–51 (Kagan); RBPh 50 (1972) 621 (Salmon); *Rev. Hist.* 96 (1972) 254–55 (Will); *Historische Zeitschrift* 213 (1971) 135–36 (Meyer); CR 22 (1972) 423–25 (Briscoe); *Mnemosyne* 28 (1975) 315–16 (Van der Veer); *Anzeiger f. Altertumswiss.* 28 (1975) 39–41 (Weiler). There were others.

9 In his famous proem (1.1), Herodotus, after promising to rescue the great deeds of both Greek and Barbarian from time's obliterating passage, adds: '. . . and other matters, including the reason they warred with one another' (τά τε ἄλλα καὶ δι' ἣν αἰτίην ἐπολέμησαν ἀλλήλοισι).

10 A good deal of work has been done on Xerxes' life, administration, fiscal policies, and architectural enthusiasms: see Granger, Kuhrt & Sherwin-

White (*Ach. Hist.* II 69–78), Matsudaira, O'Neil, Rocchi, and Tripodi. Most of it confirms and amplifies my earlier evaluation of him.

11 Plato *Laws* 707 B–C, well analysed by R. W. Macan, *Herodotus: The Seventh, Eighth, and Ninth Books* (London 1908), vol. ii, 47–48. The Athenian Stranger (clearly representing Plato himself) is joined by Megillus the Spartan in denying Cleinias' assertion that Salamis was the battle that saved Greece: ἡμεῖς δὲ ... φαμὲν τὴν πεζὴν μάχην τὴν ἐν Μαραθῶνι γενομένην καὶ ἐν ταῖς Πλαταιαῖς τὴν μὲν ἄρξαι τῆς σωτηρίας τοῖς Ἕλλησι, τὴν δὲ τέλος ἐπιθεῖναι, καὶ τὰς μὲν βελτίους τοὺς Ἕλληνας ποιῆσαι, τὰς δὲ οὐ βελτίους. The well-connected Plato is not inventing here, nor being a crusty and untypical odd man out, but simply restating an aristocratic truism that had been a commonplace since long before Marathon.

12 See Meiggs & Lewis 40–47, esp. 40–41; cf. Ostwald 336–67, 342. I am leaving the Kerameikos *ostraka* out of account here: see below.

13 I have learned a great deal from much valuable work done in this area since I wrote in the late 1960s: see in particular Balcer 1979, Ghinatti, Holladay, Karavites, Knight, Ostwald, and particularly Williams 1973, 1978, 1980, 1982.

14 Thuc. 1.22.4: τῶν τε γενομένων ... καὶ τῶν μελλόντων ποτὲ αὖθις κατὰ τὸ ἀνθρώπινον τοιούτων καὶ παραπλησίων ἔσεσθαι.

15 The particular parallel that recurs more than once in this book is the similarity between Xerxes' advance in 480 and that of the Third Reich in 1940, with interesting personal equations (e.g. Themistocles: Churchill and Thessaly/ Thebes: Vichy France). Such an illustrative line-up, perhaps understandably, sat somewhat ill with my German and Austrian reviewers. Weiler devoted the greater part of his notice to it, while Meyer (after chiding me for 'einer exzessiven Detailfreude' – most British reviewers complained of just the opposite) severely proclaimed that my modern notion of *eleutheria* (freedom) meant that I was incapable of analyzing the ancient article properly.

16 A. E. Housman, *D. Iunii Iuvenalis Saturae* (corr. ed. Cambridge 1931) xi.

17 O. K. Armayor, 'Did Herodotus ever go to the Black Sea?', HSCPh 82 (1978) 45–62; 'Did Herodotus ever go to Egypt?', *Journ. Am. Res. Cent. in Egypt* 15 (1980) 59–73; 'Sesostris and Herodotus' autopsy of Thrace, Colchis, Inland Asia Minor, and the Levant', HSCPh 84 (1980) 51–74; *Herodotus' Autopsy of the Fayoum: Lake Moeris and the Labyrinth of Egypt*, Amsterdam 1985. Detailed criticism of Armayor's thesis in Pritchett 1982, 234–85.

18 The *reductio ad absurdum* of this methodology was to argue that Ovid was never in fact exiled to Tomis, but invented the whole thing (making numerous geographical and other errors in the process) as a literary *jeu d'esprit* in Rome. See, e.g. A. D. Fitton Brown, 'The unreality of Ovid's Tomitan exile', *Liverpool Classical Monthly* 10 (1985) 18–22, well refuted by D. Little, 'Ovid's last poems: cry of pain from exile or literary frolic in Rome?', *Prudentia* 22 (1990) 23–39.

19 Pritchett 1993 10–143 offers the most detailed rebuttal of Fehling, on a

case by case basis; see also John Marincola, 'The Sources of Herodotus', *Arethusa* 20 (1987) 26–32 (more moderate, less partisan), and Gould 136–37.

20 O. Murray, *Achaemenid History II* (Leiden 1987) 101 n. 12.

21 I am thinking in terms of a comprehensive treatment by one author. As should by now be clear, I have learned a very great deal from the relevant chapters in CAH iv², especially those by Lewis, Ostwald, and Barron (Hammond's views were already familiar to me from various earlier articles); but this is not the same as a single articulated overview.

22 *Hannibal's War: A Military History of the Second Punic War* (Warminster 1978); *The Spartan Army* (Warminster 1985).

23 In this he rather reminds me of the Prussian general Von Moltke, who in 1914, when presented with a memorandum on the need for an Economic General Staff, replied: 'Don't bother me with economics – I am busy conducting a war.' See Barbara Tuchman, *The Guns of August* (New York 1963) 374.

24 See in particular 33–39: but also 50, 69, 80, 184, 196, 238 and elsewhere. This is the basis on which I am admonished (p. 39) for using what I fondly imagined to be reasonably neutral descriptive terms such as 'intelligence officer', 'reconnaissance unit', 'commando force' or 'pioneer corps'. Lazenby's notion is not restricted to military affairs either. The idea that Themistocles master-minded the reform of the archonship in order to promote the *strategeia* as a political body, and correspondingly weaken, not only the archonship itself, but also the Areopagus Council that was recruited exclusively from ex-archons (see pp. 46–47) is dismissed as 'too Machiavellian', and we are warned solemnly that it would be 'a mistake to credit Themistocles with too much foresight' (Lazenby 82–84, following Badian, who argues, on other grounds, against any long-term planning by T. in this matter). Too Machiavellian for *Themistocles*? Nor should Professor Lazenby need reminding that as late as the 19th century quite a number of senior officers appointed for reasons of social prestige did very well when it came to fighting a battle.

25 Once again I am reminded of 1940, and the uncomprehending irritation generated among French intellectuals by the (to them) wholly irrational refusal of the British to follow their lead and surrender on the best terms they could get.

26 Lazenby 50 ff., and 69, where (against all lexical usage) he claims that συναγαγόντες simply means 'rallying' instead of the tactically crucial 'drawing together' (of the two Greek wings going back to aid the centre at the Soros: cf. my account, 36–37); and 184, where Burn and I are cited as arguing that '*the Greeks rowed* north past Aigaleos into the Bay of Eleusis, where they assembled, and then returned to envelop the head of the Persian line'. This is a total misrepresentation: see p. 188 for what I actually say (that the Corinthians stood away northward under sail as a decoy movement to lure Xerxes into the narrows, in the belief that he had the Greek fleet bottled up).

27 Again, Lazenby (p. 36) downplays this kind of evidence to the best of his ability. On military matters see, e.g. Anderson, Garlan, and, best of all, Pritchett 1971–91; on naval developments Haas, Jordan, Kelly, Morrison 1974, 1984, Morrison & Coates, Starr, Wallinga 1982, 1987, 1990, Whitehead; on the cavalry, Bugh, Evans 1986/7, Worley.

28 Here, of course, we enter that grey area of looking-glass loyalties discussed earlier: the now common notion of double (or even triple) agents has made the idea (to put it no more strongly) of Themistocles playing both ends against the middle perfectly credible. Sir John Harington's famous couplet applies: 'Treason doth never prosper: what's the reason? / For if it prosper none dare call it treason.'

29 See pp. 172–74 with 293 n. 6, and cf. Lazenby 163 and 198.

30 Lazenby 161: this is very different from Artemisia's shrewd advice (Hdt. 8.68) that Xerxes should *divide his forces*, keeping half to stall the Greeks at the Isthmus while detaching the rest to effect a landing (presumably at Gytheion) in the southern Peloponnese, and attack Sparta from the south.

31 On a personal note, I should say that Professor Lazenby and I have never met; but I think we would probably get on very well if we did. We certainly have a surprising amount in common, including (on internal evidence) not only a passion for exploring odd corners of Greece on foot, which might have been expected, but also familiarity with the works of Rider Haggard; a wife who has been, fairly recently, working for a Ph.D.; and, rarest of all, a wise cat willing to accommodate itself tactfully to the clutter on a writer's desk. Professor Lazenby has also spoken more kindly of my style than (I suspect) it merits, and describes *The Year of Salamis*, in his Preface, as 'deservedly famous, combining scholarship and imagination with the ability to tell a stirring tale'. Perhaps realizing that this was overdoing it a bit, for the rest of *The Defence of Greece* he makes almost every mention of my book – and it is constantly referred to throughout – highly critical, and as a final dismissive gesture omits it from his extremely wide-ranging bibliography.

32 One well-justified reviewer's complaint (Briscoe 423–25) was that by using existing translations I had (inevitably) slipped into the acceptance, here and there, of nuances stressed by the translator but not necessarily present in the original. In fact for some while now, precisely because of this risk, I have been making my own translations of matter I cite: in any revision of the present text the translated matter will be my own version, taken directly from the Greek (or occasionally Latin) source.

ORIGINAL EDITION NOTES

PREFACE

1 First pointed out by N. G. L. Hammond, JHS 76 (1956) 42, n. 37, and Burn, PG, p. 456, n. 12.

1 Discovered in 1939 by archaeologists working on the excavation of Ostia, Rome's port at the mouth of the Tiber – not, surprisingly, in some rich man's house, but under the rubble of a small, unpretentious apartment block (Russell Meiggs, *Roman Ostia*, p. 433) – a touch which should appeal to those who see Themistocles as the patron of the Athenian proletariat. Like the 'Troezen Decree' [see p. 98 ff.] the 'Ostia Herm' at once gave rise to a vast and controversial scholarly literature. All critics agreed it was a Roman copy, most probably of the Antonine period – see e.g. R. Bianchi Bandinelli, *Critica d'Arte* 5 (1940) 17–25, G. Becatti, *ibid.* 7 (1942) 76–88. But what was it copied from? Here the experts divided. Some dated the original to the fourth or third century BC, thus firmly labelling it Hellenistic: so Bandinelli, *op. cit.* (with reservations), B. Schweitzer, 'Das Bildnis des Themistokles', *Antike* (1941) 77–81; H. Weber, *Gnomon* 27 (1955) 444–50 – but on this see the rebuttal by K. Wessel, *Jahresb. d. deutsch. arch. Inst.* 74 (1959) 124–36 – and others. However, the dominant opinion of scholars and art-historians now tends to suggest that the Ostia Herm derives from a fifth-century original portrait made towards the end of Themistocles' life, perhaps when he was Governor of Magnesia. See L. Curtius, *Mitteilungen des deutschen Archäologischen Instituts* (Röm. Abt.) 57 (1942) 78–93; F. Miltner, 'Zur Themistoklesherm', etc. (Bibliography); Calza (Bibliography, and also *Scavi di Ostia V: I Ritratti*, Pt. 1, Rome 1964, pp. 11–14); G. M. A. Richter, *Greek Portraits*, pp. 16–21; *Portraits of the Greeks*, vol. 1, pp. 97–9 and pls. 404–12 (Bibliography). Miss Richter describes this bust as 'the first real [Greek] portrait', a verdict with which the present writer would concur, though at the same time acknowledging the justice of Calza's *cri de coeur* (*Ritratti, loc. cit.*): 'Non è facile uscire di questo labirinto scientifico'.

2 These figures substantially agree with the totals recorded by Herodotus and Simonides: modern scholars tend to reduce them, but they have recently been most convincingly vindicated by N. G. L. Hammond, in his article 'The Campaign and the Battle of Marathon', JHS 88 (1968) 13–57, esp. 32–3.

3 I follow the time-scheme worked out by Burn, *Persia and the Greeks* [hereafter referred to as PG], p. 257. Hammond [JHS 88 (1968) 40] has recently attempted to make the full moon that of 9 September. I do not find his arguments convincing: the Persians had met with little or no opposition, and should easily have reached Euboea by the end of July: see Burn PG, p. 241.

4 The site of the Herakleion has been much disputed: I follow Professor Eugene Vanderpool [AJA 70 (1966) 322–3] who not only places it in the most likely strategical position, but is the only scholar to provide convincing archaeological evidence in support of his thesis. Other suggestions include the Avlona Valley and Mt Agrieliki, below the Church of St Demetrius; see e.g. Hammond JHS 88 (1968) 24–5.

PART TWO

1 So Burn, PG, p. 320, who argues that the white flax [*leukolinon*] of Herodotus [7.25] would not be strong enough. Since the weight of the rope alone would be something like 1 cwt. per yard, this seems likely.

2 For the most useful modern discussions see Bibliography s.v. Maurice and Tarn, together with How and Wells [henceforward referred to as HWComm.], p. 366 ff., Burn, PG, p. 326 ff., Hignett, *Xerxes' Invasion of Greece* [henceforward referred to as XIG], p. 40 ff. Cf. Hdt. 7.61 ff.

3 For an illuminating prosopographical analysis see Burn's excursus, PG, pp. 333 – 6, 'Members and Connections of the Achaemenid Family in Xerxes' Army'.

4 H. W. Parke and D. E. W. Wormell, *A History of the Delphic Oracle* (1956) pp. 169 – 70. As they rightly say, 'there can be no doubt that we have here the original utterances of Delphi before the event'.

5 Maintained, e.g. by Brunt, 'The Hellenic League against Persia', *Historia* 2 (1953 – 4) 135 – 63, esp. 143; challenged by Hignett, XIG, p. 100.

6 For what follows I am much indebted to the penetrating analysis by Brunt, *Historia* 2 (1953 – 4) 135 ff.

PART THREE

1 See J. S. Morrison and R. T. Williams, *Greek Oared Ships 900 – 322 BC* (1968), pp. 134 – 5.

2 Directly attributed to Ephorus [fr. 111 M = schol. Pind. *Pyth.* 1.146] who is probably also the source for Diod. 11.1.4 quoted here; the link between Xerxes and Carthage is queried by many modern historians, most recently by Gauthier, REA 68 (1966) 5 – 32, but convincingly defended by Bengtson, *Griech. Gesch.*, 2nd ed. (1960), p. 163, Burn, PG, p. 306, n. 30 and Ehrenberg, *From Solon to Socrates* (1968), p. 161.

3 The dating and relative chronology of the two main Persian War oracles to Athens are still a matter of dispute: for recent discussions see e.g. Hignett, XIG, pp. 441 – 4, Burn, PG, pp. 355 – 8, Parke and Wormell, *Hist. Delph. Orac.*, vol. I, pp. 169 – 71, Hands, JHS 85 (1965) 59 – 61, Labarbe, *Loi Navale*, p. 120, Grundy, *Great Persian War* [GPW], p. 238.

4 See now C. W. Fornara, AHR 73 (1967) 425 – 33, against the predominantly sceptical views of earlier writers.

5 M. H. Jameson, *Historia* 12 (1963) 386; cf. the same scholar's *editio princeps*, published in *Hesperia* 29 (1960) 198 – 223, from which I have learnt a great deal. The critical literature on the Troezen Decree is immense: not all items are of equal value, but the more important are cited below in my General Bibliography.

6 Close examination of the stone itself [now No. 13330 in the Athens Epigraphical Museum] has convinced me that in line 28, where Jameson originally conjectured *ka[i ta pleromata ton] n[eon]*, and afterwards substi-

tuted *ka[i tous allous kata] naun*, we can in fact read *ka[i tou]s nau[t]as [kata] naun*.

Professor E. Vanderpool now informs me (what I had previously failed to notice) that *nautas* was in fact suggested, though apparently as a conjecture rather than as a reading, by A. G. Woodhead and R. S. Stroud in *Hesperia* 31 (1962) 313, to be rejected – again as a conjecture – by Jameson, *Historia* 12 (1963) 391, n. 12. My own carelessness in scrutinising these two articles thus gave me the accidental advantage of a completely independent reading, which may at least lend confirmatory weight to Woodhead's and Stroud's proposal.

7 Jameson, *op. cit.*, p. 203.
8 P. A. Brunt, 'The Hellenic League against Persia', *Historia* 2 (1953–4) 135–63.
9 See M. R. Cataudella, 'Erodoto, Temistocle e il decreto di Trezene', *Athenaeum* 43 (1965) 385–418, a most perceptive and valuable discussion.
10 See in particular Aristotle, *Ath. Pol.* 22.8; Plut. *Them.* 11.1, cf. 21.2–4, *Arist.* 8.1. The most sensible discussion is that by Burn, PG, pp. 351–2; cf. Caspari, CR 10 (1896) 418.

PART FOUR

1 For a summary – and a brilliant demolition – of such views see now Hignett, XIG, p. 119–25.
2 See W. K. Pritchett, 'New Light on Thermopylae', AJA 62 (1958) 202–13, with pls. 54–5; A. R. Burn, *Studies Presented to D. M. Robinson*, vol. I (1951) 480–9, cf. PG, pp. 408–11; also now Pierre McKay, 'Procopius' *De Aedificiis* and the Topography of Thermopylae', AJA 67 (1963) 241–55, with pls. 49–50 and map, the latter of inestimable value for exploring the terrain *in situ*. The first traveller to map out this route was Major-General Gordon: see his *Account of two visits to the Anopaea* (Athens 1838).
3 That of W. K. Pritchett, AJA 65 (1961) 369–75.
4 See the highly ingenious speculations of T. J. Dunababin, *The Western Greeks* (1948), p. 425 ff.; also Burn, PG, pp. 481–3.
5 This paragraph represents an attempt to reconcile the apparently conflicting testimony of Herodotus [8.9] and Ephorus [Diod. 11.12.5]; but the sequence of events, and many details of the subsequent battle, remain obscure. For some cogent general criticisms – though I cannot accept his remarks on the *diekplous* – see Hignett, XIG, pp. 183–6.
6 E.g. Diod. 11.10.1–4; Justin 2.11.12–16; Plut. MH. 32 [866A–B].
7 Hignett, XIG, p. 371. His discussion of this tantalising problem (*ibid.*, pp. 371–8) is by far the most cogent known to me. *Devotio* was the quasimagical self-sacrifice of an individual or commander to spare the community as a whole: 'It is expedient that one man should die for the people.'
8 Cf. W. W. Tarn, JHS 28 (1908) 219, and Hignett, XIG, p. 189. Another

obvious candidate is the Battle of Lade (494) at the close of the Ionian Revolt.

9 This was precisely the formation adopted in July 1588 by the Duke of Medina Sidonia when bringing another Great Armada up the English Channel: cf. Morrison and Williams, p. 139.

10 So Holm, *Gesch. Sicil.*, vol. I, p. 207; Freeman, *Hist. Sic.*, vol. II, p. 199.

PART FIVE

1 Hignett [XIG, p. 100] is worth quoting here: 'This sensible observation, indignantly challenged by Plutarch, recalls Macaulay's verdict that the Highland tribes which rallied to the cause of Charles the First in Scotland only did so because the hated Campbells of Argyll had joined the other side.'

2 Themistocles' predicament at this point bears some resemblance to that of Colonel de Gaulle (as he then was) in 1940, when he acted in defiance both of his Army superiors and of the Vichy Government, with what striking results we know.

3 So Morrison and Williams, p. 124. Since Themistocles' plan *always* envisaged the evacuation of Athens, it makes the order no less callous if we refer it back to June (their explanation).

4 Herodotus (always anxious to deny his bugbear credit for any originality or percipience) attributes this insight [8.57] to Mnesiphilus, Themistocles' old tutor, in fact it almost certainly originated with Themistocles himself. See Hignett, XIG, p. 204, and reff. there cited.

5 On this point see now Arthur Ferrill, 'Herodotus and the Strategy and Tactics of the Invasion of Xerxes', AHR 72 (1966–7) 102–15, esp. 107–8.

6 Hdt. (8.97) followed by Plutarch (*Them.* 16.1) places this operation *after* the Battle of Salamis, treating it mainly as a diversionary activity, designed to cover the retreat which took place a day or two later. This cover-plan, as Burn says (PG, p. 437), seems 'improbably cumbrous', and I agree with him in following the more plausible tradition preserved by Strabo (9.1.13, C. 395) and Ctesias (§26, Henry, pp. 31–2) – though not without hesitation: Hignett's critical remarks (XIG, pp. 415–17) have considerable cogency.

7 Strabo (*loc. cit.*) provides an interesting confirmation of Pritchett's thesis when he states that the channel is about two stadia, i.e. 400 yards, wide; today, even at its narrowest point, it is rather more than twice that distance.

8 Hdt. 8.65, as interpreted by Myres, *Herodotus: Father of History* (Oxford 1953), pp. 265–6, following a hint by Munro in the *Cambridge Ancient History*, vol. IV, p. 306; cf. Burn, PG, p. 448, and see p. 205.

9 Hdt. 8.70: this crucial passage is to be clearly distinguished from 8.76.1, which describes the Persians' *second* plan, precipitated by Sicinnus's mes-

sage (see above, p. 207). Hignett (XIG, pp. 217, 406) is surely correct in his supposition that 'Herodotus, in dating their adoption of the second plan within a few hours of their execution of the first, may have telescoped the course of events'. Hignett would separate them by 'several days'. I place the first on 17 August, the second forty-eight hours later.

10 Beloch, Obst, and, most recently, Hignett, XIG, pp. 403–8, Appendix IX, 'Salamis: four historical fictions (a) The first message of Themistokles'. For an interesting rebuttal see the review by J. R. Grant in *Phoenix* 17 (1963) 301–6.

11 Our main ancient sources are Aesch. *Pers.* 355–60; Hdt. 8.75; Plut. *Them.* 12.3–4; Diod. 11.17.1–2; Nepos *Them.* 4.3–4; Justin 2.12.19–20. I do not accept Hignett's contention that 'what later writers (e.g. Diodoros and Plutarch) have to say cannot be used to support either version, as their accounts of the matter are derived from one or other of the two primary sources and have no independent value' (p. 403). How Hignett knows this I simply cannot imagine. There are details in both Diodorus and Plutarch – and, if it comes to that, in Nepos and Justin – which could not possibly derive from either Herodotus or Aeschylus; Hignett's answer in such cases seems to be that they made them up out of their own heads. This is the merest casuistry. With the larger part of ancient literature irretrievably lost to us, we cannot tell on what earlier sources Ephorus (for example) may have drawn, let alone judge their reliability.

12 Main sources: Aesch. *Pers.* 361–85; Hdt. 8.76; Plut. *Them.* 12.5; Diod. 11.17.2. The most sensible treatment of these much-disputed preliminaries is that by Morrison and Williams, pp. 140–3, 150–5.

13 Main sources: Hdt. 8.78–81; Plut. *Them.* 12.6–7, *Arist.* 8.2–6; Nepos *Arist.* 2.1; cf. Diod. 11.17.3–4. The most perceptive discussions are those by Hignett, XIG, pp. 408–11, and Fornara, JHS 86 (1966) 51–5.

14 Main sources for this order of battle: Hdt. 8.85.1, 87, 91, 94; Diod. 11.17.3, 18.1–2, 19.1–2. Goodwin long ago argued, on a point of particular syntax in Hdt. 8.85.1, that the Athenians were in fact on the right and the Spartans on the left, a view now readopted (for different reasons) by Morrison and Williams, p. 143. I am not convinced by their arguments. For a similar interpretation to mine see Burn, PG, p. 458 ff., to which (though differing from it on points of detail) I am much indebted.

15 On this phenomenon see Plut. *Them.* 14 and the highly interesting information collected *in situ* by Hammond [JHS (1956), pp. 46–9] from a seaman of the Royal Greek Yacht Club. Cf. Morrison and Williams, pp. 161–3, who add some very pertinent comments on the comparative behaviour of Greek and Persian vessels in adverse weather conditions.

16 I owe both the translation and the interpretation of this phrase to Burn, PG, p. 465.

17 Main sources: Aesch. *Pers.* 447–71; Hdt. 8.95; Plut. *Arist.* 9.1–2; Paus. 1.36.1–2. The best modern analysis is that by Fornara, JHS 86 (1966) 51–5.

PART SIX

1 So Hignett, XIG, p. 264, following a hint in H. Delbrück, *Geschichte der Kriegskunst*, vol. I (3rd ed.), Berlin 1920, p. 96.

2 Hdt. 8.108 – 9; Thuc. 1.137.4; Plut. *Them.* 16.1 – 5, *Arist.* 9.3 – 10.1; Diod. 11.19.5 – 6; Justin 2.13.5 – 8; Polyaenus 1.30; Nepos *Them.* 5.1 – 2.

3 On this much-neglected monument see Plato, *Menexenus* 240D, 245A; Plut. *Arist.* 16.4; Nepos *Them.* 5.3; also J. Stuart and N. Revett, *The Antiquities of Athens* (London 1762), vol. I, p. ix; Chandler, *Travels in Asia Minor and Greece* (London 1765), vol. II, ch. 46; Sir William Gell, *The Itinerary of Greece* (London 1819, 2nd ed. 1827), p. 303, all cited by E. Vanderpool, *Hesperia* 35 (1966) 102 – 3, n. 20, and AJA 70 (1966) 323, n. 15.

   A recent article by W. C. West (see Bibliography) argues that the *tropaia* of Marathon and Salamis were only given permanent form as victory monuments about the second quarter of the fifth century, when Athens 'restored' them; I find this conclusion somewhat dubious. At the same time, Mr West is probably right in his suggestion that they 'were the first Greek trophies to be given permanent form'. He states (pp. 18 – 19): 'In turning an impermanent marker of victory into a permanent commemorative monument, Athens reveals the enduring significance with which she endowed Marathon and Salamis in the years of the Pentakontaetia . . .' But (as I hope to have made clear) the magnitude of the achievement impressed itself very clearly on Athenian minds *ab initio*, and I see no reason (with Vanderpool) why the original monuments should not have been permanent and commemorative, a new departure to mark so famous a victory. See also now Paul W. Wallace, 'Psyttaleia and the trophies of the Battle of Salamis', AJA 73 (1969) 293 – 303, with pls. 65 – 6.

4 So Burn, PG, p. 488: the most convincing interpretation of this passage (Hdt. 8.114) known to me.

5 For these Corinthian epitaphs (already referred to above, p. 188) see Plutarch, *MH* 39 (870 E ff.) where no less than five of them are quoted *in extenso*. The Corinthian explanation of Xerxes' defeat is reported by Thucydides (1.69.5) who puts it in the mouth of their ambassador to Sparta in 432.

6 On this point see A. J. Podlecki, *Historia* 17 (1968) 274.

7 A point well made by Lattimore, p. 89 (see Bibliography).

8 E.g. Macan (see Bibliography), vol. 2, p. 343; Munro, JHS 24 (1904) 145 – 7; Burn, PG, pp. 496 – 7. Against such a view see H. B. Wright, *The Campaign of Plataea* (New Haven, 1904), p. 47, and Hignett, XIG, p. 271, n. 4.

9 Cf. Hdt. 8.144.5, and Hignett, XIG, pp. 278 – 9.

10 First advanced by Munro, JHS 24 (1904) 145 – 7; criticised in detail by Burn, PG, pp. 500 – 1, n. 34. Cf. Hignett, pp. 249 – 51, and reff. there cited.

11 See on this and other points of Agiad genealogy Mary E. White, JHS 84 (1964) 140 – 52.

12 Hdt. 9.12: my translation, except for one felicitous phrase borrowed from A. D. Godley.

13 Hdt. 9.13.65; cf. 8.53.2; Diod. 11.28.6; Thuc. 1.89; Paus. 1.18.1, 20.2; Justin 2.14.3; cf. HWComm., vol. 2, p. 291.

PART SEVEN

1   Main sources: a stele from Acharnae, found in 1932 and published by Louis Robert, *Etudes épigraphiques et philologiques* (Paris 1938), pp. 296 – 316, with p. ii; re-edited by M. N. Tod, *Greek Historical Inscriptions*, vol. 2 (Oxford 1948), no. 204, and by G. Daux, *Studies Presented to D. M. Robinson* (St Louis 1951), vol. 2, p. 777; Lycurgus *In Leocr.* §81; Diod. 11.29.3 – 4. Of the modern discussions see in particular Burn, PG, pp. 512 – 15 (whose translation of the Acharnae text I use here) and, for the arguments against authenticity, Hignett, XIG, pp. 460 – 1. Burn, admitting its anachronisms and discrepancies, regards it nevertheless as representing 'a fallible, but a real, patriotic tradition'. This seems to me a very fair assessment. Cf. my remarks (above, p. 98 ff.) on the Troezen Decree.

2   On this point see the sensible remarks of Parke and Wormell, *op. cit.*, p. 175 – 6: 'When Mardonius retreated and circled round behind Cithaeron, Aristeides had to invent excuses which would make the oracle square with the new situation . . . The Plataeans will have been glad enough for the sake of Athenian protection to assist in fulfilling the oracle literally.'

3   So Burn, PG, pp. 520 – 1, to whose masterly analysis this paragraph is generally much indebted.

4   For the Phocian guerillas (an important reference, often overlooked) see Hdt. 9.31.5. Other allusions to Mardonius's food-shortage: Hdt. 9.41, 45.2; Plut. *Arist.* 15.1.3. Artabazus's subsequent assertion that sufficient stocks were available in Thebes could only be true, if at all, for a very limited period.

5   For a good general survey see Hignett, XIG, pp. 301 – 11, and the literature there cited. Cf. W. K. Pritchett, 'New Light on Plataia', AJA 61 (1957) 9 – 28 with pls. vii–x for discussion of the topographical problems; additional details in Burn, PG, p. 519 ff.

6   Pritchett, *op. cit.*, p. 21, n. 78.

7   Reported at vast and (to us) tedious length by Herodotus [9.26 – 7 *passim*, cf. Plut. *Arist.* 12.1 – 2], who took keen interest in what we may term the Greek military pecking-order, and knew that his audience would do likewise.

8   Hdt. 9.49.3, cf. A. E. Wardman, *Historia* 8 (1959) 57.

9   Evidence only in Plut. *Arist.* 13.1 – 3; the anecdote is most often dismissed as fiction, designed to glorify Aristeides, but convincingly defended by Burn, PG, pp. 525 – 7, who compares it with the more successful *putsch* of the Four Hundred in 411, and guesses that Plutarch's source for it may

have been Cleidemus, described by Pausanias (10.15.4) as 'the oldest of the Atthidographers'.

10   Macan, vol. 2, p. 88, argued that this proved the story fictional, since Plataea at the time was in ruins. *Verb. sap.*

11   HWComm., vol. 2, p. 309; cf. Hdt. 9.50, 51.4. Military reinforcements: Hdt. 9.41.1; Plut. *Arist.* 15.1.

12   Arguments well summarised by Hignett, XIG, p. 322.

13   The exact location of the Island has given rise to much scholarly and topographical controversy. I am convinced that the only possible solution is that of Grundy, GPW, p. 482 ff., which is adopted here: cf. Pritchett *op. cit.*, p. 25 ff., Hignett, XIG, pp. 325 – 6, 428 – 9. On the other hand I cannot accept Grundy's juggling (p. 483) with the Asopus and its main tributary to explain Herodotus's curious statement that the Island was ten stades distant both from the river and the Gargaphian spring. As a means of solving historical cruxes, textual emendation is something normally to be regarded with deep suspicion; but Woodhouse's neat insertion of k (= 20) before *kai* in the passage in question [JHS 18 (1898) 57], giving a distance of *twenty* stades from the Asopus to the Island, is almost certainly correct. Both Pritchett and Hignett (two critics not noted for over-credulity) accept it without reservation.

14   So Ephorus [Diod. 11.30.5 – 6], whose account of Plataea, worthless for the most part, does contain this one undoubtedly correct crumb of information. Cf. Burn, PG, p. 536, who reaches the same conclusion independently of Ephorus (not cited by him here) and on different grounds.

15   As Burn reminds us [PG, p. 530 ff.] Herodotus was collecting information at a time when feeling against Corinth, Megara and Boeotia was particularly strong in Athens. I cannot, however, accept his theory that the entire retreat was carried out according to prearranged plan: see the fundamental objections to such a view enumerated by Hignett, XIG, p. 327 ff.

16   Regarded with suspicion by Thucydides, who picked up an error of fact in it (1.20.3): there was no such unit as 'the Pitane *lochos*'. Another glaring mistake is the assumption (Hdt. 9.55.2, in a context which presumes an eyewitness account) that Spartans voted with pebbles rather than by acclamation. Cf. Munro, CAH, vol. 4, p. 335, n. 1.

17   Hdt. 7.211: 'Amongst the feints they employed was to turn their backs in a body and pretend to be retreating in confusion, whereupon the enemy would come on with a great clatter and roar, supposing the battle won.'

18   Hdt. 9.61.2; cf. Hignett, XIG, p. 330; Burn, PG, p. 521.

19   Simonides *ap.* Plut. MH. 42 (872B – E); Hdt. 9.69; cf. W. J. Woodhouse, JHS 18 (1898) 51 ff.; Burn, PG, p. 536 and n. 69.

20   Hdt. 9.101.2; Hignett, XIG, pp. 456 – 7; Burn, PG, p. 530, n. 49. The three discrepant dates given by Plutarch (*Arist.* 19.7, 4th Boëdromion or 27th Panemus; *Camill.* 19, *Moral.* 349F, 3rd Boëdromion) are all *prima facie* too late, and probably refer to the days on which the victory was commemorated at Athens and Plataea respectively. 27th Panemus has been

computed to = 19 September (so Burn *loc. cit.*) and not (as in the Loeb ed. of Plutarch, vol. 2, p. 275, repeated in Ian Scott-Kilvert's *Rise and Fall of Athens*, p. 131) *c.* 1 August. Cf. HWComm., vol. 2, p. 331.

21 Hdt. 9.69.2, 70.5; Plut. *Arist.* 19.5; Diod. 11.32.5, 33.1; Ctesias §26 (Henry, p. 32); Wright *op. cit.*, p. 69; Hignett, XIG, p. 340; Burn, PG, p. 541.

22 To be compared, for minor discrepancies, with the list recorded by Pausanias [5.23] from the statue of Zeus at Olympia, and the battle-orders given in Herodotus [8.43 – 8, 82; 9.28 – 30, 77]. For a full discussion see HWComm., vol. 2, pp. 321 – 4; I agree, as regards omissions, that 'states whose contingents were very small were left out unless, like the Tenians, they rendered signal service'. Burn, PG, p. 544, suggests that the Lacedaemonian drafter may simply have forgotten some minor items on his list.

23 Plut. *Arist.* 20.4 – 5; cf. Parke and Wormell, *op. cit.*, pp. 176 – 7.

24 Plut. *Arist.* 21.1 – 5, cf. 10.6; Diod. 9.10.5, 11.29.1; Burn, PG, pp. 544 – 5, with n. 91; Hignett, XIG, p. 342. There is no reference to the so-called 'Covenant of Plataea' in Herodotus or Thucydides; nor was it invoked by later orators or pamphleteers (e.g. Isocrates) who would have found it a highly persuasive argument. In favour of the Covenant's authenticity: Raubitschek, TAPhA 91 (1960) 178 – 83, and BICS 8 (1961) 59 – 61; J. A. O. Larsen, *Representative Government in Greek and Roman History* (1955), pp. 48 – 50, 208 – 10; Hammond, *Hist. Greece*, p. 250. One fact they fail to consider is that such a far-reaching political decision could only be taken by the *probouloi* of the League in plenary session, not by a gathering of generals at Plataea. For the epigram inscribed for this occasion on the new altar to Zeus the Liberator, see Plut. *Moral.* 873B.

25 By Hignett, XIG, pp. 254 – 5, in a generally acute analysis of the Greek position at this stage.

26 Hdt. 9.100; Diod. 11.35.1 – 3. For the various scholarly theories cited above, see HWComm., vol. 2, p. 331; Grundy, GPW, p. 526; Hignett, XIG, p. 259. Mardonius, too, employed an Aegean beacon-chain: see above, p. 228.

27 Including tigers, if we can trust our eighteenth-century travel-writers: see esp. J. P. Tournefort's *Voyage du Levant* (Paris 1717), pp. 404 – 36, in a general excursus on Samos. Chandler, *Travels in Asia Minor and Greece* (London 1775), p. 144, similarly describes the Mycale area as infested by wild beasts, even in his day.

28 A point well brought out by Hammond, *Hist. Greece*, p. 252.

29 Hdt. 9.106; Diod. 11.37.1 – 3; Hignett, XIG, pp. 259 – 61.

30 *The Hot Gates* (London 1965), p. 20: the entire essay deserves to be read and re-read by all students of the Persian Wars, and every genuine Philhellene.

BIBLIOGRAPHY

Adcock, F. E.   *The Greek and Macedonian Art of War*. Berkeley 1957.

Alexanderson, B. N.   'Darius in the Persians', *Eranos* 65 (1967) 1–11.

Amandry, P.   'Thémistocle, un décret et un portrait', *Bulletin de la Faculté des Lettres de Strasbourg* 39 (1960–1) 413–35.

Amit, M.   *Athens and the Sea. A Study in Athenian Sea-power.* [Coll. Latomus 74] Brussels 1965. See the reviews in *Phoenix* 19 (1965) 251–2, and *Athenaeum* 43 (1965) 465–6.

Baelen, J.   *L'An 480, Salamine*. Paris 1961.

Bauer, A., and Frost, F. J.   *Themistokles. Literary, epigraphical and archaeological testimonia.* Chicago 1966.

Bengtson, H.   *The Greeks and the Persians, from the Sixth to the Fourth Centuries.* Trs. John Conway. London 1968.
Griechische Geschichte (2nd ed.) = Müller's Handbuch der Altertumswissenschaft III 4. Munich 1960.
'Thasos und Themistokles', *Historia* 2 (1954) 485–6.
'Themistokles und die delphische Amphiktyonie', *Eranos* 49 (1951) 85–92.

Béquignon, Y.   'Un décret de Thémistocle', *Revue Archéologique* (1961) 57–8.
La Vallée du Spercheios des Origines au IVe Siècle. Paris 1937.

Berve, H.   'Zur Themistokles-Inschrift von Troizen', *Sitzungsberichte der Bayerischen Akademie der Wissenschaften, Philos.-Hist. Klasse*, no. 3 (Munich 1961) 1–50.

Boegehold, A.   'The Salamis Epigram', *GRByS* 6 (1965) 179–86.

Boer, W. Den   'Themistocles in fifth century historiography', *Mnemosyne* 15 (1962) 225–37.

Boucher, A.   'La bataille de Platées d'après Hérodote', *Revue Archéologique* 2 (1915) 257–320.

Braccesi, L.

Il Problema del Decreto di Temistocle. Bologna 1968. See the review in *Phoenix* 22 (1968) 367.

Broadhead, H. D.

The Persae. Cambridge 1960.

Brunt, P. A.

'The Hellenic League against Persia', *Historia* 2 (1953) 135–63.

Burn, A. R.

Persia and the Greeks. The Defence of the West, c. 546–478 BC. London 1962.
'Thermopylae and Callidromus', *Studies Presented to David Moore Robinson* (St Louis 1951), vol. I, pp. 480–9.

Bury, J. B.

'The Campaign of Artemisium and Thermopylae', *Annual of the British School at Athens* 2 (1895–6) 83–104.
'Aristides at Salamis', CR 10 (1896) 414–18.

Calabi Limentani, I.

'Aristide il Giusto. Fortuna di un nome', *Rendiconti dell'Istituto Lombardo* 94 (1960) 43–67.

Calza, G.

'Il ritratto di Temistocle scoperto a Ostia', *Le Arti* 2 (1939–40) 152–62.

Cambridge Ancient History, vol. IV, The Persian Empire and the West. Cambridge (2nd revised ed.) 1930.

Caspari, M. O. B.

'Stray notes on the Persian Wars', JHS 31 (1911) 100–109.

Cataudella, M. R.

'Erodoto, Temistocle e il decreto di Trezene', *Athenaeum* 43 (1965) 385–418.

Chambers, M.

'The authenticity of the Themistocles decree', AHR 67 (1961–2) 306–16.
'The significance of the Themistocles Decree', *Philologus* 111 (1967) 159–66, with bibliography 166–90.

Chambry, E., and Thely-Chambry, L.

Justin: *Abrégé des Histoires Philippiques de Trogue Pompée*, vol. I. Paris 1936.

Conomis, N. C.

'A decree of Themistocles from Troezen. A note', *Klio* 40 (1962) 44–50.

Culican, W.

The Medes and Persians. London 1965.

Custance, R.

War at Sea: Modern Theory and Ancient Practice. Edinburgh and London 1919.

Daskalakis, A. V.

Problèmes historiques autour de la bataille des Thermopyles. Paris 1962. See review in CR 13 (1963) 316–17.

'Les raisons réelles du sacrifice de Léonidas et l'importance historique de la bataille des Thermopyles', *Studii Clasice* 6 (1964) 57–82.

Davison, J. A.   'The first Greek triremes', CQ 41 (1947) 18–24.

Dow, S.   'Bibliography of the purported Themistocles inscription from Troezen', CW 55 (1962) 105–8. 'The purported decree of Themistocles', AJA 66 (1962) 353–68.

Dunbabin, T. J.   *The Western Greeks*. Oxford 1948.

Ehrenberg, V.   *From Solon to Socrates: Greek History and Civilisation during the sixth and fifth centuries* BC. London 1968.

Ehtécham, M.   *L'Iran sous les Achéménides*. Fribourg 1946.

Evans, J. A. S.   'The final problem at Thermopylae', GRByS 5 (1964) 231–7.
'Notes on Thermopylae and Artemisium', *Historia* 18 (1969) 389–406.

Ferrara, G.   'Temistocle e Solone', *Maia* 16 (1964) 55–70.

Ferrill, A.   'Herodotus and the Strategy and Tactics of the Invasion of Xerxes', AHR 72 (1966–7) 102–15.

Finley, M. I.   *A History of Sicily*, vol. 1: Ancient Sicily to the Arab Conquest. London 1968.

Flaceliére, R.   'Sur quelques points obscurs de la vie de Thémistocle', REA 55 (1953) 5–28.
'Thémistocle, les Erétriens et le Calmar', REA 50 (1948) 211–17.

Fornara, C. W.   'The Value of the Themistocles Decree', AHR 73 (1967) 425–33.
'The Hoplite Achievement at Psyttaleia', JHS 86 (1966) 51–5.

Forrest, W. G.   *The Emergence of Greek Democracy*. London 1966.
A History of Sparta 950–192 BC. London 1968.

Freeman, E. A.   *The History of Sicily*, vol. 2. Oxford 1891.

French, A.   *The Growth of the Athenian Economy*. London 1964.

Frost, F. J.   'Scyllias: Diving in Antiquity', *Greece and Rome* 15 (1968) 180–5.

Gauthier, P.   'Le parallèle Himère-Salamine au Ve et au IVe siècle avant J.-C.', REA 68 (1966) 5–32.

Ghirshman, R.   *Perse: Proto-iraniens, Mèdes, Achéménides*. Paris 1963.
                       Translated as:
                       Persia: from the Origins to Alexander the Great. London
                       1964.

Gianelli, G.   *La spedizione di Serse da Terme a Salamina*. Milan 1924.

Gillis, D.   'Marathon and the Alcmaeonids', GRbyS 10 (1969)
                       133–45.

Godley, A. D.   *Herodotus*, vols. 3 and 4. London 1922, 1925.

Gomme, A. W.   *More Essays in Greek and Roman Literature*. Oxford 1962.

Goodwin, W.   'The Battle of Salamis', *Papers of the American School
                       of Classical Studies at Athens* 1 (1882–3) 237–62.
                       'The Battle of Salamis', *Harvard Studies in Classical
                       Philology* 17 (1906) 73–101.

Grant, J. R.   'Leonidas's last Stand', *Phoenix* 15 (1961) 14–27.

Grundy, G. B.   *The Topography of the Battle of Plataea*. London 1894.
                       The Great Persian War and Its Preliminaries. London
                       1901.
                       Thucydides and the History of his Age. London 1911
                       (vol. 1 reissued 1948).

Guarducci, M.   'Nuove osservazioni sul decreto di Temistocle',
                       RFIC 39 (1961) 48–78.

Guratzsch, C.   'Der Sieger von Salamis', *Klio* 39 (1961) 48–65.

Habicht, C.   'Falsche Urkunden zur Geschichte Athens im Zeit-
                       alter der Perserkriege', *Hermes* 89 (1961) 1–35.

Hahn, I.   'Zur Echtheitsfrage der Themistokles-Inschrift', *Acta
                       Antiqua Academiae Scientiarum Hungaricae* 13 (1965)
                       27–39.

Hammond, N. G. L.   'The Campaign and the Battle of Marathon', JHS 88
                       (1968) 13–57.
                       A History of Greece. Oxford 1959.
                       'The Battle of Salamis', JHS 76 (1956) 32–54.
                       'On Salamis', AJA 64 (1960) 367–8.
                       'The Origins and the Nature of the Athenian Alliance
                       of 478–7 BC', JHS 87 (1967) 41–61.

Hands, A. R.   'On Strategy and Oracles, 480–479', JHS 85 (1965)
                       56–61.

Hardy, D. A. and   'Suggested Changes in the Troizen Inscription',
Pritchett, W. K.   *Annual of the British School at Athens* 59 (1964) 30–1.

Hauvette, A.   *Hérodote, historien des guerres médiques.* Paris 1894.

Henry, R.   *Ctésias: La Perse, L'Inde, Les Sommaires de Photius.* Brussels 1947.

Herzfeld, E.   *The Persian Empire: Studies in the Geography and Ethnography of the Ancient Near East.* Ed. G. Walser. Wiesbaden 1968.

Hignett, C.   *Xerxes' Invasion of Greece.* Oxford 1963. See reviews in CP 59 (1964) 291–3, CR 14 (1964) 83–5, and *Phoenix* 17 (1963) 301–6.

Holden, H. A.   *Plutarch's Life of Themistocles.* London 1892.

Holm, A.   *Geschichte Siciliens,* 3 vols. Leipzig 1870–98.

Hooker, G. T. W.   'Their Finest Hour', *Greece and Rome* (2nd ser.) 7 (1960) 97–9.

How, W. W.   'Cornelius Nepos on Marathon and Paros', JHS 39 (1919) 48–61.

— and Wells, J.   *A Commentary on Herodotus,* 2nd ed. 2 vols. Oxford 1928.

Huxley, G.   'Kleidemos and the "Themistokles Decree" ', GRByS 9 (1968) 313–18.
'The Medism of Caryae', GRByS 8 (1967) 29–32.

Jacoby, F.   'Some Athenian Epigrams from the Persian Wars', Hesperia 14 (1945) 161–211.

Jameson, M. H.   'A Decree of Themistokles from Troizen', *Hesperia* 29 (1960) 198–223.
'Waiting for the Barbarian: New Light on the Persian Wars', *Greece and Rome* (2nd ser.) 8 (1961) 5–18.
'The Themistokles Decree: Notes on the Text', AJA 66 (1962) 368.
'A Revised Text of the Decree of Themistokles from Troizen', *Hesperia* 31 (1962) 310–15.
'The Provisions for Mobilisation in the Decree of Themistokles', *Historia* 12 (1963) 385–404.

Jones, H. L.   *The Geography of Strabo,* 8 vols. London 1917–32.

Jones, W. H. S. and Wycherley, R. E.   *Pausanias: Description of Greece,* 5 vols. London 1918–35.

Keil, J.   'Themistokles als Politiker', *Anzeiger der Oesterreichischen Akademie der Wissenschaften in Wien, Philos.-Hist. Klasse* 81 (1944) 65–76.
'Die Schlacht bei Salamis', *Hermes* 73 (1938) 329–40.

307

Kiepert, H.

Atlas Antiquus: Zwölf Karten zur alten Geschichte. Berlin. n.d.

Kierdorf, W.

Erlebnis und Darstellung der Perserkriege. Göttingen 1966.

Knight, W. F. J.

'The Defence of the Acropolis and the Panic before Salamis', JHS 51 (1931) 174–8.

Kraft, K.

'Bemerkungen zu den Perserkriegen', *Hermes* 92 (1964) 144–71.

Kromayer, J. (ed.)
— and Veith, G.

Antike Schlachtfelder, vol. 4. Berlin 1924–31.
Schlachten-Atlas zur Antiken Kriegsgeschichte, vol. 4, part i. Leipzig 1926.

Labarbe, J.

'Chiffres et modes de répartition de la flotte grecque à l'Artemision et à Salamine', *Bulletin de Correspondance Hellénique* 76 (1952) 384–441.
'Léonidas et l'astre des tempêtes', *Revue belge de philologie* 37 (1959) 69–91.
'Un Témoignage capital de Polyen sur la Bataille de Thermopyles', *Bulletin de Correspondance Hellénique* 78 (1954) 1–21.
'Timodémos d'Aphidna', *Revue belge de Philologie* 36 (1958) 31–50.
La Loi Navale de Thémistocle [Bibliothèque de la Faculté de Philosophie et Lettres de l'Université de Liège 143]. Paris 1957. See review in JHS 79 (1959) 184–5.

Lang, M.

'Herodotus and the Ionian Revolt', *Historia* 17 (1968) 24–36.

Last, H.

'Thermopylae', CR 57 (1943) 63–6.

Lattimore, R.

'Aeschylus on the Defeat of Xerxes', *Classical Studies in Honour of W. A. Oldfather* (Urbana, Illinois 1943) pp. 82–93.

Lazenby, J. F.

'The Strategy of the Greeks in the opening Campaign of the Persian War', *Hermes* 92 (1964) 264–84.

Leake, W. M.

Travels in Northern Greece, 4 vols. London 1835.

Legrand, P. E.

Hérodote: Introduction. Paris 1952.
Hérodote: Histoires vii, viii, ix (Budé ed.). Paris 1951.

Lehmann, G. A.

'Bemerkungen zur Themistokles-Inschrift von Troizen', *Historia* 17 (1968) 276–88.

Lenardon, R. J. 'The archonship of Themistocles, 493–2', *Historia* 5 (1956) 401–19.

Lewis, D. M. 'Notes on the Decree of Themistocles', CQ 11 (1961) 61–6.

Macan, R. W. *Herodotus: The Seventh, Eighth and Ninth Books.* 2 in 3 vols. London 1908.

McGregor, M. F. 'The pro-Persian Party at Athens from 510 to 480 BC', *Athenian Studies presented to W. S. Ferguson* (Cambridge Mass. 1940), pp. 71–95.

MacKay, P. A. 'Procopius' *De Aedificiis* and the topography of Thermopylae', AJA 67 (1963) 241–55.

MacKendrick, P. 'Herodotus: The Making of a World Historian', CW 47 (1954) 145–52.

Maddoli, G. 'Il valore storiografico del decreto temistocleo di Trezene', *Parola del Passato* 18 (1963) 419–34.

Marg, W. 'Zur Strategie der Schlacht von Salamis', *Hermes* 90 (1962) 116–19.

Marinatos, S. *Thermopylae: guide, historical and archaeological.* Athens 1951.

Martin, J. Jr. 'The Character of Plutarch's Themistocles', TAPhA 92 (1961) 326–39.

Maurice, F. 'The Size of the Army of Xerxes in the Invasion of Greece, 480 BC', JHS 50 (1930) 210–35.

Méautis, G. 'Thucydide et Thémistocle', *L'Antiquité classique* 20 (1951) 297–304.

Meiggs, R. and A selection of Greek historical inscriptions to the
Lewis, D. end of the fifth century BC, Oxford 1969.

Meritt, B. D. *Greek Historical Studies.* Cincinnati 1962.
'Notes on the text of the Decree of Themistocles', *Hesperia* 31 (1962) 413.

Meyer, E. 'Thermopylen', *Mitteilungen des Deutschen Archäologischen Institutus* (Athen. Abt.) 71 (1956) 101–6.

Meyer, H. D. 'Vorgeschichte und Gründung des delisch-attischen Seebundes', *Historia* 12 (1963) 405–46.

Miltner, F. 'Des Themistokles Strategie', *Klio* 31 (1938) 219–43.
'Pro Leonida', *Klio* 28 (1935) 228–41.

'Zur Themistoklesherm aus Ostia', *Jahreshefte des Oesterreichischen Archäologischen Instituts*, Wien 39 (1952) 70–5.

Momigliano, A. D.   'The Place of Herodotus in the History of Historiography', *History* 43 (1958) 1–13.

Moretti, L.   'Studi sul decreto di Temistocle, RFIC 92 (1964) 117–24.

Morrison, J. S. and Williams, R. T.   *Greek Oared Ships 900–322 BC.* Cambridge 1968.

Munro, J. A. R.   'Some Observations on the Persian Wars', JHS 19 (1899) 185–97 (Marathon); JHS 22 (1902) 294–332 (Xerxes); JHS 24 (1904) 144–65 (Plataea).
Chs. 9–10 = pp. 268–346 of *Cambridge Ancient History*, vol. 4. Cambridge 1926.

Musiolek, P.   'Themistokles und Athen', *Acta Antiqua Academiae Scientiarum Hungaricae* 6 (1958) 301–19.

Myres, J. L.   *Herodotus: Father of History*. Oxford 1953.

Nilsson, M. P   *Cults, Myths, Oracles and Politics*. Lund 1951.

Oldfather, C. H.   *Diodorus of Sicily: The Library of History*, vol. 4, Books IX–XII 40. London 1946.

Olmstead, A. T.   *The History of the Persian Empire*. Chicago 1948.

Papastavrou, J.   'Die politische Situation in Athen am Vorabend der Perserkriege und die auswärtige Politik Athens', *Gymnasium* 70 (1963) 11–18.

Pareti, L.   'La battaglia di Imera', *Studi Siciliani e Italioti* (Firenze 1914), pp. 113–69.

Parke, H. W. and Wormell, D. E. W.   *A History of the Delphic Oracle*. 2 vols. Oxford 1956.

Perrin, B.   *Plutarch's Lives*, vol. 2. London 1914.

Podlecki, A.   *The Political Background of Aeschylean Tragedy*. Ann Arbor 1966.
'Simonides: 480', *Historia* 17 (1968) 257–75.

Postan, M. M.   'The rise of a money economy', *Economic History Review* 14 (1944) 123–34.

Powell, J. E.   *A Lexicon to Herodotus*. Cambridge 1938.
The History of Herodotus. Cambridge 1939.
Herodotus, Book VIII. Cambridge 1939.

Prentice, W. K. 'Thermopylae and Artemisium', TAPhA 51 (1920) 5–18.

Pritchett, W. K. 'Herodotus and the Themistocles Decree', AJA 66 (1962) 43–7.
'Marathon', *University of California Publications in Classical Archaeology*, vol. 4 (1960), pp. 137–75. See reviews in JHS 83 (1963) 192 and *Phoenix* 16 (1962) 121–2.
'New Light on Plataea', AJA 61 (1957) 9–28.
'New Light on Thermopylae', AJA 62 (1958) 202–13.
Studies in Ancient Greek Topography: I. University of California Press. 1965.
'Towards a Restudy of the Battle of Salamis', AJA 63 (1959) 251–62.
'Xerxes' Fleet at the "Ovens" ', AJA 67 (1963) 1–6.
'Xerxes' Route over Mount Olympus', AJA 65 (1961) 369–75.

Rados, C. N. *Les Guerres Médiques: La Bataille de Salamine.* Paris 1915.

Raubitschek, A. E. 'The treaties between Persia and Athens', GRByS 5 (1964) 151–9.
'The Covenant of Plataea'. TAPhA 91 (1960) 178–83.
'Herodotus and the Inscriptions', BICS 8 (1961) 59–61.
'Die Rückkehr des Aristeides', *Historia* 8 (1959) 127–8.

Rediades, P. D. Ἡ ἐν Σαλαμῖνι ναυμαχία, 2nd ed. Athens 1911.

Richter, G. M. A. 'The Greeks in Persia', AJA 50 (1946) 15–30.
Greek Portraits: A Study of their Development. [Coll. Latomus, vol. 20] Brussels 1955.
The Portraits of the Greeks, vol. I. London 1965.

Robinson, C. A. Jr. 'Athenian Politics, 510–486 BC', AJPh 66 (1945) 243–54.
'Medizing Athenian Aristocrats', CW 35 (1941) 39–40.
'The Struggle for Power at Athens in the early Fifth Century', AJPh 60 (1939) 232–7.

Rolfe, J. C. *Cornelius Nepos.* London 1929.

Schachermeyr, F. 'Die Themistokles-Stele und ihre Bedeutung für die Vorgeschichte der Schlacht von Salamis', *Jahreshefte*

des Oesterreichischen Archäologischen Instituts, Wien 46 (1961–3) 158–75.
'Marathon und die persische Politik', *Historische Zeitschrift* 172 (1951) 1–35.

Schriener, J. H.   'Thucydides 1.93 and Themistokles during the 490's', *Symbolae Osloenses* 44 (1969) 23–41.

Scott-Kilvert, I.   *The Rise and Fall of Athens: Nine Greek Lives by Plutarch*. Harmondsworth 1960.

Sealey, R.   'The Origins of the Delian League', *Studies presented to Victor Ehrenberg* (Oxford 1966), pp. 233–55.
'A Note on the supposed Themistocles-Decree', *Hermes* 91 (1963) 376–7.

Sichtermann, H.   'Der Themistokles von Ostia', *Gymnasium* 71 (1964) 348–81.

Smyth, H. W.   *Aeschylus*, vol. 1. London 1922.

Solmsen, L.   'Speeches in Herodotus's Account of the Ionian Revolt', AJPh 64 (1943) 194–207.

Starr, C. G.   'Why did the Greeks defeat the Persians?', *Parola del Passato* 17 (1962) 321–9.

Strasburger, H.   'Herodot und das Perikleische Athen', *Historia* 4 4 (1955) 1–25.

Tarn, W. W.   'The Fleet of Xerxes', JHS 28 (1908) 202–33.

Thiel, J. H.   'Themistokles, een polemiek', *Tijdschrift voor Geschiedenis* 64 (1951) 1–30.

Treu, M.   'Zur neuen Themistokles-Inschrift', *Historia* 12 (1963) 47–69.

Van der Heyden, A. A. M., and Scullard, H. H.   *Atlas of the Classical World*. London 1959.

Vanderpool, E.   'A Monument to the Battle of Marathon', *Hesperia* 35 (1966) 93–106.
'The Deme of Marathon and the Herakleion', AJA 70 (1966) 319–23. Cf. *Hesperia* 11 (1942) 329–37

Wade-Gery, H. T.   'Themistocles' archonship', *Annual of the British School at Athens* 37 (1936–7) 263–70.

Wallace, P. W.   'Psyttaleia and the Trophies of the Battle of Salamis', AJA 73 (1969) 293–303, pls. 65–6.

Wardman, A. E.   'Herodotus on the cause of the Greco-Persian Wars',
                     AJPh 82 (1961) 133–50.
                     'Tactics and the Tradition of the Persian Wars',
                     Historia 8 (1959) 49–60.

Wells, J.   'Herodotus and Athens', CPh 23 (1928) 317–31.
                     Studies in Herodotus. Oxford 1923.

West, W. C.   'The Trophies of the Persian Wars', CPh 64 (1969)
                     7–19.

Westlake, H. D.   'The Medism of Thessaly', JHS 56 (1936) 12–24.

White, M. E.   'Some Agiad Dates', JHS 84 (1964) 140–52.

Wilhelm, A.   'Zur Topographie der Schlacht bei Salamis', *Sit-
                     zungsberichte der Akademie der Wissenschaft in Wien,
                     Philos.-Hist. Klasse* 211 (1929) 3–39.

Will, E.   'Deux livres sur les Guerres médiques et leur temps',
                     Revue de Philologie 38 (1964) 70–88 [a review-article
                     on the studies by Hignett and Burn].

Williams, G. W.   'The Curse of the Alkmaionidai' II–III, *Hermathena*
                     79–80 (1952) 3–21, 58–71.

Wolski, J.   'Les changements intérieurs à Sparta à la veille des
                     guerres médiques', REA 69 (1967) 31–49.

Woodhead, A. G.   *The Greeks in the West*. London 1962.

Woodhouse, W. J.   'The Greeks at Plataiai', JHS 18 (1898) 33–59.

Wright, H. B.   *The Campaign of Plataea (September 479 BC)*. New
                     Haven 1904.

Wuest, F. R.   'A Decree of Themistokles from Troizen', *Gymnasium*
                     68 (1961) 233–9.

Zinserling, G.   'Themistokles, sein Porträt in Ostia und die beiden
                     Tyrannenmördergruppen', *Klio* 38 (1960) 87–109.

SUPPLEMENTARY
BIBLIOGRAPHY

NOTE: This list contains all titles referred to in the Introduction (1996), together with some others that readers may find of interest. It lays no claim to comprehensiveness. In the Introduction, works are cited by the author's last name, or by name and date when there are more titles than one listed here under a single author. Capitalization of a name or names in the right-hand column below indicates an item located elsewhere in the Bibliography.

Anderson, J. K.   'Hoplite weapons and offensive arms', in: HANSON 15–37.

Arnush, M.F.   'The career of Peisistratus son of Hippias', *Hesperia* 64 (1995) 135–162.

Austin, M. M.   'Greek tyrants and the Persians, 546–479 B.C.', CQ 40 (1990) 289–306.

Avery, H.C.   'The number of Persian dead at Marathon', *Historia* 22 (1973) 757.
                      'Herodotus 6.112.2', TAPhA 103 (1972) 15–22.

Badian, E.   'Archons and Strategoi', *Antichthon* 5 (1971) 1–34.

Balcer, J. M.   'Ionia and Sparta under the Achaemenid Empire: the sixth and fifth centuries B.C.: tribute, taxation and assessment', in: BRIANT & HERRENSCHMIDT 1–27.
                      'Athenian politics: the ten years after Marathon', in: *Panathenaia: Studies in Athenian Life and Thought in the Classical Age*, ed. T. E. Gregory and A. J. Podlecki (Lawrence 1979) 27 ff.
                      'The Persian Wars against Greece: a reassessment', *Historia* 38 (1989) 127–143.
                      'The Persian occupation of Thrace 519–419 B.C.: the economic effects', in: *Actes du IIe Congrès International des Études du Sud-Est européen* (Athens 1972) 242–254.
                      'The Greeks and the Persians: the process of acculturation', *Historia* 32 (1983) 257–267.

315

Barron, J. P.   'The Liberation of Greece', CAH iv² (Pt. II, 11), 592–622.

Bengtson, H.   'Zur Vorgeschichte der Schlacht bei Salamis', *Chiron* 1 (1971) 89–94.

Berthold, R. M.   'Which way to Marathon?' REA 78/9 (1976–77) 84–95.

Berve, H.   'Fürstliche Herren zur Zeit der Perserkriege', in: *Gestaltende Kräfte der Antike* (2nd ed. Munich 1966) 232–267.

Bicknell, P. J.   'The command structure and generals of the Marathon campaign', *L'Antiquité Classique* 39 (1970) 427–442.
           'Themistocles' mother and father', *Historia* 31 (1982) 161–173.
           Studies in Athenian Politics and Genealogy [Hist. Einzelschr. 19]. Wiesbaden 1972.

Bigwood, J. M.   'Ctesias as historian of the Persian Wars', *Phoenix* 32 (1978) 19–41.

Boardman, J.,   *The Cambridge Ancient History*, 2nd ed., vol. iv [CAH iv²]:
et al., (ed.)   *Persia, Greece and the Western Mediterranean c. 525 to 479 B.C.* Cambridge 1988.

Boedeker, D. (ed.)   *Herodotus and the Invention of History* [= *Arethusa* 20.1 –2]. Buffalo 1987.
           'The two faces of Demaratus', ibid. 185–201.

Bourriot, F.   'L'empire achéménide et les rapports entre Grecs et Perses dans la littérature grecque du Vᵉ siècle', *L'Information Historique* 43 (1981) 21–30.

Bowen, A. J.   *Plutarch: The Malice of Herodotus*, with introduction, translation, and commentary. Warminster 1992.

Braccesi, L. (ed.)   *Tre Studi su Themistocle*. Padua 1987.

Braccesi, L., and   Agrigento e la Sicilia greca: atti della settimana di stu-
De Miro, E.   dio, Agrigento, 2–9 maggio 1988. Rome 1992.

Bradford, A. S.   'Plataea and the Soothsayer', *Ancient World* 23 (1992) 27–33.

Briant, P.   'Histoire et Idéologie: les Grecs et la "decadence Perse"', in: *Mélanges Pierre Lévêque*, vol. ii: *Anthropologie et Société* [ALUB no. 377, CRHA no. 91] (1989) 33–47.
           'Table du Roi, tribut et redistribution chez les aché-ménides', in: BRIANT & HERRENSCHMIDT 35–44.

'Institutions perses et histoire comparatiste dans l'historiographie grecque', in: SANCISI-WEERDENBURG & KUHRT 1987 (II) 1 – 10.

'Pouvoir central et polycentrisme culturel dans l'empire achéménide', in: SANCISI-WEERDENBURG & KUHRT 1987 (II) 1 – 31.

Rois, Tributs et Paysans. Paris 1962.

Briant, P., and Herrenschmidt, C. (ed.)   *Le tribut dans l'empire perse*: actes de la table ronde de Paris, 12 – 13 décembre 1986 [Travaux de l'hist. d'études iraniennes et de l'Université de la Sorbonne Nouvelle no. 13]. Paris & Louvain 1989.

Brown, I. C.   'Herodotus and the strength of freedom', *History Today* 31 (1981) 5 – 10.

Brown, S. C.   'The mêdikos logos of Herodotus and the evolution of the Median State', in: SANCISI-WEERDENBURG & KUHRT 1988, 71 – 86.

Brown, T. S.   'Megabyzus son of Zopyrus', *Ancient World* 15 (1987) 65 – 74.

Bubel, F.   *Herodot-Bibliographie 1980 – 1988* [Altertumswiss. Texte und Stud. 20]. Hildesheim 1991.

Bugh, G. R.   *The Horsemen of Athens*. Princeton 1988.

Burn, A. R.   *Persia and the Greeks*. London 1962; 2nd ed. (with postscript by D. M. Lewis 587 – 609) 1984.

'Thermopylae revisited and some topographical notes on Marathon and Plataiai', in: *Greece and the Eastern Mediterranean in Ancient History and Prehistory*, ed. K. H. Kinzl (Berlin 1977) 89 – 105.

Burstein, S. M.   'The recall of the ostracized and the Themistocles Decree', CSCA 4 (1971) 93 – 110.

Carrière, J. C.   'Oracles et prodiges de Salamine: Hérodote et Athènes', DHA 14 (1988) 219 – 275.

Cartledge, P.   'Herodotus and "the other": a meditation on empire', *Etudes du Monde Classique/Classical Views* 34 (1990) 27 – 40.

Castritius, H.   'Die Okkupation Thrakiens durch die Perser und der Sturz des athenischen Tyrannen Hippias', *Chiron* 2 (1972) 1 – 15.

Ceauçescu, G.   'Un topos de la littérature antique: l'éternelle guerre entre l'Europe et l'Asie', *Latomus* 50 (1991) 327 – 341.

Chapman, G. A. H.   'Herodotus and Histiaeus' role in the Ionian Revolt',
                     Historia 21 (1972) 546–568.

Cole, J. W.   'Alexander Philhellene and Themistocles', *Classical Antiquity* 47 (1978) 37–49.

Cook, J. M.   *The Persian Empire*. London 1983.
                     'The rise of the Achaemenids', in: GERSHEWITZ 200–291.

Cornelius, F.   'Pausanias', *Historia* 22 (1973) 502–504.

Cuyler Young,   'The consolidation of the empire and its limits of
T., Jr.   growth under Darius and Xerxes', CAH iv² 53–111
                     (Part I, 2–3).
                     '480/79 B.C.—a Persian perspective', *Iranica Antiqua* 15
                     (1980) 213–39.

Dandamaev, M.   *A Political History of the Achaemenid Empire*. Trans. W. J.
                     Vogelsang. Leiden 1989.
                     'Herodotus' information on Persia and the latest discoveries of cuneiform texts', *Storia della Storiografia* 7
                     (1985) 92–100.

Darbo-Peschanski,   'Les Barbares à l'épreuve du temps (Hérodote, Thucy-
C.   dide, Xénophon)', *Métis* 4 (1989) 233–250.

Delorme, J.   'Deux notes sur la bataille de Salamine', *Bull. Corr. Hell.*
                     102 (1978) 87–96.

Deman, A.   'Présence des Égyptiens dans la seconde guerre médique (480–479 BC)', *Chronique d'Égypte* 60 (1985) 56–74.

Descat, R.   'Notes sur la politique tributaire de Darius Iᵉʳ', in:
                     BRIANT & HERRENSCHMIDT 77–93.

Develin, R.   'Herodotus and the Alcmaeonids', in: EADIE & OBER
                     125–139.
                     'Miltiades and the Parian Expedition', *L'Antique Classique* 46 (1977) 571–577.

Donlan, W., and   'The charge at Marathon again', CW 72 (1979) 419–
Thompson, J.   420.

Eadie, J. W., and   *The Craft of the Ancient Historian: Essays in Honor of Chester
Ober, J. (eds.)   G. Starr*. Lanham 1985.

Elayi, J.   *Pénétration grecque en Phénicie sous l'empire perse*. Nancy
                     1988.
                     'La présence grecque dans les cités phéniciennes sous
                     l'empire perse achéménide', REG 105 (1992) 305–
                     327.

'Le rôle de l'oracle de Delphes dans le conflit gréco-perse d'après les Histoires d'Hérodote', I & II, *Iran. Ant.* 13 (1978) 93–118, 14 (1979) 67–151.
'Deux oracles de Delphes: Les réponses de la Pythie à Clisthène de Sicyone et aux Athéniens avant Salamine', REG 92 (1979) 224–230.

Evans, J. A. S.   'Herodotus and the Ionian Revolt', *Historia* 25 (1976) 31–37.
'The settlement of Artaphrenes', CPh 71 (1976) 344–348.
'Herodotus and Marathon', *Florilegium* 6 (1984) 1–27.
'Cavalry about the time of the Persian Wars: A speculative essay', CJ 92 (1986/7) 97–106.
'The oracle of the "wooden wall"', CJ 78 (1982) 24–29.

Ferrill, A.   'Herodotus on tyranny', *Historia* 27 (1978) 385–398.

Fol, A., and Hammond, N. G. L.   'Persia in Europe, apart from Greece', CAH iv² 234–253 (Part I, 3 f.).

Fornara, C.W.   *Herodotus: An Interpretative Essay.* Oxford 1971.

Frost, F.   *Plutarch's Themistocles: A Historical Commentary.* Princeton 1980.

Frye, R. N.   *The History of Ancient Iran* [Handbuch der Altert. III.7]. Munich 1983.

Gaertner, H. A.   'Les rêves de Xerxès et d'Artaban chez Hérodote', *Ktéma* 8 (1983) 11–18.

Gardiner-Garden, J. R.   'Dareios' Scythian expedition and its aftermath', *Klio* 69 (1987) 326–350.

Garlan, Y.   *Guerre et économie en Grèce ancienne.* Paris 1989.

Georges, P.   'Saving Herodotus' phenomena: the oracles and the events of 480 B.C.', *Classical Antiquity* 5 (1986) 14–59. *Barbarian Asia and the Greek Experience, from the Archaic period to the age of Xenophon.* Baltimore & London 1994.

Gershevitch, I. (ed.)   *The Cambridge History of Iran* [*CHI*], vol. ii: *The Median and Achaemenid periods.* Cambridge 1985.

Ghinatti, F.   *I gruppi politici Ateniesi fino alle Guerre persiane.* Rome 1970.

Gillis, D.   *Collaboration with the Persians.* Wiesbaden 1979.

Gould, J.   *Herodotus.* London 1989.

Graf, D.

'Medism: Greek collaboration with Achaemenid Persia'. Ph.D. diss. Univ. of Michigan, 1979 [Diss. Abs. 40 (1980) 5541A–42A].
'Medism: the origin and significance of the term', JHS 104 (1984) 15–30.
'Greek tyrants and Achaemenid politics', in: EADIE & OBER 79–123.

Granger, R.

'The life of Xerxes', *Ancient History (Resources for Teachers)* 22 (1992) 125–144.

Haas, C. J.

'Athenian naval power before Themistocles', *Historia* 34 (1985) 29–46.

Hall, E.

Inventing the Barbarian: Greek Self-Definition through Tragedy. Oxford 1989.

Hallock, R. T.

Persepolis Fortification Tablets. Chicago 1969.
The Evidence of the Persepolis Tablets. Cambridge 1971 = *CHI* ii (Cambridge 1985) 588–609.
'The Persepolis fortification archive', *Orientalia* n.s. 42 (1973) 320–323.

Hammond,
N. G. L.

'The expedition of Datis and Artaphernes', CAH iv² 491–517 (Part II, 9).
'The narrative of Hdt. vii and the decree of Themistocles at Troezen', JHS 102 (1982) 75–93.
'The expedition of Xerxes', CAH iv² 518–591 (Part II, 10).
Studies in Greek History. Oxford 1973.
'The manning of the fleet in the decree of Themistokles', *Phoenix* 40 (1986) 143–148.

Hanson, V. D. (ed.)

Hoplites: The Classical Greek Battle Experience. London 1991.

Hart, J.

Herodotus and Greek History. London 1982.

Hartog, F.

The Mirror of Herodotus: The Representation of the Other in the Writing of History. Trans. J. Lloyd. Berkeley & London 1988.

Hegyi, D.

'Der Begriff βάρβαρος bei Herodotos', AUB 5/6 (1977/8) 53–59.
'Historical authenticity of Herodotus in the Persian logoi', AASH 21 (1973) 73–87.
'Athens and Aigina on the eve of the battle of Marathon', AASH 17 (1969) 171–181.
'Boiotien in der Epoche der griechisch-persischen Kriege', AUB (1972) 21–29.

Heinrichs, J.   *Ionien nach Salamis: die kleinasiatischen Griechen in der Politik und politischen Reflexion des Mutterlands.* Bonn 1989.

Hennig, D.   'Herodot 6, 108: Athen und Plataiai', *Chiron* 22 (1992) 13–24.

Herrenschmidt, C.   'Notes sur la parenté chez les Perses au début de l'Empire achéménide', in: SANCISI-WEERDENBURG & KUHRT 1987 II, 53–57.

Hodge, A. T., and Losada, L. A.   'The time of the shield signal at Marathon', *AJA* 74 (1970) 31–36.

Hoerhager, H.   'Zu den Flottenoperationen am Kap Artemision', *Chiron* 3 (1973) 43–59.

Hohti, P.   'Freedom of speech in speech sections in the Histories of Herodotus', *Arctos* 8 (1974) 19–27.

Holladay, J.   'Medism in Athens 508–480 BC', *Greece and Rome* 25 (1978) 174–191.

Hurst, A.   'La prise d'Érétrie chez Hérodote, VI. 100–101', *Museum Helveticum* 35 (1978) 202–211.

Jeffery, L. H.   'Greece before the Persian Invasion', in: CAH iv² 350–367 (Part II, 6).

Jordan, B.   *The Athenian Navy in the Classical Period.* Berkeley 1975. 'The honors for Themistocles after Salamis', AJPh 109 (1988) 547–571.

Jouanna, J.   'Collaboration ou résistance au barbare: Artémise d'Halicarnasse et Cadmos de Cos chez Hérodote et Hippocrate', *Ktéma* 9 (1984) 15–26.

Karavites, P.   'Realities and appearances, 490–480 B.C.', *Historia* 26 (1977) 129–147.

Kase, E. W., Szemler, G. J.   'Xerxes' march through Phokis (Her. 8.31–35)', *Klio* 64 (1982) 353–366.

Keaveney, A.   'The attack on Naxos: a forgotten cause of the Ionian Revolt', *CQ* 38 (1988) 76–81.

Kelly, T.   'The Assyrians, the Persians, and the sea', *Mediterranean Historical Review* 7 (1992) 5–28.

Kertész, I.   'Schlacht und "Lauf" bei Marathon: Legende und Wirklichkeit', *Nikephoros* 4 (1991) 155–60.

Kinzl, K.   *Miltiades-Forschungen* [Diss. Univ. Wien xxiv]. Vienna 1968.

Klees, H.   'Zur Entstehung der Perserkriege', in: *Festschrift für Robert Werner zu seinem 65. Geburtstag dargebracht von Freunden, Kollegen und Schülern.* Ed. W. Dahlheim et al. (Konstanz 1989) 21 – 39.

Knight, D. W.   *Some studies in Athenian Politics in the Fifth Century* B.C. Wiesbaden 1970.

Konstan, D.   'Persians, Greeks and empire', *Arethusa* 20 (1987) 59 – 73.

Kuhrt, A.   'Earth and water', in: SANCISI-WEERDENBURG & KUHRT 1990 (IV), 87 – 99.
'Survey of written sources available for the history of Babylonia under the later Achaemenids', ibid. 1987 (I), 147 – 157.
'Achaemenid Babylonia: sources and problems', ibid. 1990 (IV) 177 – 194.
'The Achaemenid Empire: a Babylonian perspective', PCPhS 34 (1988) 60 – 76.

Kuhrt, A., and Sherwin-White, S.   'Xerxes' destruction of Babylonian temples', in: SANCISI-WEERDENBURG & KUHRT 1987 (II) 69 – 78.

Kukofka, D.-A.   'Karthago, Gelon und die Schlacht bei Himera', *Würzburger Jahrbücher für die Altertumswissenschaft* 18 n.f. (1992) 49 – 75.

Lateiner, D.   *The historical method of Herodotus* [*Phoenix* Suppl. vol. 23]. Toronto 1989.
'The failure of the Ionian Revolt', *Historia* 31 (1982) 129 – 160.

Lazenby, J. F.   *The Defence of Greece 490 – 479 B.C.* Warminster 1993.
'Aischylos and Salamis', *Hermes* 116 (1988) 168 – 185.
'Pausanias son of Kleombrotos', *Hermes* 103 (1975) 231 – 251.

Lenardon, R. J.   *The Saga of Themistocles.* London 1978.

Lewis, D. M.   *Sparta and Persia.* Leiden 1977.
'Persians in Herodotus', in: *The Greek Historians: Literature and History.* Papers presented to A. E. Raubitschek (Saratoga, CA 1985) 101 – 117.
'The Kerameikos ostraka', ZPE 14 (1974) 1 – 4.
'Datis the Mede', JHS 100 (1980) 194 – 195.

McCulloch, H. Y.   'Herodotus, Marathon and Athens', *Symbolae Osloenses* 57 (1982) 35 – 55.

McDougall, I.   'The Persian ships at Mycale', in: *Owls to Athens: Essays on Classical subjects presented to Sir Kenneth Dover*, ed. E. M. Craik (Oxford 1990) 143–149.

McLeod, W.   'The bowshot and Marathon', JHS 90 (1970) 197–198.

Mafodda, G.   'La politica di Gelone dal 485 al 483 a. C.', *Messana* n.s. 1 (1990) 53–69.

Manville, P. B.   'Aristagoras and Histiaeus: the leadership struggle in the Ionian Revolt', CQ 27 (1977) 80–91.

Martorelli, A.   'Storia persiana in Erodoto. Echi di versioni ufficiali', RIL 111 (1977) 115–125.

Masaracchia, A.   'La battaglia di Salamine in Erodoto', *Helikon* 9/10 (1969/70) 68–106.
                    (ed.) *La battaglia di Salamina: Libro VIII delle Storie*. Milan 1977, 2nd ed. 1990.
                    (ed.) *La sconfitta dei Persiani: Libro IX delle Storie*. Milan 1978.

Massaro, V.   'Herodotus' account of the battle of Marathon and the picture in the Stoa Poikile', *L'Antiquité Classique* 47 (1978) 458–475.

Matsudaira, C.   'Xerxes, Sohn des Dareios', in: *Gnomosyne: Menschliches Denken und Handeln in der frühgriechischen Literatur. Festschrift für Walter Marg zum 70. Geburtstag*. Ed. G. Kurz, D. Mueller, W. Nicolai (Munich 1981) 289–297.

Maxwell-Stuart,   'Pain, mutilation and death in Hdt VII', PP 31 (1976)
P. G.   356–362.

Meiggs, R., and   *A Selection of Greek Historical Inscriptions to the end of the Fifth*
Lewis, D. (eds.)   *Century B.C.* Oxford, rev. 2nd ed. 1988.

Merentitis, K. L.   ''Ο μῦθος τῆς προδοσίας τοῦ 'Εφιάλτου', Ἐπιστημονικὴ ΧΕπετηρὶς τῆς Σχολῆς τοῦ Πανεπιστημίου 'Αθηνῶν 18 (1967/8) 110–217.

Milton, M. P.   'The second message to Xerxes and Themistocles' view of strategy', *Proceedings of the African Classical Association* 17 (1982) 22–52.

Momigliano, A. D.   'Persian Empire and Greek Freedom', in: *The Idea of Freedom: Essays in Honour of Isaiah Berlin*, ed. A. Ryan (Oxford 1979) 139–151.

Morrison, J. S.   'The Greek ships at Salamis and the *diekplous*', JHS 111 (1991) 196–200.
'Greek naval tactics in the 5th century B.C.', IJNA 3.1 (1974) 21–26.
'Hyperesia in naval contexts in the fifth and fourth centuries B.C.', JHS 104 (1984) 48–59.

Morrison, J. S., and Coates, J. F.   *The Athenian Trireme: the History and Reconstruction of an Ancient Warship*. Cambridge 1986.

Mueller, D.   'Von Doriskos nach Therme. Der Weg des Xerxes-Heeres durch Thrakien und Ostmakedonien', *Chiron* 5 (1975) 1–11.

Murray, O.   'The Ionian Revolt', in: CAH iv² 461–490 (Part II, 8).

Nakai, Y.   'The scale of the [*sic*] Xerxes' expeditionary forces and fleet' [in Japanese with English resumé], JCS 37 (1989) 12–22.

Nenci, G. H. (ed.)   *La Rivolta della Ionia: Libro V delle Storie*. Milan 1994.

Neville, J.   'Was there an Ionian Revolt?', CQ 29 (1979) 268–275.

Nikolaou, N.   'Hérodote et le dispositif des forces navales à Salamine', in: *Stemmata: Mélanges de philologie, d'histoire et d'archéologie grecques offerts à Jules Labarbe*, ed. J. Servais, T. Hackens, B. Serrvais-Soyez (Liège & Louvain-la-Neuve 1987) 275–289.
'La bataille de Salamine d'après Diodore de Sicile', REG 95 (1982) 145–156.

Nippel, W.   *Griechen, Barbaren und 'Wilde': Alte Geschichte und Sozialanthropologie*. Frankfurt 1990.

Noonan, R. T.   'The grain trade of the northern Black Sea in antiquity', AJPh 94 (1973) 231–243.

Nyland, R.   'Herodotos' sources for the Plataiai campaign', *L'Antiqué Classique* 61 (1992) 80–97.

O'Neil, J. L.   'The life of Xerxes', *Ancient History (Resources for Teachers)* 18 (1988) 6–15.

Ostwald, M.   'The reform of the Athenian state by Cleisthenes', in: CAH iv² 303–346 (Part II 5: see esp. § iv, 'In the wake of the reforms: Athens 507/6 to 480 B.C.', 325–346).

Papastavrou, I. S.   Θεμιστοκλῆς Φρεάρριος· Ἱστορία τοῦ τιτάνος καὶ τῆς ἐποχῆς τοῦ. Athens 1970.

Piccirilli, L.　　　'Temistocle εὐεργέτης dei Corciresi', ASNP 3 (1973) 317–355.

Podlecki, A. J.　　　*The Life of Themistocles*. Montreal & London 1975.

Prestianni, A. M.　　　'La stele di Trezene e la tradizione storiografica sul decreto di Temistocle', in: *Umanità e Storia*: Scritti in onore di A. Attisani (2 vols., Naples 1971), vol. ii, 469–496.

Pritchett, W. K.　　　'Plataiai', AJPh 100 (1979) 145–152.
The Greek State at War. 5 vols. Berkeley & London 1971–1991.
Studies in Ancient Greek Topography: Part II (Battlefields) [Classical Studies iv]. Berkeley 1969.
(i) 'Deme of Marathon: Von Eschenburg's evidence', 1–11.
(ii) 'The battle of Artemision in 480 B.C.', 12–18.
(iii) 'The Hollows of Euboea', 19–23.
Id. Part III (Roads) [Classical Studies xxii]. Berkeley 1980.
(vii) 'The site of Skolos near Plataiai', 289–294.
Id. Part IV (Passes) [Classical Studies xxviii]. Berkeley 1982.
(vi) 'The roads of Plataiai', 88–102.
(ix) 'Herodotus and his critics on Thermopylae', 176–210.
(x) 'Route of the Persians after Thermopylae', 211–233.
'Appendix on some recent critiques of the veracity of Herodotus', 234–285.
Id. Part V (untitled) [Classical Studies xxxi]. Berkeley 1985.
(v) 'The strategy of the Plataiai campaign', 92–137.
(vii) 'In defense of the Thermopylai pass', 190–216.
The Liar School of Herodotos. Amsterdam 1993.

Raaflaub, K. A.　　　'Herodotus, political thought, and the meaning of history', *Arethusa* 20 (1987) 221–248.

Raviola, F.　　　'Temistocle e la Magna Grecia', in: BRACCESI 13–112.

Rhodes, P. J.　　　*A Commentary on the Aristotelian Athenaion Politeia*. Oxford 1981.

Robertson, N.　　　'The decree of Themistocles in its contemporary setting', *Phoenix* 36 (1982) 1–44.

'The Thessalian expedition of 480 B.C.', JHS 96 (1976) 100–120.

'False documents at Athens: Fifth century history and fourth century publicists', *Historical Reflections* [Univ. of Waterloo, Ontario] 3 (1976) 3–25.

Rocchi, M.
'Serse e l'acqua amara dell' Ellesponto (Hdt. 7.35)', in: *Perennitas*. Studi in onore di Angelo Brelich, Rome 1980, 417–429.

Roux, G.
'Éschyle, Hérodote, Diodore, Plutarque racontent la bataille de Salamine', *Bulletin de Correspondance Hellénique* 98 (1974) 51–94.

Sacks, K. S.
'Herodotus and the dating of the Battle of Thermopylae', CQ 26 (1976) 232–248.

Sancisi-Weerdenburg, H.
'Gifts in the Persian Empire', in: BRIANT & HERRENSCHMIDT 129–146.

Sancisi-Weerdenburg, H., and Kuhrt, A. (ed.)
Achaemenid History I: Sources, structures and synthesis. Proceedings of the 1983 Achaemenid history workshop. Leiden 1987.
Id. II: The Greek Sources. Proceedings of the Groningen 1984 Achaemenid history workshop. Leiden 1987.
Id. III: Method and Theory. Proceedings of the London 1985 Achaemenid history workshop. Leiden 1988.
Id. IV: Centre and Periphery. Proceedings of the Groningen 1986 Achaemenid history workshop. Leiden 1990.
Id. V: The roots of European tradition. Proceedings of the 1987 Groningen Achaemenid history workshop. Leiden 1990.
Id. VI: Asia Minor and Egypt: old cultures in a new empire. Proceedings of the Groningen 1988 Achaemenid history workshop. Leiden 1991.

Sartori, F.
'Agrigento, Gela e Siracusa: tre tirannidi contro il barbaro', in: BRACCESI & DE MIRO 77–93.

Scaife, R.
'Alexander I in the Histories of Herodotus', *Hermes* 117 (1989) 129–137.

Schachermeyr, F.
Die Sieger der Perserkriege. Große Persönlichkeiten zwischen Beifall und Mißgunst. Zur Problematik des geschichtlichen Erfolges. Göttingen 1974.

Schmitt, R.
'The Medo-Persian names of Herodotus in the light of the new evidence from Persepolis', in: *Studies on the*

sources on the history of pre-Islamic Central Asia, ed. J. Harmatta (Budapest 1979) 29–39.

Schreiner, J. H.	'The battles of 490 B.C.', PCPhS 16 (1970) 97–112.
Sealey, R.	'The pit and the well: the Persian heralds of 491 B.C.', CJ 72 (1976) 13–20. 'Again the siege of the Acropolis, 480 B.C.', CSCA 5 (1972) 183–194.
Sekunda, N. V.	'Persian settlement in Hellespontine Phrygia', in: SANCISI-WEERDENBURG & KUHRT 1988, 175–196.
Shapiro, A. H.	'Oracle-mongers in Peisistratid Athens', *Kernos* 3 (1990) 335–345.
Shear, T. L., Jr.	'The Persian destruction of Athens', *Hesperia* 62 (1993) 383–482.
Shrimpton, G.	'The Persian cavalry at Marathon', *Phoenix* 34 (1980) 20–37.
Sidebotham, S.	'Herodotus on Artemisium', CW 75 (1982) 177–186.
Siewert, P.	*Der Eid von Plataiai* [Vestigia xvi]. Munich 1972.
Simpson, R. H.	'Leonidas' decision', *Phoenix* 26 (1972) 1–11.
Spyridakis, S.	'Salamis and the Cretans', PP 31 (1976) 345–355.
Starr, C. G.	*The Influence of Sea-power on Ancient History*. Oxford 1989.
Tozzi, P.	*La Rivolta Ionica*. Pisa 1978. 'Erodoto e le responsabilità dell' inizio della rivolta ionica', *Athenaeum* 65 (1977) 127–135.
Tripodi, B.	'L'ambasceria di Alessandro di Macedonia ad Atene nella tradizione erodotea (Hdt. 8.136–144)', ANSP 16 (1986) 621–635. 'La Macedonia, la Peonia, il carro sacro di Serse (Hdt. 8.115–6), *Giornale Italiano di Filologia* 38 (1986) 243–251.
Tronson, A.	'The Hellenic League of 480 B.C.: fact or ideological fiction?' *Acta Classica* 34 (1991) 93–110.
Vanderpool, E.	*Ostracism at Athens*. Cincinnati 1970.
Van Der Veer, J. A. G.	'The Battle of Marathon. A topographical survey', *Mnemosyne* 34 (1982) 290–321.
Vannier, F.	*Finances publiques et richesses privées dans le discours athénien*

aux Ve et IVe siècles [ALUB no. 362, CRHA no. 75]. Paris 1988.

Vickers, M. 'Interactions between Greeks and Persians', in: SANCISI-WEERDENBURG & KUHRT 1986, 253–262.
'Attic symposia after the Persian Wars', in: *Sympotica: a symposium on the symposion*, ed. O. Murray (Oxford 1990) 105–121.

Wallace, M. B. 'Herodotus and Euboia', *Phoenix* 28 (1974) 22–44.

Wallace, P. W. 'Aphetai and the Battle of Artemision', in: *Studies presented to Sterling Dow on his 80th Birthday* [GRByS Suppl. x], ed. K. J. Riggsby (Durham N.C. 1984) 305–310.
'The final battle at Plataia', in: *Studies in Attic epigraphy, history and topography*, presented to Eugene Vanderpool by members of the American School of Classical Studies [*Hesperia* Suppl. 19] (Princeton 1982) 183–192.

Wallinga, H. T. 'Persian tribute and Delian tribute', in: BRIANT & HERRENSCHMIDT 173–181.
'The ancient Persian navy and its predecessors', in: SANCISI-WEERDENBURG & KUHRT 1987 (I) 47–77.
'The trireme and its crew', in: *Actus: Studies in honour of H. L. W. Nelson*, ed. J. den Boeft & A. H. M. Kessels (Utrecht 1982) 463 ff.
'The trireme and history', *Mnemosyne* 43 (1990) 132–149.
'The Ionian Revolt', *Mnemosyne* 37 (1984) 401–437.

Walser, G. 'Zum griechisch-persischen Verhältnis vor dem Hellenismus', *Historische Zeitschrift* 220 (1975) 529–542.

Waters, K. H. *Herodotus the Historian: His Problems, Methods, and Originality*. London 1985.

Welwei, K. W. 'Das sogenannte Grab der Plataier im Vranatal bei Marathon', *Historia* 28 (1979) 101–106.

Whitehead, I. The περίπλους', *Greece and Rome* 34 (1987) 178–185.

Williams, G. M. E. 'Athenian politics 508/7–480 B.C.: a reappraisal', *Athenaeum* 60 (1982) 521–544.
'The Kerameikos ostraka', *ZPE* 31 (1982) 103–113.
'The image of the Alkmeonidai between 490 B.C. and 487/6 B.C.', *Historia* 29 (1980) 106–110.
'Aristocratic politics in Athens c. 630 to 470 B.C.' Ph.D. diss., Pennsylvania State Univ. 1973.

328

Wolski, J.　'L'influence des guerres médiques sur la lutte politique en Grèce', in: *Acta Conventus XI Eirene*, 21 – 25 Oct. 1968 (Warsaw 1971) 641 – 647.
'Progressivität und Konservatismus in Sparta und Athen im Zeitalter der Perserkriege', *Jahrbuch für Wirtschaftgeschichte* 2 (1971) 77 – 82.
'ΜΗΔΙΣΜΟΣ et son importance en Grèce à l'époque des guerres médiques', *Historia* 22 (1973) 3 – 15.
'Hérodote et la construction de la flotte athénienne par Thémistocle', *Storia della Storiografia* 7 (1985) 113 – 122.
'Thémistocle, la construction de la flotte athénienne et la situation internationale en Méditerranée', *Rivista storica dell'Antichità* 13/14 (1983/4) 179 – 192.

Worley, L. J.　'The cavalry of ancient Greece.' Ph.D. diss., Univ. of Washington [Seattle], 1992. Diss. Abs. 53 (1992/3) 2059A.

Xydas, C. (ed.)　Ηρόδοτος, βιβλίο πέμπτο (V): Τερψιχόρη. Εισαγωγή, κείμενο, σχόλια. Athens 1991.

INDEX

*indicates a map reference

Compositor: G & S Typesetters
Text: Monotype Baskerville
Display: Monotype Baskerville
Printer: Edwards Brothers
Binder: Edwards Brothers